DIXIE SAINTS

LABORERS IN THE FIELD

DOUGLAS D. ALDER

RSC
BYU

DESERET
BOOK

Published by the Religious Studies Center, Brigham Young University, Provo, Utah, in cooperation with Deseret Book Company, Salt Lake City.

Visit us at rsc.byu.edu.

Printed in the United States of America by Sheridan Books, Inc.

DESERET BOOK is a registered trademark of Deseret Book Company.

Visit us at DeseretBook.com.

Cover and interior design by Madison Swapp.

ISBN: 978-1-9443-9420-2
Retail US: $21.99

Library of Congress Cataloging-in-Publication Data

Names: Alder, Douglas D., author.
Title: Dixie saints : laborers in the field / compiled by Douglas D. Alder.
Description: Provo : BYU Religious Studies Center, 2017. | Includes index.
Identifiers: LCCN 2017003203 | ISBN 9781944394202
Subjects: LCSH: Mormons--Southwestern states--History.
Classification: LCC BX8615.S89 A43 2017 | DDC 289.3092/279248--dc23 LC
    record available at https://lccn.loc.gov/2017003203

CONTENTS

PREFACE

This study could have never come to be if it were not for Fielding H. Harris and Melvin Blomquist, who made their contributions in the 1960s. Harris moved to St. George, Utah, from northern Utah in 1965, with the intention of making his living by tuning pianos, as he had done in the northern portion of the state. While there, he had also recorded some oral histories. Upon arriving in southern Utah, he discovered that the much smaller population was insufficient to support him and his family. He had a brother-in-law, Melvin Blomquist, who lived in southern California, where he had a successful accounting business. Melvin wanted to help Fielding and his family and suggested that he would finance an oral history project. Together they decided to interview a particular group: those born in the Mojave Desert region (below the Great Basin) around the year 1900. That would include people from about thirty villages and towns.

In 1968, Harris began his interviews. Over the next three years, he completed 425 tapings from Panguitch in the north to Bunkerville and Mesquite, Nevada, in the south; from Panaca in southeastern Nevada to Kanab in Kane County, Utah; from Orderville in Long Valley, Utah, to Mount Trumbull in northern Arizona; from Enterprise, Utah, to

Washington, Utah; and all the towns in between, such as Springdale, Rockville, Gunlock, Virgin, Hurricane, La Verkin, Toquerville, Leeds, St. George, Santa Clara, Veyo, Hebron, Pine Valley, Central, and several others. Some people he interviewed were born outside this region but moved to it later, such as a substantial group from the Mormon colonies in Old Mexico.

In 1986, Melvin Blomquist contacted me just after I moved from Logan into the administration of Dixie College. He inquired whether Dixie College would be interested in archiving the interviews, which they had transferred to cassettes from the reel-to-reel originals. We were excited and received them with enthusiasm. Seven years passed, and in 1993 I returned to teaching and research. We went to work transcribing the interviews. Another key figure then entered the picture. Valarie Johnson had recently moved to St. George from Phoenix, Arizona, where she had been involved in transcribing oral history tapes in Gilbert, Arizona. She contacted us and we immediately responded. She became officially allied with the Val Browning Library as an oral history transcriber. She soon enlisted about a dozen others as a team to do the transcribing that was completed in 2013. Fielding H. Harris recorded the interviews, and then about twenty-five years later, a team of trained transcribers, who had each done many of the interviews, typed the interviews very carefully. The interviews were then taken to the interviewees to read if they were alive or, if not, to surviving family members. After this, transcribers included their corrections, indexed the document, and completed the final typing. They are cataloged and stored in the Dixie State University Library Special Collections and Archives. The tapes are also there and have been digitized along with the transcriptions.

In these interviews, Harris faithfully followed an outline, asking similar questions of each person: "Give your full name and birthplace and date. Give your father's and mother's name. How many siblings did you have? What do you recall about your early childhood?" This sometimes led to other childhood issues. "Tell about your school life. Tell about your parents." These questions came from the file of Laura Snow Woodbury, dated 19 April 1968. They prompted the respondents to tell the story of their life. Here are some questions he asked

Harmon Gubler on 18 February 1969: "Did you enjoy school? Did you take trips? Did you learn to be a farmer from your father? Did you like farming? Did you go to college? What did you do for fun when you were growing up? Name your brothers and sisters. Where did you go on your mission? Tell about your courtship. Tell about your children. How long were you branch president? Did you help bring water into this area?" Harris asked such questions of all respondents who in turn gave often lengthy answers, describing their childhood, education, adulthood, work, progeny, and service.

Funding to support this effort was another key element. The transcribers were paid a modest amount, but because many of the interviews were more than one tape, there were about 650 tapes to transcribe. The Val Browning Library budget was a major contributor to this cost but so were private donors and the transcribers themselves who did some of the work voluntarily. The Utah Historical Society, the Utah Humanities Council, and the Charles Redd Center at BYU funded grants. The latter also did some of the transcribing. About twenty to forty files were transcribed each year. The library support staff for these two decades of work has been critical for this project, particularly Bonnie Percival, Caleb Ames, Rob Snow, James Miller, Tracy O'Kelly, Amber D'Ambrosio, Glen Harris, Daphne Selbert, Richard Paustenbaugh, and Kathleen Broeder. Elaine Alder, Leah Welker, Kimball Gardner, Tyler Bali, Mandi Diaz, Leah Emal, and Devan Jensen helped edit this book.

Fortunately, Fielding Harris was consistent, asking each interviewee the same questions but allowing them to personalize their answers. This consistency helps in the tabulation of the data, such as how common childhood death was, how many people had second or third marriages, how often fathers and mothers died in midlife, how often people moved, how many served LDS missions, how many graduated from high school, how many went to college and where, how many were active in their religion, and how many served in their community. Between these questions, the person being interviewed often included choice personal views and many stories. The tapes are a treasure of real life experiences and feelings. A chart at the end of this study summarizes the data.

All this effort enabled this extended project of social history—examining the life of the laborers in the field. The resulting book is largely a compilation of their own words, describing their life in the middle period of the development of the West. It focuses on a rather large region, one that is arid and that required arduous labor to convert to agriculture and community life.

INTRODUCTION

Dixie Saints: Laborers in the Field is the story of the common folk—the farmers and ranchers, the fruit peddlers, the road builders, the timber cutters and lumber makers, the freighters, the midwives, the mothering women and child nurturers, the quilters and gardeners, the teachers, the choir singers and band players—those whose names are on genealogy charts but are seldom in the history books. It is about agriculture before machines and hard muscle labor in gardens, farms, and ranches.

Such people in this study were not pioneers because they were not of that generation—they were of the next. Most of the thirty-plus Mormon villages in and near southern Utah had been founded by the late 1800s, with its capital in St. George. A few, like Hurricane, La Verkin, Enterprise, and Veyo, started just after 1900. The farms and town lots were already surveyed when these folks were born. The irrigation dams and ditches were mostly in use. The roads were roughed in, but there were no oiled surfaces. The outhouses were in place, but there were no sewers. Schools were well under way, but eighth grade was the end goal and many did not reach it. Reading, writing, and arithmetic were the initial curriculum, sometimes with music and drama added. Many students could only attend part of the year because they had to do farmwork in the growing season. These people were born mostly between 1880 and 1910. They lived to see an oiled road named Highway 91 end the area's isolation in 1930. Then came a transformation with the arrival of air-conditioning in about 1955, but it was a luxury for the wealthy. The I-15 freeway did not arrive until 1973, when Utah's Dixie became absorbed in the modern consumer's United States.

A similar story could be told about almost all western parts of the United States, but this one is mostly concentrated on the Mojave Desert in southwestern Utah, northern Arizona, and southeastern Nevada. It is located immediately south of the Great Basin. This desert is two thousand feet lower than the Great Basin, much warmer, and definitely arid, with only five to eight inches of rain per year. People had to survive with irrigation, mainly water from the Virgin River and its tributaries.

The story of the earlier generation, the so-called Dixie Pioneers, is well known—of building a temple, tabernacle, opera house, courthouse, and town hall in St. George, the region's capital, and a cotton factory in nearby Washington City. At the same time, whites were confining the American Indians (Southern Paiute, Hopi, Navajo) to reservations and then appropriating their hunting and gathering lands for ranches and farms. Those in construction had partly built the elaborate system of irrigation canals, and the Hurricane Canal, the La Verkin Canal, the Enterprise Reservoir, and the New Castle Project were about to be constructed. The Washington Fields Dam was already in use and had been since 1888. These engineering achievements opened a much larger area for serious farming; nonetheless, water was still scarce.

The original mission of raising cotton, sugar cane, and grapes had given way to cultivating alfalfa because in 1869, the Civil War had ended and the railroad had come to northern Utah. Cotton fabric could be imported from the South cheaper than raising it in southern Utah because it rained in the South and, because of the remnants of slavery, labor in the South was much less expensive. Meanwhile, The Church of Jesus Christ of Latter-day Saints abandoned using wine for their sacrament ceremony and shifted to water. There was still a market for Dixie wine among the miners, but the Silver Reef population dwindled in the late 1890s. Thus, raising grapes became less important, but it continued for domestic use and for selling in Nevada.

Alfalfa became the staple crop, with three to five cuttings a year. Both small- and large-scale cattle ranching produced this major export product, but the herds had to be driven seven days to Nevada to reach the railroad. A freighting business had grown, particularly in fruit and lumber. Dried peaches and figs were shipped north. Dry farming and mining were other alternatives.

Most people lived in villages like those that their New England and European ancestors lived in, which was quite different from many other settlers in the West. They rode out to their small five-acre farms, which were that size because irrigation water was so limited. The women raised gardens and fruit on their town lots, also supplying their family's needs by irrigation. These families owned their property rather than being a part of a commune. For a century, the area was dominated by self-sustaining agriculture. It was relatively isolated because the railroad never came to what came to be called "Utah's Dixie."

The larger story of the American West often focuses on the movement of Anglo-Americans to the vast areas beyond the Mississippi River. Many Americans considered the West as a wasteland, but others saw it as an opportunity. Most went there in search of free land and a new start for their lives. They knew little about the Native Americans, whose land they intended to occupy. They carried American and European culture with them and planned to implant it in the West as their forefathers had done in the eastern half of the continent.

The Mormon movement to the West was similar to this larger American effort, but there were distinct differences. The village system of the Mormons was a contrast to family life on dispersed farms, ranches, and homesteads in places like Oregon, the American River in California, Colorado, or Montana. Annual rainfall in Utah's Dixie was less than ten inches. Those living in that area adapted to that reality by establishing cooperative communities based on a regulated irrigation system like those in northern Utah. They lived in villages rather than on their farms, as was the norm for Mormons in the American West and Midwest. They became part of a cooperative religious movement to create their vision of Zion. It was a tightly organized and highly disciplined group effort. Those who settled in southern Utah and its neighboring areas did the same, but they had to adapt to the aridity, which required even more discipline.

Establishing a relationship with the Indians was central to the effort. Indians did not accept the concept of private property or fences. They lived mainly off of hunting and gathering in a pre-agricultural society that changed with the seasons. Some raised corn, but they had never herded cattle. The coexistence of the two societies was tenuous and often led to conflict.

That pioneer period throughout the West has been the subject of endless writing, folklore, music, and art. It is central to western American identity, as evidenced by western-themed movies. For example, many of those movies were made in southern Utah. However, interest in the middle period—about 1900 to 1950—has been much less impelling than the stories of the earlier decades.

Population growth was very slow in those middle decades. The high birthrate was offset by continuing emigration of many young people who went away in search of land or jobs. By 1960, there were only ten thousand people in Washington County. Few people visited the region, even though Zion National Park was available nearby. Highway 91, built over Utah Hill in 1930, was steep, and trucks found it daunting, especially in the winter. There was practically no industry to export products or attract capital. Generally, the years between 1900 and 1950 could be described as follows:

1. The people were mainly born into large families, often with as many as a dozen siblings. However, not all stayed in the region as adults.

2. Of that number of births, almost all families buried some of those offspring, either as babies or as young children.

3. Those who survived worked on the farms and ranches as children, gaining valuable experience.

4. They went to school in their villages, often in one-room schools. Those schools usually offered eight grades, but some children dropped out to work on the farms as their parents faced health problems or even died rather young.

5. Many were expected at age sixteen to enter the workforce full-time, having worked part-time in the family enterprises before

then. Some were hired out to neighbors, and some roamed widely seeking work and land.

6. Some were able to continue on to high school, but not in their village. This became more common after about 1930, but the Great Depression also limited education.

7. A few even went away for a year or two of college at Cedar City, Provo, Salt Lake City, or Logan. They were a select few. After 1911, St. George Stake Academy attracted some high school students. After 1916, it became Dixie College and had a small college enrollment but a larger number of high school students.

8. Those who went into the workforce were mainly unskilled workers. However, they had worked with animals, crops, and tools for several years before they reached sixteen. They usually couldn't inherit their father's farm if he was still alive because he had to farm it nearly until his death to support his younger family members without retiring. Being dependent on jobs meant that they couldn't control their lives, and they often had to move in search of employment—building roads, working timber, laboring on the railroad, mining, homesteading, or whatever they could find.

9. Most of these people married young, at about age eighteen. Despite their limited incomes, they began having children and some nearly equaled their parents by bringing eight or more off-spring into the world. The wives often maintained the small farms and sought part-time employment, and some had to take over the family's support when their husbands were injured, sick, or when they died young. There were many deaths of husbands or wives and that often led to second and even third marriages.

10. Through this struggle, the couples focused loyally on their children and the priority of family. The interviews later in this book include hundreds of memories of happy childhoods. All their community neighbors were experiencing essentially the same

challenges. They were very helpful to one another and were not despondent about their plight. They did not describe themselves as poor. They produced their food but functioned by barter and largely without cash.

11. The majority of these people were active in The Church of Jesus Christ of Latter-day Saints. It was central in the meaning of their lives. It drew them together in a "saintly" community. They held callings as teachers of youth, musicians, and pastoral servants to one another. Some of them were called on full-time missions to distant parts of the United States, Europe, or even the South Sea Islands.

12. Families and friends rallied to support the men financially while they were away and help their families who stayed in the village during their two- or three-year absence. Such mission calls were common, but only a portion of the families needed financial help. The temple in St. George was a big influence on these people. Many went there to be married, while many prepared and then went after a civil marraige. Others did proxy work for their deceased relatives. These ceremonies gave those who experienced the ordinances a conviction that their marriage would be eternal and that their family would have eternal links. Some people did not value that idea and did not participate. The Church standards of paying tithing (mostly in kind) and avoiding the use of alcohol and tobacco were a challenge for many, especially ranchers who lived away from the villages and often associated with cowboys who were roamers and not Mormons.

13. There was always a portion of these people who did not participate in religion. Nevertheless, they were part of the community. They worked on the ranches, participated in water companies, danced at the town celebrations, and were accepted by everyone else. Most families had at least one member in this "inactive" lifestyle. There were very few people of other faiths. The Presbyterians maintained two small congregations and two fine elementary schools with certified teachers. The Catholics

were organized in Silver Reef, but that became a ghost town by 1900. Until 1950, the region was almost without religious diversity. Some Native Americans aligned with the Mormons, but many did not. Very few of them lived in the villages. The Shivwits Indian Reservation was the home to a few hundred of the Shivwits Band of the Paiute Tribe of Utah. The Navajo lived east of Washington County with the Hopi in nearby northeastern Arizona. The arrival of the Americans was a huge challenge for them.

14. Virtually all of the interviews in this book include stories of health difficulties, such as accidents, broken bones, and disease epidemics such as influenza. Children often died of these diseases and accidents. Boys were involved with horses a lot, even with rifles, and accidents involving either or both sometimes led to deaths. Childbirth was often critical, because deaths of both children and mothers at birth were common. Almost all families buried one or more newborns.

15. There was a problem with medical care. Those in villages away from St. George or Hurricane seldom had access to a doctor and hardly any ever used the small hospital in St. George. Midwives were very important and some even helped with sickness not related to births. Herbal remedies were the main tool to overcome sickness. County school nurses inspected children for illnesses, administered vaccinations, and referred some to doctors. They even performed physical examinations. Seeking religious blessings during illness was virtually universal. Family fathers were expected to be priesthood holders and be worthy to give blessings. Sometimes families sent for a bishop or other elders to perform this ritual. These fifteen statements are but generalizations. The actual words of these four hundred people are more important. They give the reader the opportunity to be the historian, to consider the document, and to read the actual words of those involved in this period, this landscape, and this lifestyle, most of it before the industrialization of life and the absorption into the wider American landscape.

The main point of this book is that the Mormon village system is what distinguished these people from the rest of the western United States. The concept of the Mormon village began with Joseph Smith. He had established Kirtland, Ohio, and then a few towns in Missouri. They were short-lived, and soon the Mormons gathered at Commerce, Illinois. They purchased nearby land and created Nauvoo. That community and its satellite nearby towns became the Mormon communal achievement.

In the St. George Tabernacle, Susan Easton Black gave an address titled "Joseph Smith, Architect." The title caused the attendees to think of the Kirtland Temple and the Nauvoo Temple, which Smith architecturally conceived. Professor Black, however, meant much more. She described how he designed Nauvoo to be a tight, communal society where the Mormons lived and gardened in town and went out to their nearby farms to work each day, returning at night to be at home in the town. Nauvoo was also successful at developing three mills and promoting crafts which allowed them to transport goods for sale from their port on the Mississippi River.[1]

Brigham Young succeeded Joseph Smith and used his plans to design the five hundred communities the Mormons established in the Great Basin and adjoining areas. This plan differed fundamentally from the way most settlers in the US West lived, who came west hoping to settle on large farms. In the 1860s, the US Federal Government established the homestead system, enabling people to claim a whole section of land (640 acres) and live and farm there. This scattered the people widely. The result was that they were a long way from schools, churches, and neighbors.

The Mormon village, in contrast, envisioned tight communities that could be defended. Each village maintained a locally led school and church located on the town square. Because the towns were established in semi-arid regions, they depended on irrigation systems, which were also managed by town regulations. The central Church leaders in Salt Lake City were deeply engaged in promoting this tight communal system throughout what came to be known as the "Mormon Corridor." Villages were founded as far north as Alberta, Canada, as far south as northern Mexico, and everywhere in-between.

The interviews in this book came from people whose parents settled in the Mojave Desert, the arid land south of the Great Basin (see the map).

Those villages began with Fort Harmony in 1852, which was soon followed by Santa Clara and other small towns in Pine Valley and Gunlock in 1854. Then, John D. Lee convinced Brigham Young to let him establish Washington City in 1854. The upper Virgin River Valley soon welcomed Virgin, Grafton, Rockville, and Springdale. The Paiutes convinced people from Fort Harmony to join them at Toquerville. Brigham Young then decided on a major effort in the southern region. He called 309 families to found a capital city, St. George, in 1861–62. Jacob Hamblin was then instructed to proselyte and found towns in Arizona, east of Kanab. Mormon villages were also founded south of St. George—Bloomington, Bunkerville, Las Vegas, and Muddy Valley, to name just a few. Some Mormons undertook ranching on the Arizona Strip. Altogether, there were some thirty-plus communities in Utah's Dixie. Then, after 1900, more came into being as the result of major water projects—Hurricane, La Verkin, Enterprise, and Veyo. These new efforts also continued the communal village system. This information lays a framework for understanding the interviews included in this book.

Fortunately, some scholars have written about the village system that the Mormons implemented throughout the Intermountain West. One of the most interesting writers, Nels Anderson, actually lived near St. George in the decade before he became a soldier in World War I. His story is unusual because he traveled alone and did not arrive to the area until 1909. His personal story is detailed later in the book in the testimony of Joseph Terry. After attending high school in St. George, Nels went to Brigham Young University with the intention of becoming a lawyer. He was not impressed with the school, so he returned to Dixie to get two years of college. Then he returned to BYU, where his interest shifted to sociology. He obtained a job teaching high school at St. Johns LDS Academy in Arizona.

One year later, Nels volunteered to serve in the US Army in World War I. After short basic training in the US, he was shipped to England for more training. Then, he was sent to France, near the front lines. Following the war, he returned to BYU and graduated at the head of his class. Then he went to the University of Chicago and did his master's thesis, which was later published by the University of Chicago. After this, he went to New York University and did a doctorate in sociology and worked for the

Governor of New York, who at that time was Franklin D. Roosevelt. When Roosevelt was elected as US president, Nels became part of his administration in the National Labor Relations Bureau.

He decided he wanted to write a sociological study about the place on earth he loved most: southern Utah. The Library of Congress was at his disposal. He went to work, but one of his teachers at Dixie College heard what he was doing. She contacted him and told him that he must come back to St. George to write the bulk of the book. Her name was Juanita Brooks, and she was deeply interested in southern Utah history and would later become the major historian of the area. Nels did come back for a few months and worked in the local records, and then he used the Church History Library archives in Salt Lake City. The book, *Desert Saints*, was published in 1942 by the University of Chicago. It included key insights to the very generation of the interviewees in this book.

Here is one insightful excerpt:

> The Mormon frontier differed radically from other frontiers in its method of recruiting population. Utah did not have an open-door policy, as did California, during the first decade of the westward rush. Utah used every device to discourage random migration. Just any individual migrant was not welcome in Zion, not even if he could pay his way. Missionaries were sent out to every 'kindred, tongue and people' to select the emigrants Zion wanted and could use. They wanted emigrants who could accept the Mormon Gospel and make sacrifices to establish the new society.
>
> Zion did not grow on the principal of individualism; in fact, it would have failed had it been built on the individualism of California. Had the emphasis been place on such a principle, Brigham Young's following would have fled to California, even before the forty-niners. Zion had to be built by cooperative effort, and it was.[2]

This point was especially valid for settlers in the Mojave Desert. They were the closest to California, but they had learned to value the cooperative society and the village system and most chose to remain in their villages. Nels Anderson was an example of those who chose to depart, and this choice did not always please him. In his later years, he felt abandoned by the United States Government, so he moved to Canada. In the book, he suggested that the Mormons were justified in staying with the village system and the Mormon faith.

Near the end of the book, Nels quoted a letter from the President of the Church, John Taylor. It was dated 26 December 1882 and read:

> In all cases in making new settlements the Saints should be advised to gather together in villages, as has been our custom from the time of our earliest settlement in these mountain valleys. The advantages of this plan, instead of carelessly scattering out over a wide extent of country, are many and obvious to all those who have a desire to serve the Lord.
>
> By this means the people can retain their ecclesiastical organizations, have regular meetings of the quorums of the priesthood, and establish and maintain day and Sunday schools, Improvement Associations, and Relief Societies. They can also cooperate for the good of all in financial and secular matters, in making ditches, fencing fields, building bridges, and other necessary improvements.
>
> Further than this they are a mutual protection and a source of strength against horse and cattle thieves, land jumpers, etc., and against hostile Indians, should there be any; while their compact organization gives them many advantages of a social and civic character which might be lost, misapplied or frittered away by spreading out so thinly that inter-communication is difficult, dangerous, inconvenient and expensive.[3]

Taylor's letter is a fine summary of the purpose of the village system. What is fascinating is that the villages continued well into the twentieth century. Even the new towns stayed with the system. Therefore, the stories the people tell in this book are consistent with the lifestyle of their parents and grandparents. Once modern technology arrived—electricity, machines, telephones, radios, and automobiles—the rural areas stopped growing and urban centers became dominant. Anderson's book was published just as that change was under way.

Another major scholar who focused on the Mormon village system was Lowry Nelson. In 1925, he published a study of Escalante, Utah, in

Garfield County. It is part of a series sponsored by Brigham Young University. In the introduction he says:

> Utah [and its neighboring regions] is one of the few spaces on this continent where the farm-village type of community is found. It existed in the early days of New England, but with the coming of improved methods of transportation and other factors, it disintegrated. Although the agricultural village has never developed extensively in America, in the countries of Europe it is rather common. . . . The 'Mormon' village was definitely planned and established before the farm land was developed. That is to say, the first settlers laid out the village site and apportioned the lots, as their first act. They then surveyed the fields and apportioned them. The vast rural areas of the United States, on the contrary, grew up in practically the opposite manner; that is, the farms were established first, and the village or hamlet came as a secondary growth.[4]

He went on to give a detailed account of Escalante. It was settled in 1875 as a spillover from towns at higher elevation. It is 5,700 feet in elevation whereas Panguitch, the county seat, is 1,000 feet higher. Land and water were available and 11.3 inches of rain fell per year. About 123 family heads chose to come rather than being called to come by Church authority. By 1876, they had constructed a log building for a school large enough for ninety pupils and two teachers. An LDS Church branch was organized in 1877. Town planners surveyed five-acre town blocks and divided them into four-family lots. On those lots, families constructed farm buildings such as a barn, a corral, pens, and a root cellar. Eventually, the town built a canal and each family got one acre-foot of water for their garden. Livestock was their main effort and alfalfa was the farm crop. Nelson reported that frost ended around 22 May and returned around 27 September. There were 124 farms within 3 miles from town, covering 5,000 acres. Thirty or more other villages in the desert region were much similar in their layout. Nelson's study goes on to include many details about crops, economics, and social structure.

Dean L. May published an important summary of the research by many scholars who study the Mormon village.[5] One of his key points was that scholars studying Mormon towns can gain insight by studying colonial New England towns. May was especially impressed by the work of Clyde Kluckholm and Talcot Parsons, which dealt with cultural groups in the Colorado Plateau—Zuni, Navajo, Spanish, Mormon, and Texan. Thomas O'Dea was a member of that team and that work led to his important book, *The Mormons*. Nelson's large project supports the work of Donald W. Meinig and Richard V. Francaviglia that concludes that there is a Mormon culture region. May says:

> The varied body of converts from England and other parts of western Europe was not primarily agrarian but consisted of large numbers of skilled craftsmen, tradesmen, and factory workers. For many their only common experience as Mormons to the time they arrived in the Salt Lake Valley was their conversion and their long journey to the Rocky Mountains. After a brief stay in Salt Lake City they generally settled in small farming villages. There, cast into close association with other Mormons, in formal church gatherings and in less formal daily associations, they began in earnest the process of becoming Saints—of developing the unique character later scholars described in Ramah and in other Mormon villages. In detailed studies of life in Mormon villages of the past, one has a rare opportunity to discern and analyze the processes that contributed to the building and perpetuation of a distinctive subculture.[6]

Recently, a major study was published by the University of Utah Press.[7] It surveys works by many scholars, including Nels Anderson, Lowry Nelson, Andrew Karl Larson, Edward C. Banfield, Henri Mendras, Alma A. Gardner, and Nancy Taniguchi, among others. Banfield is cited in more detail in chapter 7, which discusses civic service.

The breadth of Bahr's study is amazing. He considers articles, theses, and dissertations on scores of Mormon communities over a period of 150 years. For example, he reports on the work of Joseph Earle Spencer in the 1930s. His 1935 dissertation at the University of California, "The Middle Virgin Valley, Utah: A Study in Cultural Growth and Change," focuses on the areas near St. George. He points out that some of the villages were unable to achieve the standard grid square because they were located in narrow river valleys. Gunlock, Virgin, Veyo, Santa Clara, Leeds, Rockville, and Springdale are examples. Spencer focuses on the adaptation to new developments in the 1900–30 period. Transportation and highways were improved, new equipment became available for farms and homes, more interaction with visitors happened, and uniformity declined. Modern readers will quickly realize that this was the beginning of a diversity that characterizes much of the region today.

Bahr quotes diverse authors about the nature of social class in Salt Lake City during the pioneer times. Regarding the status of women, he focuses on Jules Remy, who decries what he perceives as the suppression of women. Then he cites John William Gunnison, who says Utah women's education is "quite as free and liberal as to the other sex," and the Mormons "Give, or profess to allow, all the freedom to the females that is found in any Christian nation." Nonetheless Gunnison admits that the glory of the women is to be a mother in Israel.[8] Reading Bahr causes one to be grateful for scholars who do exhaustive research and provide it to the world.

Ronald Walker wrote an article about daily life in Mormon villages during the period 1850–1900, the era just prior to the era of these interviewees.[9] That early period was much more difficult since it involved breaking the first ground, moving newcomers into the village, and helping the desperate neighbors who needed a cup of flour to survive. Serving the sick was also difficult, because no doctors were available. Midwives had to travel very long distances and treat many illnesses. Meanwhile, men had to build the original canals and ditches as well as roads—all without heavy equipment. Building forts and the first homes was that generation's job. They even had to retrieve cattle stolen by Native Americans. Women had to weave thread into cloth. This generation dried fruit and their children and grandchildren kept that up. Essentially, it was a generation that set the tone for all subsequent generations.

An article by Joseph Earle Spencer[10] tells the details of the local geography and of the rainfall, which gave eight to thirteen inches per year. It emphasizes "the unified church leadership of community action."[11] It describes the similarities and differences of the villages, but it says that they were "designed to give everyone an equal division of available land."[12]

It mentions how the early emphasis on cotton, silk, sorghum, and wine gave way to alfalfa, as well as how the population of 3,270 in the 1800s was surpassed in the 1920s.

In his 2014 MHA presidential address in San Antonio, Glen Leonard focused on historic Mormon communities. He emphasized the role of Joseph Smith in setting the design for the later Mormon villages and his impact on Brigham Young, who implemented the plan. He mentioned that Young's experience in the Zion's Camp trek to Missouri influenced how Young organized the trek west in the 1840s and '50s. Then he told how Joseph Smith gradually developed the town layout plan after his experiences in Kirtland. Those plans were set up for Jackson County, Missouri, and then implemented more in Nauvoo. Brigham Young was involved with it all. Leonard goes on to talk about the initial communities all close to Salt Lake in 1847 and 1848, until Parowan was undertaken. He points out that there were several self-directed settlements that did not follow the plan for square blocks and wide streets.

In the second half of his address, Leonard focuses on the second generation. Many of them were from large families and the younger sons could not inherit the father's land. They often migrated to nearby lands that could be made into farms. They did not go as an organized company but on individual initiative. Leonard focuses on the towns of Davis County and its neighboring towns and shows that many communities were founded gradually. Several of these families had established farms before an actual village plan and ward were established. This situation was somewhat similar in Washington County. St. George, Washington City, and Santa Clara were done as an original plan. Then, other villages sprang from them. After 1900, like in Davis County, several Dixie communities came from individual initiatives—Enterprise, Hurricane, and La Verkin. Leonard explains that the coming of the railroad was a big influence in the Davis and Weber County expansions and diversification. Washington County was different. No railroad ever came. The first highway in that area was built in 1930 and then Interstate 15 was built in 1973. Thus, Washington County didn't become absorbed into capitalism until much later than northern Utah. Similarly, it didn't become religiously diversified until a generation or two after northern Utah.[13]

All of this information helps give context and background to the interviews included in this book. These people lived in the many Mormon villages located in the Mojave Desert. Those who lived in the village rode out to the farm every day. The communal nature of the village had a huge impact on family life; on childhood; on the work of both children and adults; on the nature of the schools; on the life of work for adults and children, men and women; on the health challenges they had to deal with; on the service they gave to their communities; on their interaction with Native Americans; and on their reception of fellow Mormons who fled Mexico at the time of the 1912 Revolution. We have focused on this topic of the Mormon village because it has impact on all these matters.

We can now look at brief excerpts from some of the whole group, in their own words. We will do so by category, but we will include many stories of selected individuals. The ones included here were chosen because a descendant had signed a release form, they illustrated the point of the section in which they were placed, and they told interesting tales. The categories we divided the stories into include the following: Family Life, Childhood, and Teenage Years; Schools; Youth and Adults at Work; Health and Sickness; Mormons Colonists of Mexico Who Moved to the US; American Indians; and Military, Church, and Civic Service Efforts. There is a final section that lists statistics regarding the interviews. To make reading easier, capitalization and punctuation were standardized, and words in brackets were added by the transcriber.

NOTES

1.   See Susan Easton Black, "The Economic Sacrifice of the Nauvoo Exodus," in *Far Away in the West*, ed. Scott Esplin, Richard E. Bennett, and Craig K. Manscill (Salt Lake City: Deseret Book, 2005), 59–79. In this article, Professor Black describes Nauvoo's economic success and the exodus from the city.

2.   Nels Anderson, *Desert Saints: Mormon Frontier in Utah* (Chicago: University of Chicago Press, 1966), 116.

3.   Anderson, *Desert Saints*, 427.

4.   Lowry Nelson, *A Social History Survey of Escalante Utah* (1925), 3.

5. Dean L. May, "The Making of Saints: The Mormon Town as a Setting for the Study of Cultural Change," *Utah Historical Quarterly* 45, no. 1 (Winter 1977): 75–92.

6. May, "The Making of Saints," 82.

7. Howard M. Bahr, *Saints Observed: Studies of Mormon Village Life, 1850–2005*, (Salt Lake City: University of Utah Press, 2014).

8. Bahr, *Saints Observed*, 108–9.

9. Ronald W. Walker, "Golden Memories: Remembering Life in a Mormon Village," *BYU Studies* 37, no. 3 (1997–98), 191–218.

10. Joseph Earle Spencer, "The Development of Agricultural Villages in Southern Utah," *Agricultural History* 4, no. 4 (October 1940), 181–209.

11. Spencer, "The Development of Agricultural Villages in Southern Utah," 182.

12. Spencer, "The Development of Agricultural Villages in Southern Utah," 184.

13. Glen M. Leonard, "Seeking an Inheritance: Mormon Mobility, Urbanity, and Community," *Journal of Mormon History* 40, no. 2 (Spring 2014): 1–57.

UTAH'S DIXIE REGION

PIOCHE

PANACA

CALIENTE

HEBRON   ENTERP

HAMBLIN

MOUNTAIN MEADOWS

CENTRAL

GUNLOCK   VEYO

PAIUTE RESERVATION

IVINS

SANTA CLARA

ST GEORC

BLOOMINGTON

NEVADA

MESQUITE

BUNKERVILLE

GLENDALE

LOGANDALE

INTERSTATE 15

A

LEGEND

COUNTY BOUNDARY	
STATE BOUNDARY	
INTERVIEW LOCATION	● MT TRUMBULL
STATE HIGHWAY	
INTERSTATE	
MAJOR WATERWAY	

SCALE

60 KILOMETERS

40 MILES

CARTOGRAPHY BY ERIC HARKER
SEPTEMBER 8, 2014

Chapter 1

FAMILY LIFE, CHILDHOOD, TEENAGE YEARS

INTRODUCTION

An article in the *Christian Science Monitor Weekly* portrayed a young girl touching a tablet screen.[1] That is modern childhood as today's parents and grandparents know. Even three-year-olds call their grandparents on a smartphone. What could be more wildly different from the likes of children between 1880 and 1930? Much has been written about childhood since then.

In the MHA Tanner Lecture at the annual meeting in 2001, Elliott West presented a fine overview of the "Children's Story," suggesting that many children suffered because of their Mormon membership between 1830 and 1870. Many were driven from their homes in Ohio, Missouri, and Illinois. Those in Europe experienced leaving that continent, crossing the Atlantic, and settling near the Mississippi River—only to then face crossing the Great Plains. Many lost parents, and all struggled, especially with hunger.[2]

West says of the early Mormon children that "the struts that had held life together suddenly fell away [when they became Mormons]. Everything altered. Power shifted instantly."[3] They became part of a new religious minority. There were fears of separation and loss of homes. He points out that the difficulties parents faced by converting to Mormonism especially had an impact on the children.

When the decision was made to transfer the Church headquarters to the Rocky Mountains, the children faced more hunger, more cold, more trekking, and sometimes more separation from parents. Disease was a huge danger, and medical care was unavailable. "Some remember the adventure and excitement, but for others it was an agony of exhaustion and short supplies, especially during the handcart disasters."[4]

West's focus on the earliest period of "Becoming Mormon" gives a firm picture that contrasts with childhood in the 1880–1930 period. Children still had trials in mid-nineteenth-century Utah, but they did not have the fears of their ancestors. Children were obviously a large portion of the settlers of Utah. Pictures, songs, and even statues about them abound in the state, but their personal statements are limited in comparison to their pioneer parents. Considerable scholarly attention has been devoted to the children, but the sources (their words) are limited. It is usually the parents who tell of the children rather than the children telling of themselves. Recently, several scholars have focused on the children. They have found a few journals, many pictures, some letters, and a lot of oral histories. Most of them are written by adults reflecting on their youth.

Once the Mormons settled in the Great Basin and established scores of cooperative villages, life changed dramatically. Soon, each family had an acre-sized garden where they grew fruit and vegetables. They also raised chickens, pigs, and cows for their daily food, and they had a farm out of town that was also their support. Stability returned, but so did intensive labor. Children were a main source of that labor. William G. Hartley tells of life in Gunnison, Utah, in the second half of the nineteenth century. There were between 500 and 1,200 people living on the twenty blocks and their expansion over those fifty years. Initially, there was an ungraded school that taught through the fifth grade with little equipment and no books. There were endless health problems and some childhood deaths. The children worked on the gardens and the older ones on the farms, but they also played with their many siblings and neighbors. They participated in the regular Church meetings and socials.[5]

Susan Arrington Madsen has written widely about childhood and has written several articles on the same topic. She authored an article titled

"Growing Up in Pioneer Utah: Agonies and Ecstasies,"[6] in which she suggests four reasons to honor pioneer youngsters. First, they were the largest minority. She quotes Elliott West, professor of history at the University of Arkansas, who wrote that "a large portion of the actors have been left out of history."[7] A second reason, according to Madsen, is to give credit where credit is due: "Pioneer children and adolescents carried a heavy load on their relatively small shoulders."[8] Third, she said that young pioneers are worth watching to learn about their interests and challenges. And "fourth is that the courageousness and optimism of the children contributed significantly to the well-being of the group."[9]

Madsen includes an example of Martha Cragun Cox, who as a child sat up all of one night in St. George with a widow's dying infant. The mother was totally exhausted from attending the dying infant for two weeks and caring for other children. She lay down and went to sleep, and Martha watched the child die. This experience deeply influenced her, and she later became a lifelong nurse and midwife in southern Utah. Another author, Martha Sontag Bradley, also wrote an article about pioneer children.[10] It deals with the impact—particularly the negative impact—of polygamy on children as the federal government attempted to enforce the anti-polygamy laws. The fathers often had to go into hiding and the children often had to lie about that. Children were considered illegitimate by the government. Sometimes, they were left to provide for themselves and even became estranged from their fathers. These children had no luxury of childhood. This is a powerful article, but it is more about the parents of the people interviewed for this book. These people came after polygamy had ended, but their parents were those children; and some who settled in this area came from northern Mexico during the 1910 revolution, where polygamy was still practiced.

Davis Bitton wrote yet another article about pioneer children.[11] He points out that non-Mormon visitors considered the Mormon children to be neglected, filthy, disorderly rebels. On the contrary, the Mormon view of children was that they were workers, were part of an eternal family, and were gifted with divine creativity. They were considered to be faithful, indispensable, and divine increase. They were to advance the kingdom of God and learn the gospel of Jesus Christ.

Bitton discusses the issue of teaching religion in the schools. The local village schools were sponsored by the towns and not the state, so members of the local congregation took turns going to the schools to teach a weekly class on religion. The high schools were governed by the state and did not allow religion in the schools. The Church organized Sunday schools and Young Women and Young Men associations to fill that gap, but attendance was only 50 percent. In the 1930s, the Church took the next step and established seminaries adjacent to many high schools for released-time religious instruction. Again, attendance of the LDS youth was less than half. Davis emphasizes that the role of mothers was pivotal in raising children, teaching them skills and especially the principles of the gospel, even to the rowdies.

The people who will tell such stories in this study, like Emma Lucinda Nelson Larson, lived mainly in villages, though some were on ranches. The central community in the region for these families was St. George, where the tabernacle, the temple, and the courthouse were located. Santa Clara was ten miles to the west. About twenty miles to the north, Veyo was founded in 1911. Nearby was Gunlock, already fifty years old. About fourteen miles north of Gunlock was Pine Valley, an important lumbering and cattle community. Even further north, people began settling in 1896 in what became Enterprise, especially after the Enterprise Dam was completed in 1910. Newcastle was nearby but did not become a rival to Enterprise as it was anticipated to be.

About six miles to the east of St. George was Washington city, the site of the old cotton factory and many farms, founded in 1854. In 1906, some twenty miles further east, Hurricane and La Verkin were founded. They were the sites of canals that were built on the side of the canyon, diverting Virgin River water into those new towns. Just north of La Verkin was Toquerville, one of the original villages, and north of there were Harrisburg and Leeds, also settled very early. Even further north, Harmony and Kanarraville were settled. Pinto was up in the mountains west of them. Harmony was founded in 1852, the first town in the county.

Hurricane, also founded about 1906, was at the foot of the Hurricane cliffs, adjacent to the Virgin River, where the Hurricane Canal came out of the canyon. A difficult trail had been built up that cliff as early as 1858, and the town of Virgin had been built at the entrance to the upper canyon. In

1860, Rockville was founded further up the canyon, and Grafton nearby at about the same time. Springdale and Shunesburg were also established then at what became the entrance to Zion National Park. Several towns in nearby Nevada were also part of the Dixie environment—Logandale, Mesquite, and Bunkerville. Some towns in Washington County had been abandoned by the time this story begins—Hebron, Harrisburg, Bloomington, and Price. The village towns were small, between 100 and 300 people. In contrast, St. George, the capital, had 1,500 people by 1900 and grew to 4,600 by 1950.

Ranching was an alternative to village living. Ranches were well developed in the western area between Santa Clara and Pine Valley. Many ranches were established on the Arizona Strip and a large one was at Pipe Springs, east of Hurricane. Others were scattered throughout the area, usually away from the villages and farms.

The farmers living in the villages left their homes in the morning and rode out to their farms. The farms were small because their existence depended on scarce irrigation water. These people were living in a desert with only five to eight inches of rainfall annually. Each of the villages, however, was located on a small stream. The limited water required that irrigation be tightly regulated. Each family was assigned a four-hour water turn once every three or four days. These villages and the water system were well established by the time this story began. By 1900, most of the villages were in existence, including a school and a church in each town (often in the same building).

Those living on ranches and the few who tried dry farming focused mainly on cattle and sheep. It was a risky business, dependent mainly on fluctuating seasons of rainfall. Some years, there was little precipitation. These men were essentially capitalists instead of being in the cooperative system of the villages. They lived away from schools and churches, which were important to them. They had to find markets for their products. But above all, they had to find water and food for their animals. They were often away from their families and community for weeks and months.

Some men tried living by working in mines. Southern Nevada had several of them, but work was often transient. Living near a mine was not conducive for family men. Sometimes, though, they went to work in the mines and came home only occasionally. They were dependent on employers and surrounded by a lifestyle often in conflict with their values.

Other alternatives included cutting timber and finishing it into lumber in mills. This was an essential industry for community building, but it, too, was seasonal, and it took fathers away from families. School teaching was a valued employment and the teachers often farmed in the summers. Those who undertook this work had to get advanced education, often outside the county. A couple of families built ice plants, and a few people tried to make a living as shoemakers. Road building and carpentry attracted quite a few, and working on the railroad drew many to that work, but they had to live outside the county. In most cases, women and children continued to maintain gardens and small farms to provide the food for the families while the husbands and older sons were away.

Central to all these people in "Utah's Dixie" and nearby areas was family life. This chapter will quote about thirty people as they describe life with their parents, siblings, and friends in their childhood and teenage years in these villages, ranches, and elsewhere. Now, let us turn to the words of people who were interviewed about their childhood.

INTERVIEWS

EMMA LUCINDA NELSON LARSON

Emma Lucinda Nelson Larson was born on 18 February 1891 in St. George, Utah.[12] "About the earliest [event] I remember was [when] my mother had a little baby. I think I was about four years old. When the baby [Charles Nelson] was about a month old, it died [from] pneumonia. I remember my father making a little casket to bury the baby in. Then about a year later they took my mother to [the Utah State] Mental Hospital in Provo [Utah County, Utah] where she remained for fifteen years.

"When the sister six years older than me married at the age of eighteen that left me the oldest [one] at home. [I was] twelve [years old.] I had to assume a lot of responsibility, but I had a lot of good brothers. They were good cooks and helped with the laundry and the housework. We got along fairly well. My father was a boot and shoemaker. He also hauled freight with a team from Modena [Iron County, Utah]. That left us children at home alone a lot. There were a number of things that we did that we shouldn't have done. We didn't know any better, but we got along fairly well.

"Yes, I had a lot of fun. I was the wild one. I think sometimes if my children had done the things that I did when I was a child I wouldn't have liked it, but I really didn't know any better a lot of times. We did have fun. We played ball. We would get out in the street in the evening and play Run, Sheep, Run and Hide-and-Seek. There were about eight or ten of us, all about the same age, and we huddled together. We had molasses candy pulls and a lot of fun.

"I went to school most of the time. In those days, there were no bakeries. You couldn't buy a loaf of bread anywhere. My father would be gone. My brothers would be away. They went to the mines to work. I would mix our bread in the morning before I went to school. When my father was home, he would write me an excuse for the teacher to let me out so that I could bake the bread. Then he [had] the teacher understand that when he wasn't there, she would have to let me write my own excuse, because I had to go home and take care of the bread. We had cows. My sister younger than me used to help. We had to milk the cows, [take care of] the pigs and the horses, and do all the chores when the men were all gone.

"I remember a lot of things about [my father.] He was a good shoemaker. There wasn't much money in those days. I remember he would take us two younger girls in the wagon and go over to Santa Clara [Washington County, Utah]. We would gather up a gunny sack full of shoes to mend or repair. Then he would bring them home and get them all fixed. He would take us back with him when he took the shoes back. It was mostly trade. I remember we used to get squash, grapes, dried fruit, and very little money. He had a farm that he tried to run. He [grew] enough hay for his own stock, the horse team, and the milk cows. He always had a good garden."

DANIEL WINDER

Daniel Winder was born on 29 April 1905 in Mt. Carmel in Kane County and lived some of his life in Springdale. He went to school in Mt. Carmel for four grades and four more in Springdale. He recalled the following: "When I was nine years old I was working for Henry Esplin who at the time was bishop of the Orderville Ward [Kane County, Utah]. I was on a ranch about a mile from this ranch and we were clearing and plowing ground. We had about forty acres cleared. Charles and Homer Esplin, Henry's boys, helped clear the ground and then they had to go down on the Arizona Strip to bring their sheep up. I stayed there at the ranch and plowed [the] forty acres with a hand plow. [It was] the first time it [had] ever [been] plowed. Anybody that knows anything about running a hand plow knows that was quite a job for a nine-year-old boy to do. Three years later, I was on that same ranch [and] I cut and harvested forty acres of corn alone. [I] had to cut it with a hoe and load it on a wagon, haul it into the yard and shock it.[13] I worked there for forty-five days and never saw a soul."[14]

MYRTLE CRAWFORD WINDER

Myrtle Crawford Winder was born in Springdale on 20 February 1908. She gives a girl's view with both fun and difficulties: "I remember before I even went to school [and] after grandma [died] my little sister Della was just a baby. Mom used to ride a horse from Oak Creek [Washington County, Utah] down to Springdale to clerk in the store and help grandpa. One morning it was cold. Mama always rode side-saddle [as] she was quite a horseback rider. As we went down [the trail], the saddle turned and mama turned and the horse started to run. The horse ran up the hillside, up on the bank, and we fell off. I took Della down to Aunt Fannie [Gifford's] place and stayed there with her while mama went back [to] get the horse. She had to go clear back to the corral to get her. When we [went] down to Springdale, I would watch Della while [mother] would work in the store and help grandpa.

"I had a cousin [Merle Crawford] my same age [and we went to school together]. The first year I guess we [arrived] home all right but the next year there were boy cousins her age, Norman Crawford, Heber Crawford, and Roger Rupert from Springdale and Edwin Stout from Hurricane. The four of us [would] find hills to climb and roll down and slide. We would be let out [of school] about 2:30 p.m. [and the other youngsters were] let out at 4:00 p.m. We would be home most of the time because we had places to go.

"I remember the last year (eighth grade when) we were to school, there was a boy there by the name of Cecil Hepworth. He would take the powder out of shotgun bullets and then cut the bullets up and make all the girls [rings]. We called them engagement rings. He would put the powder down

[on] the floor and strike a match to it; right [on] the schoolhouse floor. I don't know how he got by with it but the teacher let him do it. Maybe she couldn't handle him. One day he went up the trail and [took] some powder [from] where they were making it. He filled his pocket and then stooped over and struck a match to some [powder]. [It] burned and flashed up into the powder in his pockets and he died from [those] burns.

"Grandfather [William Robinson] Crawford had a great big barn. That was the best place that you could ever pick to play run-sheep-run or hide and seek. It had some great big swings in it and we enjoyed that. We also had candy pulls. At these parties we would have candy pulls or just go outside and play. I could play with any of the girls and some of the boys in basketball or baseball. There were four of us girls. I used to play marbles with the cousin of mine and two other boys. Sometimes the girls would be against the boys and sometimes we would do it the other way, one of the girls and a boy [as a team]. We really tried to see which one could get there first to start that marble game."[15]

MARY HAFEN LEAVITT

Mary Hafen Leavitt was born on 5 November 1877. She tells about life on the west side of the county in Santa Clara: "My mother's first husband was John Reber. He only lived ten days after they were married. They went to Salt Lake to be married. [It happened] the day after he came home. He had another family besides my mother then. She was the second wife to him. They went out in the field to see the crops after they had been gone ten days. On the way back they stopped at a little stream of water [because] the horses wanted a drink. He caught his bridle on the wagon tongue and ripped it off. That scared the horses. They had blinds over their eyes. As soon as the bridle was off, [the horses] were frightened and began to run down the lane as fast as they could go. [They] went over a wood pile and almost tipped the wagon over. It threw the husband [John Reber] out and a [wagon] wheel ran over him and crushed him. He died that night. None of the women were hurt. They all hung onto the rack. It was just a hayrack they were riding on. Mother was a widow for a year or so; then she married my father, John [George] Hafen.

"I remember lots of little things in that first home down here. I was looking over this book a while ago. My mother was a very congenial woman.

The young folks often came there to spend the evening with her. She made the most beautiful valentines you ever saw. They would come, maybe three or four of them, to get the valentines made for their best boyfriend. Each could have one of mother's valentines. They thought that was all they needed. They would often do her work while she [made] them. She taught them to crochet and to knit. So many times they would come and spend the evening with mother. I will always remember those lovely evenings.

"There was a man who came from Switzerland. He lived there. Rick Sickel was his name [and] he taught all the young folks to make baskets. [This area] was great fruit country and everybody had to pick fruit, so they had these baskets to fill up and dump in the wagon. We would often go [to pick fruit] before sunrise in a big double bed. Do you know what a double bed wagon box is? We would take these baskets along, fill them and dump them in the wagon. [When] the wagon was full, [we would] go home and spend the rest of the day cutting. It would take all day long to cut the wagon load of peaches.

"We cut them in halves and put them out on scaffolds to dry. We would fill one board at a time, and put on another board and another board, until we had the whole yard full [of scaffolds]. Then my father would take these to Beaver [Beaver County, Utah] and exchange [the peaches] for clothing and cheese. [He would] come home with all kinds of nice [items]. He was a very enterprising man. He did a lot of peddling besides tending his store. Of course, his wife took care of the store when he was gone. He had a big family. He had about ten children [in] his first family. Arthur K. [Knight Hafen] is one of his grandsons."[16]

VERA HINTON EAGER

Vera Hinton Eager was born on 14 August 1899 in Hinckley, Millard County. Several families from Washington County had moved there to start that town. She later moved to Hurricane, and these memories tell of the earliest settlement there: "In 1905, we moved to Virgin, Utah, which was Father's home town. In March of 1905, they moved to Hurricane [Washington, County] Utah [and we were] the first family to move to Hurricane. I was six years old at the time.

"When we moved on the Hurricane Bank, as we called it, it was a big, flat place. It had chaparral, slippery elm, and sagebrush all over the flat

[land]. We made trails through this to go from one place to another. While we were the first family to move there, it was only a few days until other families moved in. The first church [meeting] that we held in Hurricane was under a bowery which the men [had] built. They put the posts up and posts across. They would find cottonwood trees—which there were quite a few [of] around Hurricane—[and] put them across the top of the bowery to make shade. They would split poles and fix them for seats for people to sit on. This is where they had the first [meetings of] The Church of Jesus Christ of Latter-day Saints. They [found] a bell [and] anchored [it] to three poles. It would ring one half-hour before Sunday school meeting and Primary. My brother had to ring the bell for Primary, as my mother was the president of the Primary. It was his job to ring the bell one half-hour before each Primary. When my sister was born, he was unhappy because she wasn't a boy. He wanted a brother, so the brothers could take turns ringing the bell. He thought that he would have to ring that bell forever.

"While we were living there, we would go out on the hills. Father took up a lot of land, so we had hills to roam. While we were exploring one day, we found a place called a skeleton hole. The reason for this name is that it seemed that part of the ground had just dropped from the surface. It was a deep hole. When we found [it], it was large enough for a man to get down in there. [The men would] go down in there and pile rocks up so they could get in and out of this skeleton hole. At first, there were a lot of dead animal carcasses down there, like rabbits and coyotes. They would come running along, and they wouldn't notice this hole soon enough [and] down they would go. They would just drop down into this hole. It smelled really bad down in there. We had lots of fun down in there when the rocks were piled up so that we could get in there. We didn't have flashlights, but we would light a stick and go way, way back in for about a mile. . . . We were really quite frightened to be down in there for fear some wild animal would drop down in and it would be hungry. Maybe it would attack us! We didn't like to go down in there too [much], but we sure did like to go over there and look down in [to] see what we could see.

"We would walk over the hill and go swimming in the Virgin River. We had so much fun swimming in the river. The boys would find holes that were deep that they would swim in. [The] girls were a little bit [afraid] to go in the deep holes, so we would swim [and] wade around, and float on the river. Then we would cross the river and go over to Ash Creek. Under the rocks in Ash Creek we would find suckerfish. We would catch those and take them home. Our mother would fry them in the frying pan, crisp and brown. We would eat them, bones and all. I never remember fish being as good as those suckers were that we caught down at Ash Creek. One day, while we were going down there, my husband Thomas's sister killed a rattlesnake. [Thomas and I] weren't married at the time. All of the rest of us were frightened to death. We didn't know what to do, but she got a big stick and a rock and killed the rattlesnake. We all thought she was so brave for killing the rattlesnake."[17]

BLANCH MATHIS MCCOMB

Blanch Mathis McComb gives a city girl's view of youth. She was born on 21 July 1903 in St. George and describes the capital-city life of advantaged young people: "I remember having such a happy childhood and the fun we had with all the neighbor children. We had our little playhouse where we had divided rooms and a real little stove where we gathered vegetables from the garden and made soup. We picked Pottawattamie plumbs and pears and our mother let us bottle them. We would play that were bottling [canning] fruit. One of our neighbor friends, Wilma Church, and I used to play on the Black Hill a lot. We had playhouses there. That is why we are so fond of the smell of chaparral now because we always remember those little playhouses we had on the Black Hill.

"My cousin Helen Miles and I were very dear friends and [we] spent so many happy times together. I remember especially the time when Helen and I were eight years of age and were to be baptized. Our mothers couldn't go with us and so they fixed our clothes and we went down to the temple alone. I remember how they praised us for being such brave little girls to come that far alone.

"We had a lot of the fun days [at school]. All the [students were] together when we would go on picnics and hikes. I remember the Arbor Days over on the Woodward School grounds. There was no landscaping there but we would plant trees and make little gardens. Each class [had a] little garden. Arbor Day was quite an outstanding day. I remember the big wood piles because the furnace burned wood and the huge stacks of wood [were kept] out on the playground. [We] marched up and down the stairs. All the classes formed out in front of the school and the school orchestra [played] and we would take turns and march up those long steps.

"It was a real event to get to [Dixie] High School where we could have different teachers for each class. All through high school, I remember the fun class was chorus. We would go up to the Tabernacle where we held chorus [practice] with Brother [Joseph William] McAllister. We loved [him] so much. He taught us so much [about] music. We had the operas up in the old opera house.

"Nearly every family in town had [the] flu in 1918. I remember when we had [it] in our home. Nearly all of us [were] ill with it and I was 'out of my head,' [as] they used to call it. I remember my father administering to me and how it helped and calmed me down. Of course, we all recovered.

"I do remember one incident though. We were juniors [and] after the 'D' was put up on the hill, we came to school one morning and someone was standing at the door asking if we were juniors. They said we were not allowed to go into the building. This surprised all [of] us because we didn't know what had happened. It turned out that two boys in our class had gone up in the night and painted a '22' in the center of the 'D.' It spoiled our fun. So the letters were removed because they had marred the official block 'D' on the hill. We all joined in and went up the hill and helped erase it, although it wasn't our fault.

"All through my life, from the time when we were quite young, it seems like we had fun. We had our slumber parties on the Fourth of July, hay rides in the morning and playing down in the Seegmiller farm with Helen. All the adventures that we had are so much fun to think about. I remember Anna Miles and I were Beehive leaders [in the Church of Jesus Christ of Latter-day Saints]. We went to Pine Valley Mountain and camped. We rode horseback one day over Pine Valley Mountain with a large group from St. George. We wound up through the canyon and the mountains. I especially remember [Dilworth] Snow and the marvelous voice that he had. As we rode along the trail, single file, he would sing and his voice would just echo through the mountain. We went up over the pass of the mountain and went to Cabin Valley and back down to Pine Valley that evening. It was a lot more fun going up than it was going down, I can say that! I remember going to the dance in Pine Valley that night in their church with the lamps lighted and the old orchestra. [A] thunderstorm came up [and] we were all so frightened."[18]

LOLA BELLE DEMILLE BRYNER

In contrast to the life in St. George is this report from Lola Belle DeMille Bryner in Rockville. She was born on 21 May 1901 about the same time as Blanch McComb from St. George. Her lifestyle was different, even though they lived in the same county, and she was very positive about her family and community life: "I was born while my father was on a mission to the Southern states. In his diary he [wrote] that he saw in [a] dream the buggy that was going around the narrow dug way from Rockville to Springdale [Washington County] to get the midwife to come back to Rockville to help my mother [with] her delivery. When he received the letter from my mother stating that he had a daughter, it was no surprise to him because he knew that I had been born.

"Rockville is hemmed in by beautiful mountains on each side and the Virgin River flows down through the green little valley. I had four brothers and three sisters. We grew up here, untouched by civilization. We had a freedom that is seldom known because we were so isolated in this small town. In those days, the only means of [transportation] was by horse and buggy so we didn't travel very far. We roamed the mountains, hills, and valleys. We watched the birds, gathered wildflowers, and had a wonderful childhood in spite of the hardships which we had [to] endure, but most everyone was poor in those days so we didn't notice it.

"We also had a town Christmas party that was always special. It was held in the school building which was used for church, dances, and all community gatherings. Our Christmas party was held there. A huge Christmas tree was put on the stage and each parent would bring a gift for [their] child and it was hung on the Christmas tree. Then, at night, we all went to [the] party. They had a program. Then they would open the curtains on the stage and there was this beautiful tree. Our eyes must have looked like stars as we looked at it! Then Santa Claus would come in the door and run up the [aisle] crying, 'Merry Christmas, Merry Christmas,' and go up on the stage. He would take the gifts from the tree and call the children's names that were on the gift. Only one gift for each child was on the tree. The child would go up and get their gift and a bag of candy, popcorn and nuts that he had in a bag on his back. My father was usually the town Santa Claus. I thought this was extra special because I knew he was the Santa Claus. He loved little children and was always so kind and good to them.

"Thanksgiving time was also celebrated in a special and friendly way. We had the town dinner when we were children. We gathered in the same building and large tables were set up. The children would gather around and watch all the festivities. The food [was] brought in by each family and put on the table. I imagine we got in the way many times, and [I] remember being told to go out and play until we were called. Later, when I was a little older, I was able to help set the tables and help prepare [the food] for this dinner. This was a very special time for us which we enjoyed.

"Our home was a very humble two-room home. We used one end of it as a bedroom. We had two large double beds, and I remember mother had a trunk in between, which was always a curiosity to me. There she kept some of her most cherished treasures. We had a fireplace at the other end [of the room] and a table for us children to study [at]. A little shelf hung on the wall with our few books, our Holy Bible, and [other] important books that we had. I remember pretty lace curtains hung at the window, and we had a woven carpet on the floor and chairs and a fireplace at the end.

"The fireplace was the center of our lives. Here, in the evenings, we roasted potatoes, popped corn, and told pioneer stories. My father [grew] lots of apples of every kind. Nice juicy apples were brought in, at times, around the fireplace in the wintertime, and we ate those. Grapes that we had picked were brought in, and sometimes in the wintertime we would make ice cream in the evenings. We couldn't make it any time, only in the winter, because we did have the ice. We would get the snow and ice and put it in a large tub and get a bucket that had a bale [handle] on it. [We would] put our ice cream mixture in this, put the lid on the bucket, and turn the bucket back and forth, back and forth, taking the lid off and scraping it until it was all frozen. This was a special treat for us.

"Around the fireplace I had cousins and uncles, my father's brothers and relatives. They were musical and would play the guitar, the mandolin, and the harmonica for us. I thought the music came straight from heaven; this was enjoyable for us. I remember the home teachers coming [to our house] and we would sit around the fireplace. They would always kneel with us, and we would pray. Then they would give us a sermon out of the Bible, [a] gospel sermon, and then they would pray again before they left. I always had a good feeling and felt that the Lord was close by watching over us and that we were loved by the elders in the ward. These were some of my fondest memories of my life there.

"Another fond memory was of my father. When he was on his mission, he got [a ride on the train]. [He] knew about the train which we children knew nothing about. He got up in the morning [at our house] to build a fire in the fireplace in our kitchen stove. It became warm, [and] he would want to wake us up. He would start calling us, 'Get up, it is time to get up. Don't let the sun burn blisters on your eyeballs. Get up and be about your work.' Then he would start dancing the train dance. He would shuffle his feet slow, slow and then finally go a little faster, a little faster. Then he would say, 'It is the first call to breakfast.' And then, 'The last call to breakfast.' [He was] trying to get us up in a kind [and] pleasant way. I didn't know what a train sounded like, but later when I heard a train, I realized how real his train dance was—how much it did sound like a train."[19]

EDWARD SIRLS TERRY

Edward Sirls Terry offers a boy's view of rural living. He was born on 21 December 1886 in Mesquite, Nevada, but the family soon moved nearby to Beaver Dam Wash, Arizona. "In my early childhood my father and mother moved up on the Beaver Dam Wash. They took a farm there above the Blue Ranch. I was very small and had one sister younger than me. We worked along with the rest of the family, hard [work] at all times, grubbing ground and planting it into crops. My father was a wonderful orchard man. He planted a vineyard and orchard and [they were] wonderful. We also raised a fine garden every year. [We] raised corn, cane, and alfalfa hay. We made molasses for years and years. Even after I was married we made lots of molasses and [were known for] having the best molasses [made] anywhere in the country. We raised lots of beans. [When] we were little fellows, we used to go out after the beans had been gathered and thresh [the beans] in a wagon-box or on a canvas with a flailer.[20] We used to go out and spend hours and hours going up and down the rows picking up the beans that had [been] threshed out so none of them [were] ever wasted. My father had a few head of sheep, five head to start out with, and they kept increasing. I and my older brother would herd them with the milk cows out on the hills in the spring of the year.

"We chased the chipmunks and little rabbits. [We] ran and barked like we were dogs. They would go down in the hole [and] we would get two sticks and dig in the holes and put our nose down to the holes and smell them and go to growling and digging again. . . . When I was about sixteen years of age, I was doing a lot of trapping. In fact I trapped all my life up [until] two years ago. I'll have to tell this one trapping experience. We would [take] our coats or pelts into St. George and get the bounty on them. [There was] a bounty [of] fifty cents apiece. Old Uncle Charlie Miles was the recorder in the courthouse [where we picked up the bounty]. [One] time I brought in a bunch of hides, and he said to me, 'Edward, did you catch all of these in Utah? You know we can't give bounty on the ones caught in any other state.' I said, 'Well, I caught them all but this big one here.' He said, 'Where did you catch it?' I said, 'In Nevada.' He said, 'The law says they have to be caught in the state of Utah.' I said, 'No, the law says they have to be killed in the state of Utah.' He said, 'That is right, but you caught it in Nevada.' I said, 'Yes, but I drug him across the line to kill him.' He paid me."[21]

MARTHA VILATE HUGHES KNIGHT

Martha Vilate Hughes Knight was born on 29 January 1903 in Mesquite and tells another version of youthful fun: "Yes, we had lots of fun. We had fun when we were out of school. We had to make our own fun, because there wasn't television and things like that then. We would decide that we were going to have a dance maybe late in the afternoon. [George] Bowler, [who] was one of our schoolteachers, would play his violin and his wife [Nancy] would play a mandolin. Their daughter [Rachel] would play the piano. All the boys in town would go and help him on his farm so he would come and play for dances.

"We used to go hay-rack riding. We would take a team and go hay-rack riding. On May Day, the first day of May, they always had such big celebrations. They would go up to what was called Johnson's Ranch a lot of times and put up big swings in the trees and have sport [events.] They always had a queen and her maids. It seems as though I was always chosen to be one of the maids. I was little and was always one of the maids on these occasions. The whole town used to [turn] out.

"They had footraces. At Christmastime they would [have] sport [events] for two solid weeks. They had sports all day and danced at night. They would have different kinds of dances. The girls and the women would all have to fix lunches, and the boys would draw their names or put their tag on their toes. They would have to take them to lunch.

"Those days weren't like it is now. When they dance now, they just dance with the same person or get in a little clique. But then if a young girl went to the dance, she spent as much time dancing with the married men as she spent dancing with the young boys. Everybody danced, and they used to have wonderful times.

"If they decided they were going to have a rabbit supper, the whole town would go up to the Tunnel Point. They would have all kind of sport and cook the rabbits and have big suppers. So we had lots of enjoyment when we were youngsters. The boys used to play ball. A lot of the time the girls would stand against the boys and play ball. Then the two towns, Bunkerville and Mesquite, used to play ball. There was quite a rivalry between them. We used to stand up to watch those ball games."[22]

JOSEPH TERRY

The story of Nels Anderson gives a different view of Terry's ranch because he was a hobo who drifted there after being kicked off of a freight train but became part of the community. Joseph Terry, the rancher, tells the story: "The station then was Acoma, [Nevada]. They came to Acoma and found him on the train, and they put him off. The conductor hailed him, and they pulled the train out and [went] down the line two or three hundred yards to slow down [the train]. When the conductor let loose of him, they started the train and went on.

"This boy walked down the tracks until he [came] to Clover Valley. That was five miles below. My brother-in-law, [who] married my younger sister, was raking hay alongside the railroad there. The boy came walking along down the tracks. He went to the side of the fence and stopped close to the track. He started talking to the boy and asked him what he was doing. The boy talked to him a little but he did not have much to say. [My brother] said, 'When did you [last] have something to eat?' He said, 'I had a sandwich yesterday.' He said, 'Crawl through that fence.' He crawled through the fence and said to him, 'You go across the field to my house over there and tell my wife to fix you something to eat.'

"The boy walked across there, but going across he came to the wood-pile before he came to the house. Everybody had wood-burning stoves. He picked up the axe and went to chopping wood. My brother-in-law saw him chopping wood, and so he rode around towards the boy as close as he could get and stopped his horse. He went over and took the boy into the house. He told his wife to fix him something to eat. He had not had anything to eat since the day before. She fixed him a good meal. He ate and then he went out and went to doing chores around and worked around. The next morning my brother-in-law took him over to his parents' place over to the Wood's home. They made their home there. He said, 'Here, Father, I brought you a chore boy. You have him do your chores and take care of him.

"[Soon] Grandfather Wood said, 'This is a good boy. I better take him out to the ranch to do the chores for you.' My brother picked him up and brought him over to the ranch there, and he did the chores for us. He came to live with me there, and he took up with us. We took care of this young lad. He was very ambitious and anxious to work. . . . He stayed right with us. When they started school, they went to school, and he went through school that winter and then worked around with us the next summer. . . . The next winter my oldest brother went down to St. George to put his children in school there, and this boy went down there and went to [Dixie High] School with them. He got along nicely in school. He was very bright and active. His name was Nels Anderson.

"He lived with us in the summertime and went down there in the winter until he [was] old enough so he could branch out and take a job. . . . [Then] he went to school [at BYU] in Provo. The war [World War I] broke out, and he was called into the [United States] Army. He went in the Army and was [sent] over to England. They finally located in Germany. The war was called off while he was in Germany. He came back to the United States. He went to work here and worked his way until he finished college work in the Brigham Young University. He kept going right on from there."[23]

While at Dixie College, Nels Anderson associated with Juanita Brooks and was later able to help her obtain a grant during the Great Depression to employ women in Washington County to transcribe pioneer journals. Anderson wrote a famous book about the Mormons titled *Desert Saints*. He obtained a doctorate degree in sociology from New York University and became a key leader in the labor programs of the New Deal. During and after World War II, Nels was associated with the United States Army in Europe and the Lend-Lease Act. He was not born in the area, nor was he actually related to the people of the county, but he knew the area completely and became one of the most famous people to have lived in Utah's Dixie. In 2012, Dr. Charles Peterson delivered the Juanita Brooks lecture titled "Hopeful Odyssey: Nels Anderson." Allen Kent Powell published Anderson's World War I Diary,[24] which includes a good summary of his life. One aspect of the journal reflected his mentality at the time. He tells of using his spare time to roam in search of other Mormons, particularly some from Utah's Dixie and Arizona so they could reinforce their Mormon values.

MARY ANN STARR

Mary Ann (Adams) Starr was born on 29 October 1902 in Cedar City. She reflects on her childhood: "I remember when the lightning struck our home when I was a [young] girl. I remember when we [had a] dairy at the old ranch in Ellie's Canyon. The bear [would] pass [by] the milk house. I remember the old squaw [who] came to our home in the middle of the night looking for Thomas Urie. It was a bad storm that day. The south field ditch ran right through the top part of our lot. We had an old fireplace, but it was summer and a homemade board was put over the fireplace. It struck the chimney, and it blew the fireboard out and clear across the room. It stunned us all. My mother was sitting in her rocking chair and it turned the chair right upside down. I can remember my father jumping [up] and grabbing all [of] us. He thought the house was on fire. [He] took us down [to] the old dirt cellar [in] the back of the house. This ditch was going through our lot; it overflowed and the cellar began to fill up with the muddy water. We had to run back in the house. The neighbors had come and put the fire out. It was a mess in there, [and] the water was running around the house. I will never forget that [experience].

"The time the Indian came [we were living in] the same house. The Indian camp was south of town, and my father was off freighting to Milford and Delamar mines in Nevada. We had all gone to bed. Something woke mother up. She heard someone breathing hard. She told us all to be quiet, and she got up. She was afraid to light the lamp. She could see the outline of this woman. She asked who it was, and the old squaw jabbered and said she wanted 'Tom.' Of course, mother knew she meant Thomas Urie, the city marshal. She told her where she [would] have to go down to get [him]. The squaw told her that all the Indians were drunk and were beating up on their squaws. She had come for help. She seemed confused. Mother told her, the best she could, where to go. It was in the middle of the night, late for us anyway. She left and Mother barred the doors, because [people] didn't used to lock their doors. . . .

"I came down with pneumonia. They only had one doctor here at that time, a Doctor Green. He was out of town. I would like to mention this. We called Grandma Pryor. She was well known around here, Margaret Pryor. She was a midwife and the only doctor half of the time. My father went down on a horse to get her, and she took care of me. . . . Father asked her if she thought she could save me. She said, 'With God's help I will save your girl.' And she did. She slept on the foot of my bed for one solid week and brought me out of it. . . .

"In those days, we didn't have cars. We always had saddle horses at home though. I remember two [of them]. We called one 'Kelly' and one 'Fawn.' We practically rode them to death. We loved them. Everywhere we went we [were] either in a wagon or on a horse. The neighbor girls, my pals across the street, they had horses too. We would ride up to the old mill, up Cedar Canyon, especially for Easter. For Easter we would go up there, have our lunch, and ride our little ponies up there."[25]

BODIL MARGARET PULSIPHER

Bodil Margaret Johnson Pulsipher was born on 13 February 1890 in Colonia Juárez, Chihuahua, Mexico. Her family later moved to the upper Virgin River area in southern Utah, where her father, Nephi Johnson, had some interesting adventures with American Indians regarding Zion Canyon. She tells: "The Indians were going up [into Zion Canyon] and they wanted Nephi to come with them. . . . He said, 'Okay.' They said, 'We go now, but we come home before dark. The bad men will get us if we don't.' . . .

[I liked to] ride horses, wild ones; if they would buck, I would stay on them. . . . I didn't do it too much. I think once is about all I did. My brother rode anything, and I snuck them to the farm. . . . Yes, I was more scared than he was. I would only ride them bareback and then they could kick me off. . . . We had fairs and would give prizes to the ones who could do things quicker than the others. One time . . . they said, 'We will see who can put the harness on this horse the quickest and get it back in its place.' The same with the saddle; 'put the saddle on the blanket right and the saddle.' They got through and then they said, 'Come on, Maggie.' I said, 'I am not going to get out there.' I was always acting like I was [very] scared. I won the most prizes for a whole bunch of women, and I was just a young girl. . . .

"The boys got the chickens and roasted them and we would eat them . . . from the neighbors. . . . We used to have big family chicken suppers. You would go part way up the mountain and cook them in a bake oven."[26]

LORA ANN CHRISTENSEN

Here is a brief memory from Lora Ann Gifford Christensen. She was born in Springdale in 1881 and remembers a less combative group of friends: "It was like all one family here in Springdale and we played with everybody; we were all out together. . . . We were like one big family [when] we went out to play and have our fun. When we [were] almost grown, we went out on the streets [to] play different kinds of games. . . . Run, Sheep, Run and all [those] kinds of [games].

"I went to school here in Springdale. . . . We went to [the] eighth grade. We stayed out [of school] a few times. Some winters one of us would go, [and] then someone else would go [the next winter]. Other winters we would change."[27]

LAURA SNOW WOODBURY

Here, Laura Snow Woodbury gives a St. George version of gangs of friends. She was born on 9 March 1897, almost the same time as Lora Ann Gifford Christensen but in a larger town setting. She reports both about childhood and teenage friends, but also about work: "My childhood was a happy and a normal one. I was fortunate in having the living care and protection of both a father and a mother. As children, we had the whole quarter of the block in which to roam. At the side of my home there were large almond trees, whose nuts promised a real treat to us on the long winter evenings. Eating almonds before the cheery blaze of the fireplace was much more fun than harvesting them in the fall. I remember the time I used to spend helping pick up almonds off the ground and then husking them.

"One of our chief recreational areas is now a busy highway. It was not unusual for the [children] of our day to play in the sandy and unlighted streets on a hot summer evening. Our chief games were Run, Sheep, Run; Steal Sticks; and Come to Court. Our neighborhood pals in those days included Abel and Nettie Riding, Burt Bentley, and Willa and Chauncey Andrews, who lived directly across from our place. [Also] there was Gwen Gardner and my cousin, Polly Kemp. Often we gathered at the small, black rock house of Sister Riding's and made molasses candy and cracked black walnuts. . . .

"I remember the evenings that my grandmother, my aunt, and my little orphaned cousin would spend [time] with us, especially in the wintertime. My grandmother and my aunt raised [my cousin, Polly Kemp]. . . . We would spend [time] around the fireplace popping corn and munching on apples. We didn't have treats then [like] they have now, but we had our type of treats. . . .

"We were born [at] the end of the pioneer times. We had to carry the coal oil lamp from room to room. We had to clean the lamps, fill them, and trim the wicks. Our home was a large two-story home. I remember the first time we had electric lights. When the lights were first put in, we turned on the lights in every room in the house. Then [we] went outside to the sidewalk to look at it. That was one of the wonders of the world! . . .

"In my teens I made no attempt to shirk from the many household tasks, in spite of the fact that part of my day was spent in the school room. Wrapped in an old bathrobe, I have at times started the family washing at four [in the morning]. On many occasions I arose early enough to have most of the ironing done before an eight o'clock class at school. We had no such conveniences as automatic hot water or automatic washers. Friday afternoons after school, I could be located cleaning the upper floor of our home to lessen the Saturday's work the day following. These tasks did not hurt me and they surely must have given my mother a lift. I do not want to infer that, while I was thus engaged, my dear mother was idly sucking her thumb, for she was not. In the early part of these days, all baking, washing, sewing, etc. had to be done in the home. There were not always bakery goods and ready-made clothing to be had.

"For twenty-five years my mother entertained church dignitaries four times a year at stake conference time because father was stake president for these twenty-five years. Her duties were also many. House cleaning in the spring was really a job. It meant pulling up the carpets [and putting] new straw under them. Every speck [of dirt] that could be washed was washed, transoms included. One spring, Mother and I worked side by side from dawn to dark for three weeks before we had finished the spring cleaning. Believe me; it was clean when we were through. . . .

"One lonely Sunday afternoon, Polly and I were wondering what to do with ourselves as we stood on the David H. Morris corner, now where the telephone building stands. While I was pondering, along came Vernon and Annie Worthen and David Woodbury. An invitation to go riding with them in the Worthens' white-topped buggy was an answer to our needs. That was the beginning of many good times and a lifelong friendship with them. Soon after that, we found that we belonged to a gang of some twenty to thirty people—a gang who could any time, in fair weather or foul, go trooping into the George [and Leonora Woodbury] Worthen home, regardless of mud on our feet or regardless of frequency of visits. Any time we wanted to go [there] we could depend on being welcomed at the Worthens'. They lived across the street north of the tabernacle. I shall always cherish the fun and memories of the evenings there."[28]

ROBERT PARKER WOODBURY

Robert Parker Woodbury grew up in St. George and was born about 1875. He was interviewed after he turned ninety-two. He tells of teenage fun: "We played ball, went fishing, swimming, and [did] a lot of those things together. When we grew up and [were] a little older, the boys began to think about girls, and the girls about the boys. We used to have home parties, and there were kissing parties. I guess you would say it was unsanitary now, but we had a lot of them, and I don't remember one of them getting sick.

"We had to make our own fun [because] we didn't have picture shows or anything [like that] in those days. So we had lots of parties in the home. We would have something to do that we had to gather a forfeit, a hand-kerchief, or a pocketknife or whatever they had. After you [had] a number of them, they had to be redeemed. I had one person sitting on a chair, and the person had one of these articles, and he would say, 'Heavy, heavy hangs over your head.' The [person] would say, 'Was it fine or superfine?' Fine stood for boys, and superfine stood for girls. He would announce it and tell what he had to do to redeem the article that he had. You know there was some kissing there! . . .

"[Dancing] was the joy of my life. I started dancing when I was a young fellow [and] danced until I was ninety-two. [The] last dance [that] I went to [was when] I was ninety-two! Then I had a sick spell, and I haven't danced since. It was like missing a lot to miss a dance. We used to have those old quadrilles [where] they would have a caller. He would say, 'Fill up the floor,' and [we would race across the room]. In those days, the girls would sit on one side of the hall and the boys on the other. You would break a neck to get over to get a girl [for] a partner to dance. We did enjoy those old quadrille dances.

"[We had] a violin and a banjo or something like that, but the violin was the main [instrument]. It wasn't noisy like it is now. You could sure dance to that violin! [There were] a lot of older men that played the violin, and we had real good dances."[29]

LUCY CRAWFORD SCHIEFER

Lucy Crawford Schiefer was born on 16 December 1904 in Virgin, Utah. She also lived in Springdale and Oak Creek, and she tells about ranch life as well as community life in Springdale: "I used to run and gather the eggs for my grandmother. She was a hard worker and would work in the garden. She knew I was dependable and I would gather those eggs. Each night I would bring the eggs to her. She would say, 'How many eggs did you gather today?' I would tell her. Always she was one egg short. She would give me articles to count to see whether I knew how to count because there was always an egg missing. One night she didn't work in the garden; she sat in the laundry room and watched through the window to see what happened when I gathered the eggs. When I came to the corral gate to come out, Grandfather met me. He picked up one egg and poked a hole in the end of it and sucked his egg for the day. I came in the house and Grandmother would say, 'How many eggs did you gather today?' She kept strict count because she paid tithing on those eggs. Every tenth one had to go for tithing. Then she knew why I miscounted the eggs. . . .

"We were raised on a big ranch. To go from one side [of the ranch] to the other took quite a little while so we had horses that we would ride. Once in a while, I didn't stop for a bridle or even a rope. I would just walk out, whistle, the horse would come to me, and I would pile on. One day Father caught me out on the street that way on the highway. He gave me a severe bawling out for that. He said I had no way whatever of defending myself that way. If anything startled the horse and it wanted to ride—and I did have horses run away with me a time or two, so I knew he was right. I never stopped for a saddle if I wanted to ride the horse over the field anywhere unless I had to carry something.

"We had a big row of currant bushes across the river. This, I guess, was three quarters of a mile from the house. We would go over there in the spring and the summer and pick currants. Mother and I would each ride a horse and each carry two buckets of currants back to the house on these horses. We could put the bridle over the horn of the saddle when we had the saddle on. To go across the [Virgin] River, if it was very important, we usually rode a horse. If they were busy in the hay field, then we would have to wade [across] the river or cross on a footbridge that my father made.

"One time a cousin of mine, Nora Jolley—she was Nora Crawford at the time—waded across the river. It was a clear day. [She] carried her shoes and stockings. When we went to come back, the river was up just under our arms, and it was getting kind of muddy, [but] it wasn't too bad. We got out, and by the time we [were] on the outside, a larger flood came down. It would have swept us away if we had [stayed longer].

"Another narrow escape that I had was with my father and mother. It was on the twenty-fourth of July. We had been celebrating in Rockville. We came home, and we had pigs across the [Virgin] River in [the] orchard under the currant bushes. Father had to haul water for them because the water was out of the ditch that ran past. We dipped up water, filled the barrels, and took them up to the pigs. [We] came back and he said, 'I will fill these barrels to take to the house.' We lived about a half a mile from the river. At that time, there was no water system here. All our water [came] from the river. He was dipping up water and said to Mother, 'Whip the horses quick!' She didn't understand, so he yelled for the horses to move. They did, and when we turned to look back, a flood had gone past us. If we hadn't [moved], we may have been swept down. . . ."We had to have our own parties because there was no television or radios. We had our own orchestra through the town. Various ones [who] knew how to play instruments would get together and find their own music for dances and [events]. We always had parties, especially in the wintertime, and a dance about once a week. Friday night was our dance [night]. We always [planned] Saturday night was family night. We didn't have [a] dance or anything. My father had a home evening [on] Saturday night in my home. We always had refreshments after reading the scripture and talking over the messages from the Holy Bible, or he would give us lessons. We didn't have a lesson book that I remember back in that day. [It was] about 1915, I recall, [when we had home evening]. But he always read from the Holy Bible. Then we would have singing. My father played the organ. Some of the time we would invite neighbors in. One boy, especially, used to like to hear the tunes my father played that would jiggle the organ, he called it. The floor must not have been even so the organ would kind of jiggle on some of the pieces like 'Turkey in the Straw' and 'Marching Through Georgia.' Dad could play very good that way and he played for dances, too."[30]

DELLA HUMPHRIES HARDY

Della Humphries Hardy was also born in Virgin in 1908, four years after Lucy Crawford Schiefer, but she then moved to Hurricane as one of the earliest settlers: "I remember my mother telling [me] that the morning I was born, it was a windy March morning. We did not have a doctor in that section of the country, and they did not come out this way very [often]. All they had were midwives. This lady was the one [who] had moved in with her husband and family at the time [we had what] we called the 'oil boom' in Virgin. We had another fellow [who] used to come out there all the time for eggs and milk. He came this [particular] morning. When he came in, he saw they were feeding my older sister breakfast. He said, 'Where is your wife?' She was always there. They said, 'She is in the other room. We had us a new baby girl this morning.' Brother Lyons said, 'I know better than that.' Just then Dad said I let out one of my usual squalls, and he said, 'I guess it is true.' My father used to always say that I got my windy disposition from the month I was born in.

"I remember going into Hurricane. There was still sagebrush, boulders, and rocks. You did not drive straight up the road like you do today. You drove in and out around the big boulders. We lived on the hillside on the southeast end of town. My mother used to say that Dad would have had to hunt hard to find a place fuller of boulders and rocks. We moved into a little one-room house and lived there until my father was able to go to Virgin and bring the other home, [which was] a bigger place, down and put it on another section of the lot.

"I had an accident on one occasion. My neighbor friend and I, being so far from home [at school], would take our lunch a lot of times. We would hurry up and eat, and then [we would] run to the swings to get our turn to play. Usually the older girls and boys got the swings [most of the time], so we would try to get ours at noon. She was singing when two of the boys came through the fence and told her to get out. They wanted to swing. She would not give in. They said, 'If you do not, we will throw a rock at you with this flipper.' It did not scare her much so they flipped. Instead of hitting her, it hit me in my right eye.

"They took me home and took me to the doctor. They thought I had lost my right eye because it had pierced the flesh and the liquid had come out of the eyeball. I never see a pretty sunset that I do not think of the first time that the doctor took the bandage off this eye; it was as the sun was going down. I heard this car drive up, and I was lying on the bed in the front room. Father and Mother were out in the front yard because it was getting [to be] warmer weather. I do not remember whether it was fall or whether it was spring, but I heard this car stop. Soon, I could hear someone running. It was the doctor. He was a big man, and he came running up the walk. He said, 'Where is Della?' My mother said, 'She is in the house.' He said, 'Have her come out.' She came and took me out. He took this bandage off of my eye. The first thing I said was, 'What a beautiful sunset.' My mother began to cry. I was older before it dawned on me why my mother cried and hugged me so hard just because I said it was a beautiful sunset.

"We grew up as most children do [and] had good times. We lived close to the mountain. We used to like to climb to the top of [the] old black lava hill. It never dawned on us to wear shoes. We went bare footed and hopped from one rock to another. It was our job, along with all the neighborhood [youngsters], to herd the cows. We were always glad when spring came so we could take off our shoes and socks and get out and climb the hills.

"Children in the neighborhood used to have me cut holes in these big five-gallon cans [to] make little stoves. There we would fry meat, potatoes, onions, and cook all kinds of meals. We would invite the neighborhood [youngsters] over, and we would take our turn. We had as much fun as those who had riches. We did not think we had any less than the rest. We enjoyed life together.

"In the summertime, we used to wade and swim in the canal. When it was very hot, we would sit in the canal and go up maybe four, five, or six blocks [and] wade in the canal upstream to the next person's place that we wanted to visit. We sang all the way [and] had a good time. In those days, different ages played together more than they do now, too. The older ones were the father and the mother."[31]

ERASTUS SNOW GARDNER

Erastus Snow Gardner lived in Pine Valley all his life. He was born on 10 January 1892. Here he gives a boy's view of ranch life: "I remember when I was a boy, there used to be roundups bringing the cattle from the winter ranges. There used to be a lot of cattle owned around Pine Valley. I remember as youngsters, we just about lived to see [the] cattle come over the ridge into Pine Valley. They would string over the ridge for hours. We youngsters would go down to the lower end where the fields were and climb up on the fence to watch them come into town. They would bring the cattle right up into town [to] separate [and] each man [would] take his cattle from there.

"Ranchers from the whole southern part of the state would ride together on the ranges to gather their cattle. They would separate their cattle at what they called [the] Magotsu [Creek] corral [and] take them to the different towns from there. We would drive all the cattle that belonged to Pine Valley into Pine Valley, separate them, and each man would take his cattle to his summer range. . . .We had bears there that would kill any amount of cattle. They had hunters come in and hunt bears. They finally killed one, and the other one left, but he [had] killed thousands of dollars' worth of cattle. . . .

"I had a little gray mare, one of the best little animals [there] ever was. She was a speedy little animal too. I had gone to the upper field to get some cattle out of the field that [they] shouldn't have been there. [There was] a neighbor [who] was just a little younger than I was in a field higher up. He saw this little mare standing in the field for a long time and he came over to investigate. When he got there, I was sitting on the ground with my arms around her hind legs. I was unconscious [and] didn't know anything. . . He [put] me on the horse and led her home. Just before we got down to my home, I regained consciousness enough so that I could remember him bringing me home. . . .

"I have been [a rancher] all my life, ever since I was big enough to ride a horse, [since I] was about three years old."[32]

LUCY JEPSON ROBERTS ISOM

Lucy Jepson Barnum Roberts Isom was born on 21 September 1885 in Virgin. She tells of childhood memories of thirteen siblings: "I remember a great many things about our home life. I remember the little chores we had to do as [young] children. Every Saturday I had to scour the knives and forks with sand. We had no scouring preparations in those days. We had an upstairs room in our home. I had a brush and always had to sweep the stair steps down. I remember we had to pick up [wood] chips. We always had a pan to pick up the chips so there would be kindling to start the fires with in the morning. We had to carry in the wood. When I was a very small child, I carried five or six sticks of wood at a time and filled the wood box by the stove. We always had a wood-burning stove.

"I remember more especially the evenings that we spent together. My oldest brother [James Anthony Jepson] was perhaps ten or twelve. We would sing and listen to the stories in the evening. Sometimes we would play games like: Three in a Row, Fox and Geese, or Button, Button. [These were] some of those games that the family could play together. One of the things that I remember most is the family prayer we had every night and every morning just before we ate our meals. We would gather around the table. We always knelt and had the family prayer. As soon as the children [were] old enough to appreciate what we were praying for, they were asked to take their turn in the family prayer."[33]

AMANDA AMELIA MILNE

Amanda Amelia Hannig Milne tells a story of hard labor instead of fun. She was born in Washington, Utah, on 4 June 1883: "I worked in the cotton factory [in Washington] when I was twelve years old. I went to work at 7:30 in the morning and worked until 5:00 at night for twenty-five cents a day. That was [the] factory pay. I worked all day when I was only [twelve] years old. That was about all I did. Father died and left mother with seven children. He had a stroke and starved to death. They could not feed him like they do now. . . . [Father] started the factory, took care of the machinery, [and] oiled it. I was about eight when he died. I had to quit school and help Mother. I don't know what we would have done if it had not been for the [cotton] factory. . . . Mother was a hardworking woman [and] took care of all of us. She had a big house and worked in the factory sewing blankets. She would take blankets home [and] sit up until 12:00 or 1:00 [at night] sewing blankets."[34]

LOUIS RUMELL REBER

Louis Rumell Reber was born on 23 September 1899 in Santa Clara in a family of thirteen children, to a mother who weighed one hundred pounds. She also worked in the cotton factory in Washington. His family raised cotton in Santa Clara and in Middleton. There were so many children that four of his brothers slept in a wagon with a canvas cover and cotton to sleep on. He gives a teenager's view of the flooding problems there: "The biggest [flood] was in 1910. [It] did all the damage. It took [out] a couple of houses, corrals, hay, and grain. . . . One woman wouldn't come out of her house (Dora Iverson). . . . [We had to] pack her out in water waist deep. Water was all around her and she wouldn't [leave]. Water was out quite a ways to the hill area. [We] packed her out. [We] got her furniture out but it washed away during the night. The flood came higher during the night and took it all. There [were] some people [who drowned]. We also lost a lot of animals. [There was one horse that was washed] about one-and-one-half miles down [the river] and crawled up on the [bank] of a wash and was there for a few days before he was [found]. There was a flood in 1906, 1909, and then the worst one in 1910. This area has required a lot of hard work to make it go. There was a typhoid epidemic in 1902 and 1903."[35]

LORENZA "RENZA" BARNUM DAY

Lorenza "Renza" Barnum Day was born in Hebron and then lived in nearby Enterprise. She tells of childhood fun and adventure: "We lived on the ranch where there were lots of snakes. We killed lots of snakes. We always did a lot of fishing when we were young.

"My father owned a field that was a couple of miles from town. He used to grow a little alfalfa, corn, and everything that went in the garden. I remember there were a bunch of willow [trees] on the bank where we were one day. We went down to eat our lunch in the shade where we usually fished and there was a rattlesnake. We could see it coming down the trail. The sand was kind of deep and it never stopped. It came right toward us. It stood a foot off from the ground with its head [up], and it came right at us. My father had stood a shovel up against the willows and he jumped up, took the shovel and threw the snake [away from us]. As soon as it lit [on the ground], it came right at us again, right towards us, and he killed it with the shovel.

"We had raccoons also. I remember a 'coon' came one night. We had a bunch of little pigs. My father was out teaching this evening. Mother and the rest of us had gone to bed, and we could hear one of these little pigs squealing and squealing. It was quite dark and finally it quit [squealing]. When my father came home, my mother told him [about the squealing]. He went down to the pigpen and the little pig was dead. The next morning, he could see two [small] holes on the side of [its] neck where a 'coon' had gotten ahold of it.

"There were five girls and, next to the baby, was a boy, so he was alone. We had to milk the cows, forty of them. The two sisters, older than me, helped too. Of course, the cows didn't give [as much] milk [as] cows do now. We left Hebron [because] there was no room for any advancement or [for] any more people to live there. They had trouble with [having enough] water. They could not get the irrigation water that they needed. They had to leave and come where they could get water on their land and have more room to expand.

"I think we made fun out of most things when we were young. I remember my father and mother used to sing together a lot around the fire at night. We didn't have heaters in those days; we had a fireplace. I remember helping my Grandmother Pulsipher make [the] candles that we used. We had cook stoves, but in our living room, at night, we would sit around the fire. Father and mother would sing a lot when we were young. When we were older, we all used to sing.

"I remember the first inkling I had ever about Santy Claus. On Christmas Eve, a party [was held] at the church house and they would have Santa Claus pass around hardtack candy in a dishpan. My father was holding the handles [of the pan]. When he came up to me, I looked at his hands and I said, 'Mother, that is "pa," isn't it?' She said, 'Why, what makes you think that?' 'That is his hands. I know.' That was the first inkling I had of who Santa Claus was. I must have been six years old.

"When we went to school, we played baseball. That was the only kind of ball [games] we knew then. The girls played [baseball] with the boys. They used to choose up sides, and we would play ball. We did lots of wading in the canals. We always found something to do [even] if it wasn't any more than picking flowers on the Indian Hill.

"We always danced. Dancing was about the only public [activity] we had. We had the violin, mandolin, and the organ. We danced quadrilles and the Schottische. We also did round dancing. I would still rather dance than do anything else, if I could."[36]

LEAH BUNDY JENSEN

Leah Bundy Jensen was born in 1923 and lived at Mount Trumbull. She tells of a life of ranch work for a girl and some fun for a teenager: "I remember my older sister, Helen [Bundy], used to drive the truck a lot for Dad before I [was] old enough [and] before she left home. She would drive into St. George to get supplies. It seemed like she was the one [who] brought all [of] the diseases out to Mount Trumbull. At least she [was] accused of it! She was the first one to come down with everything that came out [our] way. She came down with the mumps, and Mama isolated her in the bedroom. Nobody could go in but Mama. She had already had [the mumps]. Eventually, we all got [the mumps] anyway. [It] seems like [the] mumps were worse those days than they are now. Our jaws swelled up so we couldn't eat for three [or] four days or a week or more.

"I remember when my dad got his first Model T Ford. He was driving it up the road, and we came to a gate. Instead of grabbing the brake, he said, 'Whoa, whoa, whoa,' and he went right through it! I thought it was quite funny. He never did get over that. For the longest time, as long as we had the Model T Ford, he would just say 'whoa, whoa, whoa' when we came to a gate.

"We always had good times on July fourth and twenty-fourth. I will always remember that my mother made us girls new dresses [for those holidays]. It seemed like [those were] the only new dresses we ever had. . . . We would go down to the schoolhouse, have races and a big family dinner, a community dinner. The whole valley, ranchers from miles around, would come. The mailman or someone [else] would go into St. George and bring out ice. We would always have homemade ice cream and a great big [feast] and then a dance that night.

"A lot of times we didn't have too much music. I know [there were] a lot of times [when] we would just have a harmonica. My cousin would play [his harmonica] as he danced and we all had a good time. I had an Aunt Edna [Bundy who] would [play] chords [on] the piano when we had [the dance] down at the schoolhouse. She would chord and he would play the harmonica. [There were] times when the young folks from St. George and Fredonia [Arizona] would come with guitars, banjos and accordions. When the Kenworthy boys came to live on the mountain, they always furnished us with good music. They were very talented.

"As a child, I thought my dad was quite hard on us. He made us work. A lot of times it seems like my cousin's dad didn't keep them busy. They would go off for a joyride or something, but we always had corn to hoe or something [we had to do]. He always had something for us to do. We were always kept busy, and I thought he was kind of hard on us. But as I look back, I don't know what more I could say, what appreciation I could show my dad than to thank him for [teaching] me how to work, because it has really been a blessing to me to be able to know how to work."[37]

AGNES MELINDA LEAVITT

Agnes Melinda Leavitt Leavitt tells of teenage fun in Bunkerville, Nevada. She calls it "the group of thirty." "We had one [child] out of every family in town. What was mine was theirs. If we decided to go down to my melon patch, we all went [there]. If we decided to go down to their [sorghum] can patch, we all went [there]. If we decided to go into the fruit trees, we all went [there]. Our parents just let us go because we were all [friends]. [We had] sorghum candy and chickens. [We had] fried chicken [and] oyster suppers. There was something going all the time. We had to make our own amusement, [and] we did. We went to Mesquite sometimes as young people. There were a lot of us. We had thirty [young people] in my crowd. There were five or six different crowds in this little town.

"We had choir practice twice a week where we met and sang songs for church. Altogether, we had about every night taken [with activity]. Some [nights were our] religion class and choir practice and our dance night. Then [we had] our parties in the spring. That about did it.

"During Christmastime, Mesquite [folks] would come over here for a day and we would go over there. You know how it is with one town against another. Aubrie and I were children and going to school. They had to have the sheriff right there to keep us in back of the line. They would run races. Some of the boys had been running races for months to get ready to run against each other at Christmastime. [We had] horse races, hose pulling, and ballgames. It was every day during [the] holiday [season]. There was not one day that was lost during the two-week holidays. [There was] a dance at night with [a] big supper. They had talent night sometimes. [People from] Overton, [Nevada], came up."[38]

LORIN "DUTCH" ABBOTT LEAVITT

Lorin "Dutch" Abbott Leavitt gives another report on Bunkerville. He was born there on 18 January 1909 and he focuses on some of his version of fun: "[We used to] steal a lot of melons and chickens! We did a lot of [horseback] riding. We had our horses, and Daddy always ran cattle. We used to do a lot of riding on the [Virgin] River for the cattle. My biggest pleasure was hunting in the valley here. I hunted duck and geese and trapped quail. [I] did a lot of trapping of coyotes [and other] fur-bearing animals here all my life.

"I made most of my spending money off of trapping. I used to love to hunt. For that matter, I still do [it]. Hunting and fishing are my recreation. [I like] any kind of dancing. A week never went by that we did not have a dance. All during school, I was in athletics, music, drama, and [activities] like that. I participated in [those activities] all the time. In fact, my wife's oldest living sister's husband, Kenneth Earl, was the thespian of the valley. He did a lot of theatrical work. It seemed like I was always with Kenneth.

"We used to play a lot of games when we were children. We had to create our own activities and recreation. We built a big bonfire out in the intersection on the streets [in front of] one place or another. That is the way we would go.

"Down at George Hunt's place, [which] is a couple of blocks away, we had a haystack. We would play what we called Willows. The game was that there would be eight, ten, or twelve boys. Lots of times, [there would be] girls too. Two [people] would be given willows. I mean they were really tangled willows. The idea was that if you could catch them, you could whip these children with the willows. You would have to run! I was after Stan Neagle. I was just getting up close enough that I could make that willow crack him every step he made. There was a stick sticking out of the haystack. I tripped over the stick and fell on an old wagon post that was laying there. The bolts were sticking straight up. [It was] the U-bolts [or] the clamp bolts. I hit that with my right knee and just opened it up for about two and a half inches. [It] let all the knee water out of there. I was about eighteen months tied up with that [injury].

"[I] broke my arm trying to crank an old Model T [Ford]. My brother was sporting his girl and I was standing there waiting for him to come out so I could crank it. I took hold of it and pulled the crank. It backfired and the crank hit me across the wrist and broke my arm."[39]

RHODA HAFEN LEAVITT

Here is another Bunkerville story. Rhoda Hafen Leavitt was born there in January 1905. She included a tender memory about her father, Albert Luther Hafen: "[We children would] go in the bedroom and start gossiping, talking low, about our friends saying this or that. I remember one time he came to the door and shook his finger and said, 'If you cannot say anything good about anybody, you keep your mouth shut. Not one word. You can talk all you want to, but if you cannot say anything good, you keep still.' He was strict on being honest and was proud.

"His old age pension was coming before he died. He would no more take that pension than anything. He was too proud to go on that pension. He made his own way. He did not want any help on the farm. They were independent. . . . He always tried to teach us to be the same way, to be honest. If we could not say anything good, don't say anything."[40]

MARIE BLAKE GUBLER

Marie Blake Gubler, born on 24 December 1901, gave a few comments about ranch life in Pine Valley: "Yes, we had fun, especially at the ranch in the summertime. There was another family [of Gublers who] lived up there that had a lot of children. We would always get together and had a lot of good times together. We even tried to hold a Sunday school. We had a lot of fun together.

"We did not have many parties at home, [but] at the ranch we used to party. Every time we would go to the top of Pine Valley Mountain, we would bring ice home and make ice cream. The two families would always get together and make a party of it.

"I used to love to go to dances. Even at the ranch, we had just one big lumber room. We would go in there and try to dance. It had a board floor, [and] it was not very smooth. We had an old phonograph that we used to play [records] to dance by."[41]

EVAN ERASTUS COOPER

Evan Erastus Cooper was born in Washington, Utah, on 4 February 1915. This meant that he was still a teenager at home when the Great Depression hit in 1929. He tells a story of those challenges: "My father grew up with very little education, but he was a hard worker and had a fairly good head on him. He was very good [doing] mathematics in his head. He could figure out a problem in his head about as quickly as most people could on paper.

"He chose farming for his career. He married my mother when they were around eighteen or nineteen years old. He farmed and freighted with horses and [a] wagon. He was a good teamster. He loved and drove fine horses. He would not have a horse that was not good to pull. If he broke one, it was always good to pull. To my father and mother were born eight children.

"My mother was about eight years old [when] her father died. She has been a wonderful mother. Her father was ill a long time before he passed away, [and] it exhausted about all they had accumulated to live on and to dope [medicate] him until he passed on. Somehow in the growing-up years, my mother developed an inferiority complex or she felt that other people were better than they were, not because they were better, but I guess because they were better clothed. They had to work hard for a living doing janitorial work and they had to haul their wood.

"My mother developed this inferiority complex and she seemed to not be able to cope with it as time went on. She passed it on to many of [her] children and gave us the idea that other children were better than we were, even though she and my father provided as good a home or average home for their family. I would say lots of times [it was] better than an average living. Before cars came along, he drove a nice buggy [with] nice harnesses and nice horses. We went for a ride on Sunday which was mostly the means of recreation and family entertainment. We had plenty to eat and plenty to wear. When cars came along, we always had a car, but still she could not accept the fact that we were an average family. I do not think anyone should feel that they are better than anyone else unless they do better, but were an average family. It was passed on to us, especially me, until I became older and began to realize what was happening to me. I do not know how the other children feel about it.

"It was here that Mrs. Sproul entered into the picture. She had a wonderful outlook on life [and] was talented in many fields. She was talented in music, drama, in singing and instrumental music. She came to my rescue and really helped me by talking to me. During the [Great] Depression years, she and her husband were on what they called an unemployed schoolteacher's program. They used to give night classes in music and drama. I took some of the leading parts in some of their plays. I am sure they gave me the leading parts to help me. With her coaching and talking too, it helped me a lot. It helped me to overcome my self-conscious inferior attitude towards people and what people thought [of me].

"My mother was a wonderful mother. She was a good cook, a good seamstress and very economical. My father could have never done for us children what he did if he had not had the kind of a wife he had. All of us were practically grown before we ever had what we called a store-bought shirt. She made them [all]. My sisters were up in their teens before they ever had a store-bought dress. She made their dresses. A lot of them were made out of older clothes, but they always looked nice. She was an excellent seamstress. She could darn trousers and [clothes] until her hands [were] so shaky [that] she could not [do it] anymore. You could hardly tell where the hole was. She could take a dozen eggs and a pan of milk and make a wholesome meal for our family.

"My job around home helping my mother was on wash day to cook and punch the clothes. We had an old puncher. Some people bought punchers [from] the store but ours was a homemade one. It was a big gallon pan put up over the end of a board and nailed there [with] holes punched all through. It had sort of a suction. The first method of washing was to fill the black tub, the kettle they called it, outside and build a fire around it. After the water [became] hot they dipped part of the water out and put it in the scrub tub. Then they put the clothes in the tub [with] the homemade soap and the lye. First, they put the lye in the water, and a scum came [to] the top. They skimmed this scum off. I think the purpose of the lye was to soften the water. Then they would cut up the homemade soap in thin threads and put it in the water. After this dissolved, they would put the clothes in and then we would punch them with the puncher. I walked a million miles around the black tub punching these clothes with suction!

Then they took the handle of the punch and sorted these clothes out of the hot water and put them over in the scrub tub [where] they scrubbed them, rinsed them and hung them [to dry].

"Our meals were always regular. At seven o'clock in the morning we had our family breakfast. The chores had to be done before seven o'clock. We had to have the cows milked, the horses fed, the pigs fed, and were washed and ready to come to breakfast. We always had our family blessing on the food. The regular mealtime and the family blessing seemed to regulate and start the day off with regularity. Our dinner was always ready shortly after twelve o'clock [noon]. In the evening we had our evening meal around six o'clock. Then the dishes were done, and we always had visiting. Neighbors came to visit, or we went to visit neighbors. That was another old tradition in the rural areas because there were not movies [and] there were no cars to go [anywhere]."[42]

MYRZA LANG BOOTH

Myrza Lang Booth was born on 25 May 1916 in St. George. She reported on the limitations of life during the Great Depression but had a positive attitude that led her throughout her life: "I only went [through] the ninth grade. When I [started] the ninth grade, that was in high school, the tuition was $10.00 then. I did not have the $10.00, but they let me go anyway. I never could raise the $10.00 all during the year so, consequently, when it came to be the tenth grade I could not go because I still owed the $10.00 for the ninth grade.

"When [my son] Lloyd [Booth] graduated from high school, I went back and took what they called GED [General Education Development] tests. These were tests made up to give to the soldier boys to see if they could go into college. I passed these, and they gave me my diploma. So I graduated with Lloyd. I did not have enough nerve to walk up and get my graduation certificate. Lloyd had gone to California to work the week before. If he had been there I think I could have, but I was backward enough that I could not get up in front of all those people. If I had to do it over I would very proudly get up, walk up and get it. I am very proud of [receiving] my diploma after [so] long [a time].

"The only times that we ever really had fun was on the Fourth of July and the twenty-fourth [of July]. We would get up early in the morning and get tin pans, and we would beat on [them]. We would go all over the streets, up and down all over this end of town—we called it Sand Town—and we would go around and beat [the pans]. We also had [a] martial band that would go around and play [music]. These are the noises that stand out in my life.

"Those were the fun noises. Usually we would have ten or fifteen cents to spend. We would go down into town and take all day to spend this money. When you finally made a choice of how you were going to spend it, then all decisions were made. You spent it and that was it. You could go home. I remember once I bought a balloon. It was one that you put helium in, and [it would] go up in the air. I was going around [town] and I was so proud of this balloon, and some little [child] broke it. He reached up and broke it. It nearly broke my heart. It was something that we did not have at the time.

"We used to go on Easter trips. Those were fun times anytime we could get a few people to go. We had a few Easter trips. For everyday fun, life was serious. I think the things that I remember more than anything else, as far as our home life was concerned, was that my mother worried all the time. We never opened a sack of flour that she did not worry about where the next one was coming from. Then it was hard to get shoes.

"We never went without food. I know Fred has told about how they were hungry at times, but we were never hungry. We always had food, but the thing of it was my mother worried about it so much that it took the joy of having it away. My mother was an immaculate housekeeper, even though we lived in three rooms and one of those was almost a pantry. Our house was clean. People used to say they would not be afraid to eat off Hazel's floor because it was that clean. We were raised with cleanliness, even though we had very little. The thing that Mama always worried about was food. She was raised at a time when—you can appreciate this—food was at a premium, but then Mama was a born worrier."[43]

INEZ HEATON HOYT

Inez Heaton Hoyt was born on 9 August 1891 in Orderville, Long Valley. "Mother was a good housekeeper. She was clean and neat. She was kind to us girls, and we enjoyed being with her. She kept our clothes neat. As fast as we grew up, she taught us how to take care of our clothes. My Saturday job every [week] was to clean out the dish cupboard. We had a lovely cupboard between the kitchen and the dining room. I had to wash all those dishes and put them back every Saturday; besides [the] other things, that was my special job. I would help with the other Saturday work.

"One time, Mother could not do much work. We were trying to build another home or add-on to the one we had. Mother and [my sisters] took in washing during the winter to help keep up so that what Dad could earn could be put on the house. . . . We would have to carry water from down [at] the creek and fill a fifty-gallon barrel each night with water after we were through washing [so that] the water would settle so it wouldn't be so roily to wash in the next day. We had a lot of that, but it did not hurt us. It was good.

"As a girl, I remember mother was sick a lot. Maybe it was because I did not like to do the work so much. It seemed like she had sick spells quite often. I know several times my father would call in his brother, Jonathan [Heaton], and they would administer to her. It always helped her. I used to wonder why they did not call him more than they did because she did suffer a lot with her stomach.

"When I was about eight years old, they took her to Cedar [City, Iron County, Utah] to the doctor. She had something wrong with her. They took me over too. They thought my heart was not good and they took me to be examined. I was all right, but she had to have an operation. They [removed] tumors from her. She never was very well after that. She lived a long time. She did a lot of genealogy work after that. In the hospital they had the elders come in, and she was relieved of suffering and helped a lot. She was really relieved a lot through faith.

"Nowadays you do not know there is a moon half [of] the time. You do not know when the moon is up or when there is [one] because there are so many electric lights. We appreciated the moon, and we enjoyed it. In the neighborhoods we would get out and play Steal-a-Stick and many [other] games in the evening. I really enjoyed those times we had together.

"We had our girls' singing group. I remember one day we all decided the day before to get our Saturday's work done early and then get together and sing the rest of the day. We had a group of girls about the same age. We got together and went down to the meetinghouse. We [asked] Brother Cox, the janitor, to let us go up into the little tower room where they rang the bell. We all [were] in there and we sang the whole afternoon. Then we wanted to do it every Saturday but they would not let us. I liked to do things like that."[44]

JOSEPH FIELDING HARDY

Joseph Fielding Hardy was born on 3 October 1908 in Bunkerville, Nevada. He tells about boyhood fun: "I remember in the summertime when those flash floods, rain and floods [would] come down [the river]. We would all go down to the [Virgin] River and swim in [the] flood. The older fellows would throw the smaller fellows in, and we would float down the river, and the older fellows would fish us out. We did not fear that we would not be caught. Nobody worried about us; we would just have confidence that they would get us out. I remember one time when the water was out, we would have to take our cattle down to the [Virgin] river to water them and drive them down during these floods. I remember one time I rode my horse out into deep, swift [water], and it forced me off the horse. I almost lost my hold there. If I had, I would have panicked because I was alone, but I held onto the horse's mane, [and] he drug me out.

"I might tell [about] a prank we pulled as teenagers. One of the men here harvested melons. He brought them up and put them right up side of his house. Then he came up to the store where we all hung out—young fellows and the old fellows. He said, 'Boys, I brought the melons all up and stacked them right up by my house. You are welcome to them if you can get in get them and get out without me catching you. I have a shotgun ready and a dog out there that will notify me.'

"Of course, we all took the challenge. We took a pound of bologna. One of the [fellows] knew the dog well, and he [went] in and gave the bologna to the dog, and the dog took off. We filed the melons out [and] ate what we could. After we could not eat any more, we cut the rest of them open and took every melon.

"The next day he came after us and was going to have us arrested. Some of the older fellows [who] were there and they heard what he said. [They told him]; 'You cannot have them arrested. You told them to get in there and out without you catching them. They could have every melon.' Finally, he turned, 'Lordy, I did, didn't I?' That was the end of it. He said, 'I will never make that statement again.'"[45]

REED PRISBREY

Reed Prisbrey was born on 16 February 1905 in Middleton and lived in New Harmony and Washington, Utah. He tells of teenagers who were somewhat wild: "We used to make our fun. There used to be a bunch of young fellows here in New Harmony. We would have parties [with] neighbors, back and forth around the neighborhood, chicken suppers, parties, or something like that. We made our fun. Sometimes we would steal our chickens from different ones. I have to tell this incident. We would choose up sides [as to] who [would] go. This one time, Pratt Prince, a young fellow who lived here, and myself were chosen to go steal chickens from Brother Schmutz. Pratt was in the coop. [Brother Schmutz] had it boarded up about half way. He [Pratt] crawled in and picked up three chickens and handed them out to me. I seen [sic] him a-coming with a flashlight, and I said to Pratt, 'Better go, he is a-coming.' I took off and he didn't hear me. The old man came up to the coop to the door. Pratt hands him two or three chickens, and he turned them loose. [He] kept turning them loose. Pretty soon, Brother Schmutz said, 'Don't you think you have got enough?' Pratt damn near knocked him down getting out. Maybe he did knock him down. He dove out of there and ran. Of course, they didn't catch us.

"We used to go out when the snow was deep in the wintertime. Maybe [after] a foot of new snow and all of us would get on horses and choose up sides. The losing side would give a dance or a party. We would go out and take the ears off the jackrabbits [and] kill them. We would chase them down in the snow. Sometimes it would be ten people deep after one rabbit. One of them would come out with one ear and the other side with the other. That is the way they would do."[46]

EMMA BRADSHAW CORNELIUS

Emma Bradshaw Cornelius was born in Woodruff, Arizona, and later lived in Virgin, Utah, where she was interviewed. She gives a childhood memory in Woodruff: "Dad had to go off to herd sheep. He had a cabin built up in the mountains. He had another man come and sleep in the wagon box and stay with mother at night while he was gone. She had two or three little children.

"One night, she woke up after hearing something outside. They had killed a sheep under a tree out in the yard the day before, and she heard something out there eating the entrails of the sheep. She got up and looked out the window and saw a big animal. She could see it because the moon was shining. She said she did not want to yell at the man in the wagon because she was afraid the animal would get her, so she kept quiet. They did not have anything [over] the doorway except a piece of cloth, and the bear could come in. It passed by the door and went on down to the corrals and got after the cow and calf. [It] scared them out of the corral, and they ran away. The man happened to hear the [commotion] and got up and went after [the bear]. It ran down to his place and killed a calf that night.

"The next night they decided they would sleep down there because they thought [the bear] would go back to where it killed the calf. It did not go back there, but it went down to mother's place and went into the house [because] nobody was there. That night, mother had gone to the man's place to stay. The bear tore up the bedding. It drank her milk and ate a piece of butter. It scattered things all over the yard like it was mad because it did not find anybody home."[47]

CONCLUSIONS

Taken together, these interviews give a picture of life for children and teenagers between 1900 and 1930, the period before modernization, in the Mojave Desert area of southern Utah, northern Nevada, and northern Arizona. The most powerful message from them is the influence of family life. Stable marriages were the dominant pattern. Children learned to work beside their parents in the home and in the field. Parents were their models, and the youth adopted their values.

The most surprising thing is what the children did not say. They never reported being hungry. They had plenty of food because their family raised it in their own garden adjacent to their house and bartered for what they could not raise. They had ample home-cooked meals with fresh-baked bread almost daily. They lived in their own houses, even if they were modest and often self-built. Most everything was made at home. Children felt adequately cared for in this barter economy. Lola Belle DeMille Bryner reflected, "Most everyone was poor, so we didn't notice it."[48]

Most families had many children, so children of all ages had nearby friends and undertook many activities together. Nature was their life, and because there was no commercial entertainment, they created their own entertainment. Many spent much of their lives with horses and cattle.

One reason they were so satisfied is that most of them lived in a village instead of out on a farm, separated from each other. They were all together, and their lifestyle lacked no imagination as they interacted. The community-organized fun, such as music, dances, town celebrations, Christmas, and Thanksgiving, was also much easier to promote in the village. At these events, everyone came, including grandparents and parents and their babies. Another form of fun was the family fireside. It was common for a family to sit around the fire at night in the darkness and sing, tell stories, and play games.

Life in the capital city of St. George differed somewhat because there were so many more people. They had the opera house where vaudeville shows were regularly performed. Dixie College existed after 1911 and had an orchestra, musicals, and a dance hall, and eventually it featured athletic teams. Some youths, however, were unable to participate in either village or urban fun because the death of a parent required them to be employed full-time.

These stories, admittedly fond memories, depict powerful family life of stable laboring families. They are positive, probably because they were survivors. The many children who died, and even the parents who died young, did not get a chance to be interviewed and may have given different views.

NOTES

1. Stephanie Hanes, "Toddlers on Touch Screens: Parenting the 'App Generation,'" *Christian Science Monitor Weekly*, 20 October 2013, http://www.csmonitor.com/The-Culture/Family/2013/1020/Toddlers-on-touch-screens-parenting-the-app-generation.

2. Elliott West, "Becoming Mormon," *Journal of Mormon History* 28, no. 1 (Spring 2002): 31–51.

3. West, "Becoming Mormon," 38.

4. West, "Becoming Mormon," 44.

5. William G. Hartley, "Childhood in Gunnison, Utah," *Utah Historical Quarterly* 51 (1983): 108–32.

6. Susan Madsen, "Growing Up in Pioneer Utah: Agonies and Ecstasies," in *Nearly Everything Imaginable: The Everyday Life of Utah's Mormon Pioneers*, ed. Ronald Walker and Doris R. Dent (Provo, UT: Brigham Young University Press, 1999), 317–28.

7. Madsen, "Growing Up in Pioneer Utah," 318.

8. Madsen, "Growing Up in Pioneer Utah," 318.

9. Madsen, "Growing Up in Pioneer Utah," 320.

10. Martha Bradley, "Children on the Underground," *Utah Historical Quarterly* 51 (1983): 133–53.

11. Davis Bitton, "Zion's Rowdies: Growing Up on the Mormon Frontier," *Utah Historical Quarterly* 50, no. 2 (Spring 1982): 182–95.

12. Emma Lucinda Nelson Larson, Oral History Interview, Voices of Remembrance Oral History Collection, file number 68-081, Dixie State University Special Collections, St. George, Utah. Hereafter cited as Interviewee Name, VOR File ##-###.

13. A shock would contain fifty to one hundred stalks of corn tied into a bundle, forming a pyramid.

14. Daniel Winder, VOR File 68-128.

15. Myrtle Crawford Winder, VOR File 68-129.

16. Mary Hafen Leavitt, VOR File 68-100.

17. Vera Hinton Eager, VOR File 68-044.

18. Blanch Mathis McComb, VOR File 68-096.

19. Lola Belle DeMille Bryner, VOR File 68-015.

20. A flailer is a small implement used to separate grain from husks and other chaff.

21. Edward Sirls Terry, VOR File 68-102.

22. Martha Vilate Hughes Knight, VOR File 70-020.

23. Joseph Terry, VOR File 69-102.

24. Allan Kent Powell, ed., *Nels Anderson's World War I Diary* (Salt Lake City: University of Utah Press, 2013).

25. Mary Ann (Adams) Starr, VOR File 69-197.

26. Bodil Margaret Johnson Pulisipher, VOR File 70-035.

27. Lora Ann Gifford Christensen, VOR File 68-131.

28. Laura Snow Woodbury, VOR File 68-007.

29. Robert Parker Woodbury, VOR File 68-038.

30. Lucy Crawford Schiefer, VOR File 69-008.

31. Della Humphries Hardy, VOR File 69-007.

32. Erastus Snow Gardner, VOR File 69-018.

33. Lucy Jepson Barnum Roberts Isom, VOR File 70-025.

34. Amanda Amelia Hannig Milne, VOR File 69-036.

35. Louis Rumell Reber, VOR File 69-056.

36. Lorenza "Renza" Barnum Day, VOR File 69-112.

37. Leah Bundy Jensen, VOR File 69-070.

38. Agnes Melinda Leavitt Leavitt, VOR File 69-071.

39. Lorin "Dutch" Abbott Leavitt, VOR File 69-072.

40. Rhoda Hafen Leavitt, VOR File 69-078.

41. Marie Blake Gubler, VOR File 69-123.

42. Evan Erastus Cooper, VOR File 69-027.

43. Myrza Lang Booth, VOR File 69-135.

44. Inez Heaton Hoyt, VOR File 68-070.

45. Joseph Fielding Hardy, VOR File 69-080.

46. Reed Prisbey, VOR File 69-206.

47. Emma Bradshaw Cornelius, VOR File 70-016.

48. Lola Belle DeMille Bryner, VOR File 68-015.

## Chapter 2

SCHOOLS

INTRODUCTION

When Mormon villages were founded in the period between 1850 and 1900, their leaders were urged by the Church headquarters in Salt Lake City to establish a school in each village. In most towns, they implemented a plan to survey the town into blocks with about eight one-acre lots in each. In the center of the town, they devoted the central block to serve as a town square. Initially, they often built a bowery there for Church and town meetings. Then they divided the other blocks into family plots. Irrigation ditches were dug down each side of the wide streets so that the families had water for their gardens. Each of the families received one of the one-acre lots and began to set up a chicken coop, a pigpen, a root cellar, and a corral. They lived in their wagon or in a tent at first, but as soon as possible they built a cabin.

Civic buildings were just as essential. Within a year people usually built a modest church and a school, often on the town square, to be a center for the one hundred to four hundred residents. Sometimes, both functions were housed in the same building. Each community elected a group of school trustees that was responsible to arrange for a place where the school classes would be taught; obtain furniture, books, and supplies; hire a teacher; and collect tuition. Because St. George was at least four times bigger than most villages, the town was divided into four wards, and each had a one-room school. There were also some women who taught school in their homes in St. George.

The majority of youth in the Dixie region attended their local school. In the 1860s these schools may have only offered three grades, but by 1900 schools were expanded to six grades, and soon eight. However, there were not eight classrooms. In some schools there was only one teacher, and all classes were in the same room. Another room was often added, allowing for two teachers and dividing the grades into two groups: beginners and advanced. Three rooms and three teachers were rarities. Many students did not attend a full year because they had to be available for the planting season and the harvest work. Also, many students had to drop out before the eighth grade to help with work at home on a permanent basis because one of their parents was seriously ill or had died. It was not uncommon for young people to quit school by age fourteen.

Initially, each community had to finance the schools. They often received some LDS Church support but little supervision from the central Church; nonetheless, religion was usually taught in the schools. In succeeding decades, the local LDS leaders in the village sometimes arranged for a religion class to be taught by a member of the congregation once or twice a week as a supplement to the school curriculum.

As political leaders in Utah planned for statehood, the territorial legislature began to appropriate modest funds to the schools. At first, each county received one dollar per student, until it was later increased. Elementary schools—unopposed by the LDS Church—began a gradual process of secularization.

High schools were a different matter. Statehood was achieved in 1896, and the state and county governments gradually promoted the establishment of publicly supported high schools. In Washington County, there were only two: one in Hurricane and one in St. George. The latter began in the Woodward School when the county added grades nine and ten a few years after the 1901 opening of the school. Woodward School, located on the town square, had consolidated the four one-room schools into a two-story building where eight grades were taught, with a teacher for each grade. When the LDS Dixie Academy began in 1911, grades eleven and twelve were added, making a full high school. The Hurricane High School began about 1918.

The LDS Church leaders in Salt Lake had made a significant decision in 1888 to establish a network of academies. They had concerns that state-supported high schools would soon take over and eliminate the teaching of religion in the schools. They wanted access to the youth in the schools in order to teach them religion. These Church schools required students to pay tuition of ten dollars, whereas state-supported schools did not. The Church appropriated substantial amounts to support faculty salaries; they also generally paid half the cost of building a two-story, multiple-classroom school. These schools soon made grades nine to twelve available to students. The academy began in St. George in 1888, but only the grades up to the eighth grade were available, and it closed in 1893. Then, in 1911, it started again, making grades nine through twelve available as well. In 1916 Dixie added a year of teacher preparation courses, beginning the first year of college. In 1917 a second year of teacher preparation was added as teacher certification standards were raised statewide.

Several people have written about Washington County schools. In 1923 Josephine J. Miles read a paper on the schools to the St. George chapter of the Daughters of Utah Pioneers.[1] She focused largely on St. George, detailing the efforts of individual teachers clear up to 1900, prior to the creation of ward Church schools. She says: "Methods and equipment improved generally, and in about 1888 there was an appropriation from the state of fifty cents per student per term of twelve weeks. This gave a little cash to go along with our pickles, broom, wood, molasses, etc., for we had to collect our own pay from the parents, furnish our own wood, clock, brooms, etc. and hire our own janitors."[2]

In 1961 Dixie College professor Andrew Karl Larson wrote *I Was Called to Dixie.* He devoted chapter 32 to the topic of schools. After focusing on the early community schools, he then dealt with the St. George Stake Academy (1888–93), the construction of the Woodward School (1901), and what became Dixie College (1911), which expanded in 1916 to include college courses for teacher preparation.

A major study is Robert Hafen Moss's 1961 master's thesis at BYU, which focuses on education in Washington County from 1852 to 1915. Moss cites Josephine Miles, Andrew Karl Larson, and Albert E. Miller (all three are historical scholars of Dixie), but he includes much more detail. For example, he includes a chart about the school population between 1888 and 1892 that shows the Silver Reef Mine brought in a considerable non-Mormon population. It is clear that the student enrollment declined as the mine began to close. The accompanying chart also shows that about one-fourth of the youth in the whole county did not register for school and another one-fourth of the youth did not attend regularly. Moss observed, "This substantial segment of the total population was not educated in the district schools, thus presenting an argument in favor of free public schools."[3]

ENROLLMENT CHART

	SCHOOL-AGE		ENROLLMENT		AVERAGE DAILY ATTENDANCE		TEACHERS	
YEAR	MORMON	NON	MORMON	NON	MORMON	NON	MORMON	NON
1888	1270	127	933	80	649	72	26	1
1889	1230	114	934	68	859	56	21	1
1890	1225	76	1034	49	622	42	26	1
1891	1236	68	1199	54	834	45	28	2
1892	1304	55	1149	44	913	33	29	2

A letter from the county school superintendent, John T. Woodbury, to the St. George stake president, John D. T. McAllister, expressed the schools' financial difficulties:

> The amount of school money allotted to Washington County for the year 1888 is $2794.00. This is apportioned to the various districts. The above money can only be used for the payment of qualified teachers. In St. George during the past winter, the pupils in the ward schools received the benefit of one dollar of this money for every term they attended school. The amount was deducted from the tuition fees of each pupil, and the bill sent to the parents only for the remainder. The short time that the schools are kept up here during the year, and the small wages paid to teachers, make it necessary that they should

spend their spare time in other kinds of employment, and [if] they cannot give attention they should do to the cultivation of their own minds and improvement in the art of teaching. The trustees have power to levy a tax of one fourth of one per cent on all taxable property in the district for the purpose of supplying the school with fuel, maps, charts, etc. But in most cases this tax is not levied, and the school runs on without these necessary aids to successful teaching.[4]

This chart is a glimpse at the financial challenges facing the schools and gives a view of teachers' salaries:

TEACHERS' SALARIES

	1899	1900	1901	1902	1903	1904	1905	1906
MALE	$46.99	$44.18	$47.50	$56.02	$62.40	$56.78	$55.69	$68.94
FEMALE	$34.31	$31.93	$32.03	$35.86	$37.19	$38.03	$38.02	$42.64

	1907	1908	1909	1910	1911	1912	1913	1914
MALE	$62.71	$67.89	$70.60	$61.70	$81.30	$67.98	$70.00	$72.68
FEMALE	$42.14	$50.77	$44.32	$49.10	$64.00	$51.25	$56.00	$57.13

Moss's concluding findings in his thesis were the following:

1. From the beginning, the major force present in the establishment and support of schools in Washington County was the LDS Church. Local church leaders were very often the educational leaders, . . .

2. The power of administering the schools rested largely on lay personnel from each community elected as district trustees. . . .

3. Financing of the schools was largely a local affair during the first fifty years after settlement. . . .

4. Many difficulties were encountered in establishing secondary schools in Washington County. Paramount among these was finance. . . .

5. The greatest achievement made during these seventy-five years was the consolidation of Washington County Schools.[5]

What is amazing is how the teaching of students began with zest in every village, even if the only meeting place was in a tent. All villages implemented the Mormon model of a local school with local trustees. Obviously, educating children was one of the main purposes of the village. People came forth to be teachers despite the severe limitations of living in the desert and the lack of money to pay them appropriate salaries. Families sent their children to schools but often had to limit their attendance so they could help farm, ranch, nurse the ill, cook, or clean. They rallied to build schools and pay tuition long before Utah became a state in 1896. By the time that free education was available to all, almost everyone was literate. Education was valued, and gradually a tax system was put in place to support it. Most of these struggles preceded the years of schooling these interviewees experienced. But even with improvements, students still attended only when they could be away from the farm or home, where work dominated life.

A personal but enticing account of education in St. George was written by Andrew Karl Larson.[6] It captures his struggles to get an education, but many other students had similar experiences. Larson lived and finished school in Middleton; he reports that school was held in the town church with two teachers: one teaching the first four grades in the basement and the other teaching the four upper grades on the main floor. He recalls scenes of teacher discipline and of his interaction with other students. He was very fond of his teachers and tells many tales about them. One of the teachers, Mr. McConnell, motivated Larson to join the band, which introduced him to Wilford McAllister, who led him further into music, especially public performances. Another teacher, Willard Nisson, carried that tradition of student activity on in the upper classes. Larson then began participating in debates. He engaged in one debate in costume. That led him into a lasting friendship with Leonard Sproul, a man who later became a community leader.

Larson also tells of learning how to do other things outside of school—peddling grain, meat, and vegetables with his "pa" on a trip to Parowan and weaving rugs with old cloth strips. He enjoyed amusements and holidays: Christmas as well as Pioneer Day, with its horse races and broad jumps. He tells about a storytelling contest at Mutual Improvement Association.

The two other contestants were smart girls from his class. He chose a short story from the *Juvenile Instructor*, and the girls chose classics. He practiced his story aloud many times at home and later recounts: "There on the Sandy Knoll I told and retold the story, narrating it with a feeling I really lived. I liked the way it sounded, and I learned where to place the emphasis, the pauses, and the speedup by some sort of instinct for an effective style of delivery. I tried not to overdo it."[7] The meetinghouse was packed for the contest. He was the first speaker, and then the two girls gave their stories, but he felt that he had won. The judges did indeed pick him, and he won the one-dollar prize.

That experience stirred him to become a reader. He read Parley P. Pratt but then moved on to authors like Charles Dickens and Hans Christian Andersen; he also read *The Last of the Mohicans*, "The Song of Hiawatha," and even the Gettysburg Address. His parents could see that learning was his forte, and despite their need for his help on the farm, they planned to send him to Dixie College, which was founded when he completed eighth grade. But they had no cash; when he finished the last year of town school, they were unable to find the ten dollars necessary for tuition nor figure out how to arrange living quarters for him in St. George. They encouraged him to repeat the eighth grade. He started but became discouraged and dropped out. The next fall, the same issue arose. They did not have cash. Then, Hugh Woodward, principal of the high school that became Dixie College in 1916, came to their house and urged the parents to sign a loan application for the ten dollars. Woodward was recruiting two other Washington City boys and suggested that they ride horses to and from school each day and avoid the cost of housing. He said that if the father could come up with five dollars, the plan could work. On that basis, Larson started at Dixie, a decision that would eventually lead him to a lifelong profession of teaching college.

Four years after the founding of the high school in 1911, Larson became a serious student there. He fell in love with literature, particularly the British authors William Shakespeare, Sir Walter Scott, and Alfred, Lord Tennyson, as taught by his teacher, Mill Ruth Carol Evans. The horse rides to school every day were difficult, especially in the winter. He sometimes felt like the English knights he read about, trying to conquer the forests and hills.

Debate also became exciting for Larson. He tells of a contest he participated in, where he and another boy, Tennyson Atkin, debated against two girls on the subject of women's suffrage. The boys took the negative side of the issue, which was tough because Utah already had women voting. The boys won the votes of all three judges, mainly because of fellow student Tennyson Atkin's knowledge on the subject. One of the judges was Nels Anderson, the school's debate manager.

Larson's ability to perform in the band led to playing college musicals that were presented in the opera house and sometimes in Hurricane. This meant that his horse ride home after the performances didn't conclude until midnight. He even played in the marching band to celebrate Armistice Day in 1918.

He alternated months going to Dixie College and months at short-term jobs whenever he could find them, trying to finance his schooling. Sometimes he went to Idaho, then to Delta, and often to Washington City. He always felt he should be in school. One fall, he and six others (young men and young women) rented a basement north on Main Street with an outdoor cranny (outdoor toilet). That year Andrew had two serious bouts of illness, one with typhoid fever and another with inflammatory rheumatism. With the help of Dr. Donald McGregor and a blessing from his father and mother, he returned to school. He was way behind in his classes, but his teachers helped him catch up.

During this time, he struck up a friendship with Katherine Miles. They did not date because he could not afford to take her out, but it eventually led to marriage. He tells of the dedication of Zion National Park on 15 September 1920. The Dixie Band, under direction of Earl J. Bleak with Larson participating, was front stage. Stephen Mather, national parks director, presided. President Heber J. Grant, Senator Reed Smoot, Richard R. Lyman, Governor Simon Bamberger, Anthony W. Ivins, Edward H. Snow, Thomas Cottam, and George Whitehead were on the stand also. Cameramen from Paramount Motion Pictures roamed about.

Andrew even tells about a student court and an appeal to President Joseph K. Nichols. The issue was a hazing incident involving the son of Archie Wallis, the editor of the *Washington County News,* and a group of students including Larson. It was tense but came to a resolution. This is but one example of the importance of student government at Dixie as instituted by President Hugh Woodward upon the founding of the college.

As a senior at Dixie, he played in the band directed by Earl J. Bleak but also attended John T. Woodbury's Bible class. He did his practice teaching at Woodward School under Lena Nelson, who later became his colleague there. Andrew Karl Larson's book is a classic, well-written illustration of the impact of education in Utah's Dixie.

A different view is to compare the schools in Utah's Dixie with those in Salt Lake City. A major scholar about education in Utah was Frederick Stewart Buchanan, who died January 2016 in Salt Lake City. He was born in Scotland, where he joined the LDS Church and came to Utah. He became a professor of education at the University of Utah. His book *Culture Clash and Accommodation: Public Schooling in Salt Lake City, 1890–1994*[8] gives a picture of Utah public education that was nearly the opposite to what happened in schools in southern Utah, northern Arizona, and Nevada villages that neighbored Utah.

The schools in Buchanan's book were all tax-supported and administered by county and state school boards, in contrast to southern Utah. Buchanan's main point is that Salt Lake City was internally diverse. After the railroad arrived in 1869, more and more non-Mormons settled there, becoming over 20 percent of the population. The mining industry became successful. As the prosecution of polygamists expanded, non-Mormons actually gained the office of Salt Lake mayor. Catholic and Protestant churches and fraternal societies grew. By the time of statehood, both elementary and secondary schools were state-supported, becoming tuition-free. In 1891 there were 209 non-Mormon teachers and 700 Mormon teachers in Salt Lake County.

Buchanan's work is worth mentioning because it is a contrast and brings perspective to the *History of Woodward School, 99 Years, 1901–2000* by Heber Jones.[9] Jones tells of the decision promoted by a lobby group led by Miss Zaidee Walker, which pressed for a professional school building to serve St. George City. She had studied at the University of Utah and seen such buildings in the capital city. The lobbying finally convinced the St. George School Board to bond for 15,000 dollars and build a two-story, eight-grade, eight-teacher school. They even stayed with the task when the costs escalated to 30,000 dollars. When opened in 1901, the Woodward School replaced four ward schools in St. George. The Woodward began with eight grades and soon added grades nine and ten. When the St. George Stake Academy opened in 1911, it was a high school, teaching grades eleven and twelve. Then, in 1916 and 1917, two years of college (teacher preparation) were added to the academy, which by then was named Dixie College. The college then included the last two years of high school and the first two years of college and remained that way until 1963, when the college moved to the new campus on Seventh East. Grades eleven and twelve remained in the old college building on the town square, under the direction of the county school board.

Another article that should be mentioned is by James Allen, titled "Everyday Life in Utah's Elementary Schools, 1847–1870."[10] He pointed out that even though schools were opened in every Mormon village, not all families could afford the tuition to send their children to the schools. Tuition was ten dollars a year. Allen says that only about 50 percent of youth attended. Also, he noted that books were generally unavailable in the very early years. Of those who attended, some dropped out. Then, he noted that by 1900 the state legislature made public funds available for elementary schools. Tuition was no longer charged, and they instituted requirements for attendance.

INTERVIEWS

Some twenty-nine students are quoted in this chapter. Not all of them went to school in the Dixie region, but most began school in a village. A few went to high school by leaving their village. Even a smaller number went beyond that. They usually remembered teachers, friends, and pranks fondly.

There were many reasons for terminating their education early— health, family emergencies, employment, and marriage. The most interesting way to understand this is to read their words. Here are a few of them.

WILFORD WOODRUFF CANNON

Wilford Woodruff Cannon was born on 20 November 1880 to David Henry Cannon and Rhoda Ann Knell Cannon. His father was a counselor in the

St. George Temple presidency and later became the president. Wilford tells: "When I was born, President Wilford Woodruff was president of the St. George Temple. My father was his assistant. Father carried me down to the temple where President Wilford Woodruff was hiding in the temple because of polygamy. He took me in his arms and gave me his name and a blessing when I was eight days old. That is [recorded] in father's diary.

"I grew up in St. George and, like other [children], I attended [the] district school. In the good old days, once a month the teacher would [hand out] a little bill [for the students to take] home to [their] parents and they would pay the bill. I was in second or third grade before they introduced [the] public school [system]. There were little one-room schoolhouses all around town. Until I was [in the] fifth or sixth grade, I attended these one-room houses. After maybe the sixth grade, we had a central school up in the top floor of the courthouse. I went there a couple of years. Then we met in the basement of the [St. George] Tabernacle from then until I finished the eighth grade.

"In 1899, I went to Cedar City [Iron County, Utah] to attend the Branch Normal School. When we went up there, we had to take 'Old Dobbin' and the shay. It took us three days to get to Cedar City [from St. George]. We took a team, [and] two of my sisters and I went up and rented an apartment in Cedar City. We took a lot of our provisions from here with us. While I had that team up there I went to the canyon and brought down a load of coal. I went out into the sticks and [picked up] some wood. My two sisters and I kept warm that way.

"The next winter the three of us went up to BYU in Provo. We went around through Modena [Iron County, Utah]. We took a train from Modena and went to Provo. We rented an apartment there and attended school that winter. George [Henry] Brimhall was the head of BYU that year. I enjoyed BYU quite a little. I wanted to study engineering, so the next winter I went up to the University of Utah. They had just moved out on the hill (where they are now) the [previous] fall. They only had three buildings at the university then. I stayed there four years [and studied] mining engineering. As soon as school was out, I left and went out in the sticks to do [work in the] mines."[11] Such is the report of a young man from the capital town of Dixie supported by one of the most privileged families.

VERDA BOWLER PETERSON

In contrast, consider Verda Bowler Peterson, who was born in Hebron on 21 November 1904: "We moved from Hebron to Enterprise when I was about a year old [not long before the earthquake put an end to the town]. There isn't anything there except for one or two old trees.

"My first teacher was Dora Woodbury. I had her for a couple of years. My next teacher was Fanny Klyman from Toquerville [Washington County, Utah]. Althea Gregerson was the next one. I had Willard Canfield and Bernie Farnsworth. I liked all my teachers. By the time I went to Bernie ([he] was more outstanding in my mind), I was possibly in the sixth or seventh [grade]. They used to have contests [at] school in writing the times tables. I won the blue ribbon [once]. I remember losing it one night. I remember getting up the next morning as soon as I could see. I knew where I had been the night before. I went to see if I could find my blue ribbon, which I did. I was tickled to death to [find] it because it meant [a lot] to me. I liked school a lot.

"I remember [the] girls used to play marbles with the boys on the sunny side of the school building. I didn't win very often. I think [the boys] cheated.

"[My] next teacher [was] Will Staheli. He was an outstanding teacher. He had a way of bringing out of you what he wanted to. In our history class there [were] two or three of us that had the history book that had the last chapter or two in it at the end of the year. I happened to be one of them. He was going to have us give the last [lesson] of the course. History was hard for me, so I [was] prepared and asked him if I could have my turn first in class that morning. He said yes. I memorized it, and I went through it. I about covered the whole thing. I didn't have to use the book. He was a good teacher. He couldn't sing, but he could sure put music over. He could make the people understand what he was trying to do. He wasn't a very good singer, but he was really good in music.

"I didn't go on to high school because, at the time, my mother had poor health and we had a large family. It was a family of twelve, and we didn't have a lot of money. They didn't hire people then like they do now. There weren't people to be hired or money to pay them. So [the] girls had to stay out of school. My older sister was not too well. I stayed out [of school] a lot. Before that, I wouldn't miss school for anything. After I had to stay out a lot, I began to look for excuses to stay out [of school]. I got discouraged and I never did go further than the eighth grade, about age fourteen."[12]

LESLIE "LES" STRATTON

Leslie "Les" Stratton was born in Hurricane on 11 November 1908. He tells of the demands of farming on a male student: "I got every bit [of schooling] I could. We usually had to work in the spring to get our crops in and we usually had to put the crops up in the fall. I did not always get a full year of schooling. When I [was old] enough to be in high school, the last four years of high school, I did not get any credit for them because I did not complete them all. I kept right on through, one year after the other and [had] all four years in, but there was no credit for the full year because I was out in the spring and the fall, for about three months of the year.

"We used to have nine-month schools, and I [went] about six months a year. I was good enough to make the basketball team. Bishop Church from La Verkin was the coach. We beat every team but St. George. We had a dandy team. I played baseball and was chosen by the county down here to represent Washington County in baseball and played at the [Utah] State Fair. I played first base. I think I was the biggest shot there because the first two balls that were knocked came straight to me."[13]

THERESA CANNON HUNTSMAN

Theresa Cannon Huntsman was born in St. George on 20 October 1885. She attended school in St. George, Cedar City, and the University of Utah before Dixie College existed: "I did not start to school as soon as I was six years old. The school was quite a ways from my home. I was small, and Momma thought it would better to wait until the next year, so I got a late start [in school]. I loved school and wanted to go. After I started, I really loved school, and I never wanted to stay out; it made me sick to be sick.

"There were schools in small houses all over town, one in every four or five blocks. We had some very good teachers in St. George. Our first teacher was Mrs. Mary Judd, and she was possibly in her thirties. She was a married woman, and she was a good teacher. The next teacher I went to was Rose Jarvis, another good teacher that I loved very much. Then

Martha Snow Keats was the next teacher. In 1901 the Woodward School started. Before that, we went to [class in the basement of the St. George] Tabernacle and to the [Washington County] courthouse for one grade. In the basement of the tabernacle we had several grades that year. John T. Woodbury was my teacher after I reached the seventh grade.

"They would make a class for us [even when a class was not available]. In that way I took several of the grades over. When it came to eighth grade, I took that over two years. The first year I was ill and had to quit, so I took it all over the next year. I did that with two of [my] high school years because I wasn't well, and my heart was bad. Then I went to Cedar [City] for a while, and I went to the University of Utah for a while, but I never did complete the college courses."[14]

DORA MALINDA CLOVE

Dora Malinda Holt Clove was born on 2 April 1894 on Holt's Ranch near present-day Enterprise. She began school at Hebron. In her interview she said: "[During] our early [education] we would go maybe five months of the year and that [would be] the end of our school [year]. We would [have] the same amount of [school days] every year and have to start over the next year. The first part of [the school year] we got done well. We had grades. We were all taught in the same room, [with] several grades in one room. We really liked it. My brother taught [in] my first [school]. [His name was] George O. Holt.

"We would have so many minutes for each class. We had arithmetic, grammar (as they used to call it), reading, writing, [and] spelling. We had part [of our studies] in the forenoon and part in the afternoon. I wasn't the best reader in the class, but I was right next to it! I was a good speller, but I wasn't too good in arithmetic. I could do it until we got up to algebra, [but] I didn't do too badly.

"When we came down here to Enterprise, I was seven years old. We went up to eighth grade. I went to [school in] Cedar City [for] one year. I really liked it, but I didn't stay and finish up. When spring came, my father had to be out on the farm, so he called me to come back and take care of the store. He had a general merchandise store in Enterprise. I worked there until I was married and [for] a little while afterwards. My husband wouldn't let me work anymore. He said he didn't get me to work in the store, he [married] me to be a housewife."[15]

ALVIN HALL

Alvin Hall was born on 17 October 1890 in Rockville and attended school there through seventh grade. He then went to the eighth grade in Hurricane. Following that he went to high school in St. George and continued his education at Utah State Agricultural College in Logan. He said in his interview: "[I started school] in Rockville. They had two teachers, a man teacher and a lady teacher. They had two buildings. My first teacher [was] Loretta Stout. They had the lower grades in a different building from the higher grades. I felt it was a detriment to have more than one grade together like that. When we went to high school in St. George, those [students] were familiar with a lot of things that we had never heard of [before]. They had taken a lot more classes than we had [available in Rockville].

"We had mostly good teachers [in Rockville]. [Some of those teachers were] David Hirschi, George Cole, Loretta Stout, [and] Jenny De Mille; [her name was] Jenny Petty at the time. I went to the eighth grade after we moved to Hurricane. I graduated from the eighth grade here. I was out [of school] several years [after that]. My dad did not want me to go to high school; he needed us on the farm. He said it was all foolishness. I waited until I was twenty-one years old, and I went to high school in St. George anyway. I went to college ten years later when I had a wife and five [children]. My younger brother [Henry Vernon] had a job in Logan running the experimental farm for the college. He gave me a job on the experimental farm. I moved [my] family and went up there. I went to school part-time and worked on the farm on Saturdays and after school. I took two winter courses there. I [took] some college [classes] while I was in St. George [too]. [I have the equivalent of] about two years."[16]

VICTORIA SIGRIDUR TOBIASON WINSOR

Victoria Sigridur Tobiason Winsor was born in 1891 in Reykjavik, Iceland. She came to America as a child and lived in Logandale, Nevada. In 1901 she was baptized in St. George. She started school in Hebron, where she lived with the Alger family. She reports: "I started school with their children.

They had a girl [who] was in the second grade. [She was] just younger than me. She and I were learning to read words on the blackboard. They claimed that I was in the first grade, but I don't know; I didn't know the difference. They taught me words with some of the other children. It was only a little while until they put me in the same class with her, and she was in the second grade. I was only a month or so in school.

"When I came down here to live with Aunt Effie and Uncle Frank [Winsor], I was in the second grade. [I had] a special tutor up there [because] they had a small school. Children learn faster in a smaller school, believe it or not. It was only a little while [before] I could read as well as their little girl in the second grade. I could read in the book. I never was a good reader, but I enjoyed being able to read as good as she did. When I came down here to Aunt Effie and Uncle Frank's to live in St. George, they started me in school about a week after I came down. They wanted to get acquainted with me first. I was started in the second grade. I was in the second grade a little while, and they put me in the third grade. I took the first three grades the first year. I still wasn't up with my age, and I wanted to be with my age. During the latter part of the year, they didn't promote me out of the third grade because I had already taken [skipped] two grades. When I started the next fall, they promoted me to the fourth grade. I was only there a little while. A. B. Christensen was the principal. He took me to the blackboard and had me do some number work. He was the one that taught me long division. He had the teachers put me in the fourth grade. At the end of the year, I was promoted to the fifth grade. Then I was up with my age, [and] I was more satisfied.

"I didn't have much to do other than to study. I studied at home. Frank was good to help me read. I didn't want to play with the other children because they laughed at me. I didn't say my words right, and they kept asking me silly questions. They asked me where my grandpa [John M.] Lytle lived, and I said, 'In Diamond Valley.' They would ask my name and would say 'Wictoria.' They laughed! I wouldn't play with the other children, and that gave me more time to study.

"I was twelve years old, I guess, when I ran a nail in my foot. I was playing hopscotch with the other children. Somebody left a board with a nail in it and I ran the nail clear through my foot between my toes. The teacher wanted me to go home, but I didn't want to go home right then; I wanted to wait until school was out. I had to walk home anyway, and I didn't want to go home without the other children. This was at recess, [and] I walked home after school. I put my arm around my brother's neck and a neighbor boy's neck, and they helped me walk home. By that time, it was quite sore. I was out of school for six weeks with that. It got [an] infection, and I nearly had lockjaw. They promoted me just the same, [and] I didn't miss my grade. They sent books home and told me to study my lessons at home. When I was fourteen years old, I moved to Enterprise and I finished my grade school [education] up there. I was the first student in Enterprise to graduate from the eighth grade.

"I didn't go to school for a few years. I was quite sick when I was in my teens. I wasn't very strong, and I got kind of thin. It was cold out there, and I had rheumatism bad. I had rheumatic fever, and that kept me from going [to school]. When I [was] better, I went to [school] in St. George. They gave you credits in units then. I took five units the first year. The next spring I was called to take [over] kindergarten, especially in the Sunday School class."[17]

ISABELLE LEAVITT JONES

Isabelle Leavitt Jones was born on 26 November 1904. She reports: "I was living [in] Gunlock. I should have started [a] year [earlier], but we were living in Las Vegas at the time [because] my father was working there. Las Vegas was just a village at that time. My mother had a bad case of pneumonia that winter, so I didn't start until I was about seven. I can remember the house [where] we lived [in Las Vegas], and there was sand everywhere. There were a few buildings going up that were quite nice sized. My father worked with his team.

"[The school in Gunlock was] a one-room schoolhouse on the hill. The younger children sat on a board that was placed [across] five-gallon cans. That was where we sat the first year [in what] was the beginner grade. They had nine grades in [the] district school at that time. George [Hebron] Bowler was the teacher [and] his wife, [Nancy Elizabeth Holt Bowler], came and helped with the younger ones [when] he was busy. He was a good teacher. He moved to Mesquite the next year.

"They called it beginners [not kindergarten]. [Children] did not go [to school] until after they were six; in fact, I was about seven. I really liked school. All our activities were [held] either in school or church. It seemed like we worked hard [and] I had a lot of [chores to do] around home. I started washing dishes before I could reach the table to wash them without [using] a stool. [This was a] necessity [because] my mother had such a big family.

"We moved in October of 1910. I was almost nine years old. [The school] was in Mesquite and was a contrast to the little one-room school-house in Gunlock. They had three nice large rooms, three teachers, plenty of books and facilities, whereas in Gunlock [we] were so limited. I feel like it was a real opportunity for us to have lived there those six school years that we stayed there. [Education] was much better. Nevada had the money to pay their teachers. I think the teachers were of the same caliber, but teachers [who] have nine grades can't give as much attention [as] if they have only three [grades].

"When we left Mesquite, we moved to Gunlock and then to Veyo. It was known as Glen Cove at that time [and] hadn't received the name of Veyo. It was just a pioneer village and only a few families lived there. They boarded up a big tent and put a stove in the middle of it. We gathered up a few benches here and there, and that was my eighth grade. It was in a big boarded-up tent, and we held our church services there too."[18]

LEMUEL GLEN LEAVITT

Lemuel Glen Leavitt (born on 23 January 1905) and his wife, Florence McArthur Leavitt (born on 1 August 1910), are an interesting comparison. Lemuel's young life was spent in Gunlock. He describes his school life: "I went to school right over here on the corner of this forty [acres] in a tent for about three years. Then a new schoolhouse was built down here. We had a wood stove and kept plenty of wood in it. We were dressed warmly, [and] I don't think we suffered [from] cold then. Emma Abbott was my schoolteacher. George Bowler was the next schoolteacher. After we moved up to Veyo, we had James Cottam for a teacher for a number of years here. He is about the last [teacher] I can remember. No, there were [two] lady teachers here, Charity Leavitt and Lavonne Davis, before we went to St. George to school.

"I went to the sixth grade [in St. George], and then I didn't go any more until the first year of high school. I went back another part of a winter after I graduated and didn't go to high school. So I went part of the winter to the eighth grade again. I did some [classes that] I [hadn't] in St. George. I never did graduate from high school. We [became] involved in other things, and I didn't go on to school, much to my regret. My dad needed me. He didn't want me to come home, but anyway I did and it was an easy way out, I guess. [That] is the only thing I can figure. [It was] just an easy way out of school."[19]

FLORENCE MCARTHUR LEAVITT

Florence McArthur Leavitt was the granddaughter of famous Dixie pioneers. Her maternal grandfather was Thomas P. Cottam, who supervised the construction of the main building of Dixie College from 1909 to 1911, and was in the stake presidency. Her paternal grandfather was Daniel D. McArthur, the famous Dixie pioneer. She did all her schooling in St. George. She said, "There was only one grade in each room. It was in the old Woodward School that is now the Woodward Junior High School, the old red-block building. My first grade was in the southeast corner on the ground floor. Edna Wadsworth was my first-grade teacher. My second-grade teacher was Mary Star. It was in the southeast corner and the other [class] was in the southwest corner of the building on the ground floor. The third-grade teacher was Anna (I cannot remember her last name right now). In the fifth grade I had Mrs. Seegmiller. She was a dandy teacher. She taught me and most of my children in the fifth grade. Harold Snow was my sixth-grade teacher. He was stake president for some time and also [the St. George] temple president later on. He was a wonderful man. I went [through] all eight grades there. My seventh grade teacher was Leland [Lee] Hafen, who was a prominent coach [at] Dixie High School and College, and also Vivian [Jacob] Frei, who was in the stake presidency and [was] a fine man.

"From the eighth grade I went over to the old Dixie College. The Dixie College and High School were combined. There I spent four years of high school and two years of college. At that time, [only] two years of college were necessary to teach. I had a teaching certificate that I [received] in the spring of 1930.

"I always liked school. I enjoyed my school. In those days, we had some programs come in, but we were more of an isolated school than we are today. We [had] to make our own fun and furnish a lot of our own programs. I think today the Dixie spirit in school is carried on, especially before the ball games. The year that the [basketball] team won and went back to Chicago was my graduating year from high school.[20] It was really filled with activity that winter. We had a lot of Dixie spirit! School was a lot of fun, and we tried to keep up with our [studies]."[21]

ELMER RODNEY GIBSON

A very different story is that of Elmer Rodney Gibson, born on 4 April 1895 in Duncan, Utah [near Virgin]. His father died as a very young man—only twenty years old. Elmer grew up in the home of his grandparents and his mother went back to live with her parents. He said that he really enjoyed his early life, working with calves and making lots of cheese with his grandmother up on the mountain. He started school in Virgin. He said that the school was a two-story rock building: "It had the tithing cellar under it. Yes, I remember when I [was] a little older, my stepdad [James Jepson Jr., who built the Hurricane Canal] was bishop, and they [collected] the tithing over there. They used to take tithing in-kind. [They would take] wheat, corn, beans, [or whatever people] had [to give for tithing]. That is where they stored it. [It was] in [the] cellar under the schoolhouse. [It] was a big two-story rock schoolhouse. The [younger] children would go downstairs [to go to school]. Then, when we [were] about halfway through [school], maybe we would go upstairs. We thought we were getting pretty big when we got to go upstairs to [go] to school. There were two teachers. [There were] four grades for each teacher.

"I got along [fine]. I thought they were good teachers; they did their best; they seemed to be interested in the students. As I think about it as I [am] older, they seemed like they were there for the children's welfare.

"[At the time], I went [to school] part-time. I left school before I [was] through [all the grades]. My eyes were a limitation, but I did not miss school on that account. I think we had five months of school [each year]. You had to get your work done [each day] before [school]. Mary [Eleanor] Jepson [was one of my teachers]. [She was a] stepsister. She was a good teacher."[22]

JOSEPH HILLS JOHNSON JR.

Joseph Hills Johnson Jr. grew up in Tropic [Kane County, Utah]. He said: "My first schooling was in Tropic. I started school after I was seven. I do remember my first schoolteacher. [She] was Maggie Davis. I got along quite well in school there with her. I remember some of my schoolteachers. The next year, after Maggie Davis taught, Sarah Ahlstrom was my teacher. They were all lovely teachers, very fine. I loved them very much. Years later, Sarah Ahlstrom came back and taught me when I was in the fourth or fifth grades. I had her two different years.

"I only [went] to the eighth grade. I finished the work [for] the eighth grade, but about two weeks before the examination that was given at the end of the school [year], I was called out of school and never did take the examination. I had to go to work. However, a few years later, after we had been in Tropic, I went to Murdock Academy [in Beaver, Beaver County, Utah] for about six weeks. I was there the latter part of October until about December 15.

"My parents were determined that I was going to get an education. That was when I was sixteen. I herded sheep that summer and earned enough money that I thought it would put me through school. Father took me to Beaver. They were building the Murdock Academy at that time. [I] and two companions went with him, and we all rode to Beaver on a load of lumber about eighty miles.

"The schooling was wonderful, but it didn't last very long. I was late starting school. I didn't [arrive] until about a month after school began because I was working. I couldn't get away. But I did start, and I remember a few things about the school that I would like to recall.

"I was put into a class of twenty girls. There were two boys and twenty girls. It was the algebra class. The teacher said that these boys could understand and grasp the algebra much faster than the girls. So he put them in a class by themselves, just two or three girls with them. But there were about twenty girls in the class. Wallace Henderson and I were put in the class with the girls, the second class or lower class. Wallace stayed with it about a week, and he couldn't take it and dropped out. I stayed with it a few more days. I had never had algebra before, and somehow, after two or three days, it came to me and I could understand it. It seemed so easy to me. So the teacher promoted me back up to the boys' class."[23]

VERA HINTON EAGER

Vera Hinton Eager was born in 1899, and her family, including her three brothers and three sisters, went to school in the earliest days of Hurricane. She recalls: "The first time that we went to school, my uncle Irie Bradshaw moved down from Virgin. He built a house which is still standing in Hurricane. After the bowery days, we would have school in one big room of his home. We would have school and church [there]. We would all be in this one room, and they would teach us. Later, when they built the first public school and church, we would have eight grades in the one big room, and one on the stage. We would go to these schools and be enrolled like the first, second, third, fourth, fifth, sixth, seventh, eighth—all of the grades were in this room and on the stage. We would have to study when it wasn't our turn to be having class. We were supposed to concentrate, keep our minds on our work, study, and do the things we should do for school while the other grade was going on out to the side of us.

"I remember one teacher, Chauncey Sandburg, would get so aggravated with some of the children. He would say, 'If you don't be quiet, I will throw you out of the window bodily.' We all thought that was the funniest expression we had ever heard. Another teacher, Morgan Edwards, would come right down [to] us, [put] his hands under our chair and make us look right up into his eyes. He would say, 'Now, what are you doing this for? Now, you behave yourself.' He would use such a tone of voice that we were just a little bit afraid of him. I had a lady teacher called Sister Miles, and we really did love her. She was such a sweet woman. I will always remember what a wonderful teacher she was.

"When I [started] the eighth grade, I went to Hinckley, Utah, to stay with my grandmother [Elizabeth Staheli] Walker, who lived there. I went to school at Millard High School [in] Millard, Millard County [Utah]. I had quite the experiences there. I had never been away from home before. My mother was one of those strict women who would never let us use powder, paint [make up], or perfume. My uncle Avery [was] a bishop [and] lived up there. He would tease me [by] saying, 'I don't believe Vera has looked in the glass [mirror] in two or three years. She has never used powder or paint. What does she need a looking glass for?' I always thought that was quite strange.

"One day, I found some wintergreen in my grandmother's medicine cabinet. I thought that it was perfume. I thought it smelled so good [that] I put some on before I went to Sunday School. I got it on fairly strong, I guess. I didn't know how to use perfume. All of the people around me would say, 'Where is that wintergreen smell coming from?' I thought: 'I guess that must be me. It must be wintergreen that I put on.' When I went home, I washed [it] off, and never did use perfume any more. No more wintergreen!

"They had girls' and boys' day at the high school. I remember one day the girls were supposed to be up on the stage. The boys would march up. As they marched, they would take the girl who was opposite with them and would march on down. This time, the one boy that everyone made fun of happened to be paired opposite of me. Nobody liked him. He was quite a kooky [fellow]. When he came up to me, he threw his arms around me and gave me a big kiss. Was I ever embarrassed! I wouldn't go out with him anymore that day. I went home, and I wouldn't go anywhere because he did that up on the stage where everybody could see us. It embarrassed me so much. Nobody liked him anyway, and I wouldn't be seen with him anymore. That was the first year of 'high,' as it was called in those days. Now it is called the ninth grade. I came back and took some of the eighth grade [classes] over again. I learned on the piano how to play a few marches. There didn't seem to be anyone else who could play a march on the piano, so I would play these marches as they would march in and out of school. That was about the end of my school days."[24]

FERN MCARTHUR HAFEN

Fern McArthur Hafen was born in St. George on 7 October 1912. She told of an unusual situation: "I went through twelve years of schooling [and] graduated from Dixie High School [in St. George]. I started the first grade [because] they didn't have kindergarten in those days. Mrs. McAllister was my first-grade teacher. She couldn't hear. She lived in two upstairs rooms [at our house]. She was a [member of the] Seventh-day Adventist [Church]. She used to come home and tell mother that I didn't take too much interest in school. I liked to watch the birds out the window. In the second grade, Marjorie Brown [was] my teacher. She later married my uncle, Clarence Cottam. I really liked her.

"She was a good teacher. She took an interest in school and really made it interesting. In the third grade I had [Elizabeth 'Bessie' McArthur] Gardner. She was my cousin. I really liked Bessie. In the fourth grade we started to do a little more writing. [The teacher] noticed [that] I would write across the paper from the right to the left, instead from the left to the right. [The teacher would] love to hold it up before a looking glass to read it. Josephine Savage was my teacher in the fourth grade. She would stand by my desk every time there was anything to write. I was left-handed, and every time I put the pencil in my left hand she would change it to the right and stay right there until I wrote [the lesson]. I think this kind of upset my equilibrium.

"In the fifth grade, I had to stay back because I slowed down. Mrs. Brink was my teacher in the first year of the fifth [grade]. The second year in the fifth grade, Mrs. [Mishie] Seegmiller was my teacher. In the sixth grade, I had Harold H. Snow. He was a real good teacher too. In the seventh grade, I had Vernon Worthen. In the eighth grade [my teacher was] Jed Fawcett. [All] through high school we had [different] teachers for every subject. I quite liked school. I received my diploma."[25]

MARY AMANDA DEFRIEZ WILLIAMS

Mary Amanda DeFriez Williams was born on 1 April 1902 in St George. She told what it was like to attend the larger schools. "I went [through the] eighth grade in St. George [in the Woodward School]. I was vice president of our eighth grade. I was the first one to graduate of the grandchildren, so Grandpa Sorenson bought my graduation dress. It was a white taffeta. I will never forget that beautiful dress. Even today, the junior high school graduation is a big event in St. George. [It has] carried through the years. My husband [Kumen Davies Williams] was a student teacher when I was in the seventh grade. [Coach] Guy Hafen was my teacher. I will never forget that he was a teacher. We have laughed about it a lot. He taught me when I was in the seventh grade. [Kumen] was going to [Dixie] College at that time, [but] I did not know him. There was A. K. [Arthur Knight] Hafen. [He was] an English teacher, [and] I thought a lot of [him as a teacher]. John T. Woodbury Jr. was another teacher that I admired; he was a history teacher. There was Mr. Barkdahl; I have forgotten his first name. He is gone now. He taught me in art. When he left here, he went to Provo to teach. He wanted me to go to Provo and live with him and his wife [and study] art. That was after Kumen and I started to go together."[26]

Mary and her friends in St. George had the advantage of attending a school where each grade was in a separate room and had a separate teacher. There were about twenty or more students in each class. They had a band in the school, and the students marched into the building each morning with the band playing. Other students, like Irvin Bryner, enjoyed describing each teacher and especially how they disciplined students. Some, who were beginners, sent the misbehaving students to Miss Lena Nelson, who was an expert in discipline. For example, she had them stand on one foot and hold an eraser in the air with the opposite hand for a long time.

CLARENCE JACOB ALBRECHT

Clarence Jacob Albrecht grew up in Wayne County, a long way from the heart of Dixie. He became a teacher in Hanksville and a Church leader and a member of the Utah legislature in 1949. These memories are of a student who was not initially focused on such achievements: "Being that we lived two miles out of town, I was not allowed to go to school when I was six years old. They kept me home and I resented this very much. By the time I was seven, I was now a full year behind the other boys and girls of my age. I will never forget the first day I went to school to the first grade. I wore a pair of new Levi's my grandfather had purchased for me and a pair of blood-red shoes. They were about two sizes too large, and the [children] my age then called me 'Dummy Red Foot' because I was in the first grade and they were in the second [grade]. It didn't take me very long to catch up with them though. I had a very good teacher who took direct interest in me. I believe her name was Mabel Baker. By Christmastime, she promoted me into the second grade, with those [children] of my age. I went on from there. I [did] quite well in school with the exception of reading. I never was a very fast reader. It was after I had [gone] through elementary school that I learned to read a little better. I had a fascinating experience when I graduated from the eighth grade. We had to go down to Bicknell [Wayne County, Utah], which was fifteen miles away, to take our eighth grade examination. This was quite a day for me. My father made arrangements that I would go with a neighbor in his car. How rich I felt when my father gave me $3.00 to spend that day!

"I went on through high school from there. It was in my high school year that I probably learned to study. I will always be grateful to Joseph Hickman, who was my uncle. He was the superintendent of schools and also the principal of the high school at the time. I had been to school about a month when he called me in his office. He said, 'Clarence, just because you are my folks, don't expect any easy things out of me.' Among the other things, he counseled me and said, 'Anybody with the guts you have has no business just loafing around and wasting your time. This work that you have done is not satisfactory. I want you from this time to learn to do the things that are hardest for you.'

"I was very active in athletics. I played basketball three years while I was in high school. I was probably the shortest center that Wayne High ever had! I played center all three years I was in high school. In the summertime, I used to play baseball. I was issued a baseball suit for the Fremont town [team] when I was thirteen years old. I treasured this very highly. I was certain nobody was going to get that suit away from me. I about killed a horse off a time or two, riding from out of the mountains to get to town on the Fourth of July for fear they would have my suit on somebody else.

"[While] in high school, during the summer months, I learned to play [the] drums by having some drumsticks I had fashioned out of rounds [from] chairs, which I made myself. Then I found an old frying pan that I tied on my saddle. As I would get off to just sit in one place to watch the sheep, I would pound on this frying pan. I drummed up enough rhythm that I became a drummer [for] the high school band through this way of learning. In my junior and senior years, I took the leading part in the high school operas. Joseph Hickman evidently had an impact."[27]

GEORGE WILSON MCCONKIE

George Wilson McConkie was born in Moab [Kane County, Utah] on 30 June 1909. He and his children were highly educated, but George wished he had gone farther: "I went through grade school at Moab and La Sal. [At] the school in Moab the grades were separate, but [in] La Sal we had two teachers teaching the eight grades in the church house. The church was [also] the school building.

"Some of the seventh- and eighth-grade boys were much bigger than the teachers and the principal of the school. I remember once or twice when the principal took a licking from some of those rough and tough boys. I remember the trips to and from school in the cold part of the winter. My younger brother [Andrew Ray], my older sister [Ina], and I rode a horse back and forth through the snow; all three [of us] on one horse [rode] through the deep snow. There were no homes in the two miles between our [home] and the school. My brother rode the tail end of the horse, and often he would find himself in the snow bank somewhere as he dropped off.

"We would have snow [as deep as] two feet. One of our pastimes during recess or the lunch hour [was to] go out in the sagebrush around the schoolhouse and catch rabbits as they jumped out from under the brush. They could not run in the snow, and we would [catch] them.

"As a rule, in those days, teachers were a little tough. I remember one especially in the sixth grade. He used to whip the students with a hose. He had a piece of rubber garden hose about three and one-half feet long and it was split into four or five strips. He would use that as sort of a cat-o'-nine-tails, and he really laid it on. It was mainly [because] a student whispered and [was] talking to his neighbor. Things were quite different then.

"I attended high school [in] Moab. I played football during my high school days. When I graduated, there were thirteen [students] in the graduating class. The fall following my graduation, I [entered] BYU. I didn't have money enough to go straight through [four years]. I [completed] the first year and then worked for a while. Then I would go back [to BYU]. I got in a total of about seven quarters at BYU, after which I decided definitely to go into civil engineering and changed to Utah State Agricultural College [in] Logan. Of course, many of my BYU classes didn't count towards an engineering degree, which required 210 quarter hours of pre-scribed work. As a result, I never graduated although I attended, I believe, seven quarters up [in] Logan. I had more college credit, but not all of the required [classes].

"At this [time], a chance [opportunity] came along, [and] I took the examination for a surveyor. I took this test [to] prove I was qualified under a test that was given all over the United States. From this test, I wound up with an appointment for geological survey [work].

"This was as good a job [as] most of our graduates from college were [finding] at the time. We[28] decided to get married, and it was probably one of the biggest mistakes of my life, not continuing with the school. The way it looked then, we decided to take the job. I had been working as an assistant on survey crews for quite a number of years [during] my schooling. That was how I made money to go to school."[29]

NATHAN BRINDLE JONES

Nathan Brindle Jones was born 27 December 1885 in Cedar City and later lived in Enterprise. He attended a one-room school in Enoch, near Cedar City. He recalled: "I was very young when I started to school. I was a barefoot boy [walking] in cockleburs and leaves. I went to school with Dave Sterling. If I remember right, it was just a one-room brick building, or adobe [blocks], with all eight grades in the one room and [with] one teacher. If she [had] just fifteen minutes with each class, she did well. You had to have a mind to not listen to the other groups and study your own book. [You had] to study by yourself to get any education.

"I enjoyed school quite a little when I was young, but after I was older, I didn't. I didn't keep up with school to learn as fast, because I was taken out to work and help make a living. I learned to read [better] after I quit school altogether than while I was going to school. I was fairly good in mathematics. I [did] that pretty well in school. I got more with my work. Even after I was married, I learned quite a bit about mathematics.

"When I was living in Enoch on [my] father's farm, . . . we never could start school until the crops were in. The older boys were out making money for themselves. [Those of us who were] young fellows had to put in the crops. The older ones helped with the living too. It just was very little [education] that I [received] because we had to work in the fall to gather crops. In the spring, [we had] to plant the crops before the school [year] was half over. We only got a few months' break. We seldom [had] two or three months for school when we were young.

"Much of the time we were not home, even though we wanted to be. You had to get out and go make a living. I was helping father with his freighting to Caliente [Nevada] or to Pioche [Nevada] and the early days of Delamar [Nevada]. I was taken away from school in the winters. You didn't get very much [education]."[30]

LELAND TAYLOR

Leland Taylor was born on 6 November 1905 in New Harmony. He recalls his schooling there: "[It was] a small [building] with one large room. All the classes from one to [the] eighth [grade] were in the one room [with] the teacher. I wouldn't have traded those experiences for any of the experiences they have in school nowadays that I am acquainted with. They were wonderful experiences to me. The only thing I resented was not being able to get any high school [classes]. I would like to have gone on, but we could not. There was no transportation for them. My oldest brother [had] some high school [education] and the next oldest [had] a little bit—not much. None of us [had] any high school [education] until it [came] down to the very youngest [in the family]. Times changed enough so that we could [have] them in school by moving to where the school was.

"They had to work, and they had to go to work early. I had to take the eighth grade twice. I always resented that. Elmer Taylor, my cousin, was the teacher when I went through the eighth grade. Later on in the summer, I was working with him and he said, 'You could have passed all right, but I knew you couldn't go to high school. It was better for you to have something to do this winter.' So he flunked me in science. He flunked me in science to make me take it over again just so I wouldn't be idle through the winter.

"The teachers had to teach all the grades. They couldn't specialize in any one grade. They had to teach them all. It wasn't an easy life. They didn't get paid too well either. I can remember Laverna Englestead; she taught [school for] quite a while. Minnie Pace was one of the best teachers I ever had. We had the three Rs and history. I guess because I didn't have too much education is one reason I like to read so well. My brother Lester [went to] the eighth grade. That is all the [education] he could ever get. But he [obtained enough] education to put himself in the [Utah] State Legislature."[31]

JOSEPH WOODRUFF HOLT

Joseph Woodruff Holt grew up on the family ranch and went to school in Hebron, a small rural town west of Gunlock. His story is quite a contrast with Florence McArthur Leavitt in her urban setting: "My first school was in Old Hebron. It is a ghost town now. My first teacher was Zera Pulsipher Terry. I went to school there one year with Zera Terry. I must tell about a little episode we had that winter. He was strict. We had lots of [older] students up in the higher grades. I was the only one [in that grade] in a room not much bigger than this room here. The school building was about twenty feet long and about fifteen [feet] wide at that time. He used to carry a big, long, three-foot [yardstick] ruler around all the time in his hand, I guess probably to keep it a little quiet. He would use it once in a while too. One day, I was doing something he didn't like; he came up and he said, 'Joseph, put out your hand on that desk there.' I put my hand up and he held this big long ruler up. He came down on my hand, and when he started to come down I jerked my hand, and he came down and hit that desk and popped his ruler right in two. A lot of the students had to laugh, that was all! They couldn't hold themselves! I made him mad, but he didn't say any more. He just let it go at that, and that was the last of the rulers. I didn't see any more rulers. That was my first experience in school.

"I went to school for about five months each year until I was about seventeen. When I was eight years old, I went to school up in Mountain Meadows [in the town of Hamblin]. That is another ghost town. The teacher at that time was old man [James Samuel] Bowler. He was the father of all these builders around here. He was a very good teacher. He used to try to get me to sing when I was a young [boy]."[32]

IRMA SLACK JACKSON

Irma Slack Jackson was born on 14 February 1893 in Toquerville. Her mother died in childbirth in 1899. She reports her school experience: "I went eight years in Toquerville and graduated from the eighth grade. They had what [was] called the schoolhouse and the church building. The church building was used for the four younger grades. They had big, long benches that could seat about half a dozen [students]—just homemade benches. [There was] a box heater in the middle of the floor. I remember I was the only girl in the class. I wanted to sit on the end of the bench, and a cousin of mine [sat] next to me because I didn't want to sit by any of the other boys. But it was all right to sit by my cousin. I would sit on the end of the bench.

"There were four grade rooms in the church. [It was] the only church that had them. [And there were] four grades in the schoolhouse, as they called it. I remember when I was in the fourth grade, our teacher was Nellie Woodbury from St. George. [She] came up there [to] teach. She put on a little operetta called *Red Riding Hood*. She made me take the part of Red Riding Hood. I knew every song from beginning to end. I [later] sang them to my [children].

"I remember when I was in seventh grade, we had Charles Petty. He was our teacher when I was in seventh grade. He [taught] the seventh and eighth grades. He had the fifth, sixth, seventh, and eighth, but he took the sixth and seventh grades up to Zion National Park. There were no roads up there and no camps of any kind. It took us one day to get there. We spent one day there, and one day we came back home.

"For graduation from the eighth grade they gave a big, one-foot-square certificate. They did [that] in those days. It came from the state. We had to take a state examination to get out of the eighth grade in those days. Then I came down here to the Dixie Academy."[33]

RHODA HAFEN LEAVITT

Rhoda Hafen Leavitt was born on 19 January 1906 in Bunkerville. She was able and strong-willed, as these stories show: "One day one of the boys, Dee Houston, came [into the school] and sat with me. Mr. Whiting [the principal and the teacher] came in and looked at me and said, 'Rhoda Hafen, will you please take another seat?' I said, 'No, I will not. I am in my own seat. If anybody moves, it will be somebody besides me.' He turned on his heel and walked back into the office. If I had been out of my seat, I would have moved, but I was not. So I did not. He could see that he was in the wrong. He sent one of the teachers back in there, [who] asked me to come in there. He said, 'Why did you not move when I told you?' I said, 'I would have if I had been wrong, but I was not in the wrong. Dee was out of his seat, not me.' He said, 'I thought I could correct a girl a lot quicker and get by with it.' I said, 'No, you did know that I was in my seat.' He said, 'I guess you are right. I apologize.'

"The school in Bunkerville by then had each class in a separate room. Rhoda met Mr. Hutchings, one of the teachers there a few years later, and he said that her group of students were the smartest he had ever met. He was a good teacher. He said, 'We did not have many books, but we really made the best use of them. That one year I taught here, there was not a high school in the state of Nevada that went as high as those students did on their tests.'"[34]

WILLIAM "BILL" CHARLES PULSIPHER

William "Bill" Charles Pulsipher was born on 24 June 1895 in Hebron, but moved to Gunlock. "I was the oldest boy; we had two outfits, and I had to drive one of them. Dad drove one, and I drove one. After I [was] a little older, I wouldn't go to school, [and] I got so far behind. You [can't] blame a fellow for that. We had it all fixed that I was going to start when school started. We were living on a ranch south of Gunlock. I said, 'I will go up every morning to school. I have to catch up.' A couple of days before school started, it just happened; everybody in Gunlock would be out of flour. Dad said, 'We have a load of grain in Ox Valley.' That is up in the mountains south of Enterprise. 'Go up and get that, take it to Modena and get a load of flour.' I got caught in a snowstorm and had to stay there four or five days and school started. When I got back with the flour, I wouldn't even go to school. That is the way it happened. I wouldn't dare go back to school and be in class with youngsters who were two years younger than me. I have gotten by and have made a good living. I am not smart.

"My wife had one or two years of high school. I did like school when I was going and didn't have to keep staying out every day or two. When I would have to stay out a day or two and then work to catch up or skip it, it wasn't fun. The only fun I had in school was playing ball. It wasn't basketball in those days; it was baseball. I had the best teachers in the world. My first teacher was Annie Miller from St. George. There wasn't a kindergarten; I went to first grade. The second teacher was Zera Terry. He lived right there and has been a teacher his entire life. He beat me on the head more times than—I wasn't much of a cutup. I didn't like to [go] out and steal chickens and raise hell like that. The most fun I had was playing hooky from school, going out in the hills and riding steers. I did pretty well in school, but I didn't get an education.

"I was inclined to be a cowboy. My dad was one all his life, and he taught me how to rope from the time I was old enough to ride. By the time I was fifteen years old, I was driving cattle for top wages from my uncle. He had quite a herd there.

"They held a religion class for a half hour every Thursday afternoon. It was not taught by the schoolteachers. I had an uncle who came there. He would come and teach the religion class. The teacher would just hold us there, and she would stay. I quite enjoyed that."[35]

ROSALIE MAURINE WALKER BUNKER

Rosalie Maurine Walker Bunker was born on 9 May 1927 in Sunderland, Durham County, England. She later lived in Bunkerville and Logan and gives a view of what the schools were like that she attended in England. "The infant school would be kindergarten through maybe the first and second grades. When you were seven years old, you went into what we call the junior school for two years. You would be about nine years old when you finished. I think that was when we had divided classes. The boys went to the boys' school, and the girls went to the girls' senior school. We wore uniforms. When we were eleven years old, we had to sit for this scholarship examination. We went to the secondary school for about three days to take all these examinations. Only so many passed. We would not know if we passed until we saw our name in the newspaper.

"Following the next summer's vacation, we would go to the secondary school. I think at the time the reason I wanted to go to secondary school was because they had six week[s] of summer vacation and the other school had only four weeks. To me, that was the big thing to grab, and it was a nicer school too. It had gardens and playgrounds. It was near our home too.

"Those who did not pass the examination would stay and go on to the ordinary school and leave when they were about fourteen years old. It used to be fourteen, and then they raised the age to fifteen. They would study ordinary subjects—geography and history. They did not study foreign languages like they did in the secondary school or take chemistry.

"The advanced school would get the cream of the students. My French teacher used to drum it into us that we were the cream of the crop. I guess there were about ninety girls who would go each year to the secondary school. There were three grades there. I always did like school. In secondary school we had a different teacher for each subject and French class. We did not start Latin until we were in the second grade. Then we took chemistry and physics, subjects that we had not had before.

"For some students who did not pass to go to secondary school, there was another school that they went to. They did more secretarial work, like typing."[36]

VERNON WORTHEN

Most of these interviews were with people who recalled their school days as students. There are, however, some who reported their experiences as teachers. Here is an interview from one of the best-known teachers, Vernon Worthen, who was born in St. George on 19 April 1885. People who live in St. George now or who visit there will recognize his name as that of the city park. Here are some reminiscences from him: "After teaching school in Glenwood one year, I returned to St. George and taught the sixth grade [at Woodward School]. The principal was Edgar M. Jensen. A number of the teachers were Misha Seegmiller, Leland ['Lee'] Hafen, Jedd Fawcett, Florence Foremaster, [and] Emma Foremaster. [I] continued teaching there until 1927, when I was asked by W. [William] O. Bentley, who was the superintendent of schools, to be principal of the elementary school, which included the eighth grade in the old Woodward School.

"In 1936 [Washington] County decided to change the program of the school, making it a six-four-four plan, with six elementary schools, four junior high [schools], two high schools, and two junior colleges. I took the [West] elementary school. I taught in the new school building from 1936 to 1955; that was [at] 100 West and Tabernacle, and I moved to that school.

"I had as high as twenty-three teachers and over six hundred students. I taught school for forty-one years [and] enjoyed every moment of the time that I was teaching. I had many experiences in school, civic, and community activities. . . . All my life, I've been very fussy about punctuality. While I was bishop, I told people if they would be there at 2:00 [p.m.], we would dismiss at 3:00. If they wanted to come at 2:15, we would stay an extra fifteen minutes. My policy [was], and I know that the teachers at school and my PTA officers made this statement, 'We knew when you had a program at the school, if you said 7:30 [p.m.], you meant 7:30, instead of dragging on until the crowd got there.' They said, 'We knew we had to be on time.'" That was Mr. Worthen's policy at the schools he led and at the many civic activities he was in charge of. After teaching for four decades, he became the city postmaster and then a full-time gardener.[37]

ROBERT PARKER WOODBURY

Here is the story of a nervous teacher, Robert Parker Woodbury, who was born 17 January 1873 in St. George. His brief remarks, at age ninety-five, give an interesting insight: "My first school [teacher] was a widow woman by the name of Sister Everts. She had the school in her home. That was my first school [experience], and I enjoyed it very much. I went through grade school and to what they called the St. George Academy. Later on, I moved to Cedar City and took [the] Normal Training Course. I graduated from [there]; then I came back to Washington County and taught school [for] fifteen years.

"I liked it. I like [students]; I like to make [things] for the [youngsters]. I had the ungraded schools. Sometimes I had all the grades. It worked on [my] nerves, and I [became] a little nervous. I [was] so nervous when the [children] made a racket in the house. Sometimes I would scold them and tell myself [that] maybe I had better quit teaching school. It affected me that way, and so I quit. I took out a loan and bought a farm on a government farm loan and farmed the [rest] of my life."[38]

ELIZABETH "LIBBY" LEANY COX

Elizabeth "Libby" Leany Cox was also a teacher. She was born in Harrisburg on 22 February 1890. She attended Beaver Academy in preparation to be a teacher. She was often afflicted by pneumonia, and she battled it with the help of doctors. She tells that she also took a six-week summer course in Salt Lake City. "I was taking subjects that were needed to get my certificate. I took reading for teachers and took a class [from] Howard R. Driggs. That was an English class, preparatory for teaching children. I took a psychology class from Professor William Stewart. The summer was very rewarding. I rode the streetcar and then walked up to the university from the end of the line.

"I came home and [was hired at] a school for the next year in Virgin. It was a mixed school all eight grades, and there were some high schoolers and graduates from the year before [who] were not able to go away for high school. They wanted me to give them more high school work. Before school in the morning, at recess and for half an hour at noon, I was giving those three big [students] high school lessons. I used one algebra book and the books I had used in high school for their text work. [I] loaned [the book] to them. This went on for a couple or more months, I don't know just how long, and the trustees found out about it. They told me that I had to quit, that I was hired to teach the elementary school or the grade school [students] and not the high school, and I could not take this on, that it was too much.

"I stayed at Strattons when I first went [there]. I went home for Thanksgiving. When I [returned], Sister Stratton was sick. I helped nurse her. It seemed like I could rub her back and her side and ease her when nobody else could. I spent a lot of time at night waiting on her. I would lay my hands on her and pray for the Lord to give her relief, and it would come immediately. [Emotional] She got so that she did not want anybody else to do that for her. I didn't know, but when the Lord would answer my prayers that way, I thought it was all right. I just prayed. I didn't attempt to use any priesthood [methods] or anything. I just asked the Lord to bless my dear friend who was ill, and he did.

"Towards spring they found out that there was no more money for the teachers. The only compensation that was available would be for the people in the town to let me board around. Sister Stratton was getting worse all the time, and doctor said she couldn't live [as] she had cancer of the liver. I hated to leave her, but it was best. I stayed at one home and then another, knowing that there would be no compensation. I finished the school year.

"I had difficulty all winter. Like I said before, I never drew a breath that I didn't have pain. At times it was very difficult for me to handle my school [work]. I had thirty-eight students [in] eight grades. They were good [students], but they were just [youngsters]. I had one boy [who] the students said, 'You will have trouble with Reub. Every teacher [who] has come [here] has expelled him from school.' I said, 'You don't come to school to be expelled. You come to school to learn. He is a good [young-ster]; he doesn't need to be expelled. You wait and see.' Not long after, they were making wine in the town. Reub came to school drunk as he could be, and [the students] came running in to tell me, 'Reub is drunk. Now what are you going to do?' I said, 'That doesn't matter, you go on out and play. When you come in from recess, we will see what we do.'

"His seat was quite close to the stove. [It was] one of those big potbellied stoves like they used to have and [we] fired it up to warm the big room. It still wasn't quite cold enough for a big fire, but there were double seats. I had him sit on the side next to the stove. Then I got one of the other boys to make a good fire in the stove. They said, 'What are you going to do with Reub? He is drunk.' I said, 'Just let him alone. He is not hurting anybody. You tend to your own business and don't bother Reub. We will make a good fire, and he will be asleep in a few minutes.' [He] was! He slept all through the school [lessons], sound [asleep] on his arm on the bench. After I dismissed [the class] and the [students] were gone, he was still asleep. 'What are you going to do with Reub?' I let him stay there, [and] after a while he woke up and went home. That took care of that!

"They wanted me to come back and teach the next year. Dixie High School had just been completed. They were going to hold school here the next winter. Father had helped quite a lot [with] the building, hauling different things. President 'Ed' [Edward] Snow was also president of the school board. He had [visited] my [class] a time or two in Virgin. I had to see him about getting a school for the next winter. He said, 'Why don't you apply for a school in St. George? Then you will be here where the boys [her brothers] can come and go to school.' I said, 'Do you think I could get a school here?' He said, 'I know you can.' If he knew, then that was all it took. He called up the principal of the school who had just asked for credentials. He said, 'She can handle anything you have.' He told her the kind of school I had taught the winter before. He said, 'You can either put her in with the little children, she would be excellent there or, if you want to, put her in the upper grades. She will handle that all right. I ended up teaching the first grade, darling little [youngsters]. I had fifty-four of them in one room. It was quite a challenge.

"That was a good winter. I loved those children; it seemed like I didn't know the town, but those children were just like they belonged to me. They would follow me wherever I went; it was wonderful. I taught three years here in St. George, three years and a half. The last winter I didn't [teach here]. I went back and taught at Leeds. I was principal of the school in Leeds. We rolled up from Harrisburg to Leeds in a white-top [buggy]."[39]

VICTOR IVERSON

Victor Iverson was born on 7 March 1897 in Washington City. He became a well-known teacher there: "When I was about seven years old, I started school. My folks kept me out until the brother next to me was old enough to go to school too. We were almost twins, only fifteen months apart. From then on, almost through our whole school life, we went to school together. We have always enjoyed each other's association and company very much.

"When I first went to school, [classes] for the lower grades were in the basement of the church house. I remember one of my first teachers was Edna Cragun. She was very strict and demanding. I also had Andrew Sproul and another teacher by the name of Eddie Mickelson. I remember so well [the] birds and animals that Mickelson stuffed and used to bring to school. [This was] very fascinating to us at the time. As we advanced in our grades, we were sent to school in the upper room of the church house; it was divided by a curtain drawn through the center. I remember one of the teachers was the principal at the time, Charles Stoney. [He] came here from Beaver. [He] was a small man, but very rigid and strict and stern. He didn't hesitate to use a good, long mulberry willow or threaten to take an axe handle to you if you didn't step the line.

"Before I was through the eighth grade, the present schoolhouse was built. That was about 1909. I spent the last two or three years of my elementary [education] there. The teacher that I remember best in that school was Willard O. Nisson. He later became a very prominent [and] fine citizen in our town. Many of the boys and girls who grew up here at this time owe a great deal to his help and guidance. Other teachers that I remember in that particular school [were] a man named Hickman, [who] came from Beaver, and Angus Sproul. I graduated from the eighth grade and went on to school at the Branch Agricultural College or the Branch Normal School in Cedar City.

"After I graduated from the eighth grade in Washington City, some other boys from out of town were going to school at the Branch Normal College in Cedar City. Because of the influence of these fellows, my father thought that I should also go to this school, although we had Dixie Normal College in St. George. My father was criticized very severely because he sent me up there [when] our own school [was] closer. I graduated from the Branch Normal—the Branch Agricultural College, which it later became—in 1916. The next year, I went to an auto mechanics school in Kansas City and spent fourteen weeks getting some training in auto mechanics. I came home and spent some time working in garages on automobiles. I seemed to lean toward [wanting more] education. After I had spent a period of time in the army, I decided to take up teaching.

"All the [education] I [received] after that was [attending] summer school or [doing] extension work. I spent a number of summers away [at] school. Three summers I spent in Logan at [Utah State University] taking some college work. Two summers I spent at the University of Utah. Besides this work, I did a great amount of extension work that was given through either one of these colleges in connection with Dixie [Junior] College in St. George. That way, I [received] all my [education]. I never did get a [teaching] degree, but I had the equivalent of a degree, [if] I had filed and made [an] application for it.

"Teaching was my primary occupation all my life. I taught school for forty years. I began my teaching career in Leeds. I spent a year out [of teaching to] go to school; then I went back to teaching again. Altogether, I put in forty years. Thirty-nine of those years I taught here in Washington City. For a number of years, I was a teacher in the school; later, I became a teacher-principal. I spent all the time as a teacher of the fifth and sixth grade, two grades that I enjoyed very much. If I was going to become a teacher again and would have a choice of grades that I would like to teach it would be fifth grade. Boys and girls in that grade are very pliable, eager, and active. They are still quite obedient; they have not grown to an age in their life when they are changing over and taking on some of the characteristics that create some of the resentments that boys and girls grow into as they become a little older. My teaching experience has been a very happy one. I couldn't think of anything that I could have enjoyed more if I were to live my life over again. I would surely like to be a teacher again.

"I have had many hundreds of boys and girls go through my [classes]. I have been directly responsible for that part of their education. Many, many of these boys and girls have come back to visit me, and they still come back. I have taught many entire families. For instance, I taught Woodrow Staheli in the sixth grade and taught all of his boys and girls with the exception of Nancy. Had I taught one more year, I would have taught Nancy. That has been the case [with] many other families in town. For instance, I taught Chris Connell and Matilda Turnbeaugh both and, later on, I taught all of their boys and girls but their youngest boy. This has been true in a number of cases, where I taught the parents and then all of their children. During my teaching experience, I taught my four youngest brothers and sisters, [Edward], Keith, Rulon, Mae, and Berniece. Also I taught my own three children, Austin, Maxine, and Mervin, in the fifth and sixth grades."[40]

VELDA DELLE LEAVITT COX

Velda Delle Leavitt Cox was born on 27 May 1902 in Bunkerville, Nevada, the seventh child in a polygamous family of twenty-two children. She said, "I started school at six years of age. I was frightened because I thought I did not know anything. When I was in school it was so dear to me. I loved it with all my heart. I had a teacher, Miss Rencher, [who] lived in Utah [in her] later years. I do not know where she came from in the beginning. She was the dearest teacher that I can ever remember having. She was an elocutionist, and so I learned at an early age to speak pieces. During [the] early years of my life, up until I was married, I read declamations in school [in] contests. I gave them before the public.

"I graduated from high school, and in those days we were poor. My father had died when I was fifteen. My mother did not have much [money to] live [on]. She had a little $7 pension at the time. We had a little stock and [some] money. Some of the older boys [received] that, so we did not have much to [live] on.

"There was a one-year normal school that they [started] in the southern part of Nevada through [the] State College at Reno. She sent me to one year of [this] normal [school] down [at] St. Thomas [Nevada], which is now covered with Lake [Mead]. I [went] a year down there. I had $15 cash during that year. My sister [Leah], [who] was a year older and was teaching school, sent me a two-piece dress and a hat to match. I wore that to school all winter by wearing it all week, coming home and cleaning it up on weekends, and going back to school. I had a taffeta dress that she bought me. I wore that to dances because I was grown up and had a few boyfriends at the time.

"I finished and was given certification enough to teach three years. I [received] recommendations from my normal teacher enough that I was placed in the district. Then we had a district in Overton, Nevada, with a superintendent, called District Number One. Since [then], they have combined Clark County [and] we are all in Clark County. The superintendent of District Number One [was] A. L. Kelly. [He] gave me a contract to teach in the gyp [gypsum] camp which is up in the White Hill, just above Glendale, Nevada, as you go through on Highway 91. It is [the] I-15 [freeway] now, but it was [Highway] 91 then. I went to this gyp camp and taught in a boarded-up tent. I had fifteen long benches and thirty-one students of all grades up [to] and including [the] eighth grade. I had boys that could not get in the door without stooping. I was a [small] girl of about 110 pounds at the time.

"I was frightened about the school because the year before they had run three teachers out [by] their meanness. Some of those [children] blew the motor car off the track. [This was] the motor car that went down the valley. They would go down at [the] noon hour and after school put gasoline on their pigs and cows and set fire to the hair. They milked their cows during the noon hour so they would not get much milk at night. They wrote dirty [words] on the tent sides. The gyp camp was [made up of] mining people [who were divorced] and people [who] had never managed their children. They were tough kids. I was frightened, and I cried hard to my sister who was older. I said that Mr. Kelly would not have given me that job. He knew they would run [me off], and he just figured I would fail at it. My sister said, 'No, Mr. Kelly is the type of person [who] knows you can handle [it], or he would not have [given you the contract].

"I was happy to have had it here, because a lot of the normal [school] students my year had to go to Utah. The wages were about $55 to $60 lower in Utah than in Nevada. I received $105 a month and they were receiving about $60 or $55. It was quite a difference, so I was happy for that reason. I went to that school, and I can say that we [did] not have [any] trouble that year.

"I began by giving them little special chores to do. I was strict even though I was young. I went in there letting them know I was boss, not them, and that I would not take any foolishness. Those boys later were delinquent all through their life and have been in jail two-thirds of their lives. I guess they are still in jail. After their mother was older, she came back and said [to] me, 'I do not know, Mrs. Cox. I do not know whatever happened that you did what you did for my boys.'

"I had one boy [whose] mother and father were divorced. He would follow the mining camps with his dad. He was [very] tough. He was not going to sing the opening [song]. . . . It was "The Star Spangled Banner," and he was going to [have to] sing the first verse. They all knew it well. He did not come up when I called him, so I proceeded to go after him. When I [was] down to his seat, he threw up his fist and clenched his fist as much as to defy me and said, 'If you try, I will give you a biff.' I looked right in his eyes and said, 'Young man, I am [very] small, but I am really tough. If you ever put your hand [or] touch me, it would be the last time for you.' He walked up to the front of the room and sang the song. It was only the Lord that was with me, really; I could not have done it on my own.

"I had an eighth-grader [who] was smart-alecky, so I expelled him from school. I said, 'You cannot come back to school until you see the superintendent,' which was down [in] Overton, and that was quite [far] away. 'You see the superintendent and make it right with him. Then you come and ask my forgiveness for the trouble that you have caused me.' He was out of school, and I heard remarks from all around the mining camp from other people that his mother was angry, and she was calling me all kinds of names, but this did not bother me."[41]

At the end of that year, Veda married David Marriner Cox. She stopped teaching after just one year and they raised a family of five children. When she was fifty years old, she went back to college and gradually worked on obtaining a certificate to teach and did so for over a decade in Nevada—but not at the mining camp.

CONCLUSIONS

By 1900 all Mormon communities in the Mojave Desert region had a school that included grades one to eight. Parents usually supported their children in their schooling. Some families sacrificed so their children could leave the village and seek housing at a place where a high-school curriculum was available.

There was a major difference between urban schools and village schools. Schools in St. George, Hurricane, Kanab, and Cedar City were in school buildings constructed for several grades, with separate rooms and different teachers for each grade. When high schools were developed in St. George after 1911, they had separate grades and soon added musical and athletic options that did not exist in the villages, which usually had only one room for all eight grades with one teacher. In the villages, each grade had fifteen minutes alone with the teacher and then was to study their reader while the teacher met with each of the other groups. That limited the curriculum mainly to reading, writing, and arithmetic. Nonetheless, the children were generally positive about their school time.

The next main observation was that students were limited in the time they could spend in school. Many had to be available for spring planting and the autumn harvest. They could not get to school until November and had to leave in March. There were other reasons students had to interrupt or leave school—mainly because of their illness or of parents.

Discipline in the schools is fun to read about. The values of the day allowed for teachers to use physical punishment. The students told many tales, such as being forced to stay in a closet, stand in a corner, stand on one foot, or be hit with willows or rulers. They enjoyed trying to fool teachers during such punishments, but clearly they respected the teachers most who kept discipline in their classes and controlled rebels.

Equipment in the schools was often limited. A few schools were taught temporarily in tents and others in log cabins. They had no desks in such situations—only benches. Books were limited in these beginning schools or schools in mining camps. More permanent schools in villages were also limited in their equipment. Even those with more than one teacher sometimes had to divide their spaces with curtains. The more established schools often expanded into two rooms or even three.

The alternative of a Presbyterian school in Toquerville and St. George was a fascinating factor. These elementary schools had one teacher, but they were certified. They attracted students because their families respected the teachers. Mostly they came for the lower grades and then went on to the town schools. These schools continued for several decades.

Religion was an interesting issue. Initially, the schools and the LDS Church were closely allied. Religion was included in the curriculum, sometimes taught by a volunteer from the local congregation. When the Church started the academy system (high schools), a regular theology class was taught by the faculty. As the state of Utah became more involved in the schools after the 1896 statehood, the teaching of religion in the schools became an issue. Eventually, the LDS Church developed a seminary system that made religion classes available adjacent to high school campuses as an independent offering.

NOTES

1. Josephine J. Miles, unpublished paper, 29 January 1923, Daughters of Utah Pioneers Museum, St. George, Utah.
2. Josephine J. Miles, unpublished paper, 7.
3. Robert Hafen Moss, "An Historical Study of the Factors Influencing the Organization of Education in Washington County, 1852–1915" (master's thesis, Brigham Young University, 1961), 101.

4. John T. Woodbury to John D. T. McAllister, 25 June 1888, as cited in Moss, "An Historical Study," 88.

5. Moss, "An Historical Study," 198–99.

6. Andrew Karl Larson, *The Education of a Second Generation Swede: An Autobiography* (Salt Lake City: Deseret Press, 1979).

7. Larson, *The Education of a Second Generation Swede*, 156.

8. Frederick Stewart Buchanan, *Culture Clash and Accommodation: Public Schooling in Salt Lake City, 1890–1994* (Salt Lake City: Smith Research Associates and Signature Books, 1996).

9. Heber C. Jones, *History of the Woodward School: 99 Years, 1901–2000* (n.p.: Prepared for the Committee for the Restoration of the Woodward School, 2000).

10. James Allen, "Everyday Life in Utah's Elementary Schools, 1847–1870," in *Nearly Everything Imaginable: The Everyday Life of Utah's Mormon Pioneers*, ed. Ronald W. Walker and Doris R. Dant (Provo, UT: Brigham Young University Press, 1999), 359–85.

11. Wilford Woodruff Cannon, VOR File 69-015.

12. Verda Bowler Peterson, VOR File 69-061.

13. Leslie "Les" Stratton, VOR File 70-081.

14. Theresa Cannon Huntsman, VOR File 69-115.

15. Dora Malinda Clove, VOR File 69-117.

16. Alvin Hall, VOR File 69-136.

17. Victoria Sigridur Tobiason Winsor, VOR File 69-014.

18. Isabelle Leavitt Jones, VOR File 69-164.

19. Lemuel Glen Leavitt, VOR File 69–168.

20. This was when the team got its name of the "Flyers."

21. Florence McArthur Leavitt, VOR File 69-165.

22. Elmer Rodney Gibson, VOR File, 70-043.

23. Joseph Hills Johnson Jr., VOR File 68-027.

24. Vera Hinton Eager, VOR File 68-044.

25. Fern McArthur Hafen, VOR File 68-108.

26. Mary Amanda DeFriez Williams, VOR File 70-052.

27. Clarence Jacob Albrecht, VOR File 68-042.

28. He and Mabel (Stephenson) McConkie.

29. George Wilson McConkie, File VOR 68-092.

30. Nathan Brindle Jones, VOR File 69-141.

31. Leland Taylor, VOR File 70-079.

32. Joseph Woodruff Holt, VOR File 68-009.

33. Irma Slack Jackson, VOR File 69-131.

34. Rhoda Hafen Leavitt, VOR File 69-078.

35. William "Bill" Charles Pulsipher, VOR File 70-036.

36. Rosalie Maurine Walker Bunker, VOR File 69-081.

37. Vernon Worthen, VOR File 68-046.

38. Robert Parker Woodbury, VOR File 68-038.

39. Elizabeth "Libby" Leany Cox, VOR File 69-132.

40. Victor Iverson, VOR File 68-106.

41. Velda Delle Leavitt Cox, VOR File 69-069.

## Chapter 3

Youth and Adults at Work

Introduction

A vital element of life in the Dixie desert was physical work. Children, teenagers, and adults spent most of their lives doing hard labor. They worked with cows, sheep, pigs, chickens, and especially horses. Horses were the key to life on farms and ranches, but also for riding to school and having fun. Both men and women did heavy labor and irrigation all of their lives except during times of serious illness. Many stayed at it until their death. Retirement was almost unheard of except for the disabled. Much of the work was with hand tools—shovels, plows, or axes when working the land, or washboards, cookstoves, or churns when working in the home.

The value of work was honored. Parents usually felt that teaching their children to succeed at physical labor was as important as having them learn in school. There were examples all around them of children who had to take on the work of their parents as early as age twelve if the parents were seriously ill or had died. If the children had the luxury of reaching the age of sixteen and graduating from the eighth grade, they needed to have the skills to take on full-time work. They needed quality experience with tools, animals, and crops to be ready for adulthood by then. Physical work was what adults did. Girls needed to be ready for marriage by age sixteen and the boys by eighteen. It was not uncommon for thirteen-year-old boys to herd cattle alone for several weeks. Girls often hired out as household help after that age.

Marriage for women did not always mean their work would be confined to the home. They usually maintained large gardens and often small farms if the husband was away at the ranch all summer. Husbands often died young because of accidents, and women had to become cooks or find some other paying job in addition to maintaining a home for the children—and there were often more than six children in a given family. Men spent their life at unskilled labor, with the exception of the few who went to high school or college or even the privileged who graduated. Those who graduated often became teachers. The other men worked on farms and ranches, but some worked on railroads, in mines, in road construction, or in custodial work. A handful became businessmen.

Most of the people in the western United States between 1850 and 1930 were wed to the land; manual labor was not unique. Agriculture was the dominant lifestyle in rural areas. The people in this story were just one part of that reality. The nature of the Mojave Desert, where these interviews were made, had its own uniqueness. The communities there, just south of the Great Basin (Utah and Nevada), were mostly distant from a railroad. That meant they had little contact with the rest of the nation. To sell their cattle meant driving a herd seven days into Nevada to reach a railroad. They also had to go to that railroad to buy tools such as plows. They were somewhat isolated because there was no oiled highway until 1930. There was no electricity or imported oil. Farming tools depended on muscles of numerous men and oxen.

Weather was especially challenging. Rainfall was limited to eight inches per year, making irrigation essential. Creating and regulating canals and ditches was central to their community life. Summers were very hot. Temperatures above one hundred degrees were standard for June, July, and August.

Range land was very important for ranchers. Because federal regulations were lax, overgrazing was common, eventually resulting in the

Taylor Grazing Act in 1937, which seriously limited grazing and reduced the size of cattle herds. Cattle rustlers on the open range were a challenge. Among them were outsiders, some of whom came to the desert to avoid law enforcement elsewhere.

Ironically, the greatest challenge in this land of limited rainfall was flooding. Occasionally, there would be serious rainstorms in the mountains above Zion Canyon and Pine Valley. This would result in flooding in the Virgin and Santa Clara Rivers. Sometimes, they would rise to ten times their normal height. Because these rivers were in the desert, their shorelines were just sand. The rivers would rise abruptly and expand widely and undermine the buildings of nearby communities and wash away growth from nearby farms. They were called hundred-year floods, but they sometimes happened every decade and still do.

By the time these interviewees were born, their parents and grandparents had found a way to survive in this desert land; but it was still a challenge for this next generation, who lived between 1900 and 1970. For example, there was a competition between school attendance and work. Children were needed on the farms, but teachers wanted them in the schools. Another issue was that there was little cash available. People raised what they consumed and bartered with each other for their needs. One example is that when fathers wanted to sell their products, they would fill a wagon and go peddling. Often, their products would include dried peaches or figs. They would drive as far north as Beaver, Utah, or the mining towns in Nevada. Generally, they would have to trade rather than be paid with cash. Interestingly, three banks were established in St. George after 1900, so some cash was obviously circulating.

Some venturous men ranged beyond the farming lifestyle and sought cash-paying jobs. This meant leaving their families to maintain the small farm and garden. Often, it also meant living in environments where gambling, alcohol, and prostitution were present. Church leaders urged the men to avoid such options, and most did; but these opportunities were alluring to young, unmarried men who did not own their own farm or ranch.

These are some of the main factors that challenged those whose words are in this chapter.

Andrew Karl Larson's book *I Was Called to Dixie*[1] is the classic book on life in early Utah's Dixie. He devotes a dozen chapters to agriculture, raising cotton, and home industry. Some agricultural initiatives were taken before 1861, but the big thrust came with the settlement of St. George, specifically to raise cotton. The many efforts, including the construction of the cotton factory, are detailed by Larson; but the gradual decline came, especially with the end of the Civil War and the arrival of the transcontinental railroad in northern Utah in 1859. This then caused the Dixie-ites to be dependent again on their small farms. Some felt that raising fruit would be the solution. Larson wrote:

> Cutting up the ripe fruit and getting it on to the scaffolds to dry was a big chore, sometimes . . . transformed into a social gathering. . . . Not all of the dried fruit went to Salt Lake City as the cotton had. Much of it found its way to the settlements in Iron, Beaver, and Juab Counties, while a considerable amount found its way to the people in Sanpete Valley. Sanpete had plenty of flour and potatoes as did the counties on the main road to Salt Lake City, and these staples were welcomed in exchange for dried fruit. Because of the long, hot summers potatoes did not grow well in most areas of the Virgin River Basin; hence this valuable food was gladly acquired by means of barter. . . . But when fruit became abundant, this article, with the molasses, cotton, and wine also in surplus, helped supply the needs for the things they did not produce themselves.[2]

The wine industry has always been an interest to those reading about Utah's Dixie. Larson gives a forthright explanation:

> Many of the towns made considerable wine. The soil and climate of Santa Clara, St. George, Washington, Leeds, Harrisburg, Bellevue, Toquerville, and Virgin City seemed particularly well adapted for grape culture. Wine became one of the most common articles of trade, for it was an item that could readily be exchanged for other things. It was paid as tithing in large quantities, and not a few gallons went to the irrigation companies in payment of water assessments. Large amounts went to Pioche, to Silver Reef, and to the settlements north; but not an insignificant amount found

its way into the innards of the inhabitants of the Cotton Mission, demoralizing the will of many otherwise good men, creating sots of those prone to alcoholism, and laying temptation in the way of the young.[3]

Then Larson gave his summation:

> But the wine industry came to a sorry end. The fact is that there were too many cooks making wine, and it found a place with silk and cotton in the graveyard of unrealized promises. The lack of a standard quality was perhaps the one big drawback. Almost everyone with a few grape vines made wine for his own use and a little to sell. They paid their tithing, too, with wine and were not always careful to see that the Lord's tenth was the best; in truth, it was too often the poorest. So when people paid their tithes in wine, there were about as many flavors and qualities of wine as there were tithe payers. When some of the poor wine was sent north for sale, it did nothing to enhance the reputation of Dixie wine or its manufacturers. Moreover the problems of personal degradation and disorganization convinced the church authorities that promotion of the wine industry had been a grave mistake. The Tithing Office at St. George discontinued accepting wine as tithing and abandoned its own winepresses in an effort to discourage its further manufacture. Its use in the Sacrament devotions was abandoned in favor of water after the evil fruits of wine had so long been evident.[4]

Larson continues and declares that a miracle then came—alfalfa. John T. Woodbury writes:

> The coming of alfalfa was the greatest boon that ever came to Dixie. When it was first introduced, early in the seventies, it was cut with a scythe or sickle. But on the virgin soils the yields were at first heavy, and the feeding problem appeared in a fair way to be solved. William Lang had the first patch of lucerne and it was reported he was going to plant five acres of it. People wondered what he would ever do with so much feed, and how he would get it cut. The latter problem was soon solved, for right after the introduction of lucerne,

they also introduced the mowing machine, and instead of breaking their backs to mow the lucerne, Isaiah Cox and Erastus McIntyre rode the machine and drove the horses to cut the lucerne. At first it was raked up with hand rakes, but later on the horse rake was introduced, and some of the drudgery of hay-making was removed. During the year 1874, the year of the "Order," a number of pieces of land were sowed to lucerne, and since that time lucerne has been about the most important crop in Dixie.[5]

The result of the coming of alfalfa was that livestock could be fed year-round. Milk, butter, cheese, and meat were available, and the cattle could also become an export product. Agriculture was king, but so was hard labor for all.

Nonetheless, the flooding problem had to be solved. Damming the Virgin River seemed to be the sensible solution, but the efforts to place dams in the Virgin River failed for years. Larson's chapter 21 details the story. Some eighteen dams were built between the late 1850s and early 1890s, only to be washed away. This threatened the desire to make large-scale agriculture possible in the Washington Fields. The story of determination that kept the people of Dixie, particularly Washington, at the daunting task is legendary. They finally succeeded, expanding the opportunity for year-round alfalfa and cattle raising. Alfalfa thrived in the red sand if it got water, resulting in four or five cuttings a year. That same reality continues to thrive in Enterprise today, supporting a huge dairy industry.

The building of mills was essential to produce flour. Larson tells of one built on Diagonal Street in St. George by Easton Kelly and Samuel L. Adams. There is a similar story about Albert Petty in Springdale. Sawmills were established in Pine Valley and Virgin. David Flanigan "had noted the fine stand of yellow pine on the East Rim of Zion while hunting there with some friends; . . . he conceived the idea of lowering timber by means of a cable running from top to bottom of the breath-taking height."[6] Flanigan later implemented that dream in 1900. By 1906, he had lowered two hundred thousand feet of lumber to the foot of Cable Mountain, as it came to be called. Like the Washington Fields Dam, this was a miracle project of determination.

Most Dixie-ites engaged in productive farms and homes. Women made all the clothes for their family, sometimes spinning and weaving the cloth. They and the children raised and prepared the family's food. Nonetheless, there were others who worked in the cotton factory, built dams, cut timber, built roads, and even manufactured wine. The isolation of the Mojave Desert caused them to produce all they needed, so they did.

All of this skilled work which Larson described was influenced by skilled labor in the pioneer period that occurred just before. Several scholars focused on their work. For example, Richard Oman wrote about Ralph Ramsay, who came to Utah from northern England. He worked on the Eagle Gate Monument in Salt Lake City and helped with the woodwork on the Salt Lake Tabernacle organ. He then moved to Richfield, Utah, to supervise the making of furniture, and then he moved to St. Johns, Arizona, then to the Mormon colonies in Mexico, and finally to Snowflake, Arizona. He trained people everywhere he went to make furniture.[7] This is an example of utilizing skilled craftsmen to train locals. One of the interviews in this chapter describes how local chairs were made, and how they were also based on European designs.

Women were adroit in manufacturing skills, especially with fabric. Charles Lowell Walker records in his journal that women made carpets for the temple in time for the dedication on 1 January 1877: "The sisters are busy sewing the carpet and getting the screen ready. All are busy pushing the good work along." Then Andrew Karl Larson adds a footnote: "The carpets for the Temple were, of course, made of rags woven on homemade looms. Discarded clothing was torn into strips which were then sewed end to end and wound into a ball about six inches in diameter. The sisters took care to see that the colors were arranged in a pleasing, artistic pattern. The balls were sacked in burlap bags or in seamless flour sacks made at the Washington factory."[8]

The presence of the cotton factory was of real significance for Utah's Dixie. Brigham Young essentially sent the 1861 company to St. George to raise cotton, based on the success of an experiment of raising it near the Virgin River. People in Washington were devoted to that crop, and cotton fields were created in many places in Utah's Dixie. Initially, the cotton crop was harvested and shipped north for sale. It was bulky and not easily transported. Once in Salt Lake, it did not attract many buyers. It became obvious that people wanted cotton cloth and not cotton balls. Brigham Young was a practical man and could see the reality. He knew that the residents in Washington County did not have the capital to build a cotton factory, so he decided to take a risk. He agreed to put up the money personally to have the factory built on the understanding that the profits from the sale of the cotton cloth would pay him back.

Douglas Alder and Karl Brooks wrote:

> In September 1865, Young announced the cotton milling project and engaged Appleton Harmon to install the factory. The project was pursued with haste. Elijah Averett was the major stonemason, though many others helped, several of them from the Tabernacle building crew. John Peck Chidester, Hyrum Walker and August Mackelprang cut timber and hauled it to the site. The first floor of the structure was completed within the year and was dedicated 14 July 1866. The dispatch with which the cotton factory was completed was amazing, since at the same time the Saints were exerting efforts to build the tabernacle, construct dams, clear land, and build homes.
>
> Machinery was freighted south and installed the last few days of 1866 under the direction of a Scottish convert, James Davidson, who had been sent to direct the project. Volunteers contributed their muscle for building a mill-race to bring the stream water to the waterwheel. By January 1868, the factory was in operation. In 1870 the building was enlarged by adding another story, a testimony to optimism.[9]

The factory employed about forty men and the same number of women, mostly young. That was not the major impact. Instead, it was the opportunity it provided for cotton farmers to sell their crop. The future seemed bright, and then the intercontinental railroad came to Utah and soon brought cotton cloth for sale. Rather quickly, farmers shifted to raising alfalfa instead of cotton. For two or three decades, the operators of the cotton factory tried to adapt it to be a general merchandising operation, but it never really prospered even though entrepreneurs Woolley, Lund, and Judd managed it.

Another recent study is about raising cattle for slaughter. A lecture by John Alton Peterson focuses on the huge tithing herd that was maintained at the fort there. It was similar to several other herds of tithing cattle, such as one at Hebron on the west side of Washington County. It could be argued that these herds were organized to keep them away from federal agents, and Peterson presents that view; but they also had practical purposes. In the case of Winsor Castle, that herd became a major supply of meat, butter, and cheese to feed the two hundred laborers who were building the St. George Temple.[10]

Many skilled workers were involved both with the herds and with the temple construction. Quarrymen produced the stones for both the tabernacle and the temple. Many of them were apprentices, trained by mentors who brought those skills with them to the Great Basin. Adobe bricks had to be made for construction of many regional buildings, such as the opera house, homes, and granaries. The adobe bricks were often made by women and children. Lumber was essential for all construction. Initially, the lumber was cut and milled in the Pine Valley mountains. By the time the temple was under way, that supply was gone, and mills had to be transferred to Mount Trumbull on the Arizona Strip. Robert Gardner was the key leader in both efforts. Again, most of the men had to learn that trade from those who had such skills before coming west.

The major point is that children grew up learning to work, but they had mentors who had mastered many skills in the generation before them.

Now let us turn to the interviews of those who were especially interested in work.

INTERVIEWS

DELLA ELIZABETH STEED

Della Elizabeth McCune Steed is an example of intergenerational labor. She was born in 1895 in Nephi but also lived in Las Vegas and Springdale. She served an LDS mission in New England and met her future husband, Glenn Wilcox Steed, there. She recalls some time of her youth: "I remember most that my father was an honorable man. He taught honesty and set the example for the rest of us. I thought he was the most wonderful man ever. He was a very lovable father. He always showed affection for us. When I was about seventeen, my mother was in the time of life when her health was not good. He had a crowd of twenty-five men on the ranch. They were putting a watering system for a place nearby that was being made into a little town. In our childhood [days], there was a spring that they had always hauled the water [from] for use in a great big barrel on a skid with a horse pulling it. They were tapping this spring and putting into a tank for this little community that was springing up over there. I went down and cooked for my father on this ranch. We had twenty-five men [working there]. I would make twelve loaves of bread every night and every morning. Many times I had to make a big square pan of baking powder biscuits to finish the evening meal. I spent that one summer there with my father working on the ranch.

"They killed a mutton every night besides the hams and bacon that they used. I learned to cook. I never [went] to bed before midnight, and I was up at five [o'clock] in the morning. I knew how to work. It was good training.

"My father was always wonderful. There was never a morning that he did not come in and put his arm around my shoulders as I was standing there with three or four fry pans going. He would come in and see that I was getting things ready and say, 'My daughter, you do not know how I appreciate you and all you are doing.' It was worth it."[11]

WALTER "WALT" WALLACE BOWLER

Walter "Walt" Wallace Bowler was born in 1876 in England. His parents heard LDS missionaries and decided to cross the Atlantic and come to Utah. He described the trip on a ship with five hundred passengers, who spent most of the time below deck and in stormy weather. He was about six years old. They arrived in the US and traveled by train all the way to Utah and on down to Milford and then by wagon to Hebron. Zera Pulsipher Terry was a missionary in England and was the reason they came. They joined the LDS Church after they came. The family brought eight children with them. One had died in England before they departed. He tells of what happened after they arrived: "There were about a dozen houses up there [in Hebron]. The first place we lived [was] a little brick place down in the end of town, [just] before you leave town. Father had a shoe shop. He could mend a shoe. He used to make boots and shoes outright from beginning to finish. He did not have any machines. He sewed them by hand. All [of the] sewing, as we called it, was with a waxed thread. He had wild hog buckles for a needle. I have seen him take a piece of white cord thread, [which was] sewing thread for boots. [He would] wax it. [He] had it blacked up, [which] we called waxed. Then on the end there were these hog buckles. They were like a needle, but they were kind of forked. He could twist them together so he had something [to sew the shoes]. Then he would make a hole with what he called a sewing awl. He had a clamp. He would make a hole and he would put the stitches from each side through [there]. That made [a] chain stitch, [which was] like a machine stitch. He made lots of boots and shoes.

"He learned his trade in England. He started up with it again right here in Old Hebron. He was one of the men [who] were sent out to colonize [and] settle the outside places. They had a dairy up in Little Pine Valley, where the reservoir is now. I was [a] cowboy and tended the cows. They milked forty cows, night and morning. [They] turned them out [as there was] plenty of grass. [They] did not feed [them]. I would start [out with] those cows after they [finished milking]. [I took them] up over the other bottom [area]. That is where the big reservoir is now. [There was] big grass and willows. [It was] up along the point that they call Cave Canyon. Then [I] came down and had breakfast. Then I would take all the calves down and put them on the hill to graze.

"Father had a chance to buy a place down in old Gunlock. A man by the name of Joe Huntsman was going to leave there. He was selling his place. When we moved down there, I had one mare and colt and a nice yearling heifer. That was my earnings for two years. When I went down there, they went towards the payment on the place.

"We stayed there for quite a number of years [and grew] some cotton. I remember going and picking cotton when it was ready. We [grew] all kinds of vegetable garden [plants]. Talk about your peaches and grapes. Mother could not stand to see the peaches fall on the ground and go to waste. We had what you call scaffolds, and we cut the pit out of those peaches. [It] kind of split them up edge ways in rows, and [we] left them until they dried. We had dried peaches. [We] did not know what we were going to do with them. [We would] just dry them and keep them from spoiling.

"I remember so well some good news. A man by the name of Edward H. Snow had been to Salt Lake City. He found a market for dried peaches. Some people [there used them] to make brandy. It was a different kind of brandy.

"We used to get $4.00 a hundred for dried peaches. It took about 400 pounds of fresh peaches to make one [hundred pounds] of dried [peaches]. That is another thing that I remember so well. Mother had peaches in pieces of sacks. [She had them in] anything that would hold a bucket or two. The whole family worked all summer. When we were through, we had a whole ton of dried peaches. I remember when they took them to St. George. Mother went down [there, and] they gave us $80 [for those peaches]. Mother carefully bought some sugar, some salt, and some spices, different things that [we] used. Maybe she bought a sack of flour.

"We used to [grow] what they called Dixie molasses. [It was] sorghum—that is sugar cane. I sat many a night [at the mill]. We had a horse-powered mill with steel rollers. That horse-powered mill had a sweep on it, and a couple of horses [were hooked to it]. [They would] go around in circles. We would have the rope tied to the horses and then to the sweep. They would pull the sweep, and the sweep would lead the horses. We would get [the] juice. We had what they called vats. [We would] put [the juice] in the vats and cook it. It would raise a green scum. We had what was called a skimmer. We would skim it and cook it and made Dixie sorghum. [That is what] we called it.

"I remember one time [that] my brother John and I took two thirty-gallon barrels of sorghum [and] went up north to trade [them] in for flour. We went to Cove Fort and over the Cricket Ridge Canyon into Elsinore, Annabella, and Richfield. We were peddling. John would drive the team. I would stop and go to each house and ask if they would like to buy some Dixie sorghum. They would ask the price. I would tell them that they could have a gallon of Dixie sorghum for a bushel of wheat or fifty cents. Lots of them gave us wheat, and [some] of them would give [money]. We sold out in Annabella and Richfield. Then we came back to Elsinore with our wheat. [We] stopped there and traded it in for flour. Then [we] were on our way home in December. It got cold and windy. We got out, took two quilts, and made us a bed one night. It [was very] cold, so we got a lot of sagebrush so we could keep a fire at night. I remember one night John woke me up. He found that one of the quilts had got a spark [on it] and burned our bed. Anyway, we went home with the winter's flour. [We were as] happy as a bunch of meadowlarks! [We] had flour to last us all winter. That was something!"[12]

NORMA BRINGHURST EMPY

Norma Bringhurst Empy was born in Toquerville in 1912. She reports about raising fruit for sale: "Quite a bit of our living was made off of our gardens and farms, especially the big fig trees that we had on our lot. We had a big row of them up one side. We had them across the top and in the corner. We had what we called the big middle tree, and that tree was enormous. I couldn't exactly say how many feet [wide] it was, but the circumference of it was tremendous. It covered a large area, and we lived right against that big black hill. There were many snakes. I never was afraid of them, because we were used to them. They used to come into our cellars. [There were] two or three kinds of snakes that Daddy would get disturbed with us if we killed them, because they cleaned the mice up and kept them down. . . .

"We used to have thousands of pounds of dried figs. The way we made our living was to make fig preserves [during] the summer. We used to have labels and ship fig preserves back east and all over. One year, we made 150 gallons. That is not pints or quarts, but gallons of fig preserves for the Arrowhead Hotel [in St. George].

"Our house [was] one of the poorest homes in Toquerville until after I was married. My folks never built a big home. We lived in one of the first houses that were built there. It was one big room with two lean-to rooms on it. I had to work; I couldn't go out playing around like a lot of the children could. It was a congregating place for the town and all of our friends. They would come down while I was ironing or doing [other chores], and we would sing, laugh and have one good time. Mother was always making molasses candy and treats for us. We were husking corn, we were quilting, we were peeling peaches or we [were] drying figs. We would be out on the lawn under the trees working, and we always had a good time."[13]

AMANDA AMELIA MILNE

An account of working in the cotton factory was given by Amanda Amelia Hannig Milne, born in 1883 in Washington: "I worked in the cotton factory [in Washington] when I was twelve years old. I went to work at 7:30 in the morning and worked until 5:00 at night for twenty-five cents a day. That was [the factory] pay. I had to work in the factory every day. My husband [to-be] was my boss. He worked in the [cotton] factory, [and my] mother worked there. I used to go down and see her. I met him at the [cotton] factory. He said the first time he saw me, I had white stockings clear up over my knees. I was just [a youngster] when I met him, but we did not get married until I was eighteen.

"We [were] married on 19 September [1909] in Washington. We had a big reception. We had it up by [the] old home on the hill. We had one hundred [people that] were invited from St. George besides [the ones] we had here. We had a big cooked dinner [with] everything. We didn't do [it] like they do now. They had all they could eat. Outdoors in the yard we had a big table with melons, peaches, grapes, and five gallons of good Dixie wine! We had planned to go to the [St. George] Temple, but [President William] McKinley was shot [on 6 September 1901] and died [on 14 September 1901]. The temple was closed so we could not [be] married in the temple. We were sealed there two or three days afterwards."[14]

ATHOLE JARVIS MILNE

Athole Jarvis Milne was born in 1877 in St. George. He lived in Washington and many other places. He had eight siblings: four brothers and four sisters. As a boy, he worked for Tom Judd in developing La Verkin. Judd was also the superintendent of the cotton factory in Washington and Athole worked for him there. He tells about that work: "He [Judd] leased the factory. He planted a lot of acreage into cotton out in La Verkin. George and I would help. [He was] the one I would work with him so much. [He] was a few years older than me. We would plant cotton by hand. [The ground] would be furrowed out, and we would plant it, water it, hoe it, and pick it. I worked there [for] about three years, and then [I] started [working] in the factory [when] it [was] sold. We would work up in the cotton and bag it. I signed up as an apprentice to take that job. I was in charge of half of the machinery. I would start the factory up and oil the shafting and have charge of all the cotton right from the seed. [It would] go through the gin, gin the seeds out, and then [get] what they call a widower's dowel. Then the lapper and they were ready for the cotton cards, where they would start by making the yarn. Cotton cards matted and did the assortment by yarn. Pitch it for the spinning frames. The spinning frames have to fix it and be ready for the looms [to make] it into cloth. They made a tremendous [amount] of it into cotton batting. ZCMI took every bit of the batting. That is where they got their cash."

Next, his life took a major change. He went into the mines: "My brother George had been put in charge of Apex Mine[15] as foreman. He gave me a job there. I worked there about half my life, I guess. He worked there about twenty years and then went to the Goodsprings Mine in Nevada for six months, where he got a dose of lead poisoning and had to quit. That put him in a wheelchair for twenty years."[16]

LEMUEL GLEN LEAVITT

Lemuel Glen Leavitt was born on 23 January 1905 and lived in Gunlock, Las Vegas, Mesquite, and Ox Valley. He tells the story of agricultural work like so many others and what it led to: "We had several ranches. The first ranch we bought [was in] Pine Valley. [It was] the Whipple place in Pine Valley, and we were back and forth between there. Then we ranched a summer or two over [in] Grass Valley at Uncle Steve Bunker's place. However, we had these other places. Sometime we [children], two or three of us, would be left there alone most of the time. [When] we moved back here, my dad took up a homestead [on] the Meadows, and we were there for a few years. Then we sold that and moved over to Ox Valley. We spent the rest of my life [there] until I married and a few years after there, just in the summers.

"My parents would come back here to Veyo and leave us all by ourselves there. I think it was a good life. It taught us a lot of things we wouldn't have [learned] otherwise. Sometimes we were afraid all right. But nothing ever ate us up.

"I could tell you one little incident that happened. My brother [Cecil] and I (my brother [was] seven years younger than me) took a bunch of horses around and went to Ox Valley early one spring. We expected our folks to come [later]. I don't remember now what happened that they didn't show up. We didn't have anything to eat. I think we had a small lunch, but we didn't have anything [else] to eat. The next morning we got up, and they still hadn't come. It was about twenty-four hours, and we were getting hungry. There was some flour there in a can. Of course, we didn't have any baking powder. The only thing I could see was some flour. I said, 'I might be able to make some hot cakes out of that flour that we [could] eat.' So I stirred some up. There was no leavening effect in [the mix]. It was unleavened bread. We couldn't eat it, so we threw it out. The dog wouldn't eat it either! We have had some experiences that were a little bit funny.

"We used horses all our lives. My dad bought a truck when I was young [and I] learned to drive. When I didn't get enough money farming, I began to look around for something to do and found a job driving truck. I did that for a good many years. Then I bought two or three harvesters, and I think I made more money with them than I ever had before or since. Then I got sinus trouble and hay fever until I couldn't operate that equipment anymore. The [children] always used to say: 'If there was a dirtier job, Dad would find it for us.' We had a couple of hay balers, [and] they were dirty. We made some money at it, and the [children went] through school. We educated our [children] the best we could. When we couldn't get them to go [to school] it wasn't much use forcing them any longer. I have run most every kind of equipment that is made for farming and most all the types of trucks and a good share of the heavy and earth-moving equipment."[17]

JOHN SEVY THOMPSON

John Sevy Thompson was born on 15 September 1892 in Tennessee. His parents joined the LDS Church, moved west, and settled in Panguitch, Utah, where he grew up and spent his life ranching. He served in World War I and later worked on many ranches in southern Utah. His father had a big herd of cattle but left the family on a trip and never returned. The family thinks he died on that trip, but they never heard. His mother tried to support the family, but John went on his own to work for ranchers as a young teenager.

He tells of ranching from both the youth and adult viewpoint. After traveling the rodeo circuit for a while, he returned home. Then he had an adventure: "I stayed on that ranch. They all left me [at] Christmastime, [and] I was alone. Two of them were supposed to come back. I was just a [young fellow] then. I never saw another man from Christmas until the next [year] on 15 April. I had 300 head of cattle and fifty head of saddle horses.

"When they came back the next spring, they all looked at each other. John Black said, 'Who is over there on that ranch with that boy?' They said, 'I guess nobody.'

"The ranger, Rob Hall, came up one day. He said, 'John, are you alone here on this ranch?' I said, 'I have been alone all winter long, Rob. I am up a stump now. I have the crops in, and I can't water it over until I get rid of these cattle. I have 300 head of cattle here, and I can't do a thing until I get rid of them.' He said, 'John, I will come up in the morning, and we will count them out and put them on the mountain.' I said, 'Okay, Rob.' We counted them out."

Thompson goes on to tell how he tried to make a living after he married Ina Alvery on 12 December 1922 in the Manti Temple. They later had seven children, but he was away most of the time seeking work: "I was cow punching and herding sheep for a long time. Then I cooked a lot. I cooked in the Army and I have cooked four years in the CCC [Civilian Conservation Corps] camp. I cooked in the summertime up here at Bryce Canyon. Then in the winter, we went down to Zion Canyon. I liked the work fine. I guess I would still be cooking if I could have taken it. I got sick down here when I was cooking. They sent me to the Veterans Hospital in Salt Lake City. The old doctor said, 'Now, John, you get out in the open and you stay there. You have enough smoke and grease on your lungs to kill a horse.' That is what put me to herding sheep. He said, 'Get yourself a job where you will be out in the open.'

"I did that until they retired me. When I lived in Boulder as a young man, I did the hardest kind of work. I carried mail on mules for eight long years. I packed up fifteen head of mules every morning with parcel post [mail]. I carried parcel post on mules from Boulder to Escalante and from Escalante to Boulder, about thirty-six miles, once a day. One day I would go to Escalante, and the next day I would go back to Boulder. I did that every winter and summer."[18]

That work convinced Thompson to go to work for sheepmen. He spent most of the rest of his life herding huge herds, some having around three thousand head of sheep. Keeping them separated from other herds was his big challenge.

RALSTON VIRDEN REBER

Ralston Virden Reber was born on 22 April 1903 in Bunkerville, Nevada. He reported: "I completed eighth grade and went through one year of high school. Then one of my brothers, Clarence, went on a mission. Wages were small in those days, and my brother and I went off to work as teenagers. [We sent] our money home to the family. I was about sixteen. We spent five years like that, sending money home to the family, and kept [our] brother on his mission. Then I came home and started working with my father on the farm. They all worked on the farm until they [were] older and married. They all went on to farm [for themselves].

"I always liked farming. I had to learn to work hard as a little fellow, and I didn't know anything else to do but common labor. As far as I went in school, I was a good student and I got good grades.

"I was thinking a while ago [about when] one of my brothers [Ira] was hurt. He was crippled [from what] they called infantile paralysis. I had been working for wages and had [about] $500 on hand. My mother and I took [my brother] to St. George and stayed there a couple of months. The money that I saved took care of the expenses. Dr. Harris, a chiropractor, gave him two treatments a day. That is to show you how [far] my money went. The two-and-a-half years that my brother was on a mission, a lot of my money went [to him] as well [as to] the home. I never regretted that."[19]

ELLEN HORTENSE HINTON

Ellen Hortense (Spendlove) Bradshaw Hinton was born on 30 April 1893 in Virgin. She was one of thirteen children, and of these thirteen, twelve grew to maturity. She recalls their life in Virgin and Hurricane: "You bet we all learned to work. We had to. We knew what jobs we had and we had to do it. My dad had been sick for a whole year before we moved to Hurricane. Mother had a baby. The house was one that had been built for polygamists. The lean-to was just resting on the cupboard. The cellars were moldy and damp. We had chills and malaria fever, so they thought [since] people were moving to Hurricane, they would move down here too. They left everything up there and moved down in 1907 or 1908. It was the very beginning of Hurricane. There were not very many people here. Dad moved a granary down from up there. He tore down his old barn. The barn was made with square nails. We lived in the granary and had two tents that first summer. Dad was not very well.

"Before we moved to Hurricane, we went up to Kolob when we were children. We would go up there every summer [to] milk cows and sell butter. He would milk cows for different people. We [went] up there every summer for several years. When we came home in the fall, we would dry peaches. We [received] a lot of store credit from that, too. We would get wagon-bed loads and put [the peaches] out to dry. The sun would dry them, and then we would sulfur them. We had a big box. We would put the trays in this box, cover it up, shut it up and burn sulfur in there [for] so long. That is where we sulfured them.

"That was to make them white so people would buy them. The sun-dried peaches were [sour]. We went up there and milked so many cows. The old milk house was [made from] a lot of logs and [had a] dirt floor. The house we lived in was just one big room [with an] attic. I used to like to go up there.

"I will tell you how we used the water. We used to bathe in a number three tub. There were twelve of us and Mother and Dad. They would add a little water every time. The first one in the tub would have the clean water. Then the next one would have to warm it up a little to make it so he could bathe in it. We would all take a bath in that tub, and then we would mop the floor [with] that water. Then we would feed that water to the pigs. You will not believe that, but that is what we did. I knew when Dad used to come down here to work on the Hurricane Canal; he would come down the first of the week and stay all week working on the ditch."[20]

RULON ANDERSON LANGSTON

Rulon Anderson Langston was born in Rockville on 4 November 1898. He tells a great story about Zion National Park: "Yes, I drove a lumber wagon one summer when I was ten years old for Frank Petty from Zion [National Park]. [It was] the lumber shipped down the old cable off the ledge. He would pick it up down at the bottom of the cable. We would go from Rockville up there and get two loads of lumber [and] back to Rockville [in] one day. It would take us three days [to go down] to St. George to deliver it and [then come] back to Rockville. I was only ten years old, so I could not harness the horses, but I could drive them after he harnessed them for me. I remember one of those trips. My hat blew off in a whirlwind and it took two trips to pay for a new hat and shirt. I earned fifty cents a day. [I had to drive the] lumber wagon, too. I worked with him a lot with the cattle before I was in [my] teens. [I earned] fifty cents with the cattle or seventy five cents if I furnished my horse.

"Another incident I want to recall is about that time in my life, when Heber J. Grant [stayed with us]. They were investigating Zion Canyon to be made a national park. Heber J. Grant was affiliated with the Union Pacific Railroad. [He] was the one sent down to investigate the feasibility. Dad met him [in] Virgin with a team and buggy. He came up and stayed at our place one night. Then he investigated and went all over Zion the next day. He stayed with us again that night. The next day Dad took him back to Virgin to meet someone from somewhere else down the [Virgin] River. [He] met him there and took him down to Toquerville. That is the way he had of getting around. He was an Apostle and also visited the different stakes at the time. I was with him in the buggy. I was too young to do much of anything else. It was about that time in my life. I remember those river crossings. We crossed the [Virgin] River thirteen times. There were places that were rough and deep. That trip was instrumental in getting it to be a national park. It was finally [named Zion] National Park in about 1912. A few years after that, we built the road. I worked on the first road that was built into Zion [National] Park. I guess I was about seventeen. I also worked on the tunnel two different winters."[21]

CHARLES MERRILL HALL

Charles Merrill Hall tells another story of labor, but not on a farm or with animals. It is about building the Hurricane Canal: "My father was one of the first ones to join the Hurricane Canal Company. He stayed with it through thick and thin. He was one of the main ones. Before it was completed I worked with him. He had the job of settling the canal. Maybe everybody wouldn't understand what that means, but if they look at the canal they would know that it took a lot of know-how to get the water down here. I worked with him during the wintertime and helped to complete the canal after it [came] down here, [by] making the [laterals] and finishing the ditch on out around.

"The canal was built along the side of the mountain in gravel, not very much dirt. [They] just blasted through the solid rock. When the water would hit that, it would go through, just like it would through a sieve. That had to be fixed so that it [the canal] would hold water [and] it would run on down the ditch instead of running out and down the side of the hill. That was before cement [was] used. When they came to a place where the water would drop too bad [low], they would get cedar bark, dig down and plug it up with cedar bark. That was the best means they knew of then to get the water. I remember how tickled my father was when they found out about cement so they could cement over these bad places. They would get people to help, [from] anywhere around here, to haul in cedar posts that had a lot of bark, and then [they would] strip it off. They would load it on [wagons and horses] and bring it down here. It took about twelve or thirteen [years to finish.]"[22]

MATILDE "MATTIE" WOODBURY REUSCH

Something needs to be included about the Arizona Strip, that area of elevated dry land just south of the Utah border and west of the Colorado River. It became famous as a ranching area, but life was tough there because of the lack of water. Ranchers often had to haul water to their homes and build small reservoirs to capture rainfall for their cattle. The area was settled largely by Mormons, but many itinerant cowboys drifted in and out. The kind of work here was almost completely ranching, and the families were spread widely apart, often on homesteads, but they ranged their cattle on federal land. Matilde "Mattie" Woodbury Reusch was born on 8 August 1890 in St. George, daughter of John T. Woodbury, a well-known educator. She married William "Will" Ruesch Jr. in 1916 in the St. George Temple. They had three daughters and two sons. She taught school in Springdale and at Dixie Junior High School and in Fredonia and Hurricane. She was used to being a teacher, but then they moved to a homestead on the Arizona Strip. It was a real challenge for her.

"Our life together was one of hardship [for] me. I had never been used to the kind of life he wanted. He and Charles Petty, a merchant here [in Springdale], and Ray Galbraith, an attorney from Salt Lake, got together and decided to take a homestead on the Arizona Strip. The other fellows couldn't go out and live on it, so they got Will to go out there and live. It proved to be a very hard life for me because I had never been used to such difficulties that I went through out there.

"You had to live on the place for three years to get [a] title to it. Charles and Ray found they couldn't do it. They didn't have any residence requirements. After we had been out there, we decided it was too much to give up. So we took it up. The grazing entry was 640 acres, and the homestead entry was 120 acres.

"In the first years of our married life, when cars were very few and far between, we went to the sawmills up on Kolob [Mountain] from there to the dry farm up at Upper Smith [Mesa], and from there to the Arizona Strip. [We] lived in a dugout. [This kind of living was] very hard on my strength, health, and endurance, but I wanted to give my husband a chance to make good on the thing he desired so much. I used to do the best I could. I remember at one time we had to ride way out in the desert. It was a couple of miles on a horse. My first child, Rondo [Ruesch], was just a baby. He is the boy [who] lives up on the corner. I remember him saying, 'What?' one day when he was a very young child. We were leaving the sawmill. At the dry farm we still had a hard life because we had to live in very difficult places. [It was] difficult [for] me. I was not very old, myself, but it was hard on me. It was the kind of life to which I was unaccustomed.

"I went to the dugout and lived in that place. Do you know what a dugout is? It was a place dug out in the side of the hill. At each end there was dirt, and up behind us it was dirt. We later built a top story to it. I used to have to descend on a ladder. We had a stove in the bottom part. It was so cold that you couldn't sit in the [area] below without feeling you would freeze. We used to churn milk from the cow. I would let it go sour. If I put it on the front of the stove, the bottle would break. If I put it on the back of the stove, it wouldn't be warm enough. I made a wire suspension and hung it from the rafter above so I could get the warmth of the heat [vapors] that went up [from the stove] so the milk would sour. I would take the bottle and shake it until the butter broke."[23]

IANTHUS SPENDLOVE

Ianthus Spendlove, born in 1905 in Virgin, captures the full life of folks in the Hurricane Canal region, particularly the later years of maintaining the canal: "When I grew up, we had lots of trouble with the canal. We always got by [somehow]. . . . [It kept] breaking. We did not have money in those days to buy cement, so we had to repair it the cheapest way we could. Some of those jobs up there now, they mix cement about one to fourteen compared to about one to four then now. Some of those jobs are still there. . . . Money was scarce. . . . They call the canal one of the seven wonders of the world. . . . My dad spent fourteen winters [working] on that canal. My grandmother Isom owned a little store in Virgin. They bought their material from her. They claim that they built that canal with her sledgehammer and her wheelbarrow. . . . I spent every summer [up there] until I was married. . . . I was well acquainted with my grandmother Isom. My grandfather Isom was shot years ago [while] out on an Indian hunt with the Indians. He was shot with an arrow. He never got over it. . . . A group of them went together out in Escalante country. While [they were] there, he was shot. I do not know if they were hunting or what they were doing. It was an Indian [situation] of some kind. . . . [It was] unfriendly Indians. [They] made the attack, and he [was] shot with an arrow. It did not kill him right out, but the effects of that arrow shortened his life. . . . He was only about thirty-seven when he died. My mother and father had thirteen children. . . . All of them lived to maturity except one [who] died when she was a baby, [Alice]. The rest were all married in the temple except one or two. . . .

"We owned a herd of cattle. We would have a sale of [the] cattle the following year. [We would sell the] yearlings sometime in the spring. [We] would get about $25 a head for a yearling. I was farming. . . . We made our own pleasure in those days with horses, ballgame, [and] rodeos. Especially at Christmastime, we would spend two weeks horseracing and dancing. One winter, especially, the Indians came in and had a hogan over here where Lindon Bradshaw now lives. They had a big camp there. They would play their sticks on big tubs. They would make their regular noise that they would make at their [pow-wows]. . . . They would dance and make their own music by rubbing sticks on a tub. . . . They would chant as they played.

"I raised fruit in the early days. [I had] strawberries and a garden. Then, on the side, I had this spray business. I used my boys to help me do custom spraying. In later years, the [Hurricane] Canal Company wanted me to run the water for the company. On 9 June 1948, I went to work for the Hurricane

Canal Company. . . . The day I took that job over, every ditch on the flat and the canal was clogged up with mud. We had an extra lot of rainy weather, [and there was] that old jumbo mud from Long Valley [Kane County, Utah,] country. . . . I stayed with that job for seven summers. I quit in June 1955 [and] went [to work] up on the [Smith] Mesa [Test Site]. [I] worked for Coleman Engineering [up there] for five and a half years. . . . I came back here and went to gardening. [I have] been raising tomatoes and gardening since then."[24]

ROWENA WHITMORE BUNDY

Rowena Whitmore Bundy also gives a view of life on the Arizona Strip. She was born on 26 February 1894 in Springville, Utah, and lived in Sunnyside and Vernal before coming to St. George and Mount Trumbull. She bore ten children, one of whom died at birth and another as a young child: "We had an awful time after we left and went out where the cows grazed. There was more curd in the milk, and we had to have something to dissolve the curd or it wouldn't digest. We had quite an experience trying to find what would work for her. We tried first one thing and then another. I felt like I couldn't raise her because I couldn't find any milk that would agree with her. I remembered when I worked for the doctor that they fed their babies Millen (a grain-type) food. We [had] the fellow at the store on Main Street order Millen food for us, and we tried that. It worked wonderful with her, so we raised her on Millen food.

"We didn't have any work [employment] out there, and we had to go in debt for a lot of things. Then he went up to Zion National Park to work and paid off the bill. We had a struggle out there on the Arizona Strip because there was nothing for you; there was no work or anything.

"Ada Adell was the next child, and she was born in St. George. She did all right, and we went back out to the Arizona Strip with her. Most of our eleven children grew up out there. It seemed like times became harder out there every year. It was drier and drier until we couldn't raise anything to speak of. We moved to St. George when the twins were eleven or twelve years old. We were the first ones to move to St. George from Mount Trumbull. My husband was trapping for the US government or for the state. My children went to school. The oldest boy was old enough, but they didn't have his grade out there. So we moved here and we have been here [St. George] at this little place ever since. My husband and I together with the boys built it. I worked for seven years in town at the Milne Motel and helped to give these younger ones a better education and the necessary things that they really ought to have. He went to Las Vegas to work down there, and that was the way we got the money to build the home and fix it up."[25]

JAMES BUNDY

James Bundy was born on 13 October 1887 in Wallace, Nebraska. He lived with his parents in Mexico and had to leave because of the revolution led by Pancho Villa. After several attempts to settle in other places, his family ended up on the Arizona Strip. He had been working at the Grand Gulch Mine: "We had to haul water from Pigeon Spring [Arizona Strip] down to the mining camp because there was no spring down there and we needed to have water for the cow. We loaded up and moved out to Mount Trumbull.

"While dad and I were freighting out there it rained. We could see the clouds and thunder and lightning further on east from the mining camp. A bunch of the fellows, six or seven of them, drove out there with their families with them. Anyway, [my wife] was along. When we got part way out there, they wanted to still go further east to what they call Hurricane Valley [on the Arizona Strip]. We divided up the hay and grain that we had for all the teams so they could go further on and they went on out. They went all around the country [area] and decided that was the best they had seen. Dad said wherever grass would grow he could [grow] grain. We thought that would be a good country [area] to move into. We did not have any machinery. In the beginning, we planted corn because we could cut that with a hoe and shuck it. Afterwards, we planted grain in the fall of the year. It was hard wheat grain [winter wheat].

"It was good for the work we did, because all we did was plow up the ground and sow the grain and harrow it. [We did not irrigate.] When we harvested the grain, you could still see the tracks of the harrow, so that was how much we did with the ground after we planted it. We never got a very big crop, but we got all we earned. All we did was plow and plant it and harvest. We never did have a binder out there. We finally came in and got a header and took [it] out there.

"We went there in 1917 and stayed there. We still have a homestead out there. My brother and James G. Bundy, our second boy, and [Vivian August] 'Pat' [Bundy], my brother, are about the only ones left there. There are folks like ours [who] had children, and some of their [children] have homes out there, but nearly all the families have moved out. They [became] discouraged when the Taylor Grazing Act was passed [on 29 June 1934]. Those whose holding [had] used the public domain were entitled to some government ground, and those [who] did not have much stock and just had the homestead were not allowed out on the public range. That discouraged them the [most].

"If we had alternated the crops [we might have had] two seasons in the ground. I still think they could have [grown] grain. There was work they could get on the outside. They could not run cattle or sheep on the public domain because they had not used it. Most of them only had a milk cow and [a] few head [of cattle] around the pasture. Most of those at the colony had a homestead, and there was not enough [land on them] to [raise] livestock on to amount to anything.

"We had five children when we [came] to the valley, and when we left there we had nine. Two children died. One of the little girls drowned, and the other one died of pneumonia, a baby.[26] The little girl was two years old when she drowned. [Denven LaVar Bundy] was the first one born [at Mount Trumbull]. He volunteered as an aviator."[27]

FREDERICK CROSS HOYT

Frederick Cross Hoyt lived in Orderville and herded one thousand sheep at age thirteen. He also worked in a sawmill, as well as in sheep shearing, dairying, and hay raising: "We were not [in school]; we had to be out on the ranch making a living. We didn't have [life] like nowadays: you could not travel fast. I helped my father [at] the sawmill when I was nine years old. He would roll the logs on, and I would run the saw. My father was a millwright and was good at mechanics. They always had him run their saw and mill. He did the rolling [of] the logs on the carriage, and I would saw them. It was just above what they call Black Rock Canyon in Long Valley [Kane County, Utah]. We worked on another [sawmill] that was across the valley. That was [Nelson] MacDonald's mill. [Later], we worked on Clyde Roundy's mill. That is where I broke my first horse. I pulled the horse over on me. It was just a yearling colt, but he came over on top of me. Father asked me where it hurt. I told him my arm hurt. When I started walking off, he started to laugh at me because I was limping when it was my arm that was hurting. My aunt [Mary] Ellen [Meeks] Hoyt was there, and she got after Dad for laughing at me when I was hurt, but that didn't help it any.

"I didn't get much [education]. I was always good in mathematics, what we used to call arithmetic. I could always tell the teacher the answer to the problem. By the time she was through, I had the answer. I couldn't write it on the board so that anybody else could get it the way I had. I could work [the problems] out, but they would not give me any credit for it because I couldn't tell them how I had done it. There was one girl in the school who was the best in mathematics. She tried to write her [problems] on [the board] and keep up with me, and she could not do it. She would get 100 percent, and I would not get anything because she could write it down.

"That is the way [education] was, and that is what it is. It isn't what you know or what you can do—it is how you do it. They didn't want you to go to the farm. They came back to how I learned how to add. I learned it myself. They are teaching it now in the schools. [With] the decimal system I could add up six rows of figures. I could figure them up and get the right answer.

"I have had a lot of outside experience. When I was thirteen years old, I was out south and west of Orderville. They took me out there and put my sheep camp at what they called a Mail Trail. [The other camp] was near Cub Spring. [The camps] were about six miles apart, and I had 1,000 head of sheep. They went off and left me there for thirty days. They left enough food, but I ate too much and ran out, so [I] had to kill my own mutton. I would go from one camp to the other and stay one day, what we would call dry, out away from it, and come back and water. The next day [I] would go back over to the other camp.

"One time when I was there, I was coming in a little after dark and my sheep were watering. All at once, my dog came as fast as he could run [and] ran right into my tent. I did not have any gun [and] did not know what it was that scared him. A little while after that, a bobcat was making a [terrible] noise. I thought it was a cougar. I did not know then that the cougar doesn't sound like that. The bobcat will make a big noise when he is around, but the cougar does not make [any] noise. They are more sneaky than that. I did not spend a very pleasant night.

"My father always sheared as many [sheep] or more than a lot of [men]. He freighted and that is where I [received] some freighting experience. He would take one of us boys each time he went to Marysvale. One year I made three trips to Marysvale and up on the divide with wool from Orderville. It took us about ten days to make the trip. . . . My mother was a hard worker too. She did a lot of work. I know more about her than I do about my dad because she was always there [at] the dairy. She used to ride the horses sideways [sidesaddle]. She would help us with the cows and dogie lambs. She was the main one with the family. She practically raised the family. She used to drive the teams out and drive them back. She rode horses, milked the cows, and made butter and cheese. She was strong and healthy practically all of her life. She did most of the teaching of us. We were always taught to pray and to depend on the Lord rather than anything else."[28]

DELLA HUMPHRIES HARDY

Della Humphries Hardy was born in 1908 in Virgin. Soon thereafter, her family moved their house to the new town of Hurricane, down the Virgin River, where the Hurricane Canal had just been completed. She tells about her work life there: "I started when I was about nine years of age to tend people's children and [do] housecleaning. I remember from twelve [years of age and] on, there was one special family that I worked for. They lived about two blocks from the schoolhouse. I would hurry home at noon and fill their black tub. They had to heat the water outside. I would fill this tub with water and put the wood and chips around it and get it all ready to strike the match to it. I would start the clothes. If I had time, I would go home and eat dinner. If I did not, I would rush back to school. I would hurry up there during [our] fifteen-minute recess and strike the match and get the water heating. When school was out, [which was] thirty minutes later, that water would be warm [and] hot enough to start washing. I would take that [load] out and use the suds and start it going. I would put on another tub of water that you would have to boil the clothes in. They would all have to be boiled and run through another [cycle of] suds and then rinsed twice. Lots of times, in the winter, I would be washing until ten o'clock at night outside. I remember one place [where] I worked, they had sickness. They had a big washing to do.

"I remember this one of them had a boy [who] was sick. She sent for her brother to come from Salt Lake City. He was a baby doctor. They were going to have to take the baby to St. George and operate. I got up about seven o'clock that morning and put the water to heat for the wash. While it was heating, I [fixed] breakfast. While they were eating breakfast, I changed all the bedding and changed the children. I got them up, bathed them and put them in clean clothes. It was on a Saturday morning. While they were eating breakfast, I did this and then I made up the beds, cleaned up the rooms in between and then back to the clothes. I would run back and forth putting clothes in and out of the washer and hanging them on the line. Then I cleaned up the house. [I] mopped and waxed the floors. As the clothes dried, I brought the one that could be ironed in and folded them down, and then I started ironing.

"In between all of this, [the sick] boy had to have hot turpentine packs on his abdomen. I would hurry in and take these hot packs into her. I do not know if you have had any experience with turpentine. If you do not keep it stirred good [and] you put your hands in it, it blisters. So I had blisters around all my fingers. I remember how that hot water hurt [when I was] doing the wash. I had an enormously big washing that day. After I got the clothes dried, I started ironing.

"Her brother and [others] came in about dark. I fixed three meals three different times for them. When her brother came in, it was ten-thirty and I was still [working]. He had gone to the place and got to sleep as he was [worn] out. It was about ten-thirty when he came in. I was still ironing. He sat there in the kitchen eating his supper while I went on ironing. He said, 'How long have you been here?' I said, 'Since seven o'clock.' He thought seven o'clock at night. He said, 'That sounds like a late time to come [to] work, is it not?' I said, 'I mean seven o'clock this morning.' He was flabbergasted! He said, 'You mean to say that you have been working here [all day]? What have you been doing?' I told him. He went into his sister and derided her for it. He said, 'This girl tells me she had been here since seven o'clock this morning.' She said, 'We just had to have it done. I knew you were going down there to take the baby for an operation, and I had to have this work done up and this washing and ironing.' He said, 'My dear sister, could you not have gotten two girls to come?'"[29]

LYDIA AMELIA BARLOCKER HUNT

Lydia Amelia Barlacher Hunt was born on 18 August 1893 in Toquerville and lived in Leeds, Harrisburg, Enterprise, and Washington. She gives a picture of fruit peddling with her father: "Peddling was the way my father made a livelihood. He would pick [the] fruit off of our trees. On our lot we had melons and grapes. Grapes were quite a thing in those days. My father used to make wine. We had a big barrel of wine and had it on the side of the wagon on a little platform that stood up and had a spout on it. All the way up [to Cedar City] he would peddle wine. The men would come out to his wagon and buy a glass of wine or a bottle of wine that he had for sale. We had big fifty-gallon barrels. That is the way he made a livelihood because he didn't work much.

"When we went on this trip from Washington City, [we went] up through the country near Leeds. There, it was nothing but a sand plot. We didn't have any highways or good roads. There was so much sand that the hubs [of the wagon wheels] would go down in [the sand]. We had a balky horse that wouldn't pull your hat off. Father made me get out of the wagon and ride this horse and gave me a stick to hit him with. I would hit him to get him to go, and he just sat back on the tongue and wouldn't pull an inch. We had to unload so [the] horse could pull the wagon out [of the sand]. He finally pulled the wagon out, and then we had to carry the fruit up the hill to put in the wagon. We had quite a trip.

"When we would go through a town, my father would have me get in the back of the wagon. We had a wagon cover on the wagon, and I would sit in the back and the boys couldn't see me. When they would see a peddler coming through town, they would think they were going to get some melons. They would all line up so they could take the melons one after the other one. I sat in the back with a quirt [whip] in my hand. They would climb up in the wagon. By the time they [climbed up] in there to grab a melon, I would hit them on the hand with this quirt. When they found out somebody was in there, they didn't bother us anymore. They did that with all the peddlers. A lot of times if [the peddlers] didn't have anybody in their wagon, they would steal all [their] melons [and] they [wouldn't] have any melons left.

"One time dad was cutting grain. We had about an acre or two acres of grain in one of the lots there where we lived. He was cutting the grain with a scythe, and I was bundling it up and tying it. [We were] too close to each other, and he cut a hole right in the bottom of my foot, along [the] side of my foot. He hollered for mother to come and help me to the house. I was laid up for a while and had to sit with my foot up. Mother doctored it with home remedies, and I dare not tell you what they were!"[30]

SAMUEL KENDALL GIFFORD

Samuel Kendall Gifford was born and raised in Springdale. He tells the story of the famed Cable Mountain there and his work on the cable: "Mr. [David] Flanigan built a sawmill on the Zion Ledges, and they hunted over the ledges. Brigham Young had made the statement that the time would come when lumber would come off the ledges, and it would sail like a hawk down the ledge. He said, 'I don't know how it will happen, but it will happen.' The Flanigan brothers [David, William, Aaron and Ron] were determined to see that this was carried out. They hunted the ledges and put three bailing wires on the top and let the wire down over what we now call Cable Mountain. [When] the wire would strike a tree limb, they would shoot the limb out of the tree with their gun until the wire was down to the natural slope of the hillside. They [would] drag it down and then let the opposite side down. They built this around some big pulleys. [They put] pulleys at the edge of the ledge and put the same kind of frame down at the bottom. It was an endless cable of 3,700 feet in length. Eventually, they added two more wires.

"My father and William [Robinson Crawford, Oliver Gifford, and Alfred Stout] bought the sawmill and put in a 5/8-inch cable. [This] made it more secure. Whenever we were working at the sawmill or running timber down the ledge, we would ride up the cable rather than walk up the hill.

"[While] they were building the lodge [at Zion National Park] and the homes around here, lumber was sent to St. George and Hurricane and

Kanab and different places. During this time, we worked [at] the sawmill. Frank and Charles Petty bought the sawmill, and continued it. I worked for the sawmill. Later my brother-in-law, [Dave] W. Lemmon, bought the sawmill and I [continued] to work for him. We would go up with bobsleds and [take] the lumber over to the sawmill at the top of the ledge. Sometimes we would stay weeks at a time just running lumber down the cable. A lot of lumber came off the top."[31]

WILLIAM BROOKS

William Brooks was a transitional person in Utah's Dixie. He mastered farming and then dry farming and eventually mining and other industrial activities. He eventually became the sheriff and later postmaster of St. George. His first wife was Nellie Marie Stephen Brooks, who died in 1932 after bearing six children. His second wife was Juanita Brooks, who had lost her first husband. They then had four children. William was born in St. George in 1891, one of twelve children. His father was George Brooks Sr., a farmer and a stonecutter with Edward L. Parry for the St. George Temple. His mother was Emily Cornelia Branch Brooks. He attended the Fourth Ward school to the seventh grade, worked on the family farm, and eventually attended both BYU and Utah Agricultural College. He reports on his wide experience:

"I never [had] a job except at home. Father had a big family, and it required our help. My brother [George Brooks] was older than I. He and I never went to work for anybody but [our dad] until we were in our twenties. I had quite a lot of [education]. I had nearly all of the grade [years]. Josephine Jarvis and Edith Ivins both took an interest in me. They gave me all the breaks they could. I [had] a lot of [education] in the grades, but I never got through the eighth grade at that time. We farmed all the time. We took up land with the companies that took up land, and George and I worked out [in] the farmlands. I was old enough to run a team and worked [for] the [Washington Fields] Canal [Company]. [We received] script for water on those projects. We worked a little twenty-acre farm there.

"It was located in Washington Fields [and was] a very successful project. We [received] seven acres from the old land, and then we [received] twenty acres from the new land. We worked our twenty acres up; we cleaned the fields and stayed there a reasonable time and got plenty of water. We made the farm profitable in our days while we were at home. The family kept coming just about as regular and systematic as any family ever did! We could keep track of each other's age by the number of children. We knew their ages. Generally, we had plenty to eat; always had plenty to eat. We had good food [and] had a good garden. We had our cows to milk and our horses to ride. We had plenty of milk and butter. We always had good food.

"I went to Modena [Iron County]. That was [so] I could help George with a little school [money]. He knew that I was getting $40 every month. That was all I got for three years. I had a good top wage [that] I was paid there. I worked for my uncle, Brigham James Lund. He married one of my mother's sisters. He didn't favor me when it [came] to the job. I worked for him out there and did what I could. The first year I was at Modena, I sent father 3,000 pounds of flour, and I repeated that the second year. I saved a little bit of money too, impossible as it would seem. I [used] my money to help Father and Mother a little bit, and helped provide for them. [The] business of stonecutting had been outgrown [run out]. There were not public buildings [being built] to speak of, [so] he went to Manti and worked on the Manti Temple. Father had a big family, all girls and quite dependent. They worked out in homes and were all fairly efficient cooks, like their mother was, and seamstresses. The oldest girl, Emma [Brooks] Ashby, went to work for the [newspaper editor]. She was a printer [at] Dixie's newspaper [*Washington County News*]. She worked there for a number of years and [received] $1.00 a day. Mary [Brooks] became a very expert housekeeper. She worked [at several] different places, where she became an efficient housekeeper."

Brooks then tells the long story of how he accompanied his brother George to BYU. He did a year of high school there at Brigham Young Academy. They earned their way through school at twenty-five cents an hour. They rented a place with five rooms in it for twenty dollars a month and had three of their sisters live with them. They went out and picked potatoes, apples, roots, carrots, and turnips. They considered it a year of comfort. William became associated with Dr. John A. Widtsoe and Dr. Lewis A. Merrill and learned about dry farming. He worked for them too: "I went to Nephi with them and [started] the Utah Arid Farm. He had

20,000 acres of ground in Dog Valley, east of Nephi. I went down there in the summertime. He had horses at the time [because] there weren't any dry farm instruments. [This] was a part of my schooling at the time. In the winter I went back to Logan [Cache Valley]. I wasn't making enough money, [so] I went to Pioche [Nevada]. It was for school purposes. I had a good summer in Pioche, [and] I [was paid] $2.50 a day. It was good wages, and I worked [in] Pioche all summer. I had some good times there." He then tells of another venture running the Chilean mill, a gold-mining operation. There, he learned to run engines. Then he went back to BYU.[32]

CHARLES HERBERT KNELL

Charles Herbert Knell was born on 25 February 1886 in Pinto and went to school there until the eighth grade. He also completed a year of high school in Cedar City. He reports, "I had a good dad. I thought he was one of the best men [who] ever lived. He was quite a prominent [person] in Pinto. He led the choir. He ran a threshing machine, [and] that was quite a thing [to do] in those days. He took the threshing machine all over the county [area] and threshed the grain both at Grass Valley and Hebron. Enterprise was just starting about that time, so he didn't do much threshing in Enterprise. He went to Pine Valley quite a lot besides going to Grass Valley.

"Dad and I got along well working together. I worked for Dad, and we had our property together. [I] worked right with him, and we both took care of the family. In fact, I bought the home that we lived in. I helped pay for [it], and we had cattle [together]. We worked together all the time. When he died, he willed everything he had to me. He had other children, but I had worked with him and owned property with him. Anyway, he made his will out to me, all of it."[33]

CLARENCE JACOB ALBRECHT

Clarence Jacob Albrecht was born on 7 April 1904 in Fremont, Wayne County, Utah. He gives some important insights into herding sheep: "When I was about thirteen [years old], I [had] my first job herding sheep. I will never forget how big I was because this man suggested I furnish my own horse and saddle. He would give [the horse] all the grain it would eat. I even had a six-shooter strapped on my saddle. When I went out to this sheep herd, I was [fairly] cocky! About the first mistake I made, I was going to see that my horse, who hadn't been accustomed to eating much grain, had plenty. I hung a couple of gallons on him, and the horse ate more than he should have eaten. He was quieted then and wouldn't eat any grain for ten days afterwards!

"I had only been herding sheep about two weeks when a [bad] storm came up. Another herd of 3,000 mixed [in with] ours in one draw. My herder and the other herders from the other outfit just moved my camp down [to] what they called Long Hollow. [The camp was] off under a cedar tree, and then they went to town to get help. If I had known anything in the world, I would have lost that whole herd of sheep. But I pushed them down. There was a ridge there, and a few sheep ran down. The storm [was] right behind them, really heavy. When I [was] down there, my camp was on the ground. Just being a green [boy], I spent all the rest of the day trying to get my tent up. I finally learned that I would have to chop the limbs away and push this back up into the big cedar trees and then anchor the back to where I could hold it long enough to get [the tent] up. It was probably a blessing in disguise, because if I had ever started doing anything with those sheep I would have lost them all. But the fact that they were just turned wild, they went on down and crawled up under the cedar trees and brushes where they could. The next morning there was eighteen inches of snow on my tent. Out of about 6,000 head of sheep, we lost 125 head. So it was kind of fortunate that I didn't know anything. . . .

"A blessing in disguise is right. There were some hard days in the future because these sheep were just ready to start lambing. We had 6,000 head in one herd. They had to be separated. There was lot of loss because of this. I went from there to the lambing ground and spent the summer on top of Boulder Mountain herding sheep. I believe this was the only time in my life where I ever saw it rain every day for thirty-one days. It did [that] year on top of Boulder Mountain. Every afternoon we would get a good rainstorm. It was not easy to herd sheep in those days because you had just a small district. There were other herds all around you. Nearly every day somebody would have to go in the corral to separate [their] sheep from the other fellow's sheep. You really had to tend to business to herd sheep in those days. . . .

"Yes, the sheep were all branded and marked. When I talk about separating, they went through a chute. As they came through, you would have a dodge gate that would dodge the one fellow's [sheep] in one corral and the other one in the other corral. You would have them all separated, and perhaps, the next day you would have to go back in the corral and separate from another herd. The herders [who] just didn't take care of business knew that they would have to go in the corral and get their sheep in a day or two. This was not good for the owners because you had the ewes weaned away from their lambs and quite a lot of dogie [orphaned] lambs in those herds because of this. One old man used to say to us, 'It is always necessary to pay attention, but the sheep will stay separated if the herders will. You will get the herds mixed first, and then the sheep get mixed. . . .'

"There were lots of coyotes in those days. I recall one time we had forty-three sheep killed one night. You really had to watch [for] coyotes every day. We always had a herder and what they called a camp-jack, a fellow [who] moved the camp. This was all done by mules. I learned when I was thirteen to tie the diamond hitch and fasten these packs on. . . .Towards night, when he knew about where we were going to [be], I would go up and shore the camp up and get the supper ready for the herder. . . .

". . . There were lots of experiences there. You learned to do a lot of things. Like in every walk of life, you did a lot of things incorrectly. One of the things that was a must was to take care of the animals and the packs. I received one wonderful expression. I went up on top of Boulder [Mountain] to herd for this man, and he was with me. When he rode up to this camp there were pack saddles, blankets, hobbles, and everything strewn all over the ground out in front of the camp. I observed that this owner of the camp just looked around. I thought I detected some disgust in his actions. We had lunch, and then he went over to his other herd. He left me there as the camp-jack. The next day, when he came back, I had hung all these pack saddles and hobbles up and had pieces of bed tarps wrapped around these so they were kept out of the sun and storms. I received the finest compliment in the world. He took me off to one side, and he said, 'I am so happy that you observed what I observed. I appreciate you taking care of these things.' This was a big boost in my life and something I have always tried to teach as I [grew] older and had sheep of my own. I always told the fellow that I wanted him to take care of things. This man said to me that day, 'You can have anything you want to eat in this camp. Just order it, but I want you to take care of it. We can buy anything if you take care of these sheep.'[34]

ERASTUS SNOW GARDNER

Erastus Snow Gardner was born on 10 January 1892. He said: "I have been [a rancher] all my life, ever since I was big enough to ride a horse, [since] I was about three years old. [Later] I had a little gray mare, one of the best little animals [there] ever was. She was a speedy little animal too. I had gone to the upper field to get some cattle out of the field that shouldn't have been there. [There was] a neighbor [who] was just a little younger than I was in a field higher up. He saw this little mare standing in the field for a long time and he came over to investigate. When he got there, I was sitting on the ground with my arms around her hind legs. I was unconscious [and] didn't know anything. He [put] me on the horse and led her home. Just before we got down to my home, I regained consciousness enough so that I could remember him bringing me home. I have had some narrow escapes.

"I remember when I was a boy, there used to be roundups bringing the cattle from the winter ranges. There used to be a lot of cattle owned around Pine Valley. I remember as youngsters, we just about lived to see [the] cattle come over the ridge into Pine Valley. They would string over that ridge for hours. We youngsters would go down to the lower end where the fields were and climb up on the fence to watch them come into town. They would bring the cattle right up into town [to] separate, [and] each man [would] take his cattle from there.

"Ranchers from the whole southern part of the state would ride together on the ranges to gather their cattle. They would separate their cattle at what they called [the] Magotsu [Creek] corral [and] take them to the different towns from there. We would drive all the cattle that belonged to Pine Valley into Pine Valley, separate them and each man would take his cattle to his summer range.

"We had bears that would kill any amount of cattle. They had hunters come in and hunt bears. They finally killed one, and the other one left, but he [had] killed thousands of dollars' worth of cattle."[35]

JOSEPH HILLS JOHNSON JR.

Joseph Hills Johnson Jr. was born on 28 July 1891 in Johnson, Kane County, Utah. He lived much of his life in Tropic, but after his marriage to Mabel Watson, he moved from job to job. He tells his story of work: "Father had a few cows, thirty [or] forty head of cattle and horses. He had a stallion that I had to stay right at home and take care of for several years. From that time on I had the responsibility of the family. It took a long time, [but] my hands finally [were] better. The left hand, the one that was frozen so hard, I could just rattle the skin on the fingers after the swelling went down. The skin had not contracted again like it was in the first place [before] it had been swollen. My fingers were smaller like I had a glove on my hands.

"I started out quite early several years before [my father died], when I was thirteen years old. Father was out in Nevada, freighting. He had a four-horse freight team for about a year. I ran the farm [that] we had about two miles from town and, with the help of a helpful neighbor, managed to get the crops in and harvested. I worked one day on our place and then one day for him for the use of his team. Then when it came time to cut the hay, he [held] things together and I cut the hay, raked it, and hauled it with his borrowed team. I worked one day for the use of the team and then had the use of it a day for myself. That is the way I started out farming.

"We had good crops for a few years. Before Father died, we went to the East Fork Mountain [Garfield County] on a ranch with a dairy herd. We had a herd of cows and we ran the dairy there for several years on what we called the East Fork, what we called the Flat Bottom, the old Beaver Co-op Ranch. There I milked as high as thirty cows [daily]. [My] mother made butter and cheese. [We] sold that. [We] put butter in barrels and crocks. There wasn't any sale for milk or cream, [so] we just had to convert it into butter and cheese. We did that for three or four years, moving to the ranch in the summer and back in the fall.

"We would take the cattle with us, and in the winter we took them to a lower altitude, lower country, where we wintered them. Then we [took] them back to the side of the mountain in the summer. After Father died, we continued that. We tried a little farming on the East Fork Mountain, but it wasn't very successful; the season was too short up there. After his death, we didn't farm any more, but we did stay with the ranch for several years."

After his marriage, Joseph had to take up many jobs: "I just tried anything I could find to do. I was away from home [a lot]. I farmed during the summer and then, about the time we had to pay taxes, I would have to leave home and find a job somewhere [to] earn enough to pay the taxes and the bills. We had to settle up and make enough so that we could farm again the next year. I was never able to make enough money to do anything. I had to work away from home, most of the time, to just keep farming.

"I went down to Gunnison [Sanpete County] to the sugar factory [and] worked there [during] the sugar campaign for three or four months. Then I went to Bingham Canyon [Salt Lake County], and I worked there for two winters as a boilermaker. Another winter I was in the building trade [doing] plastering and general building. I did that part of the time. I did most everything a few months at a time, and then I [would] go back home and take care of the farm. After we were married I bought a place in Bryce Canyon. We lived and [had a] dairy there for five or six years. Most of my family were born and raised there on the ranch. We lived there during the summer, [and] when fall came [and] school started we moved back into town."[36]

MARY ANN WEAVER JUDD ALLEN

Mary Ann Weaver Judd Allen gives the story of work from a youth perspective: "At the age of thirteen I went with my father and my five-year-old brother, 'Frank' [Weaver], on a peddling trip with a team and wagon. [The trip] took two weeks [to go] up and back to Beaver [and] Minersville [in Beaver County] and [other] northern settlements to sell produce. When we got to Cedar City, Dad was bitten by a spider, or something, that poisoned his foot. The doctor [took care of it] and told Dad to return home. [Dad] said that I could drive, [and] at my age I could do it. I had never driven a team—only out in the [desert] above Washington City to gather cactus for firewood. But I went on with him. He was determined to go, so we went on, and I drove the team. I had never unharnessed a horse or harnessed one, but I made the grade with a little help from some of the people [where] we stopped to camp. The men would come out and help. [We were] in many storms, and I used to figure the drops were as big [as] silver dollars. They would come down so big. One of the gentlemen would come out and say, 'All right, little girl, you get in the wagon, and I will take care of this.' He would unharness the team and put it away.

"On our way back, we stopped up by New Harmony, just out from [it] a ways. I had to put the nose sacks with their grain on the horses at the back of the wagon, and I had to make a campfire to fix us supper. The coyotes would come so close with their big bright eyes a-shining. I would still have to lead the wagon and the fire. Dad used to say, 'They won't hurt us as long as there is a fire around.' But there was no fire down [at] the creek where I had to lead the horses [for] them [to] drink. I was just petrified all the way down the creek and back. I saw the coyotes out from the campfire. I tied the horses up and put their nose sacks on. I thought, *Now I just won't venture out [because] it is dark, and they might come for me.* So I went back and crawled over the bed in the back of the wagon [over to] the little peephole out of the covered wagon. I reached down and [took] the nose sacks off of the horses. I got one and dragged it through [the] peephole in the back, but the other [nose sack] fell. I knew the horses would tromp it to pieces during the night. So I had to go out and get that nose sack, [and] I had to face the coyotes. But [they] didn't bother me.

"As we came along the road, in places there would be a great big snake almost as big as my arm. I would scream, 'Oh Dad, there is a big snake.' He said, 'Stop the team.' I would jerk on the reins and stop the team because it might be one [who] would bite the horse and cause trouble. Dad would tell me to wait until [the snake] crossed the path, and then I would be okay. On this trip, going up past [the] Sevier River, going through the valley to Circleville, the river was down below. Nowadays, it looks not much bigger than a cow trail, the road that we had to drive over. [As we were traveling], I saw a buggy coming. I was so scared that he was going to push me into the river [that] I stopped the team and started to cry. Dad said, 'Don't cry. Something will happen.' It was the mailman with his buggy and team. He drove up the side of the mountain, put on his brake, came and drove Dad's team past the road so he could pass me. [Those] were experiences that I had at the age of thirteen when I didn't know too much about anything, but I learned to drive the team, face coyotes, and had all of the troubles that I had. It was quite an experience."[37]

RHODA HAFEN LEAVITT

Rhoda Hafen Leavitt lived in Bunkerville, Nevada, where she was born on 19 January 1906. She tells about children working to fill in during an emergency: "When I was a young girl, I was not quite twelve when my father had to take my mother to St. George to have a baby. She was going to have my second-to-youngest sister. Hazel was her name. [They] had to go in the wagon all the way and had to stay there awhile [after] they [arrived]. [The baby] was not born as soon as they thought it was going to be. While they were gone, the whole family came down with the mumps: my older brothers, Luther, Alfred, Oak, and then all the sisters. There was myself and Rose, Grace, and Ruby. They all had the mumps and were all sick but me. I took care of all [of them], and at the same time we had the threshers [who] were going to thresh our grain.

"I was only twelve years old, but my girlfriend from across the street, Bishop Earl's youngest daughter, Vella Earl, came and helped me. [There was] a big crowd of men [who] had come there to eat. We two [girls] cooked dinners for them. We were sitting down for dinner one day, and my uncle sent his daughter up to help us. She was a grown girl out of college. Charity Leavitt was her name. He sent her up to help us cook the dinners. I can still remember how impudent and sassy we were when she came in there because we had [the men sitting] down at the table eating. She said, 'My dad sent me up here to help you cook for the threshers.' I said, 'You can go right back home because we do not need any of your help.' I remember how embarrassed she looked, but I did not think how awful it sounded. She walked out, and we did not have any trouble cooking for those threshers.

"I remember we were barefooted. We did not have any shoes. We were twelve years old, but we had more fun cooking those dinners for the threshers. I do not know how many meals, but [there were] a lot of them before they [finished] all [of the] threshing."[38]

FAY EMANUEL ANDERSON

Fay Emanuel Anderson was born on 10 July 1899 in Fountain Green, Sanpete County, but grew up in Overton, Nevada. He tells of his father: "He was a hardworking man. [He] had quite a farm. [The work] was all done with horses. [It was] slow work. I used to run the horse on the bailer for him.

They did baling then a little different than they do now. He would make little strips of wood [and] smooth them out so he could write the weight of the bale on—then he would put it under the wire. [He would] weigh the bales as they took them off the baler. When he sold it, he would just look at that slip. That was what they had to pay for. They sold it by weight. I remember when he was threshing. We used to have the threshers come. They would stay maybe a week at a time and do threshing for us. I remember all those threshers and how they did [that work]. I had to get up in the straw and take care of the straw. Mother cooked for the sheep shearers in the spring. We had the sheep-shearing plant right on the farm. When we came down here, he sold 3,000 head [at] $2.00 a head. That was in 1908. In 1912, they were $20 a head. We sold our farm for $6,000. In 1912, it went for $32,999.

"I worked in the shearing corral when I was eleven and twelve. [I would] carry the fleeces. We had a big long board floor with pens on each side. They would put the sheep in there. The fellows would shear them and throw the fleeces over the fence. I would gather them up and haul them to where they sacked them. [There was] lots of wool [that] would escape from the fleece. I would have to sweep that floor about three or four [or] maybe six times a day. [I had] to keep it cleaned up. That was hard work.

"It did not hurt me to learn to work. I had trouble with my back several years ago. The doctor took some x-rays [and] said, 'You have lifted lots of bales of hay, haven't you?' I said, 'No, I haven't, but I have handled a lot of wool or fleeces.' He said, 'You better quit work. You will be in a wheelchair.'"[39]

LLOYD BERDELL JENNINGS

Not all the people who lived in rural Utah followed the agricultural lifestyle. One such person was Lloyd Berdell Jennings, who was born on 24 January 1897 in Levan, Utah, near Nephi. As a young man he went to Amboy and Los Angeles, California, in search of work. He found it in the shipyards: "I accepted a job with a dry dock company as a paint foreman. Sometimes we would call for as many as 2,000 men or 3,000 men when they painted these ships. They would lift the ship out of the water [and] start on the keel of the boat scraping to clean it before we painted it. Then we would paint it and let it right back down into the water. By the time we had cleaned all of the shells and so forth off of the hull and had it painted with red lead, it would be back in the water. Half of the crew was on top sanding, cleaning the deck and the railings, and would paint and varnish everything on the top deck.

"This was an unusual job for a man [who] came from Levan! It was the biggest worry I ever had in my life. I enjoyed it as long as I was there. I never stayed too long. Then we moved back to Las Vegas. That was where I started in the building business [as a] contractor. While we were living in Las Vegas, our baby boy Jesse was born.

"I had a lot of experience in repair work around these plants. I felt that I was capable of building a house, [so] I started building houses. I recall the first house that I built in Las Vegas. It still stands, and was the first house I ever built. Later, construction at Boulder Dam started, and I went to Boulder City and did some contracting. I built their first community church in Boulder City.

"At the same time I was building that, I built the North Las Vegas school. I was doing quite a lot [of] work. Our home burned down. We built a new home down in North Las Vegas. We had it finished only just a few months, it was a frame house, and it burned up. My wife had always been asking me to move back to St. George. After this happened, I gave up building in Las Vegas, and we moved back to St. George. In the meantime, I had bought a lumber-yard that had gone out of business. I bought all of [the] lumber and his hardware. [So] I hauled it to St. George and started building here. I had enough lumber and hardware to build four of five homes, [and] I didn't have to buy [any] material. That gave me a boost when I built [houses] and sold them. That got me [started] in the contracting business in good shape in St. George.

"When we came to St. George, I [also] built [the St. George Café]. It is now [known] as Dick's Café.[40] I guess I just bought it to give my wife [Georgeanna] a job because she [operated] it for about two years before we sold it. It proved to be quite successful. It was a good thing. She did a nice job of running it. During this time, I got started in the contracting business. One of my first contracts was the [St. George] city and [Washington] county jail. After that, I built a good many homes, and then [did] some commercial work. My son, Leon, was in high school. He loved this [kind of] work and was very efficient [for] a boy. He could do good work as a carpenter. He worked with me all day building the jail and any work that I was doing. When he was out of school, he would be right with me. Later on, we started a little store. We had a little hardware store and started selling building supplies.

"Here in St. George, right where it is now, [was] J & J Mill and Lumber Company. When [World] War [II] came, we couldn't buy lumber, so we bought a sawmill. We bought a small mill that was producing about 5,000 or 6,000 feet [of lumber] a day. My other boy [Julian] was running some cottages [the Dixie Motel] that we had built, and [Leon] was running the gas station. Later, we bought [a] sawmill, and Julian took over the sawmill. We found that it wasn't profitable to run this sawmill. We decided to build a larger mill, and that was at Hatch town [Garfield County]. We operated that for a couple of years and found [it] wasn't profitable. The boys wanted to expand and build a bigger mill. So we moved to Virgin and put in a mill that could cut from 50,000 to 70,000 feet [of lumber] a day. The timber [came from] Cedar Mountain. We operated that mill for about two or three years."[41]

ANSON "ANDY" PERRY WINSOR III

Anson "Andy" Perry Winsor III, born in 1879 in Hebron, tells a story of combining farming with merchandising in Enterprise: "We homesteaded some dry farms over on the desert and then I started my home here. I have lived in this granary up here. I had paid for this ground during this time. I bought the different parts of this field that I now own from the family. This homestead, where our home is, was separate from the original homestead. I paid my father for that while I was working at these smelters. I was clear of debt and owned the ground, but I had no money. I landed here with $16.00. I worked over here on this dry farm and did work for others who had homesteaded there to pay for our living.

"I rolled snow into an old cellar. Up in Father's stackyard, he had an underground cellar, and I rolled snow into that and packed it with straw. Then [my wife and I] made ice cream on holidays out of that [snow]. That started us in the ice cream business. When the snow was gone, I shipped in ice from Milford and places like that [to] make ice cream. We stayed in the ice cream business for twenty-five years.

"She was a natural businesswoman. She was a success. We would get so tired and work so many hours that I would go into a barbershop to get my hair cut, they would have to wake me up when [the barber was] through. I would go sound asleep. We would leave there some mornings at four o'clock in the morning. We built this house during the time that we [lived] there. We built this house in 1926. We wanted to [leave] the farm. We had the farm paid for. We put down the first deep well in this valley. We pumped that well [for] sixteen years before they put down another well. Now this whole valley is perforated with wells. No one would believe that the water under there was worthy of putting down a pump and pumping it out. Our farm [has been] a success from the day we put that well down to this very day on account of that deep well.

"She was the business manager. The only money I ever lost was my fault, not hers. I put $1,600 into a gyp [gypsum] mine over [in] Cedar [City] and lost every cent of it. I put some in a dairy proposition over there and lost that. I took [some] stock in the Iron Commercial and Savings Bank in Cedar [City] and lost that. She objected to all of this. Still, I wanted to be the big [fellow] or thought I could boost our income faster by taking this stock. I lost it all, and every bit of it was contrary to her wishes. If I had minded her, I would have never lost any money." Nonetheless, he was completely out of debt when interviewed.[42]

LEAH BUNDY JENSEN

Leah Bundy Jensen was born in 1922 and lived much of her life on the Arizona Strip at Mount Trumbull. Her young life was also filled with hard work: "As a child, I thought my dad was quite hard on us. He made us work. A lot of times it seems like my cousin's dad didn't keep them busy. They would go off for a joyride or something, but we always had corn to hoe or something. He always had something for us to do. We were always kept busy, and I thought he was kind of hard on us. But as I look back, I don't know what more I could say, what appreciation I could show my dad than to thank him for [teaching] me how to work, because it has really been a blessing to me to be able to know how to work.

"In the fall we would take our cattle down next to the Colorado River. My older brothers had gone to [military] service, so it was just myself and my younger brother, Newell [Bundy], who was two years younger than me. We had the job of driving these cattle down. It was about fifteen [or] twenty miles or [maybe] more. I don't remember just exactly how far it was down there, but it took a long, hard day to get [there] from down into the canyon.

"We stayed there. We had to stay down there because we had to see that [the cattle had] water. There were big sandstones down there with pockets of water. We had to dip [the] water off into tubs for the cattle to drink. There was [water] down in Frog [Spring, but it] is a very steep trail, and the cattle didn't like to go down there. When the water in these sand pockets went dry, we would have to force them down. It was a steep trail, and they [would not] go unless they had to go.

"We pushed them down in there because it was so steep. I have wanted to go back. I haven't been back there for [at least] thirty years. I think back [about] all the daring things we did that winter. I know we would go down into Frog Canyon (a short way, we thought) rather than go down the trails when we didn't have to take the cattle down. We would put our feet against one side of the sandstone and our back against [the other side]. I know it was around forty-five or fifty feet we would go down [in] this way. We would have to go back up the trail, but we could get down.

"We would have a packhorse with a pack on. We would take our food down. We would come out every two or three weeks. One time we stayed down there [because] we couldn't leave the cattle on account of the water shortage. We stayed down there. We laugh about [it to] this day! We stayed down there a week after we had run out of all our groceries. [We had] flour and canned milk and I would make lumpy dick.[43] It tasted like this old-fashioned wallpaper paste. It didn't lump too well.

"I would stir it until it was too smooth, but we lived on that for a week before we could come back out and get supplies. . . . We never were afraid or anything. We always had something to do. We had to look after the cattle, we had to water them and check on them. There were about 150 of them."[44]

GORDON WALLACE MATHIS

Gordon Wallace Mathis was born in St. George on 21 December 1887 and tells his story of young adulthood. He was quite like Lloyd Jennings, an entrepreneur in the early twentieth century: "When I [arrived] home [from my mission to England], I started to work again for Nelson Mercantile Company. The manager and stockholder, Will Nelson, wanted to sell out. I finally decided to buy his stock and his home on Mount Hope [in St. George]. I borrowed the money under my dad's signature and [purchased his] home up there. It wasn't modern by any means. We started out there. We had a couple of hundred chickens, three or four milk cows, bathed in a number three tub [and] no inside toilet. That is the way we started.

"[The Nelson Mercantile Company] was in very bad shape [and had a lot of] debt. It was a rough row to hoe for a long while. I worked hard. I usually started to work at 6:00 or 7:00 in the morning [and stayed] sometime as late as 10:00 at night. Then [I would] come home and milk cows, wash eggs for market, and make butter. We had four lots. We were farming part of them too. We really put in some hard labor. But, in time, we got the business back on its feet [to] where we would buy merchandise and take [a] 2 percent discount. From then on, it started to prosper a little.

"In the meantime, my father had bought some stock [in the company from] one of the other stockholders. In the stockholders meeting, I was made manager of the corporation. I managed it for five or six years before my father and I together had acquired all the stock of the company. Then the Depression of 1929 hit. It was very severe. It wasn't so hard on trading business, but my father was in the livestock and land business, and it was hit very hard, especially livestock. [There were] not [any] sales for expenses and operation had to go on. So, actually, the trading business kind of helped support the livestock business. People had to eat, [and] we had a good trade by that time.

"In 1931, we decided to incorporate. We [put] our stock together, and my father put his land and livestock together, and we formed what is known as the Mathis Market and Supply Company. From then on we got along [fairly well]. We prospered. [There were] a lot of hard roads, but we finally got out of debt and out of the Depression.

"Now we [have] branched off into a lot of different fields of endeavor, in addition to the ranch, farming, and livestock. I was manager of the trading part and my other brother [Reed] helped with the cattle. I first went into [the] ice manufacturing business. Our basic [products] were meat and grocery.

"I was quite successful [manufacturing ice]. [This] was before we had refrigerators. We had to deliver ice [to the homes]. Then I [added] ladies' ready-to-wear [clothing] to Mathis Market and Supply Company. My wife managed that department for some time. We used to go to market and buy ladies' ready-to-wear [items]. We managed well [at that]. Then we went into [a] family shoe store, the Red and White Shoe [Store]. Prior to going into either [of] these businesses, we [were] in the cold-storage locker business. We had 380 individual cold-storage lockers. [Those] were about the first [lockers here]. [Frozen food lockers] were just starting, and it worked out very [well]. Then we [got] a Frigidaire appliance agency [and] stocked appliances. I was overseeing a lot of businesses, but I had good help and [was] more or less successful. [We had] a lot of ups and downs but [were] successful in [the end]. I had thirty-four years [of] business experience. Then I decided to lease the market, meat business, and locker business to my son, Jack [Mathis]."[46]

POWELL JOHNSON STRATTON

Powell Johnson Stratton's story is just the opposite of Gordon Mathis's. Though Powell was five years older than Gordon (having been born on 20 May 1883), his life was almost in a different century because he was riveted to farming. The Powell family lived in Virgin, and they were distanced from the consumer society of St. George. Powell tells his story: "I went to school in Virgin and completed the eighth grade. I went to Cedar City and started high school, [but] only went one year. My father was a farmer, and I followed after him. I [farmed] all the [rest of] my life. I enjoyed the school as far as I could [go]. We were poor people, and we couldn't take advantage of things that we would have liked to. I went back to the farm to help my father. We didn't have any [equipment] to work with. It was nothing like it is now. Everything had to be done the hard way.

"We had a lot of trouble from floods. There were times [when] some people lost everything they had in the floods. The [floods] didn't affect us at all. My dad picked his farm and [then] planted a bunch of cottonwood trees right above his farm around by the [Virgin] River. The river ran right around his farm [and] the cottonwood trees protected his farm. He had about fourteen acres of land, and he farmed every inch of it. It was irrigated farming, and it was good farmland. Those trees grew up and protected his farm.

"Of course, we had to work hard. There were six boys counting me and six girls. There were twelve children in the family. That created a lot of work out there. We had to have a lot of [food] out there to raise all of us children. We [grew sugar] cane and made molasses. We would take [the] molasses north [to] the farm country of Cedar City and trade it in for clothing, flour, and [items] like that to get along with during the winter. We hauled it up there with a team. We would be gone about a month. We would do that in the fall. We would make [the] molasses, load it, and [haul] it away before [the weather was] too bad.

"After mother had six or eight children, she went blind all at once. It came on that quick. I was just a [boy] and would lead her out to the outhouse because there wasn't any [inside plumbing]. I would lead her out there and back every time she needed to go. My health wasn't very good when I was a [boy], so my dad wouldn't let me [work] on the farm. Instead, I would stay home and take care of my mother. Her eyesight came back just as quick as it went. They didn't find out why because there were no doctors. They had one doctor for the whole river [area]. She was blind for about three months."[47]

VINCENT ELIAS LEAVITT

Vincent Elias Leavitt was born in 1899 and lived in Bunkerville. He dealt with the issue—farm or work for an employer: "We have lived right here ever since our marriage (1924). [We] came home and I went to farming. We were married in November, and the next July I went to work for the Nevada Highway Department. I worked for the Highway Department until two years ago [1967]. I worked ten years, and then I was off ten years. Then I went back and worked twenty-one years. I farmed and dairied those ten years. I hauled milk to Las Vegas.

"I enjoyed the highway work more. I was foreman for the maintenance in this part of the state. Being [the] foreman, I had to run all the heavy equipment—the loaders, the tractors, and the trucks. When I first went on there, everything was done with pick and shovel. When I [was] done, everything was done with machinery. [There] was a big difference, about a third of the work [that] it used to be. [We had] a lot more roads to maintain and [received] a lot better wages."[48]

GRANT WOODBURY

Grant Woodbury was born in St. George on 18 April 1898. As an adult, he had many jobs: "I went to Lynndyl, Utah, and [found] a job there. They put me in the stationary engine room. I didn't know anything about it but they put me [with] another [fellow] for a week or two [and] then they turned it over to me. I stayed there for six months, but I wasn't cut out to be bossed. I got along fine with the superintendents and the workmen there, but I couldn't stand the inspectors that they sent along the road. They [would] come in and say, 'You do it this way.' They seemed like they all came on my shift. I had to see them in the afternoon and at eleven at night. One would come one day and say, 'This is wrong; you do it this way.' I would just get it changed, and the next one would come in and say, 'This is wrong; you do it this way.' I got fed up.

"One night they took [the engine] out and didn't put any coal back in it, brought it back in, and put it on the turntable. The pipe fitter didn't arrive. I was just dragging lower and lower all the time. Finally, come eleven o'clock, the gaffer [foreman], who was taking the other shift, didn't show up. When the pipe fitter came in, he climbed up on top of the dead engine and opened the valve, [and] my steam went out just like that, that big old rusty boiler down there. I knew what the matter was, [so] I ran down through the machine shop just [to] make sure. Sure enough, there it was. I climbed up and closed the valve down and put some coal in the fire box, went up and shut mine off, and put us all in the dark. Everybody was off work. Nobody was working, only me. I worked on it until midnight chasing back and forth through the machine shop with a coal oil, not kerosene, coal oil torch, that was all I had.

"A little after midnight, the foreman came in; he saw [that] everything [was] dark. Of course, the first thing he does is to hunt the stationary engineer up. When he found me I was up on top of the boiler about thirty, thirty-five feet in the air. I got the steam back up and the water back in the boiler to where it was safe. He started to cuss, and I started to cuss too. I was just as mad as he was. But he was a nice fellow, and when he saw that I was mad he waited until I got down. When he saw me, he knew I shouldn't be there. He asked me where the gaffer was, and I told him I didn't know; I [had] never seen him. He wanted to know what the trouble was, and I told him. I went down and opened up the other locomotive in the line and got things [moving]. He got a hold of the coal boy, and he got the gaffer right quick. After the gaffer got there, he sent the coal boy down to the stationary engine room and told me that the superintendent wanted to see me.

"I went up and he said, 'Have you had your supper?' I said, 'No.' He said, 'Go up to the cook shack and get something to eat and then come back.' So I went [and] got something to eat and came back. When I went in the office he said, 'I would like you to stay all night, but you don't have to, but I would like you to.' After that, I could get anything I wanted from them. But I couldn't stand the inspectors [who] came along the road, so I quit.

"I came home and bought me a little truck, a 1917 Model T [Ford]. [I] made a truck out of it, and I spent twenty years trucking on the road. I couldn't say I really liked that. Once in a while you would have a trip that was enjoyable, but most of them weren't. I did it because I had a family to feed and I had to [work]. I had lost my truck and couldn't find a thing to do. I tried to get on with the WPA [Work Projects Administration]. They took my name all right, and they came to tell me to go to work. [But] just the day before, I [was lifting] a couple of bales of hay to feed the cows that we were milking. The bale of hay broke [open], and I landed across the top of the board fence on my ribs and broke a couple of them. The job that they had [for me] was [using] a pick and shovel job in the rocks. I told them I couldn't go.

"After a while, I got a chance at a job in the [Hurricane] high school. It was the first year of the brand-new high school. Believe it or not, [it paid] $30.00 a month. The WPA offered $42.00 [a month]. The wife and I talked it over and decided to take it, in preference to the $42.00. We [thought] there was a chance of something better there, and there wasn't on the other job. I worked one winter there, and the next spring the superintendent came to me, a fellow I was well acquainted with, had been for years. He said, 'Grant, would you like that other elementary school?' I said, 'I sure would.' So they gave me $80.00 [a month]. I worked there [about nine years]."[49]

LEAMO WEST PETERSON

Leamo West Peterson was born on 6 December 1903 and lived in Panaca and Caliente, Nevada. He gave an extensive interview about his work life at many jobs, of which some are cited here: "I was fifteen years old when I went to [work on] the railroad; I told them I was twenty-one. The first time the road master came along, I heard him, but I tried to keep out of his sight. He said to Hugh Edmondson, the boss, 'How old is that [fellow] over there.' He said, 'He said he was twenty-one years old.' He said, 'You know he isn't twenty-one.'

The boss said, 'He told me he was.' 'You know he isn't. You have him get a minor release from his parents and a release from the school board, or let him go.' I knew I couldn't get it, so I had to go, that was all. I went back again after school was out and worked there. I was working there in the fall, [but] I wasn't going to school. My parents were having a lot of trouble with sickness.

"My dad bought a pair of horses, and he said if I wanted to drive them I could drive them and he would drive the other team between the times I was going to school, but he wanted me to go to school. My parents wanted me to have an education in the worst way. They did everything possible for me to have an education. I guess I was too sympathetic. My mother was sick for twenty-one years before she died. My dad was pretty near a pauper when she died. He had spent everything he had, his cows and everything, to try and help her, and he couldn't do it. I felt like I should help them instead of helping myself."

He tells of some work while he was still going to school. "George and Joe Woodbury had a bunch of cattle and a big farm. The first job I ever [had was] working for them herding their cows. We went to school, at that time, for half a day. I herded their milk cows along with our cows over on the hill for ten cents a day. Getting them out of the corral for ten cents a day was better than just herding ours for nothing. The first two times they gave me the dollar in a check. I thought, My gosh! That bank will think that [fellow] is making a lot of money! I was that young. That was before I was even fifteen years old. I was just going to grade school.

"I used to haul gas from Enterprise to St. George and [from] Lund to Enterprise for cars. They did not even have trucks then. I took some [youngsters] with me down there one time. I was only fifteen years old. We were selling gas tanks, and the gas leaked out. You know what hot gas will do to [a youngster's] bottom. If I didn't have a mess by the time I [arrived in] Enterprise. Those fellows sat on those barrels and played around with that gas, [and] it got on their pants. I played it that way all the time in the summertime and when I wasn't going to school."

During the summers, Leamo began wandering, mostly hitching rides on freight trains, looking for jobs. He had many adventures. He went to Delta, Enterprise, and Caliente. "My brother Delbert, the brother just younger than me, and I went there one time. We heard about a job over there. We went over, [but] they did not have any work any place. They had a bunch of mules over there. They had eighty broke mules, and they brought down eighty raw broncos from Salt Lake City. We tried to get a job, but there weren't any jobs for youngsters. We went to the [railroad] depot and stayed there overnight. We went down the next morning. They wouldn't give us a job. We went down at noon, and that [fellow] said, '[Expletive], get those [fellows] out of my hair. Put them [to] doing something.' We went to work for them. They would take two of these bronco mules and put them with two others and start those old teamsters out. If you know what those old teamsters were, they were a pretty rough bunch.

"[They] put two broke mules with two broncos [and] started out [with a] Fresno [scraper]. Pretty quick, those mules would take off, and those skinners [were] going as fast as they can go. They would just throw the line there and go. Let them go, and the way the boys were riding I round up mules and when they would get away from that Fresno. We went down the canyon and worked down there for a while. I got a rock in my eye one night, and I was afraid I was going to go blind, so we quit and went home. We had a few dollars to us. We had to get a doctor to get the rock [out of] my eye."[50]

ISAAC LOREN COVINGTON

Here is another unconventional story for the time. Isaac Loren Covington was born on 20 February 1885 in Orderville. His father was a polygamist with three wives and about thirty children, and he served six months in prison for practicing polygamy. Loren went to eight grades in Orderville and became a plasterer as well as a farmer. He took up sign painting, but on the side he did landscape paintings. That is where his love was. He went to BYU and found out about professional painting. He says of his life: "I have farmed. I have worked at plastering, painting, decorating [and] sign painting. I have never been out of a job. I did some Work Projects [Administration jobs] during the Depression. One [job was] painting murals inside the [state] capitol. Dean Richards and I [worked at] that. They said if they could have [the WPA] up there, they could have it here. So they sent me to work on the [Washington County] courthouse and the public library. I did a dozen or so murals for them down here.

"I have no idea [how many pictures I have painted]. It would be up in the thousands. I have painted over fifty murals for churches, including one in the [St. George] temple down here. They are scattered from Los Angeles, up in Canada, [in the] eastern [part of] Colorado, [in] New Mexico, along the west, [and] in Salt Lake [City].

"I have done scores of pictures of Zion Canyon. I just select a place, sit in a spot, [and] paint about the same time [each] day [and] get it a little further developed. Sometimes it will take [only] the one day's work."[51]

CONCLUSIONS

These were mostly manual laborers. There were a few merchants and teachers, but most were working the land, irrigating, herding animals, raising and peddling fruit, or hiring out. Cattle ranching became a major part of the southern area. Raising alfalfa was a complement to it and occupied many families. Some herds grew large, and some people even tried to live on a homestead or ranch away from the villages. Men became expert tool workers and repairmen and craftsmen. Some became craftsmen such as shoemakers or mechanics. Several men hired out to build roads or labor in mines or work on the railroad—often as a temporary effort to raise money.

Many girls and women did domestic work for hire; some cooked as a job or took in washing. A score or more of them worked in the cotton factory. Many youth had to substitute full-time for ill or deceased parents, running the farms and ranches or maintaining the home and meals. When mothers did not have to take in work for pay, they sometimes undertook running a dairy and making cheese for sale. A few ran a bakery from home, selling or trading their goods. Some worked part-time in a café. A few taught school, either part-time or full-time.

Considering these realities, it is not surprising that parents placed a strong emphasis on teaching children and youth to work. Boys were expected to help with the harvest in the fall and the planting season in the spring, as well as full-time work in the summers. Some sought jobs far and wide. Youth in these interviews praised their parents for their devotion to work, usually modeling themselves after them. The boys started serious work at age nine and often took on a man's work by age eleven or thirteen. Boys sometimes took care of a herd by themselves at these ages. Some youth had to substitute for an ill or deceased parent. Others worked with their fathers and became partners with them for decades.

Clearly, work was the center of these people's lives, often until their deaths. They valued it but lived modestly.

NOTES

1. Andrew Karl Larson, *I Was Called to Dixie* (Salt Lake City: Deseret News Press, 1961).

2. Larson, *I Was Called to Dixie*, 345–46.

3. Larson, *I Was Called to Dixie*, 348.

4. Larson, *I Was Called to Dixie*, 349. For more information on wine making, see Olive W. Burt, "Wine-Making in Utah's Dixie," in *Great and Peculiar Beauty, A Utah Reader*, ed. Thomas J. Lyon and Terry Tempest Williams (Layton, UT: Gibbs Smith, 1995), 923–30. It focuses mainly on Toquerville.

5. John T. Woodbury, *Vermilion Cliffs* (St. George, UT: Woodbury Children, 1933), 21–22. In this source, Woodbury talks about "lucerne," which is another name for alfalfa.

6. Larson, *I Was Called to Dixie*, 270–71.

7. Richard G. Oman, "The Homemade Kingdom: Mormon Regional Furniture," in *Nearly Everything Imaginable: The Everyday Life of Utah's Mormon Pioneers*, ed. Ronald W. Walker and Doris R. Dant (Provo, UT: Brigham Young University Press, 1999), 157–74.

8. A. Karl Larson and Katherine Miles Larson, eds., *The Diary of Charles Lowell Walker*, vol. 1 (Logan: Utah State University Press, 1980), 439.

9. Douglas D. Alder and Karl F. Brooks, *A History of Washington County, From Isolation to Destination* (Springdale, UT: Zion Natural History Association, 2007), 63–64.

10. John Alton Peterson, "Brigham's Bastion: 'Winsor Castle' at Pipe Springs and Its Place in the Great Game," in *Juanita Brooks Lecture Series St. George, Utah: The 33rd Annual Lecture* (St. George, UT: Dixie State University Press, 2016). Peterson delivered this Juanita Brooks Honor Lecture on 23 March 2016 in the St. George Tabernacle.

11. Della Elizabeth McCune Steed, VOR File 69-009.

12. Walter "Walt" Wallace Bowler, VOR File 69-121.

13. Norma Bringhurst Empy, VOR File 69-126.

14. Amanda Amelia Hannig Milne, VOR File 69-036.

15. Apex Mine also featured a smelter. The mine was located on the Shivwits Indian Reservation.

16. Athole Jarvis Milne, VOR File 69-035.

17. Lemuel Glen Leavitt, VOR File 69-168.

18. John Sevy Thompson, VOR File 69-181.

19. Ralston Virden Reber, VOR File 69-068.
20. Ellen Hortense (Spendlove) Bradshaw Hinton, VOR File 70-002.
21. Rulon Anderson Langston, VOR File 70-058.
22. Clarence Merrill Hall, VOR File 69-186.
23. Matilde "Mattie" Woodbury Reusch, VOR File 68-022.
24. Ianthus Spendlove, VOR File 70-071.
25. Rowena Whitmore Bundy, VOR File 68-032.
26. The first little girl mentioned was named Cleo Fern Bundy, and the baby was named Mabel Lavell Bundy.
27. James Bundy, VOR File 68-040. James's volunteer service as an aviator included service in the US Air Corps during World War II.
28. Frederick Cross Hoyt, VOR File 68-071.
29. Della Humphries Hardy, VOR File 69-007.
30. Lydia Amelia Barlocker Hunt, VOR File 69-118.
31. Samuel Kendall Gifford, VOR File 69-004.
32. William Brooks, VOR File 68-101.
33. Charles Herbert Knell, VOR File 68-052.
34. Clarence Jacob Albrecht, VOR File 68-042.
35. Erastus Snow Gardner, VOR File 69-018.
36. Joseph Hills Johnson Jr., VOR File 68-027.
37. Mary Ann Weaver Judd Allen, VOR File 69-108.
38. Rhoda Hafen Leavitt, VOR File 69-078.
39. Fay Emanuel Anderson, VOR File 70-065.
40. Dick Hammer owned and operated Dick's Café for many years.
41. Lloyd Berdell Jennings, VOR File 68-034.
42. Anson "Andy" Perry Winsor III, VOR File 69-119.
43. Lumpy dick is a traditional pioneer recipe and is essentially a lumpy boiled pudding.
44. Leah Bundy Jensen, VOR File 69-070.
45. Lola Belle DeMille Bryner, VOR File 68-015.
46. Gordon Wallace Mathis, VOR File 68-036.
47. Powell Johnson Stratton, VOR File 68-119.
48. Vincent Elias Leavitt, VOR 69-062.
49. Grant Woodbury, VOR File 69-006.
50. Leamo West Peterson, VOR File 69-060.
51. Isaac Loren Covington, VOR File 70-001.

## Chapter 4

HEALTH AND SICKNESS

INTRODUCTION

In the early twentieth century, people who lived in southern Utah, nearby southern Nevada, and northern Arizona had to cope with heat, and they did it with moderate success. The one thing they could not control with hard labor was sickness. They did not know what later generations discovered about how illness spreads, and they had few medications and very limited health care. When the Mormons arrived in southern Utah, they encountered American Indians, especially the Paiutes, who the Mormons often turned to for help with herbs. Even though the Mormons lived in villages, they had no access to doctors. Eventually a few professional doctors set up practice in the larger population centers, mainly St. George and Hurricane; for instance, a private hospital with two doctors and ten beds was established in St. George about 1912. Mostly the people had to rely on their own resources, as the stories in this chapter detail.

Herbal medicine was the mainstay. The tradition of Thomsonian doctors in nineteenth-century United States traveled with the many settlers to the West. These herbalists were medical practitioners who gained their knowledge from traditions and a book, *New Guide to Health*, written by a Samuel Thomson (1769–1843) from New Hampshire, detailing his herbal remedies. They did not attend medical schools; instead, they obtained copies of his book and got a certificate from him. In Utah, Thomsonian practitioners were initially favored over so-called surgeons, who did go to medical school, perhaps because one of their treatments was to draw blood from the body in large amounts, based on the hypothesis that disease was spread through the body by circulating blood. Thomsonians treated illnesses with herbs; they did not cut into the body. Brigham Young, for instance, favored the herbal doctors over surgeons. However, by the early twentieth century, doctors practicing a modern version of medicine were gaining more respect, partly because more advanced medical schools in that field had been established.

In between these two practitioner traditions were midwives, best known for helping in the delivery of babies, but people often turned to them for help with illnesses. Later in the 1900s, some public schools employed nurses, and they often served whole communities, especially in attempting to limit the spread of communicable diseases.

The other theme in this chapter is the story of coping with health problems by turning to religion. A common practice among Latter-day Saints was to have elders give blessings to those who were ill. This was often done by the fathers because they held the priesthood. Sometimes a bishop or elders were sent for to give that blessing. On rare occasions, if no priesthood bearers were available, women gave blessings.

An interesting scholar who dealt with this subject of pioneer health was Dr. Wesley P. Larsen. Following a career as the dean of science at Southern Utah University in Cedar City, he retired to Toquerville, Utah, and devoted himself to studying various aspects of "the history of southern Utah, northern Arizona and eastern Nevada,"[1] such as Thomsonian doctors and local Indian medications. In his book *Indian and Pioneer Medicinal Food & Plants*, he stressed the Mormon pioneer distrust of surgeons, quoting a *Deseret News* article from 1855 titled "Let the Doctors Alone."[2] He then gives a short biography of Samuel Thomson and his impact on American medicine in the 1800s:

> Thompson [*sic*] made a successful cure for his wife in the difficult birth of their third child. About this same time, Thompson tested

the emetic Lobelia again, this time on a farm laborer. The usual vomiting resulted, followed by a rapid improvement in health, and the man felt better than he had for a long time. These successes caused much talk in the neighborhood, and he was called to attend several more cases, gradually propelling him into a large practice. . . .

His success became legend, and soon Thompson had a practice so large it was impossible to give personal treatment. Thus, he devised a system so that every family could practice for itself. This system [he] sold to individuals and groups[,] giving them . . . [a] license to practice his medicine ($2.00) and an 800 page manual ($20.00). Thompsonianism [sic] spread like wildfire over the entire American south and west. . . . Thompson claimed to have sold more than 100,000 licenses over his lifetime.[3]

Larsen tells about Priddy Meeks, an herbal doctor who moved to Parowan in 1851 and had a wide impact in southern Utah.[4] Larsen then listed many medications these herbalists used. For example, he tells about Brigham (or Mormon) tea or ephedra, a plant made into a tea that was often called *mountain rush*. The pioneers may have originally learned about the medicinal properties of the plants from Indians.[5] Larsen includes accounts of its use to regenerate languid patients. Other plants were also used; for instance, cayenne pepper was used to save frozen feet. It was a long process, but it brought heat back into the legs and feet, and after three weeks of daily treatment, the patient could avoid amputation and walk again.[6]

Larsen includes drawings of many plants in southern Utah that both Indians and Mormons used for medications and describes the Indian use and the pioneer use for each plant. For example, Mormons used horsetail to heal cuts and wounds and stop bleeding.[7] A patient would steep juniper berries for fifteen minutes and drink the juice every day for urinary tract infections.[8] A tea made from mountain mahogany was used as a laxative.[9] Oil made with mullein was often used for healing.[10] Tea was also made from pinyon pine as a diuretic.[11] Plantain leaves were ground into a juice as a remedy for burns, insect bites, poison ivy, and bleeding.[12]

By the turn of the century, medical doctors were becoming professionally educated in conventional medicine and began appearing in southern

Utah. A small book, *History of Health Care in Utah's Dixie*, was released by the Dixie Regional Medical Center in 2003 as part of the dedication of the new IHC Hospital in St. George.[13] It briefly surveys herbal medicine and midwives. Priddy Meeks's practice is described in Harrisburg, John Steele's in Toquerville, Silas Higgins's in Silver Reef, and Israel Ivins's in St. George. Midwives are mentioned, including Mary Ann Hunt Nielson, Caroline Baker Rogers Hardy, Ann Hess Milne, Mrs. William Ellis Jones (Dinah Davies Vaughan), and others.

Then the book turns to doctors that practiced what we consider conventional medicine. Dr. J. T. Affleck came from Pennsylvania, where he was trained as a medical doctor, to Silver Reef and then to St. George. In 1891, Frederick Cliff arrived, and soon after that came Frank Woodbury. These doctors were mainly in St. George but were sometimes called to villages as far away as Grafton. In 1925, Dr. George Russell Aiken established a practice in Hurricane, and Dr. Wilford Reichman came to St. George as a family doctor, specializing in births.

The big change in medicine was caused by doctors Frank Woodbury and Donald McGregor. In 1913, they established a modest hospital in St. George. Known as the McGregor Hospital, it continued to 1952. Initially, it had ten beds, two doctors, and three or four nurses. This modest medical system continued until 1952, when Washington County built the Pioneer Memorial Hospital with seven doctors and twenty-five beds. Thus conventional medicine became a parallel to herbal medicine; however, most people in the villages continued with the herbal option because St. George was too far to get to quickly. These limited medical services are mentioned by some of those interviewed below.

Nurses became a key factor in the practice of medicine. Their assistance was needed especially in births and surgery, but in recovery and treating diseases, they were central. Some became school nurses and community aides in fighting epidemics like the flu.

Susan Arrington Madsen's article "Growing Up in Pioneer Utah" gives an account of the dangers children faced:

> When J. Martin Allred was fifteen years old, a severe drought forced
> his father and him to drive their livestock from their home in Walls-
> burg, Utah, to winter on the Uintah Reservation. After a long winter

of sometimes lonely cattle herding, Martin was anxious to see his mother and siblings. Returning home a few weeks before his father, Martin experienced this reception: "We hadn't heard one word from home all winter and when I got within about one mile from home I met an old neighbor by the name of John Purcell. He began telling me of the children that had died in [Wallsburg] during the winter from diphtheria. I thought every second he would tell about some of my brothers and sisters dying, but thank the Lord there were none of them seriously sick with that dreaded disease. When I got to our front gate Mother met me and said, 'Martin, you mustn't come in as some of the children are in the worst stage of the disease.' Then Mother told me there had been 32 children die there during the winter, as many as five in one family. I was only fifteen years old, hadn't seen Mother all winter long and was so homesick to see the rest of the family. I wanted so much to take her in my arms and hug and kiss her, but she wouldn't even shake hands with me for fear of leaving a germ and I might be exposed. You can imagine my feelings at that moment and also hers." Martin's mother decided he should go away and work for another two or three months. She did not let him return home until the rest of the children were well.[14]

Jill Mulvay Derr wrote "I Have Eaten Everything Imaginable," in which she emphasizes that families were often very short of food. These people were the generation in Utah's Dixie prior to those interviewed in this book, but their stories give a good background to what their parents faced growing up.

Harmon Gubler recollected eating pigweed and lucerne [alfalfa] during his childhood in Santa Clara. "We would walk for miles to find some of the lucerne so that we could have it to eat," he said. One St. George family lived for six weeks on nothing but boiled lucerne "without even salt or pepper." Others remembered gathering dandelion greens, lamb's-quarters, wild mushrooms, rose hips, turnips, onions, and artichokes. Isaiah Cox, whose family was among the early settlers of St. George, ate "wild cane which grew along the stream."

"The Segos we children gathered and ate just as a delicacy," recalled David H. Cannon Jr., noting that "some people ate them at the table, prepared into some very tasty dishes." Isaiah Cox dug sego bulbs and remembered that "another choice wild delicacy which we dug along the river bottom was the grass nut," similar to the sego bulb but larger.[15]

Elliott West authored the book *Growing Up in Twentieth-Century America: A History and Reference Guide*.[16] He dealt with the whole nation, and the insights apply to this region. He said, "Children were in danger, first of all, because medical authorities were remarkably ignorant about the causes, nature, and treatment of diseases. Many advances in medical knowledge had been made during the previous half century, but far more still lay ahead. . . . Scientists previously had believed that diseases could be traced to such causes as 'impure blood' and deadly mists and vapors. . . . By 1890, scientists had identified the microorganisms—the 'germs'—that caused cholera, pneumonia, diphtheria, tuberculosis, typhoid, and several other maladies. This was a discovery of immeasurable value."[17] For people in Utah's Dixie, these developments still required access to doctors and the hospital. Most villages were a long way distant from both.

The people who were interviewed in this study told mostly about medicine before modernity and mostly from the village viewpoint, in which blessings and herbal medicine reigned because doctors were far away. Sometimes emergencies drew doctors to the villages, but generally this is a story of premodern health care.

Here are the words of a score of people interviewed between 1968 and 1970 when they were in their seventies or eighties. They give their memories of the period early in their lives, between 1900 and the next three or four decades, about how they and their families dealt with the issue of illness and even death.

INTERVIEWS

VERNA MAE ISOM GIFFORD

Verna Mae Isom Gifford was born in Mountain Dell near Virgin, Utah, in 1894. She grew up wanting to be a nurse. She worked for Dr. Wilkinson in Hurricane as a practical nurse and hoped to go to Salt Lake City to get formal nurse training. When the flu epidemic came in 1918, she contracted flu on a trip to Salt Lake and came back to Hurricane: "I went home and went right to [Dr.] Wilkinson's the next day to work. [We] hadn't been home only just a day or two and we had a very bad case of appendicitis there. It [had] ruptured. I helped [during the] operation. I was coming down with the flu. . . . I had the flu and had to assist the doctors [while they] were operating on this man, Brother [David] Dave Hirschi. Dr. Wilkinson came down with the flu. We had to put him to bed. Oh, I was sick! I was sick the next day. The doctor's wife was in bed. She had a new baby [and] was in bed. I took sick, so there was nobody there [who] could take care of me. There was nobody there to take care of this patient. They finally found a woman to come in and help take care of Brother Hirschi. But I had to go home. . . .

"Finally my uncle, Samuel Isom, heard about it. He was the bishop in Hurricane. He came up there and went right to my sister-in-law and said, 'I heard Verna has the flu. Where is she?' 'She is upstairs.' He said, 'I will tell you something. You get the boys to put a bed in the front room, get the heater going so she can come down in the front room where there is heat.' I had two sisters younger than me there, Ida and Reeta. He said, 'If you don't do that, I will take her home with me and take care of her.' I said, 'I won't go down to his place.' I told him right there, 'I can't go down to your place Uncle Sam, because you have had pneumonia two or three times and you have a bad heart. I wouldn't go down there for a million [dollars]. I would die first before I would go to your place. I appreciate what you want to do for me [in] helping me.' He made her fix me up in the front room. He said, 'If you don't want to go near her, just stay away and let the girls wait on her.'

"I was there in that room, and the girl [who] had been working in the house with me over at the doctor's got [the flu]. She didn't want to go home to her folks and give it to them. I was good enough to let her come in and stay with me. I was getting over the flu, and some of the [others] were coming down with it. My two little brothers [Waldon and Rulon Wright Isom] got [the flu], and I had to help take care of them. Then my two sisters [Ida Mary and Reeta Vernell Isom] got [the flu] and I had them all down. I was weak and coughing, and I had to take care of them and get them over it. This girl came in with me to stay, [and] she got over it. When she got over it, she went home. She never even stayed there to help me. I will never forget that. She left me [as] my youngest sister [Reeta] was coming down with [the flu]. She went outside and talked through the window to my brother's little girl and gave [the flu] to her.

"I was so weak I couldn't wash a dish. I couldn't sweep a floor. I couldn't do anything—only cough, cough, cough. They would keep coming down with it. Then my brother [Andrew] came down with [the flu], and he had pneumonia. My sister-in-law [Jacosa] got [the flu]. She was pregnant and lost her baby. I had two of them down and their little girl. My brother and sisters were in the other room, and nobody to help me. . . . I was so weak and tired. . . . But I got over that, and I had a chance to go all over the town and help because I had had the flu."[18]

MATILDA "MATTIE" TALBOT KOKERHANS

Accidents caused many injuries that required medications. Those who were away from doctors either had to travel by wagon long distances to get help, or use local options. Nancy Matilda "Mattie" Talbot Kokerhans lived in Panguitch, and on 9 August 1969, when she was elderly, she related this story from her memory, still able to remember the details: "The boys were digging holes in the ground [to] make [holes for] burying corn cobs for [the] Indians. [The] girls were sitting around with their dolls, watching them bury [the corn cobs]. I looked over to see how deep the [hole] was, and I reached over [as] my brother came down with the axe. [It] hit me right on the crown of the head [and] split my head open. It kind of numbed me, [and] I didn't know I was hurt until the blood began to run down my face. I [started] to scream, and the [adults] all came a running to see what was wrong.

"There was not any doctor, and it was too far to come to get a doctor, so the men went into the hills and got [some] sticky gum. They shaved my head around the cut, stuck it together, and bound it up with this sticky gum [pine gum]. It wasn't undone [removed] until it was healed. [I] never had any infection. And I don't have much of a scar."[19]

ALVIN CARL HARDY

Alvin Carl Hardy grew up in St. George, where he was born on 15 August 1902. He tells a dramatic story of surviving an accident: "We were coming home down over the mountain into Toquerville, loaded with about 3,800 [pounds] of freight. That was a wagon box and a pair of bows [with a] wagon cover, because we had flour and sugar, to keep it protected from the rain. We had a bundle of ¾ inch pipe right along the top of the wagon box, which struck out the front end over the dashboard. It had worked its way forward [as we were] coming down over the Black Ridge to where it was almost touching one of the horses. She was a very flighty animal. As we came through Toquerville, a number of boys came out and followed the wagon through town. They would hang on these pipes that stuck out behind. As they hung on them, they ran [the pipes] up and hit this animal, [and she] lunged. Just as they hit this animal one time, she lunged [as] we were crossing one of the [small] rock ditches. All of this seemed to be timed perfectly; I don't know why the timing was so perfect, but just as they swung on the pipe, the pipes hit the animal [as] we crossed the ditch. Father had told me to ask the boys not to swing on the pipe. I stood up on the dashboard, holding [on] to the bows, and stuck my head around to call to the boys; all of [these] things occurred instantaneously. As the horse lunged, they hit the ditch, it threw the wagon, and I was thrown off. I went down between the singletree and the heels of the mare, and the front wheel ran across my left hand. I feel it and see it as I think about it [now]. It just ran over me, and I turned to pull myself from under the wheel. The hind wheel hit me on the right hip and ran up across the front of my body, over my shoulder, turned me over, crossed my back and came off on the left hip on the back, which crushed the life out of me.

"Father saw me fall and threw the lines over the other horses' back, jumped and hollered, 'Whoa!' Those horses were better to mind than his children; they stopped immediately. He ran to the back of the wagon, and I was under the wheel. He drove the horses off from me, ran back, and picked me up in his arms. He said I was as dead as he had ever seen anybody. But [as] he looked into my face, holding me limp[ly] in his arms, and [not] knowing what to do, here came a lady out of the house that we were right in front of, Sister Duffins, a very fine old midwife. She ran out and grabbed me out of Father's arms and put her mouth over my face and blew like a bellows. I vomited and began to breathe just slightly, and that was all the breath I could get. She carried me in her home, and Dad called Dr. Woodbury from St. George. [He] told him what happened. [Dr. Woodbury] said, 'Brother Hardy, there is no need of me coming. If that wagon went over

that boy with that much weight on, he will be dead before I can get there.'
He told him what to do, how to poultice me. [He] said, 'I won't try to come
tonight because I will have to come with a horse and buggy, which will
take me three or four hours. But, if he is still alive in the morning, you call
me and I will come. But you can rest assured, if he is alive in the morning,
you are mistaken; the wagon didn't run over him.' Father said, 'I know it
ran over him; I had to drive the horses off from him.'

"The next morning, he called the doctor and said, 'He is alive, and I have
additional proof to prove the wagon ran over him. I have a wagon track this
morning across that body.' He came and [said] it was a miracle. He said, 'I
can't understand how you are alive.' I still couldn't breathe, and I laid there for
two weeks. There was not a broken bone in my body, but I had been crushed,
and life had been crushed out of me. I couldn't breathe, and I couldn't get
well. I would go into spasms and go out of my mind at times, and then I
would be rational. The priesthood was demonstrated there time and time
again. Every time he would call the elders—my father had lots of faith [that]
I would get better. But I would have relapses occur constantly.

"It was only a short time after that until I seemed to fade and [became]
weaker. Father felt that probably his petition to the Lord was going to be
answered, that I would not live. My mother's sister was there, Aunt Mary A.
Gubler; she was very devoted in helping [with my care]. On this particular
night, after they had [the] prayer circle for me, I passed away. Father says
I died as natural a death as my mother had died, and they prepared to lay
me out, or they did lay me out, pulled the sheets over me, and pronounced
me dead. My aunt went to the kitchen and drew the water. In those days
[it] was the custom to wash the bodies in the home, lay them out, pack ice
around the bodies and hold them for burial. She got the cloths and the
necessary equipment to wash my body and lay me out. As she applied
the wet cloth to my face, a nerve twitched in the corner of my eye, and
she stopped suddenly and called my father. She said, 'Willie, come here
quick.' Father was in the kitchen, feeling bad to think I had died, and yet
he had not shed a tear up to this point. He came running in. She says, 'I
don't know whether this boy is dead, or whether he is just unconscious.
He has been out so long, I'm sure he is dead, but I saw a nerve twitch in
the corner of his eye. Maybe there is life in that body yet.' Father burst into

tears and wept. He said, 'If there is life, there is hope. Call Brother Naegli, quick.' Brother Naegli, who was the patriarch at the time, came over, and the two of them administered to me again. [They] pled with the Lord that if it was possible, could I be made whole, and not be a cripple; if it was not against His will, to please let me live. I immediately came to, choking and gasping, and I vomited. A lot of corruption [mucus] came [from] my lungs and down in my stomach. Immediately, my breathing was restored to normal. That night, my younger brother came to visit me. I sat in the bed and he stood by my bed, and we sang [the] song 'Three Little Babes Lost in the Woods' all the way through. The next day, [I] got out of bed, dressed, and went home. [I was] well and strong. I have never felt any ill effects of that accident to this day, and I am now sixty-six-years old."[20]

EDWIN M. HIATT

Edwin M. Hiatt was born on 20 June 1913 in Jensen, Uintah County, near Vernal. They later moved to Moapa, Nevada: "The fall before we left Moapa Valley, Father was plowing a piece of ground. He [was] moving from one field across to another. There was a large irrigation ditch that he had to [cross] and a gate that had to be opened. He figured that he would pull his team down into the ditch and then get off the plow and open the gate. I told him I wanted [to get] off. I didn't want to ride across the ditch. He told me to sit still. As the horses started down into the ditch, one of the horses jumped. Just as the horse jumped, I jumped! I [landed] right down against the bank of the ditch, and the horses jerked the plow. [The plow] was a big double disc plow, [and it went] right over the top of me. It cut both legs. One leg [was] cut almost completely through the bone. The tendons in my toes were cut in my other leg.

"At that time, [the] closest doctor [was in] Las Vegas. [It] was a two-day ride with a buggy and team to get to Las Vegas. The only person was a midwife, a Mrs. Lee. She was summoned. She took a needle and sewed the cords back together and strapped me to a board. My folks [had to] keep me right flat. I was flat for almost three months while my legs healed. Then I had to learn to walk all over again. A sister just younger than me would push me. I had a little red express wagon, and she used to push me after I got so that I could [be up]. She pushed the wagon, and I would guide it. That was the way I got around until I learned to walk again. Today the only time that you [can] tell where the scar is, or where the cuts were, is if I get real dirty. No dirt sticks to these scars. You can't see the scar tissue [by] just looking at my legs. It is surely a miracle. It left my toes pulled down so that when I walk, instead of my toes being out straight they are doubled back. I walk right so that the toenails are in the bottom of my shoes. I have to keep my toenails trimmed close all the time. [I] can't let my toenails grow long at all.

"The winter Father worked [at] the sugar-beet factory in Delta, there was so much influenza. He and one other man were the only two men in the whole town of Delta that didn't have the flu. They went from home to home doing chores, taking care of [the] sick, and helping bury those that died. It was almost six weeks that our whole family, other than Father, was down with the flu. None of our family died; we all survived the flu."[21]

CORA HAIGHT COX

Cora Haight Cox was born on 15 January 1894 in Cedar City. She also lived in Orderville, Cane Beds, Rockville, and Salt Lake City. She gives further light on medical treatments: "I was a very healthy baby until I had scarlatina [scarlet fever] when I was five years old. It was not known that there was scarlatina in the country [area] then. About a week after we [had] visited in Cedar City, I had a rash break out on my chest. Carpenters who were working there said, 'It could not be scarlatina.' They never had [seen] it in that light. My mother let me go out and play. I took [came down with a] cold and was sick at that time. Mother had a hard time [trying] to save me.

"I was sick two weeks. After that, I was left with complications. I had St. Vitus Dance. That same year there were two or three others in Cedar City [who] were afflicted with St. Vitus Dance. Mother said the two children who died were not as bad as I was. She took very good care of me. She would not let anyone in the room to speak above a whisper. . . .

"My youngest sister [Lillian Bell Haight] was very ill with typhoid fever. I stayed home from school quite a bit. I was in the eighth grade and I should have been [at] school, but I stayed home and sat by her bed and took care of her while she was ill for three weeks. My mother was so busy. She had another one with typhoid fever, and there was another one just about to come down with it. She said, 'Sarah, we cannot afford to have you come down with typhoid fever, too. We have to break it up.' Three children with typhoid fever would be a terrible thing. She gave her something that broke it up and put onions on her for a poultice to draw the fever out. My sister Sarah was even delirious with the fever and had the brown stripe on her tongue that was indicative of that disease. She was cured of it in three days.

"That was quite an experience. My sister [Sarah] nearly died with the typhoid fever. When she [became] so bad and bloated, the doctors almost gave her up. They called in the elders and she was administered to. Her fever left soon after that and never did rise again. That was certainly a testimony that the administration worked."[22]

JULIA MAY WILLIAMS WILKINSON

Julia May Williams Wilkinson was born on 9 May 1890 in Kanarraville, Iron County, near New Harmony, Washington County. She tells a story that could happen as easily today as then: "When my oldest son was a little boy, he swallowed a shingle nail. I was very worried. He was about six when he swallowed [it]. I don't know how in the world he came to it, unless he put things into his mouth. I don't know what else. I prayed and prayed and the doctor said to give him whipped potatoes. He lived on potatoes until he [was] rid of that shingle nail.

"I was very grateful for my blessing [and] having my prayers answered. When he was a young boy, he went to Mutual one night. He was playing outside with the youngsters. It was the fall of the year, and they had some pine nuts, [and] they had given him a few. He was laughing and cutting up with the rest of [the youngsters]. He came home in a little while. I said, 'Lex, what are you doing home so soon?' He said, 'Mom, I hate to tell you this, but I've inhaled a pine-nut shell [in] my lung.' I said, 'Oh, no!'

"I was so frightened. I called the drug store to ask my brother-in-law to see if my husband happened to be there. He used to go down there and talk to him quite a bit. My brother-in-law, Mike McCormick, said, 'Julia, Percy wasn't here. What is wrong?' I told him and he said, 'I'll [go] right out and find him, and I'll send him home.' He sent Percy home. When he came, I said, 'What will we do?' He said, 'Get a doctor.' We called Dr. Prestwich. My husband had a brother living in Cedar [City] who was a doctor, but he happened to be in Salt Lake on business, so we called Dr. Prestwich. [He] said,

'We can't operate here. We don't have the [equipment] to do [it]. I would advise you to get in touch with your brother, the doctor, in Salt Lake. You have a lot of confidence in him, and he will do all he can for you.' He said, 'Have this boy develop a cough, and one of you give him a right-smart slap on the back when he coughs, and that will probably jar [the shell], and he might [cough] it up.' So that is what we did. He said, 'You [should] get [in] touch with your brother right [away], Percy. If there is anything I can do, I'd be glad to do it.' He left, and we called Dr. Wilkinson in Salt Lake. He told us to be sure this boy developed a cough and slap him on the back when he coughed.

"I stayed right there with my son all night and lay down on the bed by him. Every time he coughed, I would give him a smart slap on the back. The next morning I was up early, and my husband went to work. I couldn't keep off my knees. I felt like I had to be on my knees praying every minute. We didn't have a big home, just a few rooms. I would kneel down in our dining room. Finally, my son called and he said, 'Mom, come in here to pray. I want to hear you pray.' I knelt down by his bed and did my praying. I fasted and prayed all morning long.

"At noon, his father came home for his lunch. He said, 'How is Lex?' I said, '[He] still has the pine-nut shell.' He said, 'What should we do, should we call the doctor?' I said, 'I would call Dr. Wilkinson and let him know how he is.' While we were talking, Dr. Wilkinson called us from Salt Lake. [He] said, 'I want you to put this boy on a bus and send him to Salt Lake. I was coming home today, but I'll stay over and meet [him] at the bus [station], and I'll take care of him. I'll take him to the clinic, and we will do all we possibly can for him. I'll do for him just like I would my own son.'

"We were talking about it, and Lex started coughing. I ran into the other room to give him a slap on the back. He looked up at me and smiled and said, 'Mom, here is the pine-nut shell.' I said, 'Thank [you], Heavenly Father for that.' I ran to the other room and said, 'Daddy, Lex got rid of his pine-nut shell. I've never seen anything work out quite that fast.' We were all very grateful."[23]

JESSIE HELEN JENNINGS GIBSON

Jessie Helen Jennings Gibson, born on 30 April 1887 in Rockville, gives this short memory: "I had pneumonia when I was around ten. That winter was a wet winter, and we didn't have enough money to buy all the [overshoes] and things that we needed for the family. My feet were wet most of the time, and that is how I [came down with] pneumonia.

"I don't remember any part of it except the first day and then toward the [end] when it was about the last of it. I was unconscious a lot of the time. I remember that first day. I came home from school early and [had] my lessons ready for the next day. Around sundown I was tired and decided I would lie down and go to sleep [so that] when it was time to get supper, I would be ready to help. When I woke up, I had a high fever, headache, and pain in my lungs. That was the first of the pneumonia. I didn't remember any more until [I was] nearly [over it]. We didn't have doctors. Most of the doctoring was done by handywomen who had families of their own and learned a lot of [information] that way, practical nursing. My side was sore where they plastered it. They used plasters. I don't know what they put in them."[24]

CHLOE GENEVA "GENNIE" VAN LOWEN BUNDY

Here is a story not likely to be heard today. It is about the Arizona Strip and the well-known Bundy family. Chloe Geneva "Gennie" Van Lowen Bundy was born on 12 July 1888. She lived in Douglas, Arizona, and the Mormon colonies in Mexico before moving to the Arizona Strip, the high-cattle country immediately south of Utah, near the Colorado River. She married James Bundy in 1909 in Arizona, and they moved to the strip. Her story is one of many births—fourteen of them. "I was happy to be pregnant each time because [when] my first boy [was] born, the doctors told me that I could never have any more. [They said] that I must not have any more if I wanted to live. They told my mother and my husband [these things]. I did not know anything about [this] for three or four months. When my mother told me what they had told them, that I was not to have any more, I just laughed at them. I said, 'Do you know that the Lord wants me to have a lot of babies? I am going to have a lot of babies. . . . '

"We did. We had this other baby coming, and we were very happy about it. We came down here to St. George to be where there was a good doctor. He was born on the same day that my last baby was born on. William Fay was [born] on February 12, 1916. This [baby] was born on February 12,

1918. [It was] the day that [the previous] baby was two years old. I said, 'His name is to be Lincoln.' His name was Lincoln Delmar.[25]

"As time went on, I was pregnant again in another two years. Each two years I had a baby coming. This time it was another baby boy. [His name was] Denven Lavar. I had been very miserable all the way through [this pregnancy]. My husband thought he should get us into St. George, where we could have a good doctor. I kept telling him that I could not stand to go, but he said that I would have to try. He fixed up springs and mattresses and pillows, and he got me onto them. We went four or five miles, and I said to my mother, 'I cannot go another step. Have Daddy turn around and take me back home.' She insisted that he do that.

"He turned around and started back when I said, 'Mother, get me off of here. The baby is coming and I cannot stand it. I cannot take it.' My husband threw off a mattress and got me off onto it, and the baby came. [It came] with a heavy profusion of flow and some terribly large chunks. [I] passed out. I did not know anything more about it. I was inspired to have a bundle fixed. Being a nurse like I had been, I had everything fixed. My mother took care of the baby. My daddy sent one of the children on a horse and across the valley to get Martin Iverson. He had always been a horse doctor, and he came and helped Mother to fix me up. He fixed the baby up and wrapped it up. Then they put the lines or ropes right around the mattress and hoisted me, mattress and all, right up on the wagon. Then Mother told Daddy to take us home and do it fast. There was a heavy thunderstorm coming up. Daddy got those horses into shape and took off. [He was] lashing them every step of the way to go [faster]. Mother held my hand [and felt] my pulse all the time. [She] was very much worried because she could not feel a pulse. I did not know anything about this."

After her fourteenth baby was born in 1932, she made these comments: "We knew that would [be the] finish because I was past forty-five years old. That had been a good many years that I had put in having [and] raising babies. I am just seventeen years and six months older than my oldest child, and now I was forty-five [years old]. That had been a good many years [for] babies. During the time of having my family, I had acted as midwife to a good many others. I had brought a good many babies [into the world] while nursing. [Also, I was] taking care of different accidents and hurts and all, [and] it had taken me in all different ways. [I had gone] by horseback and cars. One time my husband had to put me in the back of the truck because the snow was so heavy and deep that it would not track . . . This was not a money-making job. I never [received] anything. I never made any charge. Sometimes, some of them would give me something, but it was just a help [to them]. We went on living there."[26]

LUCINDA ESTELLA HALL REIDHEAD JACKSON

Lucinda Estella Hall Reidhead Jackson was born on 17 February 1890 in Washington City. She lived in several other towns. She tells of a childbirth situation: "When my first baby was born, he went into colic convulsions when he was two weeks old. He [would] just go from [one] convulsion [to] another. He had two hard convulsions and the midwife that I had, she gave up. She said, 'If he has another [one], he will never live through it.' She had done everything she could for him and nothing did any good. My father was there, so my father and her husband administered to my baby and named him. He seemed to be better, but only for just a few hours, and then he [became] sore again.

"She spent all of her time with him. I was sitting in my chair by the bed, and I had my baby on the pillow. He was a very little baby. I said that I had some [of this solution] that is already prepared. But she didn't want to give it to him because she was afraid that she shouldn't. I said that it wouldn't hurt him. My mother raised us on that from the time we were born. It won't hurt. So she said, 'If you want to be responsible for it, why go ahead.' So I had her bring me a half a cup of water and a little bit of sugar. I put this appetite in it. I had cut it in brandy. I put a little bit in that water and fed that to him with a spoon, as much as I could when I found him aroused so he could swallow. From then on, he got better. I was forty-five miles from a doctor, and I didn't have a cent of money to send for a doctor."[27]

HANNAH ELIZABETH HEATON ROUNDY

Hannah Elizabeth Heaton Roundy was born on 29 December 1894 in Orderville, and also lived in Alton and Panguitch. She had thirteen births and many of them died. Her husband, Myron Ervin Roundy, ran sheep and farmed. She tells of a wagon trip that was nearly a disaster: "It was when my second child was just a baby in arms, and he was taking us back and forth so much. He came to me one day and said, 'Hannah, would you like to go to Moccasin and help put up your mother's fruit?' They had fruit out there. 'Take some bottles [jars] of your own to fill. If you do, I will take you out, and you can fill some for yourself and help with your mother's.' We went out and got our bottles all filled. My sister, Clarissa [Amy], went with us. When we [were] ready to come home he brought [us] back [in] two wagons. One of our cousins was out there, a girl, [so] my sister, Clarissa, and this girl drove one of the wagons with just one team. Daddy had loaded it up with melons, fruit, and [items] like that to bring back to the people in Alton. The outfit he drove was a double-bedded wagon and had two teams, one lead team like they have. He had it quite heavily loaded. One of the horses in the lead team wasn't broke right good. They had to handle him a little [more] carefully, but we got along just fine until we stopped at Yellow Jacket [Kane County, Utah] at noon. Father said, 'Hannah, you sit still with the children.' We had my little baby brother in the wagon with Areta. 'You sit still and keep the children in the wagon until I get the horses undone so we won't scare this new horse.' We just sat there and kept quiet.

"He undid the tugs and the snaps to the reins, then stepped back and went to pull the line over that lead horse's back. It scared the horse [and] he just whirled and kicked Father. He went in the air and came right down on his chest and neck. [The horse] broke and ran loose from the other horses. The other horses just stood there. Father was lying there, unconscious. The girls, when they drove up, saw it, and they came running up [to] where I was. I jumped out and laid the baby down beside my little brother and Areta and told them to watch him. We worked with Daddy all we could—did all we could think of doing. [We were] out there in the hills and timber and wilderness [with] no help whatsoever. [With] that fractious, unbroken horse, and Daddy in that condition—I said, 'The thing to do is to pray.' We just put our arms around one another, stood over Daddy and just talked to the Lord the way I am talking to you. We told him our condition, [that] we were out there in the wilderness, miles and miles from anybody, [we prayed] for him to overrule for our good, [to] give us the wisdom to know what to do and what was for the best. We begged for assistance the best we could ask in those conditions.

"We worked with him awhile. Finally, one of us went out around the horse, worked it back to the other horses, and got him standing there kind of calm by the horses. We decided that we would try to get them hooked up again. We hadn't eaten a bite, hadn't given the horses a drink, or a bite of hay. We traveled all before noon in the hot weather and sand country. We finally got the horse turned around like it should be with the rest of the horses. One of us stood without hands holding his bits, while the others checked him up, hooked up the tugs, and got the line all back in shape. One of us stood there and held that, while the other two of us got Daddy up in the wagon. I can't understand it to this day, [but] I think it was the power of the Lord. We knew Daddy was unconscious [and] didn't realize a thing, but he would not lie down. He was going to sit in that seat. I just left the little children in the back of the wagon, and I sat there with my arms around him. He insisted on holding the lines. We drove along exception-ally good, but every once in a while he would say, 'Where are we going? I can't see any; we are out traveling this time of night. Where did we come from and where are we headed for?' [He asked] different questions like that, all the way along the road.

"When we came to the Mount. Carmel dugway, the old-time dugway from Kanab down into Long Valley—I guess you don't know anything about what it used to be like—but it was just a one-wagon, rough road. It was just wide enough for a wagon to go along; that was all. When we were going down the hill, Father would always adjust his brakes, tighten his brakes and the brake blocks so the wagon wouldn't roll onto the horses and cause trouble. I knew Daddy always did this, so I just sat there, almost shaking and praying that things would turn out alright. I had planned on all I could. If I could get him to sit in the wagon, to stop the horses and then get down myself, because I had watched him do it, adjust the brakes myself, but he wouldn't let me, not on your life. He got down out of the wagon, crawled under there, and adjusted those brakes himself. He got up and drove the horses down that dugway just as good as he ever did.

"We crossed the creek, and just after we crossed the creek, a man on horse-back—and it was dark—came off a side-hill, greeted us and we knew him. I told him what had happened. He said, 'I will get around by the side of your daddy.' He turned and went around the wagon and rode right along the side of Daddy until we got to the Green, a little ranch just up on the [Virgin] River from the dugway. His brother lived there, and they happened to be threshing, with an old-time horse-powered thresher. They were four or five men there with their teams. They had stopped there for supper when we drove up. This Brother Allred, [who had] come along with us, got off his horse, ran in the house, and told them that he needed some help, that Brother Heaton had [been] hurt. Half a dozen of them came running out there, picked Daddy up and took [him] into the house. He just went—just like a dead man. They didn't think he would live until morning. Uncle Alvin [Heaton], Father's brother just younger than him, said, 'He is alive, but I don't know how long he is going to be alive.' He was that way all night, but in the morning he rallied. How we got down that dugway with him like that, and then going off completely just as soon as he got where there was help—I just can't understand, unless it was the power of the Lord. He had answered our prayers."[28]

OREN RUESCH

Oren Ruesch was born on 29 December 1894 and lived in Springdale, Virgin, and Mount Trumbull. He tells about the many floods on the Virgin River in Springdale: "It was terrible. They didn't have a way to build dams to make them stay. Usually every flood that would come would take out the dam. We would have to build it again. I helped build a lot of them.

"I had one experience when we were working on Mt. Trumbull. We had a boy [Jay Ruesch] who wasn't well when he was born. He had a growth in his throat. We administered to him. He had twenty-four convulsions in one night. He had this growth or something in his throat; we administered to him and he bled. [When it was over,] his ears bothered him awfully bad.

"When we were out on the mountain, he was two years old. We got up one morning and my wife noticed swelling on the back of his ear. I told my boss, 'We have got to get this boy to a doctor.' The car's gas tank had a hole in it. The gas had leaked out. There wasn't any other car on the mountain. The only thing [available] was a team and wagon. [It] would have been a three-day journey. We said, 'We can't wait three days. That [swelling] has to be lanced.' We felt his head and there was a soft place on the back of his ear. Brother Stout and his wife and my wife and I went into the house and wrapped up the boy on her lap. Walter [took] a hold of his hands, and his wife [took] a hold of his feet. They just held him so that he couldn't move. I had a good sharp pocketknife; I never carried any other kind. This one had a blade about that long.

"Yes. I wrapped the knife in cloth so there was only about that much of the blade showing, so that I couldn't make a mistake and injure him. I also used a razor to help cut it. We lanced it and [the swelling] was green when it opened. The stink was terrible. We cleaned it out, [put] a piece of gauze into it, and it never did close up again. It healed like that, only he had ear trouble from then until he died.

"Another [fellow] came out on the mountain after a load of lumber. He had his front-load wagon loaded and was going to pull a back wagon. He had a four-horse outfit. He [was] down guiding the shoe over the winch on the front wagon [and] he missed the winch. His horse pulled it, [and] he broke his collarbone. He was eighty miles from nowhere. Walter Stout and I took him to the house, and we set his shoulder and bound him up [with] tape. He stayed there until we [went] home so he could get his outfit home. We had two other fellows that had quinsy or throat trouble, and we lanced both of their throats. Anybody who had it couldn't breathe.

"One of my boys, Clair [Ruesch], who is next to the youngest [of those] that [are] alive, was living in Virgin. [He] was walking around on stilts. He attempted to kick a hoop off from the gate out in front so he could get out. He missed it, tipped over backwards, and broke his wrist. I set his wrist and told him I was going to take him to the doctor. He said, 'No. I don't want to go to the doctor. You and Uncle Alma [Flanigan] can administer to me.' We set it and when he took [off] the splints, he was getting along [well].

"He went out to a party one night, the girls pushed him over, and broke it again. I said, 'This spells a trip to the doctor.' He said, 'No, I won't go to the doctor.' He was eight or ten years old. I said, 'This is going to hurt this time.' I got a push-stick board, and [the wrist] was bent down like that. I [found] a pretty stiff board and put it along that one wooden bend, and another one on the other side. I said, 'We are going to have to do this up good and tight,' and we did. He is all right.

"I have had both of my wrists broken. We had an old fellow in Springdale who set [one of] my wrists. For the other one, I went to a doctor, but it is not straight."[29]

GEORGE CHAMP HENRIE

George Champ Henrie was born in Panguitch on 12 April 1912. He gave a brief report about recovering from pneumonia: "In my sixth year I had typhoid [fever] and pneumonia together. They told my folks they did not think I would ever make it. But I did. I was probably stubborn enough. When I went to school, they would make me come home and sit on a chair. It went on that way for a couple of years. Father and his two brothers—one brother was president of the stake, and the other brother was a bishop— [were] talking about it. They [thought] I was so weak, and I was not any good anyway. They decided to have me take exercises. They had me get up early in the mornings and walk around the house. This went on for years. When I quit, I was running around the house thirty-seven times.

"I think [exercise] is what happened. I carried that weak heart for a long time, and I outgrew it. I always thought it was the exercise [that strengthened] it more than anything else. It was decided among the three brothers. They thought something had to be done, and that is what they decided to do, which was against the belief of the doctor. But it worked."[30]

NEUCILE BOYTER HENRIE

Another account of self-treatment is from Champ Henrie's wife, Neucile Boyter Henrie. She was born on 26 December 1917, also in Panguitch. "After Champ and I had been married about five years, we were expecting our third baby. We had two little boys [Jerold George and James Carl Henrie] and while they were [very] dear to us, we really wanted a baby girl so much. Champ's only sister [Fern Henrie] died when he was a young boy, and he could not remember her. We wanted a little baby girl so badly. When our third baby was born, it was a little girl [Florence Henrie]. She was a little angel. She had a lot of black hair and was so cute. But she had a little twisted foot, which took a lot of the [joy], not the joy, but you could not help but have feeling for it. The doctors told us not to feel too badly about it and not to worry about it because lots of things could be done [to correct it]. As soon as she was old enough, [the] doctors would put her little foot in a cast, and she would soon be able to walk. But we still felt bad, and I can remember, as I lay in bed, I would rub [her] little foot and hold it. We did not go to hospitals. We had the elders and we prayed about it. By the time she was able to walk, she was like any other child."[31]

JOSEPH HILLS JOHNSON JR.

Joseph Hills Johnson Jr. was born on 25 July 1891 in Johnson, Kane County. He lived in Tropic, and he went to school to the eighth grade there. He reports on the problems he had riding to school: "I was working for my board. I had seven cows to milk, thirteen horses to feed, pigs and [other animals to care for]. We had to be at school at 8:45 [in the morning]. On a cold morning in December, I went out and milked [the] cows and got ready to go to school. I tried to move the buggy, but it had been a cold night. I hadn't greased the wheels of the buggy, and the wheels wouldn't turn. I had to pry them off and get some grease on so the wheels on the buggy would turn. I had to take two girls to school. When I [arrived] there, I tied the horse up and [went into] school just as the class was commencing. I ran up to the stove [because] I felt so cold. The teacher came along and I said, 'Mr. Snyder, I won't be able to do very much English this morning.' He said, 'What is the matter?' I said, 'My hands are so numb I can't hold a pencil.' He looked at me and jerked me away from the stove and took me outside of the building. [He] called someone else, and they rubbed my hands in the snow for nearly a half-hour, it seemed to me. They were frozen, just frozen stiff. That was about December 17 or 18. My hands were frozen. I suffered with that more than any particular suffering I have gone through, I guess.

"One hand was just [white]; there wasn't any color in it. It was completely frozen. I had a glove on that hand. The hand that was uncovered I had been using more, and it wasn't quite so frozen. I went to the doctor with those frozen hands, and he fixed them up as best he could. [He] put them in oil and wrapped them in cotton, and I was required to hold my hands above my head to ease the pain. I had to hold them up over my head for two or three days. I stayed with the family, my sister, and her family up at the fort. I sent the horse back to [the person] he belonged to, and I stayed there at the fort for two or three days. I went to the doctor several times, and he would treat my hands again.

"There was about three feet of snow on the ground at that time. We were about eighty miles from home and were rather homesick. George Graff, who was from Cannonville [Garfield County], and I decided we would like to go home. We arranged for horses and he saddled my horse for me. I [mounted] and hooked the reins over my arms [with] my hands up; I had to hold my hands up for any relief at all, and we went single file over those miles to Panguitch [Garfield County]. [It was] nearly forty miles, I guess. [It] was just a narrow trail in that snow. We [arrived in] Panguitch that night and stayed in the hotel. The next morning, we [mounted] our horses and went on to Tropic. [We were] within about a mile of Tropic and met a delegation that was coming out to meet me. They had heard that I was coming. They had been calling Panguitch [and] knew that we had been there. [They] told me that [my] father had died. It was a shock. I didn't know that anything was wrong. I had never heard of anything. When he was on a mission in the Southern states, he had contracted malaria. Just as regular as the spring months would come around, he would have a relapse."[32]

WILLIAM NUTTER HINTON

Here is a really short account by William Nutter Hinton, who was born on 4 October 1889 in Virgin and reported from an experience in Colonia Morales, Mexico. "A wagon must [have] run over my foot and smashed it while I was in Mexico. There were no doctors. [We] just put salve [on it]. [We put] wagon dope on it [and] kept it bandaged. I guess [we did that for] two or three weeks. It [was] all right. My mother took care of it."[33]

JOSEPH WOODRUFF HOLT

This is a brief account of self-treatment by Joseph Woodruff Holt, who was born on 25 August 1885 on Holt Ranch near Gunlock. "I was at summer school up at Mountain Meadows. The next year, I was back with Arlo Higgins again. I had a teacher by the name of Shockman. He was [of] German nationality. He was another very well-educated man, I thought. He was kind of musically inclined too, but he didn't try to get me to sing. He was also kind of a doctor, setting bones and so forth. I had one wrist broken while he was there, and he set it for me. I also had what they call a carbuncle right on my arm there. The first one came on the back of my neck. I got the blood out of that some way or other. I had another one come around the back of the neck. It was the darndest place to lance. But he lanced it and did a very good job of it. The next one I [had] come on after school; [it] was out right on the arm here [and was] about the size of a hen's egg. My father had to lance that." Joseph also said that he had several broken bones, and some were not set because no doctor was available.[34]

WILLIAM VAUGHN JONES

William Vaughn Jones was also born on Holt's Ranch and lived in Hebron, Gunlock, Pine Valley, Grass Valley, and Veyo. He was born on 7 January 1900 and says, "I suppose that I had a touch of the same disease that my mother had. At least I remember that up to the age of six and maybe past, I used to carry a bottle of cough medicine in my pocket all the time. I had a bad cough most of the time, and I would have to take a swallow of this cough medicine often. I might mention that one of the things my step-mother did for me was one of the best things that could have happened to me. We were limited in space in our living quarters, and quite often it was necessary that we boys would sleep out in a tent or some place in the open. I think that was the best thing that could have happened to me, and I overcame the cough."[35]

JOHN MATTHEW HUNT

John Matthew Hunt was born also in Hebron, but two decades earlier, in 1878. He described the health of a young boy: "I was very fortunate in accidents most of the time. While I was growing up, I used to break wild horses when they were two or three years old. I used to do a lot of riding. In fact, the boys around Old Hebron [had] me break the horses so they could ride them. One time after our fields opened up, we used to turn the horses in the fields above Old Hebron, there was [one] horse [that] was kind of a dogey, [a bad-looking] horse. Three of us boys were going up there after the cows. We were walking up there, talking, and this horse was standing still. We noticed it standing [there] sound asleep, and he didn't know we were there. I told the boys, just like all other boys would do, 'Just watch me. I will get on him before he wakes up.' I jumped up onto him, kind of on the stomach, just threw my leg over. He thought some animal had him, and he started to buck. He threw me up in the air. I came back and kind of threw a little bone out on this leg. It has never been put back, and I can't bend it now like I should.

"I had measles when I was about seven or eight years old and got through that okay. That was about all the sickness I had, outside maybe chickenpox and other diseases that didn't amount to much in [those] days. I had typhoid fever when I was twenty years old. That really about got me. It left me with big veins in this leg. I have always had to wrap my leg, [from] my ankle up to my knee, to keep the veins from swelling and [giving] me [pain]. The doctor over in Cedar wanted to operate on [the veins], but I didn't let him. The specialist came down from Salt Lake and examined my leg. He said it was a good thing I didn't because mine was the type that an operation would injure it more than do [any] good. So I never [had] it operated on."[36]

GWENDOLYN BRYNER SCHMUTZ

Gwendolyn Bryner Schmutz was born in 1898 and lived in Lund, Nevada. She gave another brief experience: "After Papa died, this was still in Lund, Nevada, Mother was out chopping wood, milking cows, and taking care of the outdoor chores. She brought in an armful of wood. Usually, she took care of those things on Saturday. But something had happened, and she didn't get to do it Saturday and had to do it Sunday morning. As she brought in the wood, I was sitting on the floor getting dressed. I went to the door screaming that something was biting me. Mother came running in. A scorpion had been brought in with the wood that morning. This was wood that had been brought down from the hill. I remember she got a heavy towel and actually pulled [the scorpion] off of my foot. It had bitten me. I can still remember the swelling that came up on [my] foot that [the] scorpion [bit].

"It was very painful. We happened to live next door to a neighbor, John Whipple. Mother called him and he came over the fence. They called a group in and administered to me. I was unconscious for three days. They held a prayer circle. It was in the wintertime. They had a tub of ice water and a tub of hot water, and they moved me from one to the other to try to overcome the effects. I remember they gave me brandy. They had to do something to counteract the poison. I[t] was like I was drunk. I remember feeling that Mother always regretted it, but they had to do something, and finally, I awakened. They had tried for three days and had someone sit right over me constantly. I don't know how many times I had been administered to. Everyone in the town had held prayer circle for me."[37]

MARY JANE MORRIS TRUMAN HOLT

Mary Jane Morris Truman Holt was born on 14 March 1896 in Hamblin, near Mountain Meadows. She lived at Holt's Ranch and in Enterprise, Pine Valley, and Grass Valley. She went to the eighth grade in Enterprise and later went to Salt Lake City for a year's training to be a nurse. She gives some insights on health from a nurse's view in southern Utah.

"Holt's Ranch is between Enterprise and Mountain Meadows. Mother went there to teach school [the] winter of 1896. Papa went to Pine Valley and bought a log house and tore it down. As he was tearing it down, he marked every log so that he could remember [how] to put it back [together]. He hauled it to Enterprise. He rebuilt the house that winter while Mama was teaching school. He took the money that she made to buy the nails, the windows, and the doors [for] the house. He finished it up [as] school let out on the last day of February, and I was born on March 14, 1896."

In her interview she also described her schooling and then her life as a nurse in Enterprise: "We didn't have doctors, we just had midwives. I delivered more than 200 [babies]. I kept track of [over] 200, and then the doctors started to [deliver babies]. Doctor Graff and Doctor Prestwick from Cedar City would come over and deliver the babies. I would take care of the [baby and mother] afterwards. At that time, the mother stayed in bed ten days. You had to bathe [the mother for] ten mornings and bathe the baby [for] ten mornings. So it was a big job after the baby was born. . . . There used to be a lot of trouble with milk leg, a painful swelling of the leg soon after childbirth due to thrombosis of the large vein. The mothers were weak when they started trying to get around. Now there are different ways to take care of the mothers. We didn't know anything [then] if they started hemorrhaging. Nowadays, they don't worry about that because they can stop [it], or give them a blood transfusion if they need it. All we knew [then] was to keep them lying quiet."[38]

MARIAH DELILA VAN LEUVEN ALLDREDGE

Mariah Delila Van Leuven Alldredge was born on 11 November 1882 in Aurora, Sevier County, Utah. She married Isaac "Ike" Alldredge from Deseret in Millard County, and they roamed Mesquite, Hinckley, and several other places. Ike wanted to farm, but he also did blacksmithing and mining, always looking for employment, but he always wanted to get back to Deseret to farm. They went back there, but didn't have a place to live. She said they moved every month. She tells of the illness of her son Verl.

"The [children caught] the whooping cough in school, and he was subject to croup. When he [caught] the whooping cough from them, he also had croup with it. He went into acute pneumonia. Three different doctors said it was impossible for him to live. I sat up in bed with him up over my shoulder for three weeks. I never lay down. I was just sitting up with him over my shoulder. If I laid him down, he would go as black as black. He couldn't get his breath at all. I lived under prayer constantly for him. He couldn't eat anything. He was eighteen months old at this time. He had forgotten how to walk. He [was] so weak he couldn't walk. His little eyes were just set back in his head. It just looked like it was impossible for him to live. There was a man [who] went by in his wagon [with] a load of hay. He went home and told his wife, 'Sister Alldredge's baby won't live tonight. I can hear him breathing clear out in the street.' He was breathing so hard. We had him out under the tree where he could get more oxygen, more air.

"That night, the ward teacher came. He came alone that night. I don't know why he didn't have a partner with him, but he was alone. He was a wonderful man. He said, 'Sister Alldredge, is there anything I can do for you?' I said, 'Yes. I wish you would administer to my baby.' So he did, and while he administered to him, the baby opened his eyes and smiled. That was the first change he took for the better. His name was Charles Woodbury. Verl began to get better from then on. That was the first night that he slept normally. For weeks he hadn't slept, hardly a bit. I just held him constantly in my arms. I didn't dare lay him down.

"My husband's sister [Susie Alldredge Theobald] was a first-class nurse, almost the same as a doctor. She put him in what they called a creosote steam. She put him under that two or three times to bring him back to life.

He went right off as black and dark. She put an umbrella over him, covered this up with a sheet, and put the creosote steam under it, and that would be [like] an oxygen tent. In those days they didn't [have] oxygen like they have nowadays. That was his oxygen tent. That would bring him back to life again. She brought him back three times that way. Oh, if I didn't have something to go through! I went down until I weighed 112 pounds. People can't believe it. Like my sister, she finally took a picture of me as I was working one day. It was so horrible! I was just hysterical, but I was going through something to make me that way.

"Verl became better from then on. It left him with hard breathing for months. My brother Ed and his wife [Dorothy Van Leuven] came over from Eureka to visit me. He said, 'Oh my land, Sis, I would take that [baby] to the doctor right now.' I said, 'He is well. He is well now.' 'Well and breathing like that?' I said, 'Yes, it is getting lighter. I think eventually he will come out of it. His breathing is getting better, and that sound is getting less.' It did, and after a few months he could breathe naturally. But he had that for a long time.

"That was a great testimony. Because I tell Verl now, 'You were saved for something. You have eight lovely children. You performed a wonderful mission.' He had a boy on a mission and just now sent another one out. They are living the gospel as near as they can. He was faithful."[39]

MILO GOLDEN CAMPBELL

Milo Golden Campbell was born in Escalante in 1910 and later lived in St. George. His wife, Alporta Allen, gave birth to twelve children. He tells of a memorable experience about the birth of his oldest son Milo Kay: "I have a sad and great experience to tell about Kay. When it was time for him to come into the world, my wife was unable to have Kay. So my good doctor told me what the deal was [with her delivery]. We were in my brother's home in Richfield. He said, 'Milo, we can't save them both. Now which one do you want?' I said, 'Of course, I want my wife if that is the case.' He said, 'Let's you and I go into this bedroom and kneel down and have a word of prayer.' We went in there, and he took the lead in the prayer. He told the Lord that we wanted help.

"We came out, and I rolled my sleeves up with the nurse and the helper. We had a real scrap to take Kay. She did not dilate. When we finally got Kay into the world, we thought he was dead. [It] looked like we had pulled one eye out [and] pulled one arm out [of his socket]. His head was flat and he was a pitiful sight. The doctor started to work with him. I said, 'Oh, Doctor, don't save him. Don't save him. I don't want him to live as an invalid. There is no other way out.' He turned to me and he said, 'Milo, shame on you. Do you know we asked the Lord to help us? And that is not the half of it. I am a doctor. Where there is life, there is hope.' I said, 'There is no life.' He said, 'I don't know that yet.' He worked with that boy one solid hour before he [could get] a cry out of him.

"As that boy grew into manhood, he was a perfect specimen of a healthy athlete today. You can see his scars just a little."[40]

ALPORTA CAMPBELL

Milo's wife, Alporta, also born in 1910, gives her version of the same story: "Milo Kay Campbell, our oldest son, was born in Richfield at [John] Larvin [Campbell], Milo's oldest brother's home, [on] September 4, 1932. The doctor was Otto L. Anderson, an osteopath physician in Richfield. When I started labor, they administered to me. Dr. Anderson was one of them that put his hand on. When they were trying to get the baby, they turned him three times, trying to get him and couldn't. So the doctor said, 'It is either the mother or the baby.' They would try [to] save one. So Milo said, 'For sure, I want you [to] save my wife.'

"They had the instruments laid out, sterilized, and ready. They were going to take the baby in pieces so they could save my life. The doctor said, 'Let's try once more.' He stood up on the bed, and Margaret and Milo held me down. This time they got the baby, but in doing so, they were afraid they injured an eye. It was so swollen and bloody, and [they] had pulled his little arm out of place. By the time I saw him, he was quite dark and swollen. His little head was all out of shape. He was really quite a sight.

"When the doctor [delivered] him, he started dipping him in warm and cold water because there seemed to be no life. [He gave him] artificial respiration [and] said, 'Milo, there is one thing sure; he can't be normal. He has to be mentally retarded. We have simply injured him too badly.' Milo said, 'Why try to save him?' The doctor looked at him and said, 'Milo, we administered to your wife before we started. Not only my doctor's profession tells me to keep working, but my priesthood [does] also.' To Milo that was a very humbling experience. [Now] to see [Milo] Kay [today]—I guess he has been our very healthiest child, as normal as could be. To see him has been a real testimony of the power of the priesthood and what it can do for us."[41]

JOSEPH AURELIUS HASLAM

Joseph Aurelius Haslam was born on 28 December 1902 in Cedar City, but lived in Kanarraville. He tells of the impact of working in mines: "I got to where I needed a steady job, and I had to get out and look for work. I had a few cattle of my own and was mainly working to pay the fee bill for them. I couldn't work fast enough to do that. I leased them out and went out to Yerington, Nevada, and found a job in the Anaconda Copper Mine. It was an open-pit copper mine. I stayed there for about seventeen years. It was a pretty good job. They retired me from that job, and I came back to here to Kanarraville.

"My lungs are no good. Being in the rough dust gave me emphysema. There was quite a bit of quartzite in the mine. You run a drill and create a dust like that and that dust, raw and fresh, is the very worst kind. You are working right in it, and you have to breathe it. It is very hard on you. Since I retired, I am just no good. I can't do anything. I have a hard time to breathe all the time."[42]

VIALATE LEAVITT WEBB

Vialate Leavitt Webb was born in Gunlock on 6 July 1903. She recalls: "I remember quite distinctly after having had scarletina [scarlet fever] that my ears were so infected. They were running [discharge] for a long while after that. The doctors said that probably caused my eye and ear trouble all through life. It was not so much that my ears were hurting, but I can still remember [they] were running. After the folks moved to Las Vegas they took me to two doctors to see if they could stop [the discharge]. [That] was about 1907, I think. The doctors said that was probably the cause of my eye trouble. For a long time, my folks didn't seem to know what was my trouble. I can remember not getting as good marks as they had expected. I can remember being at the back of the room, and all at once the teacher invited me to come up to the front of the room, and I got along so much better. I could hear and see better. When I was about eight years old, [my parents bought] me some glasses. I wore glasses until I was grown, and then I decided they didn't look so good, so I went without them for a good many years. But when my sight began to get worse, I [wore] glasses again."[43]

ANNA CRAWFORD ISOM

Anna Crawford Isom was born on 7 August 1881 in Virgin. She married George Howard Isom and they had eleven children, two of whom died at childbirth. She tells about her mother and her son: "Mother had St. Vitus' [Dance]. It left her badly crippled, so she could not sew or write or do anything like that. They sent her to school [when] they thought she was over it. When she would take a pencil and start to write, it would flip across the room. She could not control it. She never tried to write after that. She [had] me do her writing sometimes when I was old enough. When she started to get better, she begged her father to pray for her to die. She did not want to go through life like this. He said, 'I cannot do it, now, you will get well.' She said. 'I will try.' So she tried, but she would soon be back praying to die again. Finally, he said, 'I am going to dedicate you to the Lord. Let him do as he pleases about it.' He placed his hands upon her head and was going to ask the Lord to take her. He said he was surprised when he put his hands on her head. The first words he said were, 'You will get well.' She began to mend from there."

After she married, her son had muscular dystrophy. She said, "There are very few who have died from it. They live through. He [was ill for] twelve years. George wanted the boys to stand him up on his feet. He said, 'I believe if I could get onto my feet, then I could stand.' So the boys took him on one side and one the other and lifted him up. But he could not stand at all. He said, 'It is twelve years since I [have been] on my feet.' That is one trial this boy has had to go through. Wayne had that proud spirit that his father had. He hated to give up. When he found he had to give up, then he [did] it in the right spirit. I think Wayne has really done wonderfully to try to accept what he could not avoid."[44]

LAVON LEFEVRE JONES

LaVon LeFevre Jones was born on 12 October 1909 in the Uinta Basin, but moved to a farm in Washington Fields with his family. He told of his little brother, who was a year younger: "When he was twelve years old, he had appendicitis. Of course, we always blamed it on the pomegranates. We had a lot of pomegranates around the place, and he ate lots of pomegranates. We thought maybe the seeds got caught in his appendix. That was the story we heard from Father. Nobody knew how to operate, and he got gangrene, and it killed him."

After LaVon married, he moved to Bundyville on the Arizona Strip. He recounted an accident while cutting down trees to build his home there: "As [the tree] went down, it forced the bottom of the trunk around, and it broke loose from the one I had cut, and came towards me. I backed up, and it stood me right against the one that had been cut before and pinned me in there. [It] broke my leg; broke that bone right off above my ankle and pinned me there. It didn't hurt at the time because it was so numb. I could reach the axe—I still had it close—and I took the axe and pried and prayed, and prayed and pried at the same time and got free. I hopped on my horse and unhooked the tugs. Just as soon as I stepped on my foot, it just went like that, and I knew it was broken. I hopped over and made the tugs on the horse, jumped on him, and went down to where I had the other horse hobbled, down by the wagon. We had him hobbled [and] grazing. I turned him loose so he would tag me, [didn't want] to leave him up there alone, and then I headed for civilization. I had to go up a hill half a mile or so before I [could] start down to the closest sawmill.

"The pain started to show up and it was getting so that I passed out and could feel that I was going to black [out]. . . . I got to the top, and it was steep from [there] down for seven miles or better. The horse would walk [and] throw [jog back and forth] him like horses do. Every time he threw it, that was hitting [the] bone, and I was about to fall off a dozen times and crawl in, but I knew I couldn't get there that way. So I stuck it out. I went down to the sawmill where LaVon Stout was working. He went down and got Ervin Woods, [who] had an old 1929 model Chevy, which was a good car in those days. He came up and took me down to Bundyville, where we lived. I had a 1929 Ford Coupe down there. My wife [drove us] to St. George. It took us seven hours to come in because she had to go slow [because of the] pain. They laid me on the table at the hospital. Mary didn't think they made [plans] to touch anything, I guess. Anyhow, she shaved my leg while [the doctor] was getting ready to set it. [They] didn't give me an earthly thing! I had to hang [on] to keep from passing out."[45]

CONCLUSIONS

These Saints' biggest obstacle was maintaining health. The death of children, and sometimes mothers at childbirth, was common. Living in the small villages placed them out of reach of the few doctors most of the time. Accidents were a major problem, several involving horses. Many of them came from driving or riding on a wagon and then being thrown off and run over by a wheel. The result was a broken leg or shoulder, or worse. These were among the more severe problems, but most were dealt with without a hospital. There were also times when someone was accidentally shot by someone wielding a gun, but survived with intense family treatments. Snake bites were common. Usually, people were confined to bed and given various ointments and survived, but others died. Working in mines caused serious lung diseases. Homespun surgery such as lancing carbuncles sometimes worked, as did setting bones. Using natural smoky gum sometimes worked to heal severe cuts. Rubbing frozen bones with snow was better than using hot coals.

Birthing was a highlight in virtually every family, yet it was anticipated with some anxiety. Most children were born with the aid of a midwife. Midwives were also often sought out to help with ailments and accidents. Diseases were also common. The most dramatic was the flu epidemic of 1918. Knowledge about how diseases were spread was not available. It was natural for children to be infected with measles, whooping cough, scarlet fever, diphtheria, or pneumonia. Medical help was definitely limited. Almost everyone reported that they sought spiritual blessings for the sick. They told many tales of amazing recoveries which they attributed to priesthood blessings.

NOTES

1. Wesley P. Larsen, *Indian and Pioneer Medicinal Food & Plants* (Toquerville, UT: privately published, 2004), 163.

2. "Let the Doctors Alone," *Deseret News*, 24 October 1855, quoted in Larsen, *Indian and Pioneer Medicinal Food & Plants*, 71.

3. Larsen, *Indian and Pioneer Medicinal Food & Plants*, 71–72, 91.

4. Larsen, *Indian and Pioneer Medicinal Food & Plants*, 75–77.

5. Larsen, *Indian and Pioneer Medicinal Food & Plants*, 84.

6. Larsen, *Indian and Pioneer Medicinal Food & Plants*, 91.

7. Larsen, *Indian and Pioneer Medicinal Food & Plants*, 22.

8. Larsen, *Indian and Pioneer Medicinal Food & Plants*, 26.

9. Larsen, *Indian and Pioneer Medicinal Food & Plants*, 38.

10. Larsen, *Indian and Pioneer Medicinal Food & Plants*, 40.

11. Larsen, *Indian and Pioneer Medicinal Food & Plants*, 44.

12. Larsen, *Indian and Pioneer Medicinal Food & Plants*, 46. Dr. Larsen also published *Paiute Scrapbook*, 2001, a collection of essays and quotations from such people as John Wesley Powell, William R. Palmer, Alva Matheson, John Steele, Frederick S. Dellenbaugh, Thomas Moran and several more about the Native Americans in the Mojave Desert and their medical experiences.

13. Douglas D. Alder, *History of Health Care in Utah's Dixie*, ed. Terri Draper (St. George, UT: Dixie Regional Medical Center, 2003).

14. Susan Arrington Madsen, "Growing Up in Pioneer Utah," in *Nearly Everything Imaginable: The Everyday Life of Utah's Mormon Pioneers*, ed. Ronald W. Walker and Doris R. Dant (Provo, UT: BYU Studies, 1999), 324.

15. Jill Mulvay Derr, "I Have Eaten Everything Imaginable," in *Nearly Everything Imaginable*, 228.

16. Elliott West, *Growing Up in Twentieth-Century America: A History and Reference Guide* (Westport, CT: Greenwood Press, 1996).

17. West, *Growing Up in Twentieth-Century America*, 55.

18. Verna Mae Isom Gifford, VOR File 68-060.

19. Nancy Kokerhans VOR 69-146.

20. Alvin Carl Hardy, VOR File 68-126.

21. Edwin M. Hiatt, VOR File 68-069.

22. Cora Haight Cox, VOR File 68-135.

23. Julia May Williams Wilkinson, VOR File 68-023.

24. Jessie Helen Jennings Gibson, VOR File 68–137.

25. A book was recently written about Lincoln Bundy, a fighter pilot who was shot down in World War II. It is by Lyman Hafen, titled *Far from Cactus Flat*.

26. Chloe Geneva "Gennie" Van Lowen Bundy, VOR File 68-039.

27. Lucinda Estella Hall Reidhead Jackson, VOR File 69-139.

28. Hannah Elizabeth Heaton Roundy, VOR File 68-051.

29. Oren Ruesch, VOR File 68-002.
30. George Champ Henrie, VOR File 69-184.
31. Neucile Boyter Henrie, VOR File 69-184.
32. Joseph Hills Johnson Jr., VOR File 68-027.
33. William Nutter Hinton, VOR File 70-011.
34. Joseph Woodruff Holt, VOR File 68-009.
35. William Vaughn Jones, VOR File 69-163.
36. John Matthew Hunt, VOR File 69-113.
37. Gwendolyn Bryner Schmutz, VOR File 69-158.
38. Mary Jane Morris Truman Holt, VOR File 68-008.
39. Mariah Delila Van Leuven Alldredge, VOR File 68-035.
40. Milo Golden Campbell, VOR File 68-109.
41. Alporta Campbell, VOR File 68-115.
42. Joseph Aurelius Haslam, VOR File 69-192.
43. Vialate Leavitt Webb, VOR File 69-160.
44. Anna Crawford Isom, VOR File 69-178.
45. LaVon LeFevre Jones, VOR File 69-103.

Chapter 5

MORMON COLONISTS OF MEXICO WHO MOVED TO THE US

INTRODUCTION

In 1852, after the Mormons became established in the Salt Lake Valley and nearby areas, their leaders publicly announced the restoration of plural marriage as previously practiced in Old Testament days. That immediately alarmed people in other religions in the United States. The new Republican Party launched a platform against "the twin evils of barbarism—Slavery and Polygamy."[1] They put pressure on the federal government to intervene in the federal Territory of Utah to terminate polygamy. President Buchanan was convinced of the necessity to take action. In the summer of 1857, he sent one-quarter of the army to enhance the role of the federal government in the territory and to replace Brigham Young as the governor.[2]

On the way, the US Army encountered several difficulties, including an early winter and Mormon raiders who destroyed their supply wagons. They had to winter in the ruins of Fort Bridger, something they had hoped to avoid. During that winter, Colonel Thomas Kane (who was not a Mormon) undertook negotiations with President Buchanan and was authorized to travel to Utah to achieve a settlement. He was successful in getting Brigham Young to agree to step down; be replaced by a Buchanan appointee, Alfred Cumming; and to admit the army into Utah. Young accepted Cumming but required the army to relocate a long distance from any Mormon settlement. Thus the army remained at Camp Floyd until the outbreak of the Civil War, at which the soldiers left Utah to fight for either the South or the North. It was a peaceful solution for the Mormons to what could have been essentially a localized civil war, one not about slavery.[3]

The army's departure because of the Civil War did not end the political battle over polygamy. Congress enacted an antipolygamy law in 1862, but the Latter-day Saints dug in their heels and defended the practice of plural marriage because they believed it was their right under religious freedom. However, a massive journalistic campaign continued to attack the practice and Congress continued to deliberate. Finally, in 1882 the Edmunds-Tucker Act was passed, which authorized actions that aimed at disestablishing the LDS Church and forcing an end to polygamy. The LDS Church officials were faced with a choice of moving the Church from the United States once again or terminating polygamy. Federal officials actively worked at enforcing the law, imprisoning many men who were practicing polygamy. Church leaders often went into hiding. In 1890 Wilford Woodruff, LDS Church President, issued a manifesto disallowing the performance of further polygamous marriages. That brought about a cooling of the conflict but not a final settlement.[4]

During the 1880s, some Mormons looked for other solutions. They did not want to abandon any of their plural families. They wanted to escape harassment from federal marshals. One interesting option was to move to Mexico, where such arrests for practicing polygamy did not occur. Several Mormon villages were established in northern Mexico, not far from the US border. As the years went on, especially after 1890, more people moved to those colonies. Several wards were organized there, even a stake. One of the most interesting aspects of the Mormon colonies in Mexico is that the Church called Anthony W. Ivins from St. George to go to Mexico and preside over the colonies there. Ivins was a respected leader in Utah's Dixie. As a youth he was the romantic lead in the St. George Opera House. He was later mayor of St. George and a counselor in the St. George Stake presidency. He was a major rancher on the Arizona Strip and an avid friend to the Paiute Indians. His wife was the daughter of Erastus Snow, the founding leader of St. George and an Apostle. He was a monogamist. His cousin was Heber J. Grant, who later became the President of the LDS Church.[5]

The reason to mention all these details is that many of the people from those Mexican LDS colonies moved to the communities of the Mojave Desert, in or near southern Utah, to escape the Mexican Revolution of 1910–11. They were much later interviewed by Fielding H. Harris in the years 1968–70. So their stories are included in this study. Most of those who were interviewed were offspring of polygamists in Mexico. Some of their parents did not practice plural marriage but did live in those colonies. These interviews mention the Mexican Revolution of 1910–11, the impact of Pancho Villa's soldiers on their settlements, and the colonists' escape to the United States. Some of them settled in Long Valley (Orderville), on the Arizona Strip, and throughout the Mojave Desert area.[6]

Considerable scholarly study has been devoted to the Mormon colonies in Mexico. Among them is an early book by Thomas Romney, *The Mormon Colonies in Mexico*, published in 1938, at about the same time that the people in this study were in their mid-adulthood.[7] This book has already been cited with previous information. Dr. Romney lived in the Mormon colonies of Chihuahua and Sonora for about twenty-five years. He wrote the book upon the suggestion of Herbert Eugene Bolton at the Bancroft Library at the University of California, Berkeley.

Dr. Romney details the story of the colonies of Sonora, Díaz, and Juárez in the 1880s and even tells of the early missionary work in Mexico City. He explains how the Mormon village system was instituted in the northern villages, with each family receiving one-and-one-fourth acres in the town and twenty acres near town for farming. This land was free. It was given to the first one hundred settlers as an incentive to attract people to come there. Dr. Romney reported that John W. Young bought 150,000 acres around Colonia Díaz to attract Mormons, and about one thousand people came by 1900.

Anthony W. Ivins, George Williams, and John Nagle were instrumental in helping the settlers who came to Sonora in 1892. Colonia Dublán was established there near a railroad. A man named Lewis Huller purchased 73,000 acres in order to start the settlement. By 1912, twelve hundred people lived there.

Dr. Romney emphasizes the role of Anthony Ivins in Mexico. As a young man, Ivins fulfilled two preaching missions to central Mexico, during which time he became intimately acquainted with the natives of Mexico and developed a love for them that was abiding. He goes on for four pages praising President Ivins, especially for his great impact on the Mexican colonies. Ivins was later called to be an LDS Apostle and then member of the First Presidency as counselor to Heber J. Grant.

Dr. Romney describes the establishment of an LDS academy in Juárez. It opened in 1897 with 291 students, Guy C. Wilson as principal, and four other teachers. The academy included nine grades. It is still in existence. All of these factors—the land, the number of settlers, and the school—give evidence that the colonies in northern Mexico were thriving when the Mexican Revolution began around 1910.

Romney concludes by describing the events that led to the Mormon exodus in 1912—the challenges to the Díaz presidency by Madero and Salazar. To that point the four thousand Mormons in Mexico had gradually gained the respect of native citizens, but the arrival of Pancho Villa in the northern region led President Junius Romney to instruct the members to leave Mexico. Many intended to return to Mexico, and some indeed did. Others continued north, and a few even settled in or near Washington County, Utah.

A more recent study is *Mormons in Mexico* by F. LaMond Tullis.[8] In addition to what we learned from Thomas Romney, Tullis points out that Brigham Young switched his original missionary assignment at the Mexico City area to the northern Mexico border near 1875. Oaxaca, south of Mexico City, was moderately welcoming to them, but there were some conflicts among the missionaries over Dan Jones's leadership style. Tullis includes an issue about Dr. Plotino C. Rhodakanaty, a convert to the Church who became a substantial force in the Church. As a local leader he wanted to establish the United Order and to focus the mission on central Mexico. This controversy sank itself. The Church leaders in Utah decided to focus on the northern Mexico area and did so by appointing Anthony W. Ivins as mission president. The focus then became of founding several colonies in northern Mexico.

In 1890 President Woodruff issued the Manifesto as an answer to the 1887 Edmunds-Tucker Act, which threatened the very existence of Mormonism in the United States. The Manifesto was very unsettling to many people who were practicing polygamy. Some saw moving to Mexico as a solution to their marital situation. The inflow was symbolic. As many as six Apostles lived in the colonies in the 1880s in an attempt to avoid legal prosecution for practicing polygamy. As people flowed to the colonies, they brought skills and capital with them. Tullis suggested that there was an economic shift from communalism to capitalism.[9]

Tullis then analyzes the rise of the Mexican Revolution. He pointed out that Mexican President Díaz supported the Mormons cautiously, but he was very critical of the Indians even though the Mormons were supportive of them. Tullis also emphasized that most Mexicans hated the United States for stealing their lands in the Mexican War, exporting their oil, and supporting President Díaz, who was rapidly losing popularity. The revolutionaries against Díaz came into the Mormon colonies seeking food and supplies, but they did not intend to kill the Mormons. Nonetheless, the Mormons were in a no-win situation because they were such a small minority and because they were foreigners. Tullis details the many conflicts between the Mormons and the revolutionaries and the central government in 1912, and readers can quickly sympathize with stake president Junius Romney, who ordered the evacuation that led most Mormons into the United States as refugees.

A significant study was made by Bill Smith called *Impacts of the Mexican Revolution: The Mormon Experience, 1910–1946*.[10] He pointed out that both the Mexican government and the Mormons were thinking of creating settlements in northern Mexico. Some Mormons were trying to escape from federal antipolygamy laws. They saw northern Mexico as a sensible site.

The Díaz government in Mexico City was concerned that the state of Texas might try to expand into northern Mexico. They had visited Salt Lake City and were impressed. They did not limit themselves to Catholicism. They had already invited Protestants to Mexico. In 1879 the Díaz government sent an invitation for Mormons to move to Mexico. Díaz liked the Mormons once they came. They were industrious and paid their taxes. Smith pointed out that most Mormons in the Chihuahua colonies specialized in agriculture, but some developed industries and sales outlets. The Catholic press attacked polygamy, but the Díaz regime equated it with concubinage, which they ignored. He also tells of Mormon efforts in central Mexico, which irritated the LDS Church leaders in Salt Lake City. Those leaders shifted LDS priorities from central to northern Mexico, although missionary efforts continued in Mexico City.

Díaz had been Mexico's president for several terms. In 1910 he was challenged by Francisco Madero. Díaz was pronounced the winner in a questionable tally. That stirred many liberals to rally around Madero and begin a revolution. Much of the military action occurred in northern Mexico where Pancho Villa led rebels. At first the Mormons felt they could avoid the conflict because Díaz was favorable to them, but eventually they decided to flee to the nearby US border because of Pancho Villa.

These excellent studies will help current readers understand why Mormons fled Mexico and came north, some then being interviewed in their new home in southern Utah or nearby by Fielding H. Harris and included in this study. Those interviewed were largely children in 1910. When they settled in the United States, the children did not become polygamists, but many of them had polygamist parents. There were nearly two thousand who fled the colonies. They settled all over the Mormon Corridor. A few families chose to come to Utah's Dixie, especially on the Arizona Strip and Long Valley. Here are their words.

INTERVIEWS

JAMES BUNDY

James Bundy was born on 13 October 1887, in Wallace, Lincoln County, Nebraska, but came to southern Utah with his parents. He was well known during his later life there on the Arizona Strip, but as a youth he lived in Old Mexico and married his wife, Chloe Geneva Van Leuven, in the Mormon colonies. He tells many stories about farming and ranching and working in mines and smelters before their escape back to the United States because of the Mexican Revolution.

He was a real storyteller. Here is a short account: "When we went to Mexico, we stopped at Naco, Arizona. Dad had a job freighting there to raise a little money to go on to the colony. He drove one team, and

I drove the other [team]. We hauled supplies out to Canenea [north, in Sonora, Mexico, below the border]. It was about fifty miles from Naco. I was not yet fourteen [years old]. I saw twenty mules hooked onto one wagon; they used big, old wagons. I do not know why they were built [like they were]. I would say the rear wheels were six feet in diameter. They would hook up as many as ten mules; they were what they usually put on those wagons. When one of them got stuck, they would bring back another team of ten mules to pull them out of the mud. They were Mexicans mostly [who] drove those outfits.

"They were hauling supplies out to the mining camp and hauling ore back to the smelter. They did not have a smelter. I do not know what they [did] with the ore when they got it to Naco, [which was] twenty miles further east. Naco and Douglas were on the Arizona–Mexico border. The ore [from] Bisbee, Arizona, was hauled to the smelter, but [the] ore brought out of Canenea, Mexico, was before that smelter was built. [It] was likely shipped up to Globe [Arizona] or Tombstone [Arizona] or wherever they had a smelter.

"After we had been there from April to October, Dad [came down with] typhoid fever, and he could not go [on, so] Roy and Lillie [Belle] went with me with [the] other outfit. I always drove one outfit. I think we only made one trip, and then Roy [came down with] typhoid fever. I can remember sleeping on a little cot with Roy. When he was delirious, he would sit up in bed and pound on me trying to drive horses. [Omer] 'Dick' [Bundy], my younger brother, Lillie [Belle], Roy and Dad [had] typhoid fever, but I never [did]. After they [were able to] travel, we started for the colony. We [arrived] down [at] Colony [Morelos] on October 13, 1901, the day I was fourteen years old. My brother Chester was born that night.

"The Van Leuvens' place was the first place we [came] to as we [came] into the mesquite bushes. The country [area] was covered with mesquite [bushes]. They lived in what [was] called a jucal [mud and wattle construction] made out of posts. [They would] stand posts on end and place creosote—no, what do they call wild cane? It is a bamboo cane they put over the rafters and throw dirt over the top of that to build a home.

"We had a tent when we [arrived] in the colony. It was on a Sunday afternoon, and after church they pitched a tent. They all [came] to help, and my [future] wife's sister came down to wait on Mother and do the housework. They teased [my] dad about going to Mexico to get a polygamous wife, but he never got [one].

"I went to school down [in Mexico] because it was a habit more than to get an education. In the summertime, I would go to Bisbee [Arizona] and work. I started working as a tool nipper first and afterwards I got a job mucking. . . . I would go back to Mexico and work in the summer and go out to the colony and go to school to be home and among the school [youngsters] more than for an education. I am sorry to say [that]. One of the dollars would buy me four dance tickets!

"I told you [that] the first job I had away from home to earn any money was washing dishes in a survey camp. The survey camp came down there to survey the railroad [that was] laying out a track to run down to Montezuma, Mexico. It was supposed to come down through the colony, but it was never laid. That was the first job I ever had where I drew any money. I [was paid] $35 a month. Our meals were furnished, but we had to carry a roll of bedding. We had a tent to sleep in. I came back home and [went] where there were rails, but not with the survey camp. They disbanded about thirty miles from the railroad.

"I never took any of the girls serious. I would go out with one girl one night and go out with another the next night. I never took any girls serious until after I quit school and went out to Bisbee, Arizona, to the mining camp. Chloe Geneva Van Leuven Bundy came out there, and that was when I really settled on her. A judge in Bisbee married us [on] August 23, 1909. [We] stayed there and [I] worked for about a year. Then we went back to the colony.

"When our fourth child was born, the little girl, was when the rebels came and ordered the colony out. The [people] all came out, but some of them went back in. We had some grain in the bin, and we had about a dozen head of cattle. I bought Dad's brand, and that is what I gathered up. We had about a dozen head of them, but by the time they went back in there, the rebels went on through [the area]. They would have hauled the grain out, but the local Mexicans had moved the grain from our bins to their bins. When I went to gather the cattle, I do not remember just what they got, but I got thirty-one dollars in American money for what cattle I had down there. We loaded up and moved out to Mount Trumbull [on the Arizona Strip]."[11]

JOHN JENSEN

Here is a short memory of leaving Mexico by John Jensen, son of John Christian Jensen, who was born in Denmark. He and his wife, Abigail Christina Abbott, were married on 24 November 1909 and had fourteen children. He tells about his father in Mexico. "We were just lucky. My stepdaddy had all kinds of offers. [President Porfirio] Díaz was the ruler. Dad could [speak the] Indian and Mexican [languages]. He learned those languages. He [Díaz] wanted him to come up and offered him all kinds of [things] to run a big ranch that he had there. In those times, they [had] people working for them and they would peon them [use them as unskilled labor]. They would get them in debt to them, and they would not let them off. Daddy said, 'No, I am afraid you will get me peoned and I never could get away.' He [Díaz] promised that he would not, but Dad would not take it. We moved out of there just before that trouble started."[12]

MIRIAM ADELIA COX WILSON RIDING

Miriam Adelia Cox Wilson Riding was born on 18 August 1878 in Fairview, Sanpete County. She spent a period of her life in Mexico, and that is where she married her first husband, David Johnson Wilson, on 1 July 1895. She had seven children by him and four by her second husband, Franklin Dobel Riding, whom she married after Wilson died. Her interview gives some insightful information: "I was in school one afternoon [in Mexico] and our bishop came to the schoolhouse and asked if I could come out. The teacher said I could, so I went out. He told me about a good man, [and] he thought I ought to pay attention to him. He gave me a lot of good words, good information at that time. So the children wouldn't ask me what he talked about, he had some mowing machine knives for my father to put on his mowing machine. I never had seen him [Wilson]. He lived in Colonia Díaz [Chihuahua, Mexico]. He came to our place and asked father's permission and visited. He was very kind, very nice, a good honorable man. Father told him that I was the only housekeeper he had. I was seventeen then or just about, [and] he couldn't spare me.

"So [David Johnson] Wilson knew of a widow, [and] he thought it would be good for her and Father to meet. Father said if she would come and stay for a couple of weeks and see about it, he would pay her for working for us for two weeks. Brother Wilson brought this widow to our home. After two weeks was [over], Father sent me to town with the wagon to get the bishop. The bishop came over, this lady made a cake, and they were married. She was Belinda [Marden] Kendrick Rowley. Kendrick was her maiden name. She was from England. She was a widow and had two children. [Her] little girl had the same name I did. Father sent me and Victor with her back to Colonia Díaz to get her things. She was a plural wife, and her husband had a big family."

MARIAH DELILA VAN LEUVEN ALLDREDGE

Mariah Delila Van Leuven Alldredge was quoted in the chapter about health and sickness, but she also had a good story to tell about Mexico. She was born on 11 November 1882, in Aurora, Sevier County, Utah: "My father [was] wearisome about his farming and thought he could do better by becoming a school teacher. He was always educated highly. So he went to the normal school to get a diploma to teach in school. He had to mortgage our home and the farm to do this. Things didn't turn out like he planned it to be. He [received] his diploma for teaching and taught for a while. It wasn't so successful, and we were about to lose our home. So he sold it and we went to Mexico. We had relatives down there, and some of them had come back and put [talked] things up so beautiful to him that he [had] the Mexico fever. He had two families, and he thought by going down there he could take both his families down there and live with them in Mexico. He served four months in the penitentiary for the other wife. We went down, but it was forty years before I ever saw my other brothers and sisters.

"We had quite a hard time of it. We had some relatives in [Colonia] Dublán. That was where we headed first. We went to the custom house [at the state] line [in Deming]. You had to go through the custom house to [cross] from the United States to Mexico. We were there for two weeks waiting for President Ivins to come and help us through. We couldn't have [gone] through without him being there to help us with the Mexican [Consulate]. He eventually came and [took] us through, and we went on. Father [had] chartered a freight car for our furniture and horses and [other possessions]. My two brothers went with them, and then Father chartered a car [on a passenger train] for the family to go in. We [arrived at] Deming, and that is where we [stayed] for two weeks. Then we went on to [Colonia] Dublán. Mother's cousin lived there—a wonderful family. He used to be our bishop in Aurora and was a wonderful man. So we went there and stayed awhile. Then [we went to Mother's] brother and sister who were living over in [Colonia] Galeana.

"Harry Paine was the bishop's name. His wife [Ruth] was my mother's cousin. Her brothers and sisters lived over in Galeana. My aunt Chloe [Geneva] was sent there and my uncle, Edmund [and Ellen Durfee and Celestia Spencer] and their families. So we went over there. We thought we would go over and see what we would find there. When we [came] over there, we didn't like the situation, so we only lived there a couple of months and came back to [Colonia] Dublán again. Father [bought] a lot there. We lived in a tent and wagon covers until they [made] homemade adobe [bricks] and made us a four-room house. We were happy to get moved into that house.

"When we lived there, it was hard. There was no wood in the country. All the wood that was there was just fine, little mesquite trees about as big as your finger. That was what we had to feed our stoves and do our cooking and baking and all. It was quite a tedious job [as the wood was] full of thorns and slivers. So that was discouraging. The land we had was fertile, very fertile, but there wasn't enough water, and we couldn't obtain enough water. Father and the boys dug a well, and he made a wooden pump, mind you. It had a great big long handle on it that you pumped the water out. Then he made troughs to catch the water in [to flow] out onto our garden. We pumped the water out of that well and watered our garden. We had a lovely garden. We even made a strawberry patch. Oh, the lovely strawberries, great big strawberries! You could hardly put one in your mouth without mashing it! They were so large and delicious. It was lovely. Everything grew there just wonderfully well.

"[We needed] water and wood. There wasn't enough water. I don't know what the people are doing now for water. I believe they are building more wells, but I'm not sure. It was big open country. My, how the wind would blow down there, too!

"We heard about [the] country over in Sonora, [and] what wonderful wood they had over there. So my father and mother [went] in our little buggy and took a trip over to [Colonia] Morelos, Mexico, to Sonora, to see what the country was. They fell in love with it because they could keep warm over there. They could make a fire to keep warm. The wood was gorgeous all over the land, great big trees, great big round trees that were just cut down. It looked good to us! So he bought a lot there. They turned around and came back and sold our home, and we moved to [Colonia] Morelos. We were there several years. No matter where we went, it wasn't long until—if you are active in the Church you don't have to be one place very long until you have more [positions] than you can take care of. I wasn't there long until they pulled me in as secretary there. Then I served as counselor in MIA.

"The Mexican [rebellion started in about 1910]. The Mexicans started fighting there, and they were taking everything. The insurrectionists were taking everything that they came to. They would kill and take your property away from you. They were led by Pancho Villa. We had to get out. The President of the United States [William Howard Taft] and [the President of] our Church advised the people all to leave. That is why we left. We thought it was going to be a short time and we could go back and obtain our homes again. But it never did. People in Dublán and [Juárez] did go back in. They have quite good colonies down there now, I think. But the [people from Colonia] Díaz never did return. The people over in our country, [Colonia] Morelos [in] the north country, none of them ever went back there to live. They just dilapidated the whole country. The Mexicans kept the farms and houses."[14]

THOMAS EAGAR

Thomas Eagar was born in 1898 in Eagar, Arizona. He spent his boyhood in Colonia Morales, Mexico, and shared his experiences in his interview in 1968 in St. George, Utah: "They moved [when] I was two years old. I don't remember much about when we crossed the line into Old Mexico. We moved sixty miles over the line. The Mexican government sold ground to the Mormon people for settlement. There had been ranchers and Mexicans living there. The [Mormon] families came in quite rapidly, quite a few at a time. As they came in, they were assigned some of [the] old houses to live in. We happened to join up with some neighbors by the name of Ray.

"We liked the Mexican people, and we paid no attention to all these quarrels. It was a forced issue. They said we had to either join the [Mexican]

Army or move out. All the young men had to [join] the army. That was what the big quarrel was about. You had to give them everything you grew. We were coming from the field one night. We [had] taken our horses up two miles to the field. We were coming back from hunting quail. We watched 20,000 soldiers go down the other road. We were up on the foothills. There was a cut-off road up there that we used to drive the horses to the fields. We were sitting there. There were a lot of quail in that country. There were millions of them. All at once, there was a bunch of soldiers [who] came around the point, right onto us. The first thing that I [thought] about was running. I ran into some thick brush, and they hollered, 'Halt!' My brother stopped. He had the gun. He was seven years older than I was. He stopped, but not me. I ran into the brush. They told him that they were going in after me if he didn't get me back out. I let him plead a little while, and then I came out.

"They wanted the gun, but when they saw that it was a shotgun, they finally decided that he could keep it. They just turned us loose. I [was] up to almost fourteen. I had to take most of the horses to the field and back. [My dad] gave me a little mare. She was a mean little brute, but I thought that she was the best little critter that ever lived. She used to throw me off. I would get on her and start for the field, but I was always walking when I got there! The same thing [would happen] when I got on her [in] the field. I would be walking when I got back to town! That was the first year. Then one day Dad said, 'I will break her for you.' He got on her, and I had never seen him ride harder in my life. And he was a cowboy! He got on that little mare, and finally she got out into the middle of the canal, and how she would buck. He pulled out all the leather there was to hold on to that mare because he didn't want to get wet.

"I was riding her [one] night. I got so I could ride her. I thought that I could ride anything on earth that had hair on it! These soldiers hollered, 'Kin Vivi.' I was supposed to tell them who I was in favor of, which side [I was on]. If I had just said 'Muchacho,' that meant 'a boy,' and [they] would let me go. I dug that little mare. I thought that I could outrun them, and so I took for home. I guess several hundred men were yelling after me. By the time I [came] home, my dad [was] there. He had heard the ruckus, and guessed what it was. He [had] the gate down, and I just went around the granary. Of course, the soldiers were there in just a minute. But I repented quickly. He lectured me strong enough that night. I didn't run from soldiers no more! It is a wonder they didn't shoot me. That was their duty. If it had been an American soldier, they would have shot me for running. I don't understand it yet why they didn't shoot me. If there were any shots fired, I didn't get in on them. I was going too fast.

"Just not [long] after that, my brother, [William] 'Will' [Nutter] Hinton, had a little brown mare. She was the best little racer you ever saw. We had her in this field. A Mexican, or somebody, came in and got on a mare, and [left]. Will got on a sorrel horse and took after him. When he [went] up to Cucha Verche, which is seventeen miles away from home, [a fellow in a] house up on the hill said the soldiers were coming after him. [The horse] was still running. Will knew he couldn't catch the little mare. He thought that maybe the people at the house on the hill knew the mare and maybe they would stop them. They didn't, so he turned around and came back. He knew that he couldn't catch her, because she was long-winded.

"We had a big melon patch that year. We grew lots of melons, and lots of peanuts. We grew lots of everything [that could be] grown in Mexico. We would sell these melons. If [the melons] weren't ripe, they would eat them anyhow. Dad taught even the younger [children] that dorealis were two bits [twenty-five cents]. These little brothers and sisters of mine would say 'dirty Alice.' And they would give them a quarter and would pick their own melon. My dad's last family was all little fellows. They could remember 'dirty Alice.'

"Before we left there, my brother Will and I dug a big hole and buried all of our treasures. We have never been there after them yet. I think some of them would be in good condition. We put lots of [items] in glass bottles. They would be good. It has only been sixty years. There is one thing that I would like to have, and that is my mother's reader.

"My mother just knew how to work. She wasn't what you would call a foxy cook, but when the Church started, they told her she was the best cook they had ever had. That is [when] they would come to our place. We ran President Ivins's cattle, so he was there quite a bit. Thomas [Romney] was there quite a bit, [and] Pancho Villa was there quite a bit. He was a great big, good-natured Mexican. He was a nice guy to talk to. He would do anything for us. According to standards nowadays, you would say that he was an igno-rant Mexican. He wasn't a diplomat. That is why he made that one mistake about going into the United States to get horses and vittles. Of course, he took a bunch of wild Mexicans in there. We don't know whether that was done by his orders or not. I saw one of his lieutenants in Las Vegas in 1956. He said that was not done by Villa's order. Villa was blamed for it [because] he was with them. They went over there and were going to buy [items], and instead they robbed, stole, and killed. We never thought anything very bad about him or any of [those] other generals. They treated us nice."[15]

DORETTA MARIE IVERSON BUNDY

Doretta Marie Iverson Bundy was born on 1 December 1887 in Washington City and married Roy Bundy on 5 September 1907. Shortly after their marriage, they moved to the Colonia Morelos, Sonora, Mexico: "My husband's brother [James Bundy] had bought a lot or a block [of land]. It had a small two-room rock house. One room had adobes put down or brick for a floor, the other didn't have [anything] but loose dirt. I made a hard floor out of [it] with a little water. It had poles across the top and reed canes and dirt on that. [There were] not any windows. It had a fireplace.

"It was kind of tough, but my husband got work to buy household furniture; we didn't have much of that. My dishes were kind of laughable. My mother-in-law [Ella Anderson Bundy] was a very nice lady. She went with me to the store to get utensils to use. I remember I bought two or three granite iron plates, white plates, and old metal knives and forks. I bought a couple of them and spoons. I had a frying pan, so you see I didn't have very [many] dishes. I remember my mother-in-law felt kind of embarrassed. She was well-acquainted with the storekeepers; but she said I was a very saving girl and I didn't have any more money to spend. She gave me a dozen chickens, and we traded the phonograph for a cow! My father-in-law [Abraham Bundy] was quite a gardener, and he [grew an] early garden [of] peas, onions, and radishes. I would help the girls pick the peas in the morning. People would come there and buy [peas] for dinner.

"I remember we didn't have any refrigerators down there. Nothing [was] very convenient, but there was a piece of brick out of the wall that left a little cupboard. I had a curtain hung up [over] that. I remember one day I had a bowl of peas left after dinner so I put it in the cupboard. In the afternoon, I decided I would have a dish of peas. I took a dish full of peas and started eating them. I remembered I didn't have any pepper. After

I had eaten a bit, I noticed some little black specks in [it] and I looked closer and [there] were little fly worms. They hatch in a hurry! I guess [for] twenty years I couldn't eat or stand to look at peas.

"Mexico was a wonderful country. [We stayed] about four or five years. [We left] because of the trouble with the revolution in Mexico. We had plenty of meat because my husband would go in the hills anytime and get a deer. [Or he] would go up the river and come back with a sack full of fish. He used to love to do that. He would get his horse, take a couple of gunnysacks, go up the river, and come home with [fish]. He would scatter fish all along coming home. He gave to everybody. So we all fared well. There was a mine, the El Tigre Mine [in Sonora, Mexico], that was up in the mountains. [It was] twenty-five or thirty miles [from our home]. He got a job up there.

"One day my sister-in-law [Chloe Geneva Van Leuven Bundy] said, 'Let's go visit them up in the mine.' Her brother, Lafayette Van Leuven, got horses and took us up there. It was a hard ride [up a] steep mountain dugway. . . . When we were ready to [come] back, my husband said he didn't have any idea that we could make it up there. 'How about coming back up and staying this winter?' Of course, I had to come home and get clothes and my little boy that I had left with my mother. I came back up. I lived in a big, long apartment house. There [were] Mexicans [who] lived in those rooms. I had two rooms by myself, and I made friends with the Mexican ladies. They were very nice and treated me fine. They would bring me in some of their Christmas cookies, and I would give them some of mine.

"Then the revolution broke out down there. I don't remember what year that was. When they started fighting, we could see the main part of town a mile up the canyon. We could see the rebels on one side and the others on the other side, and we could hear their shooting, firing back and forth.

"My husband had a spyglass and [went] out [to] the woodpile and laid there and watched it. They came to get what they could out of the mine. They built bricks after they separated the gold out. They made one-hundred-pound bricks. When the fighting started, they took these bricks and threw [them] into a big tank of water to hide from the rebels.

The rebels came down and got all the provisions they wanted out of the store. A local Mexican told them where they put the brick. They ran the cyanide water all out on the ground down the canyon and got the brick, but they had no way to haul it out, only by burro. Two bricks were almost too heavy for a little burro and one [brick] wouldn't stay on [the burro]. In the rush to get out of the steep canyon they [were rushing] the burros, and months later they found where [the burros had] wandered off in the canyon and died with the bricks on their back.

"I was there for a couple of weeks [afterwards]. I was the only white woman there. The bishop in Morelos (that was the town we lived in) sent horses up there [and said] I better come home with him. When I came up there I had the two children, one in my arms and one on the back of the horse on the saddle. When he [Ivan] would get sleepy, Brother McCall would take him on his horse. The people in Morelos were looking for the rebels to come into town. They wanted my husband to stay up there and work and bring word down when it looked like they were coming our way. He stayed there, but the rebels came in from a [different] direction. They came into town and made our church and schoolhouse their headquarters. They would kill a cow right on the street [in the] churchyard.

"They were a decent bunch of soldiers. They would go around town buying eggs, butter, meat, and bread. I remember one day a soldier came to my place. He had a brand-new rifle that had [been] smuggled across the line. He was quite proud of it. [He] had a belt [that went] up here and round there. [It was] full of cartridges. He showed me his gun and how fast he could throw the shells out, and then he passed [the gun] to me. He thought I would be scared and run, but I took his gun and I threw [cartridges] out as fast as he [did]! He praised me. We tried to be congenial with them and tried to not be afraid because you didn't want to be afraid.

"The people in Colonia Morelos were not safe. President [O. P.] Brown was in Douglas, Arizona, and was to send us word when it was advisable to move out. There were people with their horses hitched up, ready to leave. Brother Brown told my husband that if he stayed up there he would see that his family [was] moved to town. We [received] word we were to leave and everybody was ready. We [went] just a little ways out the first night [and then were gone]."[16]

ALTA ROWLEY PERKINS WILCOX

Alta Rowley Perkins Wilcox was born on 28 October 1900 in Colonia Díaz, Chihuahua, Mexico. She was one of thirteen children. One of the children died at birth while they were traveling to Mexico and was buried beside the road. Some of her schooling was in Mexico. She remembers mostly the problems with the rebels: "I don't remember much about [my teachers] in Mexico. There were other things I was more interested in. I remember the trouble they were having with the Mexicans all the time. I remember one time we were coming home from school and someone said the rebels were coming. We got under a bridge [over] the ditch, and they ran over the top of us. We [could] hear the clatter of the horses going over the top!

"They used to come into town and pick out the best horses and take them. Dad had lots of good horses, and he always took good care of them. He had one that was special to him. [There was] an old lime kiln that [was] used to burn lime in, and he took his horse down there and threw hay over him to hide [the horse] from the Mexicans so they wouldn't take him. No one tried to stop them from taking the horses. I think they were afraid to [do that]. There were more Mexicans than there were white people. They had two or three skirmishes, and one man was killed.

"These men were under the leadership of Pancho Villa, and they were stealing, taking everything they could lay their hands on, and shooting up the place. Before we left, the schoolhouse bell was kept quiet so that [it] could [be] used as a signal [for] all the men [to] come to the church house. Sunday morning about six o'clock the bell rang. All the men got up, dressed, and went to the schoolhouse to see what the trouble was. A man had ridden from the town of Dublán, all night on horseback, to tell them that the rebels were headed [our] way to set fire to the town. We were to be out of town by ten o'clock that morning. We hadn't had breakfast. [Some of] the women and [children] were still in bed. The men came home and gathered up what they could in four hours without having their breakfast. In six hours [they] gathered their teams and wagons together and met outside the town in wagon boxes. We [went] to Hachita, Mexico. That first night it rained on us all night, it just poured down. Everybody [was] in wagon boxes.

"Most of them had covers [blankets], and a lot of them had tents that they pitched. I remember Dad pitched a tent. [We] had a folding cot, and my grandmother slept in the tent on the folding cot. Mother [was] in the wagon box with [the children]. I don't think Dad went to bed. He stayed up all night to keep us from being washed away! It was in July. I don't remember enough to know. It just happened to [storm, and] it really rained on us. A bunch of older boys were left [in Colonia Díaz] to look after things in case [the rebels] didn't come. They [were] to keep the stock fed and take care of things in town. But [the rebels] came and shot at the boys and chased them clear across the border. [They] shot one boy's horse out from under him. He got on another close by. My older brother, Claude, was one of the boys that stayed. He was sixteen years old. [The rebels] came and set fire to the town and burned it down. [They] shot the eyes out of the pictures on the walls. First [they] destroyed everything they could. If you go there now, you can still see [the ruins].

"We stopped in Hachita and [stayed] in tents. The government put up tents and [gave food] rations for a while until people could gather their senses together and decide what they wanted to do and where they wanted to go. They thought they could go back in a few days, but it turned [out] they couldn't. The town was burned down, so there was nothing to go back to. They [stayed] there and waited, deciding where they wanted to go. Dad had [a] brother in Tucson, [Arizona], so he decided to go [there]. The government charged him fifty dollars a head [for] duty on his own horses, and he was still an American citizen. He raised his horses from colts, most of them, [and] they charged him fifty dollars a head [for] duty to get them across the line. He had to [find] somebody to [set up] his bond because he didn't have [the money for] his bond. He went to Tucson.

"My mother lived in a tent and cooked on a campfire until [he] sent the money back to pay for the horses. [He] paid the bill off, [and] then we moved into a house that a Mexican family had moved out of in Tucson. Dad worked on a big ranch [where they] raised all kinds of grain. He was there quite a while and [became] foreman of the [ranch]. They called it Rolling Hills, [and] he was foreman. They used a lot of horses and mules, and he was good with [them].

"But there wasn't church there [so] that we could go to Sunday School. We were going to school with more Mexicans in Tucson than we went with in Mexico. Dad and Mother weren't satisfied with it, so they saved their money, all they could. Dad was making pretty good money for those times. They paid in twenty-dollar gold pieces. Mother had a little baking powder can, and every nickel left over, every twenty dollars she could get ahold of that she didn't have to have, she would drop in this can, enough to move on. When the can [was] full, they decided they had enough to buy hay, grain, and food for [all] of us.

"[Dad] had a sister that had gone to Blanding from Mexico. Blanding was just a new town [and] hadn't been settled very long. She wrote and told him that she would host him. So we went to Blanding. [We were] thirty days and nights on the road."[17]

ANNIE EAGAR COVINGTON

Here is a story of a polygamous family that had to leave Mexico but continued to maintain more than one family with grave difficulties. Annie Eagar Covington tells of their Mexican experiences in Colonia Morales: "We went on, [and] nothing happened on our trip into Morelos, Sonora, Mexico, that I know of. Everything went well until we [arrived] there. Down in there is a wild country. The Mexicans were starting to build up [the] little town of Morelos. This is the place my father headed for. He had that all spotted. They put my mother in a mud house that the Mexicans had built. That was all they had. We lived in there, and the girls got lice in their hair from the Mexicans' house. Oh, my mother about died! I will never forget how she would have to hunt for lice. My father built a house and got us into it. It was just a Mexican house like the other one. We lived there. For a year we didn't have food. My father couldn't [grow] anything. He had a truck, but there was nothing [grown]. We didn't have much to eat. He had wheat that he had taken down there and we would have to grind it [in] the coffee mills. My mother had eleven children, and he was gone most of the time.

"We didn't have any bread to eat. We had potatoes, but Father didn't plant fruit trees. They didn't know what fruit was down [there] in those days. Finally, there was a man [who] came through the country and stopped there. [He] decided to move in and live there. His name was Wilson. He put up a mill of some kind that you could run with a horse. It would grind wheat [so we] could make bread. Oh boy, we thought we had it! We had some bread. We didn't have to grind on that old mill anymore.

"We never had any sickness. I remember the women and children were crying because the mill was afire. The mill burned to the ground. Somebody burned the mill to the ground. Here we were again, having to eat coarse bread until they could build another mill.

"Then we [were doing] good again, and my father had a farm down close to this big river. He had a field by [the river] and a big chicken coop there [for his] chickens. He had quite a lot of grain and had a big crop planted. That flood just cleaned it right out. My mother sat there in [the] chicken coop there trying to protect all the chickens in that coop. She wasn't going to leave there. They had to get her on a raft and take her out of there. She was going to stay there and go down the river! We all went up on the hill because it looked like [the water] was coming to demolish the town. My mother sat on the edge of the hill. That night we slept in the schoolhouse because the whole town [was] nearly covered with water.

"Then my father decided he wanted to ranch. So he got a ranch. We called it Uncle Sixtus's Ranch. One of my uncles had it [earlier]. He wasn't really my uncle, but he was always called Uncle Sixtus, and the ranch was named after him. My father got it, and we lived there a year. We raised a big crop there. That was when my father decided he wanted to get another wife. A man came into the country with four girls. They were all old maids. One married the bishop, one [Emily Jane Lee Eagar] married my father, and one married the bishop's brother. The other married a Romney from up in the mountains.

"I remember one time my father went after a lot of our cattle, and horses were stolen when they were starting the war. My father took the boys and went out to hunt [for the animals]. He was gone for a day. When he didn't come home, I remember, my mother and my aunt were pacing the floor and crying and crying. They just knew the Mexicans had killed them. Finally, [my father and brothers] came [home], and they were not hurt. They had their animals.

"My mother was usually alone a lot of the time because my father would go down in town and stay with the other wife because she was a pretty young girl. One night another flood came down the canyon. We could hear the roaring of the flood. It was getting dark. My mother ran in the house and told us all to come in. She barred the door with some boxes, a chest or two that she had, and put the table over against it. Then she put some of the bedding up there and told all of us children to get up on that and pray. She climbed up there, and we all sat around on that [pile] praying. That wall of water hit that house, and [it] went right down. It hit the door and went down through the windows and doors; it went everywhere. We just clung to the walls. The next morning I got up, and everything we had was gone. We spent the morning picking up our clothes and everything we had. My mother went back to town, and we lived in a home there.

"One night, Mother wanted to get to the bottom of this thing. My mother brought me over to the neighbors. We knew there was a war. All around us was trouble. Somehow or another, it didn't bother any of us. We didn't realize anything had ever happened. My aunt [Emily Jane Lee Eagar] had died and left five little children and nobody to take care of them. The baby wasn't even named when her mother died. She died soon after the child was born. My father got a little place and put me [there] to take care of these children because I was closer to my mother. He and she just didn't get along and had separated. So I took my father's children, and I was taking care of them.

"All at once I could see an army coming. It just scared me terribly, and I ran as hard as I could go for my mother and took these little [children]. My mother wasn't home. The soldiers came right in. They just threw my father's [place apart]. He had his crops all in; there was fruit on the trees. They had watermelons. These Mexicans just turned their horses into everything. They did that with every house. I was so frightened to see so many and to see they went through everything we had. . . . I went around the corner of the house to get my mother because I was afraid to stay all alone with all these little children. I just [went] around the house and ran into a great big [Mexican] officer! He laughed. I pushed him just as hard as I could push him. I crawled through the fence and ran for Mother. My mother came home. I was twelve years old. I had started taking care of those little children all alone. I took care of them all the time she was sick, too.

"My mother just came home, and we stayed in the house and minded our business and they [the soldiers] minded theirs. They didn't often do anything to us. They stayed for a solid month in that town. They put a cannon right over our house and another one on the schoolhouse steps. They [prepared] for battle. They spent their time marching up and down the streets and all through the bushes.

"We were in communication with the church authorities all the time. They were telling what to do. Some wanted us to come out, but the bishop couldn't stand to leave his mill, store, and all of his property, so he said, 'Stay.' He kept staying, and we didn't know any minute when we would be killed. The men would leave town to be out to catch the other army. If we did have to leave, we would leave at a minute's notice.

"One night we [received] word to get out of there and get out of there quick because there was no time to monkey [around]. I remember all men were off on guard duty. They were all scattered all through the country. My brothers, Thomas and Lee, took one team and harnessed it up. We put all of my things [and] these five little children I was raising into this wagon. My brothers drove it. My mother's two oldest boys had come out there. The oldest boy had died of pneumonia in Mexico. The other two boys had already come out [earlier] and were living here. My mother had my brother Will out here. He was the only one of the Hinton children [who] stayed with her.

"We left and we [came] to this first big river. It was raining. It was a pitch black night and just pouring down—raining and raining. The women and children were all crying. My mother was sick. We camped out as far as we could go the first night. It rained all night and we just sat there. My brother Walt always said the only place he had to sit was right in the water. It trickled right down his back and all night long went down his backbone. We couldn't sleep, and there were just women and crying children because they were leaving their home and everything they [owned]. We didn't know what was in store for us.

"The next night we camped at this big river, and it was swollen [by] so much storm. My mother was [very] sick. She was really sick that night. There was still wailing and crying. The bishop [received] word that they had entered Morelos. There were 5,000 soldiers [who] had entered Morelos, and they were fighting. They had left two women there because they didn't have a wagon [or any] way of bringing them and their children and [the women] were pregnant. They jumped on horses and went back and got them out in the night. They sneaked them out of there. These women had been hiding, and they brought them out.

"The [United States] government knew that we were coming. There were 150 families that they knew were coming. They told them to put up tents for 150 families, a little tent community, [in] Douglas, Arizona. We [came] there. We were there all day in that boiling hot sun, trying to get through. They had to examine every wagon and everything. They would almost strip you to see that you were not hiding anything. You couldn't take any ammunition across. My father had a place; he would always hide all of his guns in the willows.

"We crossed over the river the next day and went on. When we got into La Prieta we were there all day long getting through those two custom houses. [As we left], they gave each family a tent to live in and water was piped along every so often. Twice a week there would be big government wagons with two spans, four mules to a big government wagon, loaded with food. They would bring it there, but it only [had] beans and potatoes, just what we were used to. We weren't used to anything better. That was good. We were really living! We also had [items] I had never seen before. We [never] had any fruit. We hadn't ever seen any, so it didn't matter. The first apricot I ever saw was after I came out of Mexico.

"We stayed in our tents in Douglas a month. They would come twice a week, and we would have to take our pans, go out, and they would dole us out enough food to last until the next time they came. This went on a month until the government could decide what to do with us. Finally, the officers came and told us that if we wanted to save our outfits and go with teams and wagons, they would give us papers showing that we were Mexican refugees. [Or] we could go by train to where we had to go. My mother wanted to come here [to Utah] because her people were here. She had a little family. Her youngest little girl [Hazel] lives over at Toquerville and was about three years old. She doesn't remember anything about Mexico. [Mother] came here to her people. The day that she left, my father wanted to go and see the family off. They were still his children. He told me to stay by with the other little family while he went [to] see my mother off. That was the hardest part of my life. I didn't think I would ever bawl.

But I did cry when I had to stay there alone and couldn't go and see them go. I never saw them [until] a good many years after that.

"They came here to Hurricane. 'Will,' my brother, built my mother a home and she came here [to] live [with] her little family. I went with my father to Arizona. He wanted to save his animals, so two other families went with us."[18]

OMER DICK BUNDY

Omer Dick Bundy, born 30 November 1891, gives a boyhood experience in the revolution: "This revolution started down in interior Mexico and gradually came up to the border. Pancho Villa and his generals came into the colonies in Chihuahua. They didn't treat them too badly over there. One or two men were killed over at Colonia Díaz. It wasn't anything like lots of things that were going on in the armies now. Even though they were rough-looking men, they still respected our American women. You have to give them credit for that.

"President [William Howard] Taft of the United States and President Joseph F. Smith of the Church advised us to leave. The women and the children and lots of the men left. Nineteen of us young fellows stayed down there with the hope that the Federals were going to come around on the train."

Bundy goes on for several pages, telling of their adventures hiding from the armies of rebels who wanted their guns, ammunition, and saddles. Bundy and his friends had many close calls but were able to evade them. "We went down through that canyon and nobody disturbed us. We headed for the Arizona line. [We were] about eighteen miles from it, down in a mass of mesquite. It was afternoon by this time and we were quite hungry. Dave knew there was a ranch over there. We decided to go over there and see if we could buy some jerky and some corn that they had. We went over there and found three more of our men. The Mexicans were friendly to us. They knew some of our men. They told us, 'Don't go up the valley.' You could see the railroad bridges. They were built down in Mexico. They made the little bridges out of timber, big beams across small washes. The rebels had gone ahead of us and set them all afire. We could see through there for about fifteen miles.

"There were three of us when we left the ranch. 'Dick' Huish and the Haney boy overtook us at the fork of the trail. Then we came up onto the top of this hill, and there were Moroni Fenn and Zane McNeil. That made seven of us. We went down to this ranch to see if we could buy beef, and there were three more: Hank Jones, and I can't remember the fellows that were with him. That made ten of us, and we had sixteen head of loose horses besides the one that we were riding. We were trying to get out with two choice horses.

"Then we milled along back away from the valley about a mile and a half until about one o'clock. We were within three miles of Agua Prieta. We decided we better stay there until daylight, and then we would make a run for the Arizona line regardless of where the custom house was. If we were put in the 'pen' it would be better than losing our outfits and maybe getting into a fight. We stayed there until it began to get light. Press Jones had a pair of field glasses, and he could see dust forming down in the valley. We were back about a mile and a half from the valley. We sat there ready to go and tried to decide what to do, whether to take a chance and go straight through to the line and not go down there to the custom house, or what.

"Then it became light enough, and he said, 'That isn't any army.' We thought it was the rebel army saddled and ready to make an attack on Agua Prieta. 'That isn't any army. That is a big herd of cattle.' We stayed there until nearly sunup. We could see then it was cattle and cowboys with them. We decided to go down there. As we approached, the foreman of the outfit came on a lope to meet us. He said, 'I am glad to see you fellows. I am sure glad to see you. I have a job for every one of you here. Come down. I will have them make some coffee and biscuits. There is plenty of fried meat left from breakfast. Come on down and get something to eat.' We were willing to take that part of his advice.

"When we were through eating, we told him we didn't want a job. We wanted to get the horses across onto the Arizona side. He said, 'They have called the fight off at Agua Prieta. The rebels have gone back down into Sonora and you won't have any trouble there.' So that is what we did. I had to leave the old Spanish Mauser and several other guns as they were Mexican property. We couldn't bring them across without paying duty on them."[19]

WILLIAM SHIRLEY BLACK SR.

William Shirley Black Sr. was born in 1889 in Millard County, Utah. His family moved to Mexico after his mother died in 1899 from complications from a birth. William was ten years old. The baby survived, and the family took care of her until the father married Artemissia Cox two years after the birth. He reports: "She had three sisters living in Old Mexico, so she and my father went down there to visit. While there he decided [this] was a far better place to raise a family than where we were. For that reason, we moved to Old Mexico.

"When we first [moved] down there, my father sent me to Juárez Stake Academy to go to school. I came down with typhoid fever. [I had] a hard spell of it and recovered. [Afterward I] went to work in the sawmill. I worked there a little while and took a setback, had it all over again. I spent over a year there, just being sick. My father was killed down [in Colonia Guadalupe, Chihuahua, Mexico, over] a water question. My brother and I went up there to get water, the Mexicans run us off. We went home and my brother got a gun. [We] went up there and took the water. The Mexicans ran home and got a gun and came back, and my father came up there just in time to [be] shot. So we were left with my stepmother and the family. We came out [of Mexico] in 1912.

"Soon after that they started this war and the insurrection. In fact, my first wife and I came up to Salt [Lake County, Utah] and were married. We went back on the train. When we got back [to] her home in Colonia Díaz, we heard some gun shooting in the night. [We] woke up to find out two Mexicans had robbed the store and came out with bundles in their arms. The officer in charge there got a man or two out to help him. They tried to stop them [by] shooting in the air, but they wouldn't stop. The two Mexicans got on their horses and ran, with their bundles in their arms, down the street. [One] of the Mormon men thought they were really having a battle, so he got out in the street and took a shot at them. He killed one of them [and] he fell. That day, Brother Harvey, one of our Mormon men, went out to his farm, and the Mexican relatives of this fellow who was killed beat him to death with a shovel. That day I was going to ride my horse back up to where we lived in Colonia Dublán. They found out I was going to go, so they wanted me to take the word up to the stake president about the trouble down there.

"I had to ride through the Mexican town to get out on the road to go up to Dublán. The bishop there decided they would send two or three of the boys along to protect me going through town. Then they decided I would be in more danger with a group of us than I would be alone. So they asked me to go alone, and I did. I rode through the town and when I got up to the edge of town I trotted through. Some men hollered at me and tried to stop me, but I didn't stop [and] nobody followed me. After I got through the town, I went pretty fast from there on for a long while as long as the horse could take it. I [came] to Dublán in the morning just as the sun was coming up. Before I got there I was so sleepy, I had to get off and trot ahead of the horse and lead him to keep awake. When I [arrived] there the bishop put me to bed for a while. Then he took me with him, and we went up towards Colonia Juárez and met the stake presidency there to talk over the situation down in Colonia Díaz.

"I want to mention one man who meant a great deal to me down there in Mexico. My father owed a debt of 1,200 dollars of Mexican money to buy the home we had. After he was killed, Edmund Richardson bought the note. He had borrowed money from President Anthony Ivins. Edmund Richardson traded some mining stock for these notes. He told me that if I would work a year for him, he would call it square. So I did. I worked a year for Edmund Richardson. He is one of the finest men I ever knew. He was a lawyer [and] took care of most of our troubles with the Mexicans down there. [He was a] Mexican lawyer. I want to also mention when I spent one year [at the] Juárez Academy after my father died, two of the men whom I thought a great deal of was Charles McClellan and Guy C. Wilson, who was principal of our school."[20]

CONCLUSIONS

These stories about Mexico are important to include for several reasons. First, all of these people later lived in the Mojave Desert region after they left Mexico and were interviewed in one of those villages. Secondly, their lives in Mexico were similar in that they lived in villages and worked mainly in agriculture. They kept close contact with Utah and were supervised by LDS Church leaders. The difference was that they were surrounded by Mexicans and eventually expelled by them during the Mexican Revolution.

About nine communities were established in northern Mexico to provide them an alternate location. In general, they thrived, but many who moved there had real challenges getting established. Not all Mormons who went to the colonies were polygamists, but its practice was central to the colonies. The LDS Church even allowed people there to be married into polygamy after the 1890 Manifesto based on the logic that it was not prosecuted in Mexico. Mexico did not legalize polygamy, but they accepted the children of second and third families as part of the original family. Those interviewed were children of polygamists when they fled to the United States between 1910 and 1912; they experienced firsthand the trials and blessings of living in Mexico in a polygamist family.

They reported that their families got along fairly well with Mexican families nearby. The problem that eventually drove them out of the country was the Mexican Revolution. The rebel side was led by Pancho Villa, and his troops were often located near the Mormon colonies. The interaction between the two groups varied. Some of these testimonies told that the revolutionaries came to them and bought food. Others told of armed rebels coming and stealing all their crops. These settlers were instructed by local Church leaders to be ready to flee to the US border. Sometimes the threat was real; other times it was a false alarm. Most of the settlers did not want to leave. Their large families were well established in the Mormon colonies. Some of the wives had as many as ten to thirteen children. They had put a decade or more of labor into their settlements. Some came directly to the area near Washington County. Others did not come to Dixie initially but did later. Like the other settlers in Dixie, these people too were laborers in the field. Once they moved, they fit into the Dixie culture immediately.

NOTES

1. See Thomas G. Alexander, *Utah: The Right Place* (Layton, UT: Gibbs Smith, 2003), 124. The 1856 Republican National Convention in Philadelphia (the party's first year), passed a resolution to prohibit "the twin relics of barbarism"—polygamy and slavery. See Bill Federer, "Twin Relics of

Barbarism: Polygamy, Slavery," *World Net Daily*, 5 July 2015, http://www.wnd .com/2015/07/twin-relics-of-barbarism-polygamy-slavery/.

2.   Alexander, *Utah: The Right Place*, 124.

3.   Alexander, *Utah: The Right Place*, 124.

4.   Alexander, *Utah: The Right Place*, 124.

5.   See Thomas Romney, *The Mormon Colonies in Mexico* (Salt Lake City: Deseret Book, 1938); and F. LaMond Tullis, *Mormons in Mexico* (Logan: Utah State University Press, 1975).

6.   See Romney, *The Mormon Colonies in Mexico*; and Tullis, *Mormons in Mexico*.

7.   Romney, *The Mormon Colonies in Mexico*.

8.   Tullis, *Mormons in Mexico*.

9.   Tullis, *Mormons in Mexico*, 60

10. Bill Smith, "Impacts of the Mexican Revolution: The Mormon Experience, 1910–1946" (PhD diss., Washington State University, 2000).

11. James Bundy, VOR File 68-040.

12. John Jensen, VOR File 69-058.

13. Miriam Adelia Cox Wilson Riding, VOR File 68-113.

14. Mariah Delila Van Leuven Alldredge, VOR 68-035.

15. Thomas Eagar, VOR File 68-045.

16. Doretta Marie Iverson Bundy, VOR 68-026.

17. Alta Rowley Perkins Wilcox, VOR File 68-072.

18. Annie Eagar Covington, VOR File 70-007.

19. Omer Dick Bundy, VOR File 68-030.

20. William Shirley Black Sr., VOR File 70-031.

## Chapter 6

AMERICAN INDIANS

INTRODUCTION

Like virtually all other areas of the United States, the lands that European Americans settled on belonged to American Indians. The new arrivals assumed the right to claim those lands and impose their concept of civilization there, much to the disadvantage of the tribal people. The European system was based on agriculture, plowing the land, planting seeds, and nurturing the plants to be harvested—wheat, potatoes, fruit, cotton, and alfalfa. They also had domesticated pigs, goats, horses, cows, and chickens—some housed in barns, pens, and coops adjacent to their homes. They established permanent villages, homesteads, or ranches based on a concept that American Indians did not recognize—private property. This created a huge cultural clash. The Indians depended on hunting and gathering, living in wickiups, and seasonal goings and comings of tribal clans. Individual private property claims to land for farms, ranches, and villages, along with the new settlers' system of fencing was a direct challenge to the Indian culture.

Mormons brought European American methods (private property with permanent homes) with them to the Rocky Mountains. In addition, they set up irrigation systems that required control of streams and the establishment of permanent dams and ditches. They included cattle ranching and sheep herding in their way of life. It was dependent on grazing large numbers of animals beyond their farms seasonally— moving over considerable areas of so-called public lands. The sheep herds often included hundreds or even thousands of animals. A problem the Mormons created, however, is that their animals ate the seeds on the open range that the Indian women were accustomed to harvest to make flour. In southern Utah, that undercut the American Indian lifestyle, particularly of the Paiute tribe that was located there. One result was that the Paiutes changed some of their economic efforts and took on the strategy of raiding the sheep and cattle herds to provide food for their people. Mormons considered that as theft and could easily have engaged in a war against the Paiutes, but they restrained themselves.

Brigham Young called several missionaries to the Paiute tribe in the 1850s. Of those missionaries, Jacob Hamblin is the best known. He and his colleagues baptized many of the Paiutes and worked to further their culture and ally them with the Mormons. Because of the many villages that were established by the Mormons and the cattle herds that were fostered, the clash over grazing lands quickly arose. Hamblin argued in defense of the Paiutes, claiming that the Paiutes deserved the portion of the cattle they were taking for the right of the Mormons to use their lands for grazing. This contest between the two civilizations was ongoing, but the Mormons knew they needed an alliance with not only the Paiutes but also the other American Indians.

Southeast of Washington County, across the Colorado River, the Navajos had a large nation. North of them were the Hopis. It was absolutely essential that the Mormons avoid a war with those tribes. Even more, the Mormons needed the Indians as allies in a possible conflict with the federal government.

A war did indeed break out, known as the Black Hawk War. It started north of the Mojave Desert, in central Utah, and lasted four years. Some of the conflict spilled over into the southern area. The Mormons employed a strategy called "forting up," meaning that many of the settlers in smaller villages were instructed to move to the larger settlements to defend themselves. These events impacted areas such as the upper Virgin Valley, so one group of Mormons that had to move were the Grafton and Springdale people to Rockville. The men would go back to their farms in the daytime but return to the central village at night. A negotiated settlement was achieved. The lesson in all of this was that the Mormons and the American Indians needed each other.[1]

The tragedy of the Mountain Meadows Massacre in 1857 near Cedar City resulted from a complex series of events. About five years before that tragic event, Brigham Young called Jacob Hamblin and others such as John D. Lee to influence the American Indians. He hoped to restrain the Indians from raiding immigrant companies that were passing through southern Utah on their way to California. Had he not done that, the federal government likely would have sent troops to defend those immigrants, and the presence of such soldiers was something the Mormons wanted to avoid. When the federal government sent an army to northern Utah in 1857, the Mormons essentially went to war with the US government. Brigham Young, in an effort to strengthen the alliance with the Indians in the south, lifted the restraining order on raiding the immigrant trains. He tried to influence the immigrants to avoid the southern route by going the northern way, but not all of them wanted to do that. The Fancher party from Arkansas was one such group. As the Fanchers moved along the southern trail, they were increasingly frustrated because the Mormons in the villages they passed refused to sell them feed for their cattle. The Mormon leaders had instructed the villagers to store their feed in case federal troops came against them.

Along the way, the Fanchers met Jacob Hamblin, who was traveling to Salt Lake City. They asked Hamblin where they could find grazing land for their cattle. He recommended the Mountain Meadows area just southwest of Cedar City. By then, the Mormons in the Cedar City area had become furious with the Fanchers. They wanted to prevent them from getting to California because they would likely complain intensely about the Mormons and urge the federal army to go to Utah to punish the Mormons. The militia leaders in Cedar City claimed that the Fanchers were mobilizing in the Mountain Meadows and should be attacked. They enlisted Indian agent John D. Lee to convince the Paiute Indians to join with the Mormons in attacking the Fancher party. The Indian motive was to obtain their large herd of cattle. All of this occurred in September 1857.

The Mormon and Indian attack on the Fanchers did in fact happen, and it is considered the greatest tragedy in the history of the area. Recently, a significant book with greater understanding of the tragedy has been published.[2] The distinguishing aspect of this book is that it is based on documentation that was not previously available to other authors. The collections at the Church History Library in Salt Lake City were made available to them, something Juanita Brooks—an American historian and author who wrote about the Mountain Meadows Massacre—hoped for but was unable to obtain. The three authors were appointed to write the study by the Church with the understanding that it would be published by a national press without intervention by the Church. The authors also used sources in several national archives. They were able to determine which men were involved in the attack and what the role of the Paiutes was. They worked hard to find the names of those who were killed. They disproved the story John D. Lee told Brigham Young about the immigrant party poisoning a waterhole near Kanosh. According to the story, the Paiutes ate meat from cattle which had drunk the poisoned water, leading to the death of several Paiutes. Unfortunately, he said, this motivated the Indians to attack the Fanchers at Mountain Meadows. The authors also uncovered new information about Nephi Johnson's role in the event—translating instructions so the Indians would know when to attack, as well as actually giving the order. They concluded, however, that Isaac Haight ordered the killings. Richard E. Turley Jr. has continued their research, particularly about the two trials of John D. Lee.

An earlier source of information about American Indians in southern Utah is "Indian Relations on the Mormon Frontier," by Juanita Brooks.[3] This article indicated how important Juanita's future works would be. She points out that Brigham Young encouraged the Mormon settlers to attempt to prevent the Paiutes from selling their children to Mexicans and Utes who wanted to take them to Mexico and sell them as slaves. The Paiutes sometimes made these deals because they were destitute. He suggested that the Mormons buy the children and raise them to prevent such slavery. Young said, "No person can purchase them without their becoming as free, so far as natural rights are concerned, as persons of any other color."[4] The children were to be equal members of Mormon society. Brooks wrote that a law passed in 1852 by the territorial legislature required that such Indian children should be clothed and sent to school between the ages of seven and sixteen.[5]

Brooks wrote the following:

> Very early the Indians sensed the genuineness of the Mormon attitude, and often sold or gave their children to them. Indian mothers would then know where their babies were and be assured they were given good care. In her later life, Ann Chatterly McFarlane used often to tell of the time when an Indian mother ran into her house in Cedar City and thrusting a two-year old son toward her said, "Hide him, quick!" and disappeared out the back door. Ann had not time to find a hiding place, so she lifted her long, full skirt and but the baby under, telling him to stand on her feet and hold to her legs.
>
> Almost before she had him placed, the warriors came, searching for the child. Mrs. McFarlane pretended not to understand, and in answer to their questions shook her head and pointed off in the opposite direction from which the mother had gone. The men went through the house, searching in every corner, under the bed, in the cellar and closets. In the meantime she went about her work, the child beneath her skirts as quiet as a quail. After a few days his mother returned and took him away.[6]

Why did the Paiutes respond positively to the Mormons? One reason is that the federal agents came up with the idea of Indian reservations. They felt it would be wise to move Indians to lands that were less desirable for Americans. In the case of the Paiutes, the federal officers wanted to move them to the Uintahs. The Paiutes were adamant about not leaving their sacred red sands, and they did not want to live with the Utes. Their resistance was eventually successful, but the Paiutes knew the Mormons would not leave the area either. Brooks said, "Perhaps it was not alone the teachings of the Mormons that had caused the distinction in the minds of the natives. The Mormons planned to stay in Utah permanently, and it was necessary for them to cultivate the friendship of the Indians if they were to be safe, especially in the smaller, scattered settlements."[7]

Brooks cites Brigham Young's policy of friendliness with the Indians: "When you go among the Lamanites, deal with them honestly and righteously in all things. Any man who cheats a Lamanite should be dealt with more severely than for cheating a white man. . . . I am sorry that some of our brethren have been killed by the Indians, but I am far more sorry that some of the Indians have been slain by the brethren."[8]

There was often a lack of sympathy for the Indian viewpoint. For example, after a group of Navajos killed Dr. J. W. Whitmore and Robert McIntyre on 8 January 1866, a company commanded by James Andrus murdered a group of innocent Paiutes. Paiutes seemed to be a liability because the Mormons sometimes had to feed them. This charity continued until 1891 when the US government purchased a tract of land for a Paiute reservation in Washington County.

Juanita Books raised the issue of the fate of the adopted Indian children. She points out, "A surprising number of Indian children in white homes died in childhood or early adolescence; they seem to have had little resistance to white man's diseases, especially measles."[9] Albert Hamblin, Jacob Hamblin's adopted Indian son, was an example of a promising youth who died in his twenties. She also observed that seven of the adoptees returned to live with their Paiute community in adulthood. Juanita gave several examples of such.

Then there are stories of intermarriage. She mentions Janet, who was purchased as an infant by Silas Smith of Parowan. As a young adult, she received an offer from a middle-aged polygamist to marry him. She refused, saying she only wanted to marry Dudley Leavitt, also a polygamist. George A. Smith convinced Leavitt to take her as his fourth wife. They had eleven children.

An article by Catherine S. and Don D. Fowler points out that the practice of childhood slavery in the period before 1860 also kept the population from expanding. The Utes not only took the children away, they also brought material culture items such as knives, kettles, tipis, guns, and eventually horses. Fowler and Fowler write:

> Apart from the official policies of Brigham Young, individual
> Mormons and non-Mormons in Utah held varying opinions about
> the Indians, most of them consistent with general American views

of the period. These ranged from common stereotypes of Indians as lazy, shiftless, thieving savages of little worth, to more positive attitudes noting their basic industry, intelligence, and educability. Many felt that although they were basically 'savages' the Indian could and should be taught 'civilized' ways even though most considered this would be a slow process. Few whites advocated a policy of complete integration as the two cultures were held to be too far removed from each other. Mormon ideology regarding the origin and identity of the Indians generally was responsible for some favorable attitudes and policies toward them, but it may also have been a contributing factor in maintaining a degree of social distance between the groups. Gradually, a place for the Indians was prepared within Mormon society as a whole—a place as an unskilled labor force to be tapped upon mutual consent and a position of association but not integration into local settlements."[10]

A contrasting group of Native Americans are the Hopis because their lifestyle and achievements were much more like the Mormons. They lived in permanent dwellings and engaged in agriculture. They were peaceful and stable. Jacob Hamblin and the LDS Church leaders were anxious to include them in the Mormon sphere of influence, even to entice them to come across the Colorado River and live in Utah. Fifteen missions of Mormons were sent to the Hopis under Jacob Hamblin's supervision, but the Hopis refused to leave their land. Hopi traditions spoke of bearded white men who would come to them and live among them. The Hopis were friendly and listened to the Mormon message, but did not respond to it.

But Hopi friendship had its limits. This was particularly true when food was in short supply. Without food or trade goods, their welcome quickly wore thin. "Judging from Mormon accounts, the Hopi were fixed in an otherwise fluid frontier; . . . most of them did not travel widely for trade or any other purpose."[11]

W. Paul Reeve's book *Making Space on the Western Frontier*[12] is a significant source for those wanting to know about the Paiutes. He argues that the Paiutes were steeped in their chosen space. Their religious beliefs claimed that God placed them in the Mojave Desert, a land full of sand

and desert mountains, and they refused to depart. They had a rich sense of community based on geography and religion. In this way they had much in common with the Mormons. They understood the Mormons more than they understood the miners. The Mormons were agriculturalists; the miners were not. The Mormons would stay; the miners would not. But the Mormons could not win the Paiutes to their view of land as a place for farms. Their worldviews clashed. The Paiutes did not fence the land; they roamed it. Only seldom did they irrigate it. The result is that the Mormon expansion on the land drove the Paiutes into a corner which eventually forced them into wage labor. Either they had to settle on the Shivwits Reservation, established in 1891 near Ivins, or they had to find low-level wage jobs. Reeve states, "The attempts of government officials to redefine Paiute space clearly failed to take [not listening to strangers] into account. For most of the nineteenth century, the Moapa Reservation proved useless to the Paiutes. They therefore reinvented their economic space, incorporating their new neighbors (Mormons and miners) into a mixed system. While that system fixed the Paiutes at the lowest rung of white economic ladder, it opened fresh ways to supplement a subsistence economy. More importantly, it allowed Paiutes to stay on their homelands."[13]

Ronald Walker notes in his article[14] that several recent scholars have taken a critical view of early Mormon actions: "Since pioneer times, Mormons have seen their acts toward the Indian as kindly and well meaning, and the majority of Mormon historians when crafting an occasional chapter or article have spoken with this viewpoint. They liked what they saw, or at least unconsciously accepted the cultural assumptions of which they were a part. This tendency has led to what might be described as the traditional view of Mormon-Indian relations. Begun by Hubert Howe Bancroft, Orson F. Whitney, and B. H. Roberts, it has continued in our own time with such scholars as Juanita Brooks."[15]

Walker then goes on to describe the work of recent historians, such as revisionists Floyd O'Neil and Stanford Layton, who are highly critical of how Mormon settlers related to the American Indians: "O'Neil and Layton see the Mormons' land hunger as voracious, their motives suspect, and their effect on the Indians 'devastating.' Brigham Young, in turn, is viewed, especially in his dealings with Washington-appointed territorial officials, as arbitrary and ultimately ineffectual. The authors, however, concede some Mormon peculiarity: 'Mormonism's stormy mid-western experience, its New England heritage, its scriptural base, and its schizophrenic view of government in the nineteenth century combined to create its own script that was acted out on the Utah Stage.'"[16]

Sondra Jones provides a landmark study on this subject.[17] She reviews the clashing interpretations of those who see early Mormons as sympathetic to the Indians and those who see the Mormons as hostile to them. She said: "Mormon settlers faithfully followed Brigham Young's instructions, in particular his orders to feed rather than fight the Indians, and did their best to teach and civilize them."[18] She noted, "Scholars castigated Mexican and Ute slavers, but wrote favorably of Mormon efforts to rescue and redeem Paiute and Gosiute children by fostering or indenturing them into their homes."[19] Jones is favorable to John Alton Peterson's *Utah's Black Hawk War*, referring to it as "the most comprehensive and detailed chronicling of Mormon atrocities to date."[20] Jones discusses a book[21] written by Ronald Holt, saying, "Holt drew attention to the paradox that 'the negative consequence of being helped could be as pervasive and profound as those of being exploited.'"[22] She also criticizes the actions of Ernest L. Wilkinson and Utah senator Arthur Watkins, who used the federal government to limit the Indians' claims to land.[23]

Though she included the many criticisms of the Mormon relationships with Indians, she has some positive words to stress: "No historian can escape the influence of their own perspectives, including this writer; however, after thirty years of being pulled through the interpretive tides of revisionist opinions about Mormon-Indian relations, I would argue that, while spattered with injustice and abuse, the pattern of Mormon-Indian relations still differed to a *significant* degree from Indian relations elsewhere on the American frontiers, particularly during the first fifteen years of Mormon settlement."[24]

The most recent and most ambitious work on American Indians in the southern Utah region is Todd Compton's *A Frontier Life: Jacob Hamblin, Explorer and Indian Missionary*.[25] Instead of dwelling on Hamblin's village building efforts at Santa Clara, Compton concentrates on Hamblin's efforts as an explorer. He describes expedition after expedition in the southwest region, often across the Colorado River—the grueling hiking on narrow trails and steep canyons, the continual illnesses, and the lack of water and food, all while dealing with various Indian languages. Hamblin's goal in doing this was to plant new Mormon settlements in the regions where Navajo and Hopi Indians were in control. These were beyond Santa Clara and Kanab, towns that Hamblin had founded. They were also east and south, in distant places in the desert where few white men lived. This was clearly a mission to bring Zion further into the desert and to expand the boundaries of Zion. These were to be places for possible new settlements as well as places of refuge should the Mormons have to leave the Salt Lake and Utah Valleys.

Next, Compton ventures into interpretation. He argues that Hamblin's missions were not acts of individualism, nor were they what Frederick Jackson Turner argued was the motive of Americans who explored the West, which was to obtain land. There was no profit motive, nor were the explorers attempting to create a monument to themselves. Instead, Compton argues that Hamblin's efforts were communitarian. He and his fellow explorers were planting a Zion version of community in a vast landscape. These missionaries were not on a salary, and they had to finance the effort themselves, often seeking aid along the way and usually living from the land. Individual accomplishment is usually considered the mode of the settlement of the West. Hamblin spent his life promoting communitarian achievements, an approach that was a natural outgrowth of the Mormon village system.

While some explorations in the US West were funded by the federal government, Hamblin's were not. They were not funded by the Church, either. Church leaders did issue the call for these explorations, but they did not allot any finances to help with the task. Just as the Mormon villages came about by a call from the Prophet, they were not the result of a financial appropriation. If settlers accepted the call, they then had to use all of their own talent and finances to create a Mormon village. That same mode was the base of the several missions Hamblin and his colleagues undertook into the US Southwest.

When the Hamblin-led companies contacted the Hopis, they were welcomed. Hamblin knew that the Hopis were somewhat similar to the

Mormons. They lived in villages, often carved into cliffs, and they used irrigation to raise crops. The Mormon explorers were hopeful that the Hopis would become Mormons when they learned about the Book of Mormon. Initially, Hamblin and his companions felt this was possible. The Hopis hosted them and even agreed to let a couple of missionaries stay with them for a year. When Hamblin returned in a year, he was disappointed. The Hopis had no intention of leaving their villages or their religion. They would not cross the Colorado River and be with the Mormons.

The Navajos were another story—they were hostile to the Mormons. They claimed that the Mormons had killed three of their men in central Utah, and they wanted to kill Hamblin as revenge. He skillfully convinced them to send one of their respected elders to the site. When he returned, he confirmed Hamblin's story (that Mormons were not the killers). Unfortunately, twenty-year-old George A. Smith Jr. was ambushed and killed by Navajos on one of Hamblin's missions, which was a definite setback for the missions.

Another problem with the Indian-Mormon relationship was that Indians were in competition with groups of Mormons who had very similar values as the Indians did. The Indians felt they were in sacred land. They spent their efforts for their group, not just their family. Both Indians and Mormons were convinced that they were being directed by their God. They differed on many secular things, too—farming, fencing, dwellings, and schools. Compton causes his readers to consider Indians more sympathetically.

The people who were interviewed by Franklin Harris in 1968–70 had some contact, though not a lot, with American Indians, mainly Paiutes. They include a few limited comments in their interviews, but here they give a spectrum of attitudes about the Indians.

INTERVIEWS

LAFAVE JONES LEANY

LaFave Jones Leany was born on 26 May 1907 in Duchesne but lived in Tabiona, St. George, and Bloomington. She tells about her mother's encounter with Indians: "An Indian man came to our house with a little girl about my age. We were two or three years old. She was sick. I think she had pneumonia [and] lung congestion. My mother put mustard plasters on her, soaked her with tea, and doctored her until she was feeling pretty good again. She said to the Indian [man], 'Why don't you give me this little girl? She is about the age of my little girl, and they could be companions.' He said he could not [because] it would hurt him, and he pointed to his heart. It would hurt him in his heart. She died within a week or so after he took her [home].

"There were also a lot of Indian squaws around that part of town. [They were] down the creek. They would come to my mother with a piece of cloth and want her to make them a dress. So she would make them a dress. She would say, 'Now you go home and take a bath. Clean up before you put this dress on.' They would not [do it]. They would just put the dress on top of another. [They put] one dirty dress on top of another. They would have four or five dresses on at one time."[26]

GEORGE WILSON MCCONKIE

George Wilson McConkie was born on 30 June 1909 in Moab, Utah. Throughout his life, he lived in LaSal, Salt Lake City, Elko, and St. George. He was directly involved with Indians through the LDS Church: "Soon after we came to St. George, a Stake Conference was held. It was announced that there [was] some Indian handiwork in the basement of the tabernacle [that] they would like people to see. Being interested in Indians, I dropped down in the basement and met Lucy Graff. The first thing I knew, I had some Indian work [to do] here too. Altogether, I spent about ten and one-half years working with the Paiute Indians in Elko and here. My wife was also involved in the Indian work [for] about the same length of time.

"For a while we were assigned as missionaries [to the Indians]. We were under the Stake Mission leader. Then I was Sunday School Superintendent at the reservation for some time. Later, when [the LDS Church unit] was made a branch, I was made branch president out there. We enjoyed it very much and we had many Indian friends. A few of them still drop in to see us for a visit. Lots of them come in when they have trouble and need a little help.

"We have taken four different Indian children into our home at different times, one at a time. [We] tried to help them out a little. Sometimes it seemed to be quite effective and other times not. Two of these [children] we took on our own, and the other [two] we received through the [LDS] church placement program. The boy we had last year is attending BYU this year. We are very happy with [how] he is doing and anxious to see him make the most of his life. He seems like one of our own, Jonathan Probashini. He came from down in Gallup, New Mexico, area. He is a fine boy [and] is looking forward to [serving] a mission. His objective is to become a school teacher in the Gallup area."[27]

FREDERICK CHENEY VAN BUREN

Frederick Cheney Van Buren was born on 26 September 1883. He tells a very different story because his father fought in the Black Hawk Indian War: "My father fought all through the Blackhawk Indian War. He was not only a good farmer; he was a good Indian fighter. He had a code all of his own. For instance, they came back from Grass Valley, where he had killed three Indians. He had been sent to guard a trail. When the shooting stopped up on the hill, his partners went up there. They hadn't any more than left [when] there come four Indians down the trail. He shot at them with his gun, but he said he didn't think he even frightened them. He knew that something had to happen. So he sat down and took his cap and ball six-shooter, put his elbows on his knees and shot as they came up. One of them fell, [but] they kept coming. They didn't know where the shots were coming from. As they came on, he shot and down [went] another [Indian]. The other two saw him, and they detoured and ran across [to the hill]. As they ran over the hill, shot at the two. He [shot] one of them in the heel. They caught two Indians and were going to execute them in Nephi. He didn't know it was the same Indians. The Indians told him [because] the Indians knew him. He was delegated to shoot these two Indians and he wouldn't do it. He wouldn't shoot a tied-up Indian. He said that if they would turn them loose he would try to get his share, but he wouldn't shoot a tied-up Indian. He didn't want to be executioner, so he was court-martialed. There wasn't much they could do because they needed all of the men and he was a good Indian fighter. It wasn't very serious."[28]

JOSEPH AURELIUS HASLEM

Joseph Aurelius Haslem was born in Cedar City in 1902. He gives a child's view of Indians there: "I can remember at times the Indians would get drunk and go on a rampage. They didn't do any harm to the white people, but they sometimes would get in a fight among themselves and hurt some of them. The white people were a little leery of them. I know my mother knew them pretty well, and she was a little worried about them. They would come around our place quite a bit. They worked for us on the farm once in a while and played here a little bit. They were from the Paiute Indian Tribe of Utah, I think. Some of them were very good. They were one or two of the very bad ones from the early days who were still alive that lived there. I remember one that was named Marycatch. He was a mean-looking Indian and wasn't sociable like the rest of them. At times there would be one of them at a time who would work for us. They would work around the farm for a little while, maybe a week or two."[29]

LAFAYETTE HALL

Lafayette Hall from Rockville, born in 1888, tells a short tale about American Indians. "I was advanced to the teachers [quorum]. As quick as I [was] in the teachers [quorum], they had us go around with the older men to teach us. I had a smart companion [David Lemmon] who was an Indian who had been raised by the whites.

"In the early days here, the California Trail went from the east to California. The Navajos would come here and steal the Paiute children. Then they would sell them to the people coming through. They would take them to California and sell them as slaves. They had quite a slave trade here. Even some of the Navajos, when they were raiding the Paiutes, were hard pressed for something to eat.

"Brigham Young advised the Saints that they could trade for those children [and] raise them in their homes. I might tell a little instance that happened to my folks in Rockville. One night the Navajos were here. They were camping a little below town. It was quiet, [and] they heard something outside. It was a little [Paiute Indian] squaw with her baby. It was several months old. She said, 'You keep my baby? The Navajos [are] here. You keep my baby?' They said, 'Yes.' In the corner [was] a pile of rags, [and] she laid her baby in that pile of rags. That [baby] would stay there all day and not make a whimper. It would look at you and [fix] its eyes at you, but it would not make a whimper. After dark, [the mother] would slip in and feed that baby, and it stayed until the Navajos left."[30]

GEORGE CHAMP HENRIE

George Champ Henrie was born on 12 April 1912 in Panguitch. He tells the story of their Navajo foster child, Linda Reese Curley: "While [our son] Wallace was on a[n LDS] Navajo Mission, he took a liking to [Linda Rose Curley] and wanted us to take her [in the] school program, which we consented to do. I believe my wife said [she was] eight. I thought she was nine.

"Anyway, this is her sixth year with us. We have enjoyed her a lot. She is good to mind [and] good to help. We had always heard the statement about 'Honest Injun' and I believe it. She has been the [most honest person] in the world that way. One day she wanted some money for lunch. I gave her too much, and I thought she could just use the rest of [the money]. I gave her fifty cents too much, and she handed me the fifty cents back.

"We have never in her life sent her to a store but what she comes right back and hands us the change. 'Linda, do you want the nickel?' She looks and laughs for it. She has always [received] the kind of marks in school that I wish I could have [received]. I wish I had put forth the effort so that I could have [received] that kind [of grades]. She likes to take part [in activities]. She likes church and church activities. She likes games. I used to be amazed. When she first came here, she was not accustomed to all our different games, cards and checkers. Finally, she would catch on fast and just loved them. She would make us sit up and take notice too. We took her over to Usher's one night and played Yahtzee. None of us had ever played Yahtzee. She beat about her share of those games. It was the first time we had ever played it. She tries to figure things out as she goes."[31]

EMMA JARVIS MCARTHUR

Emma Jarvis (Cottam) McArthur was born on 27 December 1882 in St. George. She tells about Indians in her neighborhood: "Daddy developed one block east of Grandpa near where the Indians camped. They lived across the street here in their wickiups. They were [from the Shivwits band of] the

Paiute [Indian Tribe of Utah]. They were friendly. I wasn't afraid of them. At Christmastime I always saw to it that we had enough bread and meat [so] that we could divide with them Christmas morning. There [would be] seventeen to twenty standing there [at my door] wanting something to eat for Christmas. We went out and danced with them a few times. When we moved a little farther east, we used to have one of the squaws help me with the washing. We used to wash [our clothes] on [a wash]board. For a big family we would have clothes on the three big [clothes]lines and on the fence, north and west of us.

"The squaws liked to work [and] they only charged us $1.00 a washing. When I was a little girl, Mother only paid the squaw $0.25 but she was satisfied. She did the rubbing and Mother did the rest of it. When I paid the squaw $1.00, she did it all but hanging [the clothes] out.

"They never talked much about [the gospel]. As far as I remember, they kept quiet while you [were] asking the blessing. Often they would set by us while we were eating.

"Sometimes we would feed them at the table, but they would rather sit off by themselves. They liked something sweet like honey or molasses. They [called honey] 'bee molasses.' They liked honey better than molasses."[32]

NORMA BRINGHURST EMPEY

Norma Bringhurst Empey was born in Toquerville in 1912. She tells this story: "I remember my Grandmother Bringhurst telling me of an instance. There was an Indian, and he was kind of a mean Indian. Everyone was afraid of him. He came into town drunk one day when everyone was gone. He got a hold of the baby before Grandma could get there and he was going to throw her. Grandma picked up a knife and went for him. [She] told him that she would kill him if he did. He was so taken aback and shocked that he just put the baby down and left. He came back many times and told her [that] she was the bravest squaw in the world. If it had not been for her he would have done something bad. He thanked her for her courage.

"There were many [times], especially up at Rockville where this type of [event] happened. . . . There was a great many people who lived in fear all of the time of [Indians]. Toquerville itself was named for Chief Toquer, the chief of the Indian tribe that lived near there. That is where Toquerville got its name."[33]

BODIL MARGARET PULSIPHER

Bodil Margaret Johnson Pulsipher was born on 13 February 1890 in Colonia Juárez, Chihuahua, Mexico. Her father was Nephi Johnson. She tells briefly about her father taking the Indians into what is now Zion National Park near where they lived. The Indians feared going up into the canyon: "They worried, stewed, and coaxed, 'No we still have more to see.' He stayed in there for a long time. He came back out and they were pretty near scared. They thought it was his spirit. They knew he wouldn't [survive].³⁴ He said they were crying. They didn't believe it. They had never been up there. I think from history [he was the first white man who had been up there]. They never did find anybody else unless it was lately.

"[When] they finished the tunnel [in 1930], they made up through there, they had me come up. My grandson was old enough to drive a car, [so] he took me up. We had a [good] time. There were people from around [who] took care of the party. They dedicated it."³⁵

MARY ANN (ADAMS) STARR

Mary Ann (Adams) Starr was born on 29 October 1902 in Cedar City. She tells a frightening experience: "The time the Indian came [we were living in] the same house. The Indian camp was south of town and my father was off freighting to the Milford and Delamar mines in Nevada. We had all gone to bed. Something woke Mother up. She heard someone breathing hard. She told us all to be quiet, and she got up. She was afraid to light the lamp. She could see the outline of this woman. She asked who it was and the old squaw jabbered and said she wanted "Tom." Of course mother knew she meant Thomas Urie, the city marshal. She told her where she [would] have to go down there to get [him]. The squaw told her that all the Indians were drunk and beating up on their squaws. She had come for help. She seemed confused. Mother told her, the best she could, where to go [to find him.] It was in the middle of the night, late for us anyway. She left and Mother barred the doors because [people] didn't used to lock their doors."³⁶

CONCLUSIONS

There was clearly a double relationship between the white people and the Native Americans. On the one hand, Mormons were at war with Indians for four years. Some, especially men, became Indian haters and were involved in killing Indians. Interestingly, their hatred did not transfer to Indian children. On the other hand, Mormons living in villages interacted with the Paiutes and Navajos often. Sometimes these contacts were friendly, while others involved confrontations. Tragically, three members of the Berry family at Pipe Springs were murdered. They are buried at Grafton.

Some of the whites had interesting extended relationships with American Indians. Several of the whites adopted Indian children, either permanently or during their school years. One family included an Indian mother, and another had a member who was part American Indian. But even then, those natives were often not considered as equal. Undoubtedly, the whites felt that the Indians were primitive, and this in turn hurt the child.

The American Indian values often clashed with the whites. Some of them moved seasonally and did not recognize federal or private ownership of the open lands. Whites also wanted to use those lands for grazing their cattle and sheep herds. This often led to clashes.

The Mormon settlers had both a fear and a fondness for American Indians. Those who lived close to them gradually entered into a working relationship with them, trading, interacting, and hoping they would become Mormons and farmers. The children were the key element. Both Indians and Mormons hoped to help the Indian children. The Mormons wanted them in their schools and even in their families, while the Indians wanted to preserve their long-standing values and culture.

NOTES

1. For more information on this conflict, see John Alton Peterson, *Utah's Black Hawk War* (Salt Lake City: University of Utah Press, 1998). It is well balanced, considering both American Indian and Mormon interests and involvement.

2. Richard E. Turley Jr., Ronald W. Walker, and Glen M. Leonard, *Massacre at Mountain Meadows: An American Tragedy* (New York: Oxford University Press, 2008).

3. Juanita Brooks, "Indian Relations on the Mormon Frontier," *Utah Historical Quarterly* 12 (January–April 1944); 1–49.

4. Brooks, "Indian Relations on the Mormon Frontier," 7.

5. Brooks, "Indian Relations on the Mormon Frontier," 8.

6. Brooks, "Indian Relations on the Mormon Frontier," 14–15.

7. Brooks, "Indian Relations on the Mormon Frontier," 18.

8. Brooks, "Indian Relations on the Mormon Frontier," 21.

9. Brooks, "Indian Relations on the Mormon Frontier," 33.

10. Catherine S. Fowler and Don Fowler, "Notes on the History of the Southern Paiutes and Western Shoshonis," *Utah Historical Quarterly* 39, no. 2 (1971): 93–113.

11. Fowler and Fowler, "Notes on the History of the Southern Paiutes and Western Shoshonis," 186–87.

12. W. Paul Reeve, *Making Space on the Western Frontier: Mormons, Miners, and Southern Paiutes* (Urbana: University of Illinois Press, 2006).

13. Reeve, *Making Space on the Western Frontier*, 83–84.

14. Ronald Walker, "Toward Reconstruction of Mormon and Indian Relations, 1847–1877," *BYU Studies* 29, no. 4 (Fall 1989): 23–42.

15. Walker, "Toward Reconstruction," 24.

16. Walker, "Toward Reconstruction," 26.

17. Sondra Jones, "Saints or Sinners? The Evolving Perception of Mormon Indian Relations in Utah Historiography," *Utah Historical Quarterly* 72, no. 1 (2004): 19–46.

18. Jones, "Saints or Sinners?," 23.

19. Jones, "Saints or Sinners?," 24.

20. Jones, "Saints or Sinners?," 29.

21. Ronald Holt, *Beneath These Red Cliffs: An Ethnohistory of the Utah Paiutes* (Albuquerque: University of New Mexico Press, 1992).

22. Jones, "Saints or Sinners?," 31.

23. Jones, "Saints or Sinners?," 32.

24. Jones, "Saints or Sinners?," 34–35, emphasis in original.

25. Todd Compton, *A Frontier Life: Jacob Hamblin, Explorer and Indian Missionary* (Salt Lake City: University of Utah Press, 2013).

26. LaFave Jones Leany, VOR File 69-125.
27. George Wilson McConkie, VOR File 68-092.
28. Frederick Cheney Van Buren, VOR File 69-098.
29. Joseph Aurelius Haslem, VOR File 69-192.
30. Lafayette Hall, VOR File 69-177.
31. George Champ Henrie, VOR File 69-184.
32. Emma Jarvis (Cottam) McArthur, VOR File 69-166.
33. Norma Bringhurst Empey, VOR File 69-126.
34. Rather, they *thought* he wouldn't survive being in the canyon.
35. Bodil Margaret Johnson Pulsipher, VOR File 70-035.
36. Mary Ann (Adams) Starr, VOR File 69-197.

## Chapter 7

SERVICE—
MILITARY, CHURCH,
AND CIVIC EFFORTS

INTRODUCTION

If there was anything that bound the people of these villages together, it was their membership and activity in their church. Not all of them were devoted believers. Some were not involved in church at all, but most were. The LDS Church was the center not only of worship but also of entertainment, compassionate help, health care, burials, celebrations, and some of the education. The most demanding service was when people were sent to serve full-time missions outside the Great Basin area. Men were often called to leave young families while they proselytized in distant lands for two or three years. Families usually had to work the farms, support themselves, and send their husbands and fathers some funds because their missionary service was voluntary, not reimbursed by the Church. Young men and some young women were also called prior to being married. Single young people, married men, older couples, and some older singles (widows and widowers) served in Europe, the Pacific, and most parts of the United States and Canada.

Equally demanding was a call to preside over a ward or a stake. Members of bishoprics, stake presidencies, and high councils devoted many hours every week for several years to their congregation members, also as volunteers. Other callings included teaching in the various Church auxiliaries, providing music, and visiting all of the members each month. Some people spent many hours serving as temple workers or patrons, especially in their later years. The Church members supported each other in health problems, and the elders were regularly called to give blessings, as were patriarchs. Members of the Relief Society were in charge of preparing bodies for burials, as well as many other forms of service. Most of all, everyone was a neighbor; all were bound by friendship and fellowship. Sharing with those in need was the norm, including with American Indians and anyone passing through. Some people in these communities were not active in religious matters, but they were an integral part of the village or town.

Each of the various towns needed citizen service—mayors and council members, water canal company directors and committee members, postmasters, cemetery sextons, election judges, road builders and maintainers, and school board members. Almost everything the town needed was dependent on volunteer service.

Of the seventeen people who reported in their interview that they served in the military, mostly during World War I, none went into detail about their time in the military. There was one important man from the St. George area who did serve, but he was not interviewed. His name was Nels Anderson, and he is mentioned in detail in two or three interviews of others (see Joseph Alma Terry, VOR File 69-102). At age twenty-nine, after teaching at the LDS Academy in St. Johns, Arizona, Nels voluntarily enlisted in the army. He was much more mature than most of the American troops. He decided to keep a diary, even though the military leaders discouraged the practice for fear such a book would fall into the hands of the enemy. Nels protected his diary, which survived up to today. It has recently been published.[1]

Anderson's diary mostly tells about the daily life on or near the front in France in 1918, but also describes some training weeks in England. His account is insightful. In his diary he captures what many men from Utah, Arizona, and Nevada experienced if they got to the war front in France. To vent his frustrations, he wrote letters home, some of them to his adopted families in Dixie and some to his colleagues and students in St. Johns, Arizona, or his fellow students at BYU. In one letter he commented: "Several of the fellows are reading the Bible. It seems that men will swing over when they are in danger. They are humbler and more prayerful once they are face to face with the stern reality. This isn't general, but it is true of many of the fellows. It is good to turn ones thoughts to God in case of danger but it is better to have done that before. A fellow has no time to pray when a ship is sinking; he must act then. His praying should have been done before."[2] He goes on: "I had quite a talk with some fellows this morning on Mormonism. It is surprising how little some fellows know about us. He told me that he heard the Mormons believed in free love. He was surprised when I told him that marriage was the most sacred ordinance in our church."[3] Another account was more reminiscent: "These lighthouses along the [English] shore make me think of Sam Brooks. His dad was born in a lighthouse somewhere along this coast."[4]

In another letter he wrote, "I attended a good service this evening. After service the chaplain urged the fellows to join some church before crossing the channel. . . . He was a very liberal preacher."[5] A more practical comment Nels made was: "I have new reasons for being thankful that I am an American. . . . I am thankful too that I don't use tobacco."[6]

Here is a more detailed account of his constant searching for comrades from his Utah-Dixie homeland and their Mormon values: "I was fortunate in finding 353 Infantry as I hunted up some of the Arizona boys who were with me at detention camp. I found Guy Rencher, . . . Johnny Slaughter, . . . [and] Lehi Smith. . . . I got to see two Mexican boys from Springerville: Salazar and Padilla. Smith says they are good soldiers. Smith and I walked about town. I broke my last $1.00 to buy a book for a diary."[7] Memories were also an important way to keep links with the homeland. On Utah's Pioneer Day, 24 July, Nels wrote in his diary:

> If I were back home I would have a big time today. They may be having a celebration as it is but I am satisfied they are not having the good time they would have if the boys were home. 10 year's ago today I went to my first pioneer programme at Enterprise. I heard Grandpa Woods speak of his journey across the plains and the entrance of the pioneers into Salt Lake Valley, July 24, 1847.

I was impressed with the talk. It was not a sermon as much as a plain talk of experiences. I found myself in love with the old man and in sympathy with the people who suffered such hardships that they might build homes out there in the desert where the howling mobs would not molest them.[8]

For LDS servicemen in all wars, being with fellow believers was important. Here is an example from one who later became a significant author and government official soon after his military experiences in Europe:

I put in for a pass this morning [and] no sooner had I got the pass till I was put on a detail to carry powder. I carried my share quickly and beat it. I started off toward a place called Neuf Chateau to get trace of the 342 machine gun outfit. There is where Bushman is. I ran upon his outfit quite accidently. He has been less than 3 miles from here all the while.

I ate dinner with him and then the two of us started for (Rimaucourt) We were lucky to get a truck and the result was Bush and L. L. Smith and I were together all afternoon. We couldn't stay long as I had 4 miles and he had 6 to get back to our outfits for retreat. Bush and Smith both come from Snow Flake [Arizona] so they had quite a reunion. Smith is very homesick. He was married only a week before he came to the army. It is just 3 months ago today since the three of us met at Holbrook to entrain for [Fort] Funston. It did me good to meet those fellows today. We agreed that we could get more joy from living our religion than any other source especially at this time of uncertainties.[9]

Then there was the future. Nels tells how they made plans: "Last night I had a good visit with Bushman. We talked over the school proposition. We decided that the officers training would not teach us anything useful so we thought that if we got home in February or March we could go back to school at home and finish with a few hours to the good."[10] That is what he did. Nels graduated from BYU as student body president and went to the University of Chicago for a master's degree, NYU for a doctorate, and then began a long career with the federal government. He wrote a landmark book, *Desert Saints*, about the Mormons and later became a professor of sociology in Canada and lived to age ninety-three.

The stories of the fifty-four people quoted in this study who served LDS missions are included in their interviews, whereas those seventeen individuals who served in the two world wars merely mentioned their service and did not give details. Of the group of missionaries, seventeen who served were women, some as wives, some as widows, and some as single women. The men included many who were young and single, but several were married, whose family stayed at home and supported the father in his service. Some men went in later years.

The missionaries were not professional clergy men; they were not salaried. They were self-supporting, although they depended largely upon the hospitality of the people in their area. It was called "travelling without purse or scrip." If they were married, their family at home had to support itself and even send some money to the missionary. Often their local congregation helped them. The missionaries' purpose was to proselyte and convert people in their assigned area to join the Church. They worked closely with Church members in those lands to build up congregations and help people become devoted to the restored gospel. Many of those people then immigrated to the United States, sometimes reestablishing contact with the missionaries. The missionaries usually served two years, but some stayed longer and some for a shorter period. Some had to learn a new language. Many experienced considerable rejection and had to examine their message closely. It was a time of major growth and sacrifice for missionaries. Their experience as missionaries clearly introduced them to the idea of service, and that service often continued throughout their life.

Mormon missionary work began when the Church was founded in 1830. By 1900 missions existed throughout North America (including Mexico), northwest Europe, and Polynesia. In 1901 President Lorenzo Snow renewed the emphasis on taking the gospel into all the world. Heber J. Grant of the Quorum of the Twelve Apostles dedicated Japan for the preaching of the gospel that same year. Francis M. Lyman, also of the Twelve, dedicated the lands of Africa, Finland, France, Greece, Italy, Palestine, Poland, and Russia for missionary work. The result is that some of the people interviewed for this study served throughout the world. An extensive focus of volunteer service was the village LDS Church. It was completely run by a service mentality; no one received pay. Virtually all active members had some kind of responsibility—teaching classes, visiting families, singing in the choir, helping the bishop, giving blessings, taking youth on outings or coaching them in athletics, putting on drama productions, cleaning the Church building and repairing it, preparing diverse celebrations, and even building Church facilities. All of it was service, even done by the Daughters of Utah Pioneers, the Sons of Utah Pioneers, and the Chamber of Commerce. Everyone was involved. In these interviews, almost all of the folks mention some sort of service in which they participated.

Community service is much more difficult to describe. It is not difficult to understand that each of the villages where these people lived had to maintain a water system, support a school with a school board, set up a city council and mayor, create a cemetery, construct one or more parks, build roads, choose a justice of the peace court, erect a post office, hold celebrations with music and bands, and maintain religious congregations. In addition, there were wider efforts from organizations such as the Red Cross, the Daughters of Utah Pioneers, and Sons of Utah Pioneers. Some people served larger constituencies, being members of the state legislature, the Chamber of Commerce, or the Farmers Association. Most of this service was voluntary. Certainly the extensive service in the LDS Church was all voluntary and included most of the members of the congregation. It included serving as a bishop or one of his counselors, leading the Relief Society (women's organization), teaching Sunday School, leading or teaching in the Mutual Improvement Association (youth organization), visiting all the families each month, attending to priesthood responsibilities, and more. All organizations needed community service. It was taught to the youth and expected of all community members.

An important book by Edward Banfield, *The Moral Basis of a Backward Society*, was written about this service in Mormon villages. The author lived a short stint in Gunlock, Utah, where he keenly observed the Mormon village system. Then he did an extensive study of village life in southern Italy. He began the study by describing life in a Mormon village. Quoting the *Washington County News*, he listed the public events that were happening that month: the fund raisers, the recreational activities, the library matters, and so on. It was clear that there were opportunities for all to serve and opportunities for all to benefit. Then he turned to examining the Italian villages. Such public service did not exist there. Certainly, public service is not unique to Utah, Nevada, and Arizona, but it is clearly crucial to the entire Mormon experiment in the Great Basin and the areas nearby. The people who were interviewed and included in this study are examples of the life of service as well as the life of hard physical labor.

For example, water was essential in every village, but it was scarce. It had to be regulated so that all people had access to it. The common experience in the western United States was that those settlers who arrived first claimed the water. Others who arrived later had to work out deals to get some of it. That was not the Mormon system. *A History of Washington County: From Isolation to Destination* devotes its seventh chapter to the subject of water.[11] It quotes extensively from Elwood Mead and Ray Palmer Teele's work *Report Irrigation Investigations in Utah*.[12] The chapter on the basin of the Virgin River is by Mead's assistant, Frank Adams. He says: "The type of institution in the Virgin Valley is essentially cooperative, as it is elsewhere among the Mormons. . . . If water for irrigation is to be distributed, the only way the settlers know is to work together until each man has his rightful share. Thus it is that a forbidding country has been made fruitful where individual effort would have failed. . . . The farmer of the Virgin River is the farmer of small means and modest wants. Yet his 5 acres of alfalfa is his fortune."[13]

Adams discovered that the farmers of Washington County had not filed their water claims with the court recorder. Water, under the laws passed by the territorial legislature, was distributed by the county selectmen (now called county commissioners). These men served as the 'guardians of the streams' and were charged to distribute the water with equality and fairness based on the demonstrated need of the farmer."[14] The local village farmers were not worried about anyone coming in and claiming their water because everyone in the village worked together and would not allow it. Nonetheless, Adams urged the farmers to file on their water with the government.

The reason for including these academic studies is to emphasize that water was central to the villages and their development of dams, canals, and ditches, as well as their sense of equality. No one was allowed to preempt water. It was regulated by local water companies and a water master in each village, who were all volunteers.

The building of the Hurricane Canal, the La Verkin Canal, the Enterprise Reservoir, and the Washington Fields Dam are examples of huge efforts. The Hurricane Canal began with one hundred volunteers led by James Jepson of Virgin and John Steele of Toquerville. Over a decade the workforce dwindled to about a dozen. Eventually, Jepson convinced the LDS Church to grant them modest funds to finish, and it led to the founding of the city of Hurricane and eventually the opening of two thousand acres south of the town to major agriculture.

The story of the Enterprise Reservoir reveals a parallel process. Orson Huntsman lobbied for years in the western part of Washington County and finally won the approval of the St. George Stake presidency, despite the opposition of some citizens, to build a reservoir that would divert the water of Shoal Creek away from Hebron and onto the desert so that it could support the proposed community of Enterprise. With the support of the presidency and Anthony W. Ivins, volunteers rallied to the project along with a promotion committee that included Thomas Judd, James Andrus, Isaac C. Macfarlane, Zora P. Terry, George M. Burgess, and Alfred Syphus.

Alder and Brooks comment: "Huntsman was not an aggressive capitalist. Rather than seek profit from investment, he hoped to benefit a whole community and only be one of those who gained access to water and land. The initiative and persistence of Orson Huntsman, the sustained and skillful labor of Chris Ammon [the builder], the support of stake leaders, the investment of scores of local people in the Hebron/Enterprise area, and the foresight and resources of Anthony Ivins and many others brought about a marvel, the Enterprise Reservoir."[15]

These stories illuminate the big communal projects, but there were daily small ones that were the lifeblood of each community. Post offices were located in almost every village. They had a part-time postmistress or postmaster. Mail was not delivered to the homes; people came to the post office to pick up their mail. The result was that the post office became a social center and the person behind the counter knew everyone in town and often passed on messages. The village cemetery was managed by a sextant and other volunteers. The roads were sometimes built by volunteers. The town council members were volunteers and they had many responsibilities. The county sheriff was paid, but he often appointed volunteer deputies. The canal companies were composed of volunteers. The town school board members were appointed volunteers. They had to build or maintain the schoolhouse, hire the teacher, collect the tuition, and help the teacher find housing. The town survived on community service. During the period of these people's lives there were two world wars. Men were drafted, and some volunteered. About a hundred from the Utah Dixie area served in World War I for the short period of 1917 to 1918, and about one thousand served during World War II from 1940 to 1945.

INTERVIEWS

The following interviews of these people include comments about all these kinds of service.

MILITARY SERVICE

DAVID ORIN WOODBURY

David Orin Woodbury was born on 30 April 1895 in Salt Lake City, but he grew up in St. George, where he graduated from Dixie Academy in 1915 and then went on to do two years of college there, concluding in 1917. His father, John T. Woodbury Jr., was a teacher at the college. The son became a school teacher after his military service and then became a contractor. He also served a mission to England. After his short career as a teacher, he began a long career as a contractor, building homes and businesses in St. George, constructing an annex for the temple, and remodeling the temple and its grounds. He built the West Ward chapel and then worked in Mesquite, Boulder City, and California on commercial buildings. He built five dwellings in Zion Canyon and many business facilities in St. George and Enterprise. In this excerpt from his interview, he gives a very realistic view of his experience in World War I: "In 1918, after I received two years of college at Dixie College, I volunteered to [serve] in the [United States]

Army. My father told me there was a call for 250 Utahans to go to the University of Colorado at Boulder to receive special training in electricity and safety work. Frank Harmon and I volunteered to go and take this training. We had two months training and were learning Morse code and how to operate the radios that we had at that time. They were very inadequate [compared to] today's standards. We didn't send a voice [transmission]; all we could send was a telegraph signal. We had to learn to send our messages that way.

"After two months, we were sent to Camp Dodge, Iowa, where the Eighty-Eighth Division was ready to go across the sea. The way it was set up, they put fifteen men in each regiment; I was placed in headquarters company with three or four infantry in the same platoon. [Early in] August, we landed in France. We continued training for about a month. From there, we started towards the central Alsace front [in France]. While we were in France, I was taken ill with the influenza that was sweeping the world at that time.

"After about a month, we continued on and we finally landed in Hicken, a small village in central Alsace. In order to get there we had to walk and carry our packs of approximately sixty pounds. I was so weak from the flu that I could hardly walk. At one of the villages [where] we stopped along the way, my buddy Herman Winstead and I went out around the town and found where we could buy a few eggs. We took them to cook and offered to share them if he would cook [them]. It seemed like it was a terrible recuperation there.

"We went on from there to the front. I was stationed in the company headquarters as a radio operator. There were three men [who] were stationed there: [Corporal?] George Forshee and I handled the station. We each took four-hour shifts. My shift started at 12:00 noon and went until 4:00 p.m. and [from] 12:00 midnight until 4:00 a.m. The other men took the other shifts. Our equipment was a storage battery, a coil, a wire around a wood core, a wire attached to a gleaming crystal, and a telegraph key. Messages were sent by using the Morse code of dots and dashes.

"One day while I was off duty, I went with a runner to the front lines, which were on top of a small hill ahead of our station. When I arrived the sergeant was going out to check the outposts, so I went with him. We were going along the middle of the trenches, and a German airplane came flying over. We heard a burst of machine-gun fire from the airplane. When we arrived at the outpost, the soldier said that the bullets had kicked up dirt into his lunch, but had missed him.

"The first night in Hicken we were billeted inside old buildings. We always kept our gas masks close at hand. When I went to bed on the floor, I put the mask by the side of my bed. In the morning it was gone. I found it at the end of a rathole with the sling pulled into the hole and chewed up a bit. At the rear of the house where the radio station was, we found a garden that was ready for harvest, with vegetables, potatoes, carrots, etc. We got a fry pan and some lard from the cook and had French fried potatoes and other [items]. In a small village nearby, we found someone in town with cabbage all shredded and ready to make sauerkraut. The people evidently had been driven off before they had time to finish.

"One day, two other men and I were sent to regimental headquarters to take a telephone for repairs. We had to walk the distance of fifteen to twenty kilometers. On our way back, a car came up behind us on the way toward the front. We hailed it down and asked for a ride. It stopped very quickly. The [men] did not say a word, but they let us get in and ride. They were in French uniforms, and we assumed that they were French soldiers. We got to the town Hicken in the front. We passed them through the guard and sent them on their way.

"Afterwards, I got to thinking that probably these were German spies who were trying to get back across the front. The intelligence they took back was one of the things that stopped the war. It was not too long after that, that the war ended.

"Later, we were moved to the Western Front [in France]. We passed through the town of Nancy and Toules, and on to a small town called Merville. Here, we [received] our own battle packs which consisted of reserve rations, ammunition, and very little else. We waited for three days to receive orders to move up. The orders never came, [but] at 11:00 a.m. on November 11, 1918, the armistice was signed. We got the word out; we worked the balloons in the woods. We were listening to the continuing artillery bombardments, but at 11:00 a.m. it started to taper off until it stopped.

"In a short time we were moved to a small town called Treveray [France]. We waited here for six months for a chance to come home. In May 1919 we sailed for the United States in a small vessel called the *Henry R. Lowery*. On our trip home we became very seasick after a short distance out. It took eleven days to cross the North Atlantic and to be back on our own soil. We were sent to Camp Hamilton, Long Island [New York]. While here, we [received] passes and went into Atlantic City [New Jersey]. At the YMCA we met Clinton Larson [high jumper from BYU] and Creed Haymond on their way to Europe to participate in the Olympic Games. We were mustered out at Fort Russell, Wyoming, on June 13, 1919, just thirteen months from the day I enlisted."[16]

FREDERICK CHENEY VAN BUREN

Frederick Cheney Van Buren was born on 26 September 1882 in Manti, Sanpete County, Utah. He taught school in Beaver County. He reports his experiences during World War I. "I was in the Utah National Guard for two years. It was a cavalry unit then. We were bivouacked at Fort Russell in Wyoming. We had a mean horse that we called 'the Kaiser.' He finally got away and stepped on a board. He put two men in the hospital [who were] trying to take that board with the nail out of his foot. We let him go and they caught him afterwards. I think they killed him. I don't know.

"Once I was trying to curry him when the major came along. He swore at me and said, 'Private, don't you know anything about horses?' I stepped back and saluted him and said, 'Not that kind, sir.' He said, 'Give me that currycomb.' I gladly handed it over to him. He went up [to the horse] and swore. He slapped that horse on the ribs with that currycomb. The horse whirled and kicked him right in the back of the hip. [It] broke his hip and knocked him about fifteen feet. He didn't say any more. I suppose he went to the hospital, and they fixed him up. He learned the hard way.

"This was during World War I, and we didn't leave the United States. I shot two years in the national rifle matches. One year was in Fort Perry, Ohio, and the other year was in Caldwell, New Jersey. We were shooting on the 1,000-yard range, and the wind was blowing about thirty-eight miles per hour cross range. Nobody was hitting the target, let alone the bull's-eye. When it came my time to go down on my target, I followed a lady who was shooting with her husband, E. T. Crossman. He was the rifle-man for the Winchester Repeating Arms Company of New Haven, Connecticut. She got up before he did. I heard him say he was going to hold on the bull's-eye and let it hit where it pleased. He shot, and they pulled my target that I was going down on and marked the bull's-eye on it. I thought that the wind was blowing his bullet off sixteen feet, so I went down and aimed at the bull's-eye on his target. I made nine straight bull's-eyes, which was the highest score made on the rifle range that day out of 3,800 fellas, but it was just a dunce's hunch. I happened to hit it right.

"They offered me the rank of captain to see if I would make another enlistment. I told them I wouldn't go back if they gave me the whole army. I had had enough. My life's occupation has been in physical education."[17]

BENJAMIN BRINGHURST

Benjamin Bringhurst was born on 7 June 1891 and lived much of his life in Toquerville, where he went to school in the old church. In his later life he was on the town council in Toquerville. He tells of his military experience in World War I. "My cousin Stanley Duffin and I joined the United States Army. We were stationed at Fort Douglas [in Salt Lake City] quite a while. Then [we] moved to Camp Kearney [in San Diego, California], and from there we went overseas [to Germany].

"We started out for Glasgow, Scotland, [but] after a while [we received] word that we were going to Liverpool, England. We landed in Liverpool, England, late at night, and it was raining like pitchforks. The British were there to haul us to camp, but our colonel wouldn't let them. [He] made us walk in the rain all night. Finally, we [arrived at] the camp. I remember a sand-rock wall that was built around there, and it was caving in. [There were] some little pup tents—it was sure storming. [There were] little straw mattresses the shape of your body from your head down to your feet. We laid on [those] for the night. They got [us] something better the next day.

"[After] a while, [we] went across the English Channel over to France. I was giving all the boys a sandwich as they came on the boat.[18] When it was over, an [African American] told me, 'When they catch your life jacket they will court-martial you.' I said, 'Have you got one for me?' He said, 'I will get you one.' And he did. We were on the English Channel all night long because we had to dodge the mines. Finally, we landed [at] La Havre, France. I was cooking for the boys, and after a while, I [came down with] influenza. Colonel Webb wanted me to go to the hospital; I told him I didn't want to go to the hospital. I said, 'If you will let me stay outside in the hot sun, I will get rid of the flu.' I didn't want to go [to the hospital] because there were so many [soldiers] dying from the flu there. He said, 'If you are not better by morning, we will have to take you in.' I went behind the stables where we kept the horses and sat in the sun. [I] just sat there all day long. I didn't want anything to eat, but I did drink coffee [and] it helped me. He came by the next morning and said, 'How do you feel?' I said, 'I am doing all right. I am helping in the kitchen now.' He said, 'Okay.' I [stayed] out of the hospital, and I think it saved my life.

"We took food down to the German prisoners along the shore, who were fenced in with wire. I had to take my turn going down there to take their food. The end of the war soon came, and we were released."[19]

HOMER YOUNG ENGLESTEADT

Homer Young Englesteadt was born in Denmark and immigrated to the United States and came to Panguitch, Utah, and later Orderville, Washington County. He went to a one-room school in Mount Carmel through his eighth grade year and then four years of high school at Murdock Academy in Beaver. He had spent a summer herding sheep on the Arizona Strip, but then World War I came. "I was in the first draft in World War I. My brother just older than me, Clarence, was called. He had just [been] married. I [convinced] him to let me go in his place; I kind of wanted to go with the first bunch anyway. I had been out [with] the herd all summer and had quite a bit of money. I just felt like it was my turn to go, and I wanted to go. We had such a nice bunch to go with.

"We had to all meet in Kanab. It was twenty miles over to Kanab, and you couldn't go on horseback. If you went, you had to go with the mail run. It was a little buggy that took you a long while. That morning I borrowed a horse from Mr. Landon—a nice horse—to ride over there. I can just see him over there now, bidding me good-bye. You didn't think of it in those days. He was the only one [who] felt bad; I didn't feel bad.

"We went to Camp Lewis [Washington], and we were there first. There were just a few barracks built there then. It became a big camp, a very good camp. We had a set of very good officers. It seemed like everything clicked for us. Soon after that, we started to drill out. I was put in charge of the machine gun [group]. We had a little squad. We would always be out by ourselves. Then we soon [went] overseas. I had [a] sixteen-man group; we were in charge of the machine gun. We had a machine gun battalion, we called it. Ours was a squadron. The machine guns were to protect the heavy artillery from the airplanes; that was our job.

"We were trained so you could tell the speed of the airplane, about how far it was, in just a second. You had a little [scope] you sighted to. It was quite a thing. I had a group of sixteen men there, [and] they were just perfect. You didn't have to tell them to do anything. I was a corporal, but they gave me all these men. We called them a platoon in those days. They were so good. Whenever there were any military funerals or a man died in their outfit, they would have me give the military funerals for the boys. I remember one trip we buried thirteen [who] died with influenza. There were a lot of them [that] died [from] the flu over there. They would get [very] sick. I never had [any] of it when I was over there, not even a cold all the time. I was in the military about two years."[20]

GRANT ZENIS KEYES

Grant Zenis Keyes was born on 14 February 1895. He lived in Sevier Valley, Ogden, Pioche, and St. George. He had seven siblings—two died as babies and a brother who died at age twenty-five. He married Janet Bracken on 20 October 1919, and they had seven children. Reflecting on his life, he said: "The brother [who] was eight or nine years older than I was killed in France in World War I . . . June, the oldest boy went to Texas on a mission in about 1901 or 1902. My brother and I both went to France in World War I, and I was the one [who] came back.

"We went together to Camp Lewis in Washington.[21] We were there for about three weeks and [were] given all kinds of shots. [One] day, they gave us [a shot] and called us out in line. Shots affect lots of people. We were standing in line, and he [Pete] passed out. You could see them [standing] and then all down the line, and they packed them in. They told all those [who] were [standing that] they were being transferred to Camp Kearny [San Diego County, California].

"The fellows [who] passed out stayed there at Fort Lewis, and he was one of them. They were put in the 91st Division, and we were attached to the 4th Division. We were [at Camp] Kearny until August 4, and then sailed overseas. He was put in the 91st Division. We went in [enlisted] May 26, and he was shipped overseas July 3. That was not much training. We went into the trenches September 26, and he was wounded September 29 and died November 10, 1918, the day before the armistice was signed.

"I was more fortunate. I was with the 145th Heavy Field Artillery from Utah. There were 1,135 [soldiers] from Utah, from there up to 1,500; most of them were from Idaho, and a few from Montana and maybe Colorado. It was called the 145th Utah Heavy Artillery.

"We did not see actual combat. We were fortunate in that way. In World War I [nearly] all of the artillery was horse drawn. When we got over there, our [unit] was one of the first to be motorized with caterpillars. We were trained; they would give us orders to retreat, [and] we could be moving in about two and a half or three minutes. We were trained on caterpillars instead of horse-drawn machines. We were all ready for the front lines, expecting a call any minute, when [we] were called out one morning about ten o'clock and told that the war was over. That did not make us feel unhappy. B. H. Roberts, you have read his [books], was our chaplain. We [arrived] back in Hoboken, New [Jersey] on January 4 [1919, and] it was January 29 [1919] before we were released at [the John A.] Logan College there."[22]

EARL TOLTON HARRIS

Earl Tolton Harris was born on 7 November 1889 in Beaver. He tells his experience in World War I: "Three days after we were separated and sent to our outfit, I was never far away from the front, but that I could hear the guns roar until the armistice was signed. I was there around four months up at the front. I was in the 2nd Division. They were shock troops, and they had to be shocked about every third day. The United States Marines were in the 2nd Division, one regiment, I mean. I had all kinds of experience at the front. We would get back far enough to delouse us once in a while. We would have to have new clothes. We never were out of the hearing of guns. I was there just as they stopped the German drive on Paris, France.

"We were right there where the Germans were retreating so fast that they weren't putting up any resistance. The Germans were coming down the highway four abreast in closed columns. We couldn't get up the road. We had to get out in the fields. We couldn't get in with the artillery. We had engineers and the light machine guns, and they were up in position ahead of the Germans. The Germans were coming down the road in formation. The scouts sent word back that there was someone just ahead of them. They started to deploy and came up over the ridge and our machine guns just mowed them down. When I went to the outfit, they stopped on the road about a half mile from our camp. I could walk back to my camp on dead Germans from there and not step on the ground. They just slaughtered those Germans. That was the turning point."

Harris remained in Europe for four months before returning to the United States. His lengthy report tells much about horses. He was experienced in managing horses before the war, but did not want to continue to manage them in the army. He tried to get out of it but was often pulled into the horse side of the army. He told several fun stories about that.[23]

LDS MISSION SERVICE

CHARLES "CHARLIE" RICHARD SULLIVAN

Church service was central to the lives of many people in southern Utah. One of those services was going on a full-time LDS mission. Charles "Charlie" Richard Sullivan is one example. He went on an LDS mission to the southern states just two weeks after he married Grace Lenzi McAllister in January of 1900. He tells a story that undoubtedly influenced his decision to serve a mission: "My father would let me go out on the Arizona Strip with him. I went out there with him when I could not ride a horse alone. It was about twenty-five miles out there. When we went out to ride, brand calves, or look for cows, we would take a wagon and take some food along with us. We might stay out there for a week or ten days sometimes. I was not big enough to ride a horse, so I stayed in camp and was a camp tender. . . .

"I learned how to cook a little out there. One time I thought I did not know what to cook. I thought, 'I will cook a little rice.' We had tin [pans] to take out there with us, so I put on a pot and put some water in it and some rice in it. . . . Before long I had more rice in the kettle than I had water. So I took some rice out and cooked some more rice. Anyway, I learned you did not need much rice when you were going to boil some rice. It took mostly water. I learned how to cook rice, potatoes, and onions.

"When I was twelve years old they ordained me a deacon. It took twelve deacons to make a quorum. We had a quorum; I was in the first or second or third quorum. We were down in the Virgin River one day having a little fun. They were building a dam across the river to turn the water out so it could water the crops. Before this, I had been going out with my father occasionally, and I was just a camp tender.

"My father said to me one day, 'I think maybe this trip out we will take a horse and saddle for you.' I said, 'That will be fine. I would like to be a good cowboy.' In the meantime, I had been going out with him [and] just sitting around. At night, as a rule, the cowboys would have to get their horses hobbled. They would sit around the campfire and tell about experiences they had had. One night, [one] of the men [who] was a good Latter-day Saint said, 'Today, fellows, I was so mad that I just did not know what to do about it. If I had sworn at those cattle I was afraid you would laugh at me because [of] the way I handle swear words. I am not used to swearing. If I had been a little more used to swearing, I would have sure sworn today. We had those cattle in a bunch of oaks, and I could not get them out.' I thought to be a good cowboy you had to learn to swear. We had some cowboys [who] were pretty good cowboys, and they knew how to swear. I thought, 'If I am going to be a cowboy, I have to learn how to swear dramatically.'

"We were down swimming at the [Virgin] River one day. Every time the fellows would come around—I was about the [youngest] one there— they would splash water on me, and I would swear at them. It happened this day that the president of our deacons quorum was there swimming with us. He was a few years older than most of us were. He [took] me off to one side and said, 'Charlie, I was surprised at you today. Here you have just been ordained a deacon, and you hold the priesthood. To hear you swear like you were doing does not become a deacon very well.' So there I was between two hot waters. If I was going to be a good cowboy, I had to learn to swear. If I was going to be a good deacon, I must not learn how to swear. My family did not swear much. So there it was. I either had to be a good cowboy or a good deacon. . . .

"I thought that over quite a bit. What has helped me all my life is what that president of that deacons quorum told me about deacons: deacons held the priesthood, and priesthood holders [should not] swear. I had to study about that. I went to my priesthood meetings and tried to learn what deacons had to do. We had to work differently than what they do now. We had coal-oil lamps. It was the deacons' chore to keep those coal-oil lamps filled with oil and the chimneys clean. We would have to do that every Saturday to get ready for Sunday. I was getting a little older and a little wiser all the time. I finally decided that I would rather be a good deacon than a good cowboy.

"I never regretted that. That one little incident changed me. I do not know what I might have been if I had kept on [trying] to be a good cowboy. I finally decided I would be a good deacon. I quit swearing. I have tried to keep from swearing.

"I have been a good cowboy. There was one time when I was growing up that I did not think I had to get off a horse for anybody, that I could do anything on a horse anybody else could do. We had a lot of cattle there. My father was a pretty good cattle man; he handled them well. It took a lot of good judgment to handle a lot of cattle. I have worked all my life with cattle."[24]

HARMON GUBLER JR.

Harmon Gubler Jr. was born in Santa Clara on 24 September 1880. He had eleven siblings and went to school in Santa Clara and Cedar City and eventually attended BYU in Provo. He tells about his mission experience: "I went to Switzerland. I was over there a few days short of two and a half years. When I [arrived] in the mission field, Levi Edgar Young was the mission president. I [came] in there after dark. I went alone from Liverpool [England] to Zurich [Switzerland]. I got there and I found the place. When I [arrived] there, President Young said, 'I do not know where I am going to send you, Brother Gubler. I have not decided where to send you. Do you want to go any place around here for two or three days? Next Sunday we are going to hold a conference in Bern [Switzerland].' The headquarters were in Zurich. He said, 'If you have a place you want to go for two or three days, you are welcome to go and see what you can see.' I said, 'I have a cousin [John Wittwer] here on a mission. He is here somewhere; he is supposed to be [here]. I would not mind going to see him.' He said, 'He is down here about forty or fifty miles. You go down and stay with him for two or three days if you want to. Be over in Bern for conference. I will tell you where to go.'

"When he told me he did not know where he was going to send me, he said, 'I might send you to Berner Oberlands.' That was out in the country [where there are dialects]. He said, 'How would you like to go to Berner Oberlands?' I said, 'I do not know anything about Berner Oberland. All I know is that they have four or five [returned] missionaries over in Santa Clara. They tell me they have a different language in every town. When I [come] back from my mission, I want to study languages and German is going to be one. I do not think I can learn German up in the Berner Oberlands.' He looked at me kind of funny. I said, 'I will tell you one thing. I will go any place you want me to go. If you want me up in the Berner Oberlands, that is where I am going. I told you why I did not want to go up there, and that is the reason I do not want to go.' He said, 'It would be nice to go up there and look at those glaciers during the winter. It is nice country up there.' I said, 'That might get old, looking at those glaciers all winter.' When we [came] to Bern, he said, 'I am going to send you up to Berner Oberlands.' I said, 'Okay, that is where I am going then.'

"In ten months he was released, and I was still up in the Berner Oberlands. I thought I would stay there for the rest of my mission, but in about three weeks, I was transferred to another town. I was glad to get out of [there]. There are a lot of nice people up in the Berner Oberlands, but they did have a mess in their languages there.

"I studied my German. Some of the older men [were] a little sarcastic and asked me why I didn't talk like they talked up there. I would tell them [that] they could not say much. I told them I was going to go to school. The women were nice; they did not bother me. The girls tried to help me learn German; some of them tried to give me German lessons. They did not know German too well, but they did the best they could.

"I got along in the Berner Oberlands. I made a lot of friends up there. I did not make many converts. I did not make many converts anytime when I was in the mission field.

"When I was there, I preached. I preached Joseph Smith to them. I preached the restoration of the Church. I did all I could to help them. I [had] a lot of friends. I was in one little town there called Burgdorf. My brother-in-law [John Hafen] had been there and another young fellow from Salt Lake City. He was a [boy] about eighteen or nineteen years old. They took them out and sent me up there. I had been there. When they told me to go up there, I told my conference president that I did not want to live [there]. I would rather [live where] the missionaries were living. We were living out in the sticks over a cow stable. They had the cows in the bottom, and the family lived upstairs. They had a room upstairs where they held church. That is where they lived too.

"I told them I did not want to live out there. I wanted to get up in town and be around the people more, and I would see more people. He said, 'You can go up to town, but you [will] have to pay rent there.' I knew that. He said, 'That is not all. If you want to get a room in town, get a room there and hold church in town.' I said, 'That suits me.' He said, 'We will pay for the church, but you [will] have to pay for your room.' I said, 'That is all right. I expected to pay for it.'

In that town I did not have very many people, but I increased my numbers. I had over about sixty-three percent increase [in] numbers. I was there eight months alone. Once in a while a missionary would come in and maybe stay after church or something like that. I was there alone."[25]

GLEN WILCOX STEED

Glen Wilcox Steed was born on 26 July 1896 in Farmington, Utah. He spent his early life in Farmington and other towns in northern Utah. Later in life he lived in Rockville, Washington County, where he was interviewed. As a young, single man he went on a mission to the eastern states. That is where he met Della Elizabeth McCune, who was also serving as a missionary there. Following their missions, they began a courtship and were married. He reported: "We went to New York City, having been called to the Eastern States Mission. Elder Bitter and I were sent down to the Northwest Virginia

Conference with headquarters in Fairmont, West Virginia. I spent a couple of years there roaming the hills [of] West Virginia. In the winter we would work the towns, and in the summer we would go out without purse or scrip and try [to] live off the land. Sometimes we were lucky and [could] get green apples. We met a lot of fine people. We had a little church at what is called Smith Creek now, a short distance from Franklin, West Virginia. In the spring and fall we would make the trek from wherever we were [during] the winter or summer for conference. We would always have a nice time getting together to talk about our experiences.

"I remember one time we were having a baptismal service, [and] there were two or three people being baptized. I thought it was a good idea to have a general airing [meeting]. We tried to get the word around and started before the baptism. There must have been 100 or 150 people gathered. They called on an Elder Neilson from Canada to give a talk before the baptismal service. He got up and got really excited, [and] was quite enthusiastic about his talk. He said, 'Persecution, we thrive on it, we invite it.' When he was finished, they called on Elder Wilkerson from Lovell, Wyoming, to give the prayer. While he was praying, someone hit him in the forehead with a rock. He went up to Elder Nielson afterwards and said that it was all right for him [to] brag about thriving on persecution, but he would like him to take it, not have it passed on.

"It was while laboring [in] Clarksburg [West Virginia] that I met my wife. We had three elders there at the time. Elder Pace was our conference president; they called them conferences in those days. He had received word that there would be two lady missionaries. One would stay with us and the other would go to the Southwest Virginia conference [with] headquarters in Charleston, West Virginia. We [received] the word that they would be there on a certain train at a certain time. The conference president and I went down and met the train that they should be on, but no lady missionaries were on it. We asked about other trains and they said that there [were] no others coming from that area. We went home and decided that something must have come up [and] that they [were not able] to make it.

"The next morning we were holding church; we had a hall rented over a café. We had to go down early in the morning and sweep out the cigarette butts, carry out the spittoons, and get ready to hold church. We had seven or eight people who always came to church. While I was giving the lesson, we heard a commotion at the door. There was a little hole in the door that you could push open to see if you wanted to let the people in for the lodge. We notice that it moved, and in came the two lady missionaries. One of them was Della [Elizabeth] McCune, and the other was a Sister Snow from Snowflake, Arizona.

"We abided by mission rules. I wasn't thinking about girls anyway, and she wasn't thinking about boys necessarily. There was Ida Hunsaker there from Ogden, Utah, before the girls came. She heard us tell about going through the Smoke Holes on the way down to the church in Ziegler [West Virginia]. When President [Walter P.] Monson, our mission president, came down to the conference, the girls asked him if they could go through the Smoke Holes with some of the elders. He said that he thought it would be wonderful, that those people had never seen any ladies from the outside world. He thought it would be a splendid [event]. There was nothing we could do but try to take them through. [Since] I had been through several times, the conference president asked if I would [take] them through. When the weather broke and it was time for us to meet for conference at Ziegler, we started on this [journey], which [would] be like 150 miles. We went as far as we could on the railroad to Petersburg, West Virginia."

Steed recounted a lengthy story about their adventures trekking through the mountains, often with no roads. It took them hours, but they finally arrived at the home of a family named Shirts, who were friends of the missionaries but not members of the church. This family lived out in the back country, where they hunted possums and coon. The Shirts hosted them for three days. The sister missionaries helped Mrs. Shirts with her sewing.

"They called it Smoke Holes because it was so removed from any course of travel that, during the Civil War, there would be deserters and guerilla groups who [went] back in there. There were saltpeter mines in there, and they would mold their bullets. You could look across the country and see a swirl of smoke and knew there was someone [in] there, but it was rather risky to go and see who. They called it the Smoke Holes for that reason. So this country was rough this way.

"Whenever we went through there, we had to sing until we couldn't sing any more. They loved to have us sing. We always held meetings; they called [them] gatherings. They had to hear some preaching. They passed out the word through grapevines, which were quite effective. The people live back in the woods and to go in there and try to find the people, unless you knew the trails, you would be at a loss. . . . Word went out like wildfire, and that evening they came down and gathered around and listened to them sing until they couldn't sing any more.

"While [we] were there, [we were aware] of conditions [and how the] people were desperately poor. The men would get a little flour by going out in the valley to work for fifty cents a day. That is still biscuit country down there and they had to have biscuits for every meal.

"After two years in West Virginia, I was transferred to Vermont and spent five months there. [The] headquarters were in Burlington [Vermont] on Lake Champlain. [I] went to Barre [Vermont] and was there off and on for a while. They sent Elder Anderson and me down to Bennington [Vermont] for two or three months. Afterwards, we were released and came home. The flu [1918 influenza epidemic] was pretty bad, and when we [arrived] home they didn't even have conference that spring. On the way home we visited the Hill Cumorah [Pageant in New York] and enjoyed the trip there very much."[26]

DELLA ELIZABETH MCCUNE STEED

Della Elizabeth McCune Steed was born in Nephi on 23 June 1895 and lived several places, including Springdale. She was called on a mission from Nephi right after high school at age nineteen: "I was called to go to the eastern states. It came as a shock to me. I was not interviewed or anything. I had no idea [I was going to be called on a mission]. I received a letter in the mail; that was the only [way] I knew about [the] call. I went to the mailbox, and there was this large envelope from the Church. It was calling me on a two-year mission. I guess my bishop had sent my name in, but I had not been interviewed or told anything about it. I really wanted to go.

"My first call was to Baltimore, Maryland, for one month. Then I spent six months in Pittsburgh, Pennsylvania. From Pittsburgh I was transferred to Lynn, Massachusetts. I had a sick spell, and President Monson transferred me to the Joseph Smith farm in Vermont. Brother and Sister Brown were there in charge of the farm. I spent a month or six weeks at the farm recuperating from this illness that I had. My companion was an elderly lady—Marie Hasselman. She was in her fifties. At the time I was assigned to go to her, all the other missionaries said, 'We feel sorry for you, an old maid like that,' but she was a wonderful person. She was one of the most wonderful people and was most understanding. She had been a guide on Temple Square for years. She had great understanding and knowledge of the gospel. I let her do the talking. I felt that I was so inexperienced and she had had so much experience.

"In our tracting, we met a wonderful man and daughter. His wife had passed away. He was a state senator in Massachusetts. He was a very brilliant man. We visited him all the time. He was a man who would ask questions. [He would] draw you out. I was a young girl and had not had as much experience. I would sit by and let this sister, Marie Hasselman, answer the questions. They [were] wondering if I could talk [or] if I knew anything.

"When she was transferred, I had a new companion. She was a new girl from the West to start with me as a missionary companion. How I dreaded to go back to these people. We arrived at his home, and as usual he and his daughter were there. He started with the questions. There was a question, and I would answer.

"[Then] here comes another question. He was testing me because I had been so quiet with my other companion. There would be another question. Finally, he came with a question. He asked me about his son who was serving in Germany. He said, 'My son, if he kills somebody, is he going to be held accountable?' A verse came to me from the Book of Mormon, and I repeated it to him. I said, 'Your son is fighting for the right.' I think it would be with him as it was [with Nephi]. I will never forget this Mr. Quinn. He sat down as I was answering, [and] he leaned out of his chair toward me. His face began to open up into a smile. I sat back. He said, 'My goodness, you have come through. You have it in you. You had never said a word while Sister Hasselman was with you. I wondered if you knew what you were doing, but you have it in you.'

"Later, President Monson sent word that he was going to keep me another three months. He wanted me to take vocal lessons in Boston. He wanted me to study before I came home. He thought, with my voice, that I should study. Then the World War I broke out, and I received a call from him to prepare to go home." Della recorded that she met her future husband, Glenn Wilcox Steed, who was serving as a missionary, but they did not communicate romantically. She thought he was not interested in her. Their romance did not begin until they were both home.[27]

MILO GOLDEN CAMPBELL

Milo Golden Campbell, born in Escalante in 1909, told an incredible story about his son Cline: the boy nearly died at birth but survived miraculously. The father said: "He [received] his [mission] call to Japan. On this call, I [received] a special letter from President David O. McKay. It said, 'Brother Campbell, your boy has been handpicked through a circle of prayer for a special mission, and his headquarters will be in Japan.' We felt good about the [call]. I knew that he was that kind [of boy]; he was always the kind of boy that if you could steer him in that direction, he would go. When he [arrived in] Japan, it was the first time we knew that he was called into Korea. [He was] one of the first missionaries to establish that mission permanently. There had been a few missionaries in there all right. While he was there, he had a lot of trouble [convincing] himself that he was a missionary. He was there [and] almost came home a time or two through trouble he had with different ones. [He had trouble with] mission district presidents and missionaries. Finally, after he was there a year, he was sent up to Pusan [South Korea]. He called it a kind of a little jail town. He finally gained his testimony [there]. The greatest words that ever came to me [were in a letter that came from him], 'Dad, now I know what I am here for.' He filled a great mission there. He baptized over thirty [people] into the Church and [performed] marriages [for] a few [of them]. He came back into Korea and was the district president. When he came back home, he joined the [Utah] National Guard and was picked to be a chaplain. He went back there and spent a year. Now he is home again. He is a great speaker."[28]

FRANK BARBER

Frank Barber was born in Centerville, Utah, in 1882 and later lived in Hurricane, Washington County. He quit grade school when he was eleven years old and went to work on the farm. "My daddy came here from England broke. He had to [find] a new job of some kind. He [received] fast offerings from the ward, and he [received] part of the fast offering that the other fellow didn't get. So I quit school and milked cows. I milked twenty-two head of cows with my hands for eleven dollars a month. The Davis County Nursery was operating in Centerville. [The] Smith brothers were running it; they were neighbors of mine. Three men came in there and bought out [the] Smith brothers, [and] I worked for them for thirteen years.

"One day I went down alone to Centerville. Centerville was my home in the heart of Davis County. I went in the house, looked up on the shelf, and there was a letter marked Frank Barber, from Box B. I took the letter down and it said you are due to be ready for the Central States Mission on such-and-such a date. I hadn't been up there to work, and I had missed a week and I didn't have time, so they gave me an extension of a week to get my teeth fixed up and [for] me [to get] ready to go.

"I went to Salt Lake City and reported and readied myself. I only had 140 dollars. There was a carload of Mormon missionaries on their way to the field. Four of us went to Cheyenne, Wyoming, and were transferred back into Kansas City, [Kansas]. The other forty went all over the world.

"When we [arrived at] Kansas City, they took all our money away from us. When I left, they said this is without purse or scrip. I had 1,100 miles to go. The Central States Mission included Texas and Louisiana and those places. I was sent to Sherman, Texas. The clerk there gave me a grip full of books and a package to take to the elders [who] were there. I could hardly shut the grip because I couldn't get all [the items] back in. I only had eleven dollars in my pocket. When I [arrived] down there, I got off the train at Sherman, Texas, no instructions, no schooling, no elder training, nothing but walk out in the field and change your overalls and get ready and go. They sent me alone to Sherman, Texas. I didn't have any more sense than to think some Mormon elder would grab me by the arm and take me home. But when I [arrived] there I didn't know anybody, and nobody knew me.

"I sat on a bale of cotton all day. I [had] a sandwich when I was starving, [but] I dared not spend my money. I sat there until midnight, [and] one of those southern cyclones came up over the country and roared like a ball of fire. All of the bricks in the chimney came down. Furniture was shaken to pieces. There was a little central depot. They came running in there and said, 'Where are you going? We are leaving here.' Of course, I didn't want to sit all alone in that failing house. Something said to me: 'You go around the back of this house and see what you find.' There were two horses prancing, scared to death, hooked to a cab. The thought struck me [that] the man was asleep in the cab; 'go wake him up.' I woke him up, and he took me uptown. I got off and sat and looked out the window until daylight. Then I went back down to the depot for fear some Mormon elder would come to get me. That is all the sense I had at that time.

"We didn't have any training like they have now, so nobody came. In the afternoon of the second day, a young man came up to me. We [began] talking, and I told him who I was and what I was waiting for. I looked at my watch and wondered if I better sell it and go back to Independence, Missouri. He said, 'Come down and see us. We usually shoot Mormon elders.' My heart came up in my mouth, and I took his address. The next morning, I took a little train and went down there. It had to go up and down in the mud. It could hardly travel. I could walk as fast as it could go. When I got off at the depot, it was just evening. The sun was just setting. I stood there and asked about this young man. They said, 'No, nobody [is] in this country that we know of [by] that name.' So there I stood. An old man walked up to me [and] took me by the arm. He said, 'You look like you are lost.' My voice quivered, and I knew I was about to shed a tear. He said, 'Come, go with me. I will take care of you.'

"So he took me across the road. He and his wife [had] a rooming house. He showed me a room. There was just a board partition; there wasn't any plaster in it. He took me and showed me my room. He said, 'Make yourself at home, and I will get you some supper.' He [brought] me a beautiful, lovely supper, and I sat there and ate it. While I was eating it, he went outside and gathered in all of his friends that he could find on the street and in the homes and said, 'We have a new man here. We want to hear some Mormonism. Come on over.' The house just filled right up to the door. Can you imagine me preaching a sermon to that bunch of men? I could sing a little. I sang 'Oh, My Father' [and] 'An Angel from on High.' I told them a little here and a little there as I could think about it. When I [was] through, we went to bed. It was nearly one o'clock in the morning before they left.

"I slept just through the room from the old man and his wife, and after we had been to bed a half an hour or so, they started in. 'Poor boy. Poor boy.' They kept it up until broad daylight—'poor boy.' Can you imagine me sleeping under conditions like that? As soon as daylight came, I was up and out on the street. He got me breakfast, showed me around the town and was good to me, just like a father. He was good to me, and I stayed there two days. I wrote to the office before I left for Sherman. I said, 'I am without money. If I don't hear from you in the next two days, I will be back to Independence, Missouri.'

"I went up the third day and [received] some mail, and there was my letter, telling me that there were eight Mormon missionaries working in that city [Sherman, Texas]. I didn't know it, and they didn't have enough sense to tell them [I was] there. I went back down to the old man and told him, 'I will have to go now. I have the information where I [am] to go.' He looked at me. He helped me pack my grip. Halfway to the depot, he sat it down and said, 'I can't go any further.' Tears were rolling down the old man's cheeks, and he just cried like a baby. He and his good ol' wife left me just that way, and I never [could] get back there. I found those eight missionaries."[29]

LAFAYETTE HALL

Lafayette Hall was born on 31 December 1888 in Rockville, Washington County. He went to grade school there and then went to Dixie College, where he graduated from high school and played basketball. While in high school, he dated Mary Bertha Wood Hall. He said: "She had a lot of fun that way [with me and] was game for anything. We got along [fairly well]. I went with her that summer, [but] did not get [serious] at all. In [the] fall, I was called to go on a mission.

"I had heard quite a little bit about the hardship [the missionaries] had in some places. I was not anxious to go. I was bashful and did not think I could do any good, so I was not anxious to go. They finally talked me into it. When I decided to go, I would go where they sent me. I did not care if it [was] the end of the world. I did not see how I could do any good. I guess they picked out the safest place [where] I would fit in the best—right out in the Ozark Mountains, out where it was too rough for most of the elders to go. That is where I liked it, so that is where I went on my mission. I remember there were some elders [who] got up in there and one fellow they used to move around quite a bit. They saw a fellow way back in the woods, the sticks. He said, 'Are you fellows lost?' I guess he knew who we were. 'Aren't you lost?' I said, 'No, we are Mormon elders.' He said, 'I guess you are not lost.'

"Yes, he had likely kept them before. On that mission I had a lot of good experiences. We learned how to be diplomatic, [and we] made a lot of friends. I did not baptize anybody, did not convert them; I just made friends. That was about it. I had the ground and made a lot of friends, but I was not anxious to convert them, to baptize them anyhow. I want[ed] them to be converted before I baptized them. I thought they ought to know more about it. I could have baptized one [person]. I did not have anything to do with converting him. The mission president called and told us there was a couple [who] wanted to be baptized. So we went up and saw them. I had a young companion with me. 'You can baptize if you want, I [will] not. They are not ready.' He said, 'The mission president told us to go baptize them.' So we baptized them.

"I had a good pair of legs then. I could walk with any of them out in the Ozarks. I had a good line. I could generally find a place to stay. We got that route depending on the people, and when we would get in we would generally stay with friends. [We were] careful; we did not try to antagonize them. I went in the area in two places where the elders had been mobbed. There was one man [who] lived in our ward. He did not fit in, and a mob [went] after him. He had a bullet through his hat while it was still on his head. We were the next elders in there, [and] some of them were a little hostile, but I treated them like I treated a mustang. I was careful first until I could get them [to] where I could handle them. They responded [fairly] well. I never had any trouble; I could have had all right a time or two, if I had said the wrong word, but I learned not to say the wrong word. Always say the right word."[30]

JOSEPH FIELDING HARDY

Joseph Fielding Hardy was born on 30 October 1908 in Bunkerville, Nevada. He graduated from high school there and later studied civil engineering. He described being called on a mission: "I guess the reason I was so old (twenty-five) [was because] I was inactive. I didn't go to church for several years. I had a habit of smoking like a lot of young fellows fool around and get into. I would take a little drink when we would go to a dance. A schoolteacher from Providence, Utah, came down to teach school here. I started to go with her and [with] her encouragement I quit my habits. The last smoke I ever took was on December 23, 1932. [In] March 1933 I [received] my mission call to [the] eastern states [from] President [Heber J.] Grant.

"I enjoyed my mission very much. I will relate another experience that I had. There was [a] lady [that] I did not help convert; the lady missionaries converted her. She could not speak; she lost her voice, [but] she could write and listen. Through reading the literature [she learned that] if you join the Church and [are] baptized, these signs should follow. One of them was she could speak and could do these things. She asked for a baptism with the purpose that she could get her voice back. She told us that after it was all over. I hosted the baptism, and her faith was so great [that] we elders [and] the missionaries [wished] we would have had that much faith. Before the baptism, we went [by] ourselves and prayed that we would have the faith that the lady could have her voice back after baptism.

"They baptized her, and we drove about sixty miles from where she lived, Newberg, New York, to Poughkeepsie, New York, where they baptized her. They came back to her home and confirmed her in her home. She tried to speak, but she could not speak, but she could play the piano. She started to play and was singing Church hymns. Finally, she turned to the song 'Catch the Sunshine' and started to play and sing it. Nobody sang but this woman. I met her twenty-five years after I had been on the mission. I went back and she could still talk—and I mean talk! That is another experience I had [of] the healing power of our Heavenly Father."[31]

ALVIN HALL

Not all who were called on missions served for two years. Alvin Hall, born on 17 October 1890 in Rockville, also lived in Hurricane after it was founded fifteen years later. He went to grade school in Rockville, but went to Hurricane for the eighth grade. Then he completed high school in St. George and studied a year at Utah State Agricultural College in Logan. He married Ann Pickett, 19 December 1916, in the St. George Temple and was active in the Church all his life. He was ordained an elder when he was married at age twenty-six. He was the father of seven children. He served in several Church callings, including president of the high priests quorum. He reported: "Our bishop kept telling us that the high priests [would] be expected to furnish a mission [fund]. They asked us in priest-hood meeting class who would donate towards a mission. Some ran out [of the room]! Most said they could give so much, [which was] maybe five dollars. I agreed to send five dollars to anyone who could go. [The] bishop kept asking me who I thought would be good to go [on a mission]. I made some good suggestions. All the while, I was talking myself right into it. Two of those high priests each gave five dollars for one month. That was it, but the Lord provided and we had money to spare. We got along okay. That was all right; I [received] the blessings.[32]

"[My wife] still had two children here at home. She stayed [home] to take care of them. I went to [the] West Central States Mission, [with] head-quarters in Billings, Montana. I spent four months of the time in Minot, North Dakota. It was the highlight of my life. It was wonderful! I loved the mission president. I hit it off with him. He was an old stockman [and] we could talk the same language . . . I had a lot of respect for President Sylvester Broadbent.

"I did not baptize one person [in those six months]. There was an older man [who] knew the gospel and had good faith in it. He wanted to be baptized and wanted me to baptize him. I kept telling him not to put if off too long and [that] I was ready. He could not quite [leave] his tea and coffee alone. He said he would not put off too much [longer]. One morning they found him dead in bed. So I did not even baptize one person while I was out [on my mission]. I felt like I did more good with the [young] elders than I did with anybody else. [I did well], especially for me.

"[I did] not [lose] financially or otherwise. I had one thousand dollars and had my debts well paid. I asked my wife if she could do [it] for six months on four hundred dollars and she said she thought she could. That would leave me six hundred dollars [total, and] one hundred dollars a month. Some of the elders, one or two, used to try to borrow money of me. I told them, 'I had just about enough to go on and not a cent to lend.' I used to go to the bank up there once a month and write out a check for the amount that I needed for that month. I had the money here in the bank when I left. I would not lend to them. . . . So I told them I was keeping the rules.

"The mission president wanted me to stay longer. I said, 'I just made arrangements to leave for six months. It would be nice to see my wife.' He said, 'You can have your wife here. I will furnish you with all the means you need.' I said, 'I just made arrangements with the older boys to be gone for just six months.' If he would release me, I thought I ought to go home then, so he did. I would have liked to have stayed. I really enjoyed the work, and he treated me so good. I [later] served on two stake missions at different times."[33]

LOCAL CHURCH SERVICE

Serving as a full-time missionary was an intense form of Church service. There was another type of Church service, and that was when members were called to serve in their local congregations as a choir director, scoutmaster, Sunday School teacher, ward teacher (similar to a home or visiting teacher), priesthood quorum leader, clerk, member of a bishopric, or any of a number of other callings. Some callings required only a few hours a week, while others, such as bishop, were much more demanding.

JOSEPH ALMA TERRY

Joseph Alma Terry, born in Mesquite, Nevada, in 1886 tells of his life on Terry's Ranch, near Enterprise, Utah:

"I have [always] tried to be active [in the Church]. I was appointed bishop of the ward. That is a funny incident the way it came about. I [received] a letter from the stake presidency on Wednesday evening. It said: 'We will be up to Enterprise to hold [a] conference meeting and set you apart as bishop of the Enterprise Ward. It just upset me. I was thrown right up into the air. I could not control myself. I did not know what in the world to do. I was not prepared [to be] a bishop. I could not figure out how in the world they had ever come to locate me in such a position as that, because the bishopric was quite a prominent thing. At that time, the Clover Ward over there belonged in our district here and we had to visit over there. There were one or two families [who] still lived up in Old Hebron. Our Terry Ranch [was] up there. I told my wife, 'I will have to turn that down. I cannot accept it.' She said, 'We will pray about that, and we will see what to do about that.'

"I had a wonderful [wife as] helper, the most wonderful companion that anybody could ask for. We went on, and still I had not made up my mind. The stake presidency came out, and they drove here to my place. I met them, and they said, 'We will go over and open the meeting and set you apart as a bishop.' 'No,' I said, 'I could not accept that. Do not [plan] on that.' The two counselors were wonderful friends. The stake president was set in his mind, all right. He was not going to change any. The two counselors kept encouraging me. We went over to [the] meeting, and they took me up on the stand with them. I had been active as a Seventy in the ward and visited around a lot. They took me up on the stand, and after the meeting opened, they said they had come to reorganize the ward and make me bishop. I just practically wilted. I did not know what to do, but I could not turn it down then the way it was [presented]. So I accepted it.

"I was bishop for fifteen years. I do not know whether they did not want to make a change or whether they could not find anybody [who] would accept it or not. But I went on!"[34]

JANET BRACKEN KEYES

Janet Bracken Keyes was born on 18 April 1897 in Pine Valley. She married Grant Zenis Keyes and had eight children. She tells briefly about her Church and civic service: "I was Primary president for a number of years.

I was first counselor in the Relief Society under two different presidents here in Central. I gave the literature lesson for about twenty years. That was here at Veyo since we joined the Veyo Ward. I have belonged to the Daughters of [Utah] Pioneers. I joined the Andrus Camp in St. George and [attended] for several years. I really enjoyed that. I was on the March of Dimes [committee] a couple of times. I was postmaster for several years."[35]

GILBERT DELOS HYATT

Gilbert Delos Hyatt was born on 26 July 1889 in Parowan and lived in Cedar City, St. George, and Central. He had twelve siblings. He married Mary Laverna Holt in 1915, and they had six children. He taught school for five years in Central and then became a dentist and practiced in Parowan. He extolled the example of his father: "He was a good man. He was honest and always taught honesty to his sons and daughters. At times, he would draw them together and give them lectures. One particular incident [was when] we were out in the woods getting firewood. We had one valuable mare that Walter Mitchell offered 150 dollars [for]. Father would not take that for her, although that would have paid his debts. We all chastised him for not taking it. He said, 'Well, you know that she has this distemper, and she might have died. Then if she did, how could I have ever repaid Walther Mitchell for her?' He was too honest to take advantage of a sale when the mare might have died. Yes, he taught us strict honesty at all times.

"My wife was interested in [the Church] more.[36] She influenced me partly, and then the home missionaries had some influence. We had two missions to the Shivwits,[37] Indian[s] northwest of St. George. My wife and I [served missions there]. I was superintendent of the Sunday School in Sevier County for a while. In St. George, I was secretary of the high priests quorum for a couple of years. I was also a teacher in the high priests quorum in Sevier County. Now I go to the temple often. I have enjoyed Church work."[38]

MATA GUBLER ENCE

Mata Gubler Ence was born on 8 October 1897 and lived in Santa Clara, Pine Valley, and Ivins. She married Herman Ence and they served on the Shivwits Reservation: "I was president of the Relief Society for four or five years.[39] Then I was president [of the Relief Society] up on the [Shivwits] Indian farm. It was in the stake then. I was the first Primary president in Ivins. I was Primary president twice and Relief Society president on the Indian farm and in MIA to the Indians. We had the best time of our lives. We were in with Brother and Sister John Smith. She was a beautiful singer. He played the piano for me to dance, and we had more fun. My husband had turkeys, so we gave them a big turkey supper for Thanksgiving and Christmas. Then they would dance. They liked my man. Now, whenever they (the Indians) see us, they always holler hello to us."[40]

MELVINA BELLE HAMMOND BRINGHURST

Melvina Belle Hammond Bringhurst was born on 5 August 1887 in Toquerville. She had six siblings. She married Henry Bringhurst on 20 March 1907. They had four children who lived to adulthood and three who died as babies. They loved Toquerville; they lived, farmed, ran a store, and raised a strong family there. She related briefly her Church activity: "[I was the president of the Relief Society for] thirteen years. [I was] secretary in Primary and secretary in Relief Society [and a] counselor in Mutual. I think I was [a] counselor in the Mutual twice. [I was] counselor in the Primary twice. I have taught some Sunday School classes and have been a visiting teacher for the Relief Society for a long time."[41]

LAURA STUCKI GRAY

Laura Stucki Gray was born on 1 September 1903 and lived in Santa Clara and Veyo. She married Mathew Gray on 26 December 1929 in the St. George Temple. They had three children, one of whom died at birth. She was always active in the LDS Church and made the following comments about her service: "We have always gone [to church]. We always went down in [Santa Clara] too. We go to church now in Veyo, seven miles from here. When I first married, I was a counselor in the Relief Society. I think Ramona was about one-year-old. Matt would take care of her when I went to meetings. I took her [with me] most of the time, but sometimes I would leave her home.

"I was a Sunday School [teacher] for years. I can't tell you how many! I was work director and [prepared] the visiting teachers' lessons in the Relief

Society for several years. My sister was president of the Relief Society [at one time]. I have been the representative in Veyo for the *Relief Society Magazine* for about fourteen years. I have also been a visiting teacher. Matt, Ramona, and I used to be in a choir they had in Veyo. I belonged to the Singing Mothers in Relief Society.

"I have [worked] at the [voting]-poll [booths]. I have collected fees [donations] for various [community] drives."[42]

MATTHEW "MATT" GRAY

Her husband, Matthew "Matt" Gray, reported a similar lifestyle. "Yes, I have worked to help this community develop the town of Central. I worked on [the] pipe and water system for about three or four miles, up to the end of the mountain over here and up to the head house up here. I helped build a trench. I helped in the development of roads in the community. I helped in everything if they need[ed] any help. I built my life right here. I also work in the Church. I have done temple work. I work in [the] baptismal [room] right now. I have to go see the bishop and get the teenagers and take them to the temple for baptismal. That is my job every third month. I also have done some [ordinance work].

"I have been a member of the superintendency of the Sunday School and was superintendent of the MIA. I have been on the town board for years. I have been in on all the activities [that went on in the town]."[43]

NINA VENICE SPENDLOVE STRATTON

Nina Venice Spendlove Stratton was born on 8 May 1912 in Hurricane. She went to high school and graduated there. She married William Cumon Stratton on 3 October 1933 in the St. George Temple, after a five-year courtship. They spent their life farming and raising cattle. She tells of a life of Church activity: "I was a teacher in Primary for a while and then in the presidency. I was in the presidency of Mutual. [I was] in the presidency of the Relief Society. I was not the president. [I was the president] in the Primary and the MIA. I taught theology in Relief Society for a while. That was one time [when] I had to keep studying. I taught Sunday School. I was chorister in Sunday School once. I was chorister in junior Sunday School. I have been [junior Sunday School] coordinator for a few years. I have worked in the junior Sunday School for seventeen years, but it was a year or two after I started that they asked me to be the coordinator. I have done a lot of work in the Relief Society too.

"We were called to go on a short-term mission to Northern California in 1962 and 1963. [It was] in the winter. We spent all our time in San Jose. We took Susan with us [and] she went to school. It was a time when they had to send old folks on missions because all the young men were in the [military] service. We really enjoyed it and made a lot of friends. We just got [involved], and our six months were up. We were able to baptize a few people, [but] not as many as we wanted to. It has been so long that I have forgotten. We heard about some [who] were baptized after we left.

"When we came home, they put him in as president of the stake mission for a while. We were both stake missionaries and then somebody else was put in [as] president. [I went to the temple] with the Primary class, [and] we baptized for the dead. We used to go down quite often. Then we were called to be ordinance workers. I did a little knitting for the Red Cross during World War II. That is about all."[44]

LYDIA AMELIA BARLOCKER HUNT

Lydia Amelia Barlocker Hunt was born on 18 August 1893 and lived most of her life in Enterprise. She and Nephi Hunt were married on 10 September 1912 in the St. George Temple. He worked on the Ivins ranch near Enterprise. Her father, Alfred Barlocher, had raised fruit in Enterprise and did a lot of peddling. Lydia and Nephi had eight children, two of whom died: one was stillborn and the other died at age three. She reported on her Church activity: "I was [the] first counselor in Primary for three years and twelve years as a teacher, that would be fifteen years. I taught Sunday School for twelve years. Sometimes I had the same students in Sunday School and Primary classes. It kept me hunting a lot of stories to tell them.

"I was attendance secretary in MIA for about three years. I have been a Relief Society visiting teacher for around fifty years. My husband was in the presidency of the Genealogical Society [of Utah]; I was his secretary. We were in for three or four years. Then he and I did home teaching too. I also taught genealogical work. I have done around 1,400 names in the temple and have done lots of sealings; I never kept track of those. I will be seventy-six [on] August 18, 1969 and I go down [to St. George] every Thursday morning and come back after the first session in the evening. I do three names a day, and I do some sealings in between. I love temple work."[45]

AMELIA COOPER WOODARD

Amelia Cooper Woodard was born on 3 September 1896 in Panguitch. She had a tough life because of the illnesses that decimated her family. She overcame typhoid fever as a child. She married Art Woodard, and they had four sons. One son, Dale, had a bad heart and had to be cared for, but he grew to adulthood. Then her husband died in 1934. He had sheared some wet sheep and got pneumonia and died at age forty-four. She had to raise the four boys and did so by cleaning houses for people and bringing their laundry to her own house to wash. She earned one dollar a day. Her sons grew up, and three of them served in World War II. Through it all she was active in the Church. She recalled: "Opal Hatch was president of the Primary when I was her second counselor. Then I was her first counselor for a while. That was during the war when they didn't send any instructions. They sent a little packet out, and we had to build [on] that. We had a good [and] successful Primary. I enjoyed every bit of it. She and I taught Sunday School for ten years together. We enjoyed that too.

"I taught religion class when I was young. Not long after I was married, I taught religion class. Becky Orton taught with me. She is ninety-seven [now], or maybe more than that, but she is that old anyway. We had a nice religion class, but they took that out of the schools, and you can't teach that anymore. We taught for two years, [and] that was a good experience.

"Then they called me as a stake missionary. Minerva Worthen and I were together for two years as stake missionaries. She was older than I, but she had always been a close friend. We had a nice experience. There weren't too many people [who] were not Mormons in our town at that time. We visited and we learned more than they did. We really enjoyed it. We had one lady [who] wasn't a Mormon. I worked for another lady [who] was her neighbor, and they weren't Mormons either. We visited their homes anyway. She had two little boys, and she sent them to Sunday School. This one little boy enjoyed it. She made sure that they couldn't be Mormons, but she sent them to Sunday School anyway. We had to give

[a] two-and-a-half-minute talk. This one little boy was [very] interested in Sunday School. He wanted to get right in and take part. I asked him this day, 'Would you like to give one of the two-and-a-half-minute talks?' He said, 'Yes, but my mother won't let me talk about old Joe Smith.' I said, 'Have I taught you anything about old Joe Smith?' We had been [teaching] the Ten Commandments. He said, 'No, I don't think you have.' I said, 'Do you think your mother would let you give a two-and-a-half-[minute] talk on honor thy father and mother?' The next Sunday he was up here at nine o'clock, ready to go to Sunday School with me. He was tickled to death!

"I have been a teacher in Relief Society ever since Blair was a baby, [except when] I have had some sick spells and worked out of town. I was literary class leader with one of my neighbors, Sue Walker, for about six years. I still work in Daughters of the Utah Pioneers. I am secretary now [for Garfield] County. I was elected city recorder. I have served one year of a two-year term."[46]

WILLIAM MALEN COX

William Malen Cox was born on 21 October 1896 and lived in Pine Valley. He concluded his interview with these comments: "I would like to say this about the Church. The Church made me. I didn't have a great deal of education, except what I [received] in the Church. They taught me how to conduct a meeting; they taught me how to stand on my feet and talk; they taught me how to organize and handle [a meeting]. Being a bishop, I learned a lot of things and it enabled me after that to do the things in civilian life that I did. The fact that I made a good success of being Farm Bureau president and being president of Washington County Cattlemen enabled me to be elected to the Utah legislature.

"Let me say this, the way to happiness, the way to progression, and the way to lead a good life, is to follow the teachings of the Church. Make the Holy Bible your guide, be honest and help your neighbor. Joseph Smith said this statement when they asked him what a good Latter-day Saint was. He said: 'He is first a good husband and father, he is second a good neighbor and he is third, a good member in his community.' I have tried to guide my life by that. After I went to the temple a few times and recognized what the vows of consecration meant, I have never refused a call of my Church. Whatever they asked of me to do, I did. I have never refused a donation to my Church. When I could contribute, I did it. I believe I have lived about as happy a life as the average man."[47]

WILLIAM VAUGHN JONES

William Vaughn Jones was born on 7 January 1900 at Holt's Ranch near Enterprise. He attended a one-room school in Gunlock and then went to Pine Valley. He reported an interesting thing about his health: "I had a bad cough most of the time, and I would have to take a swallow of this cough medicine often. I might mention that one of the things my stepmother did for me was one of the best things that could have happened to me. We were limited in space in our living quarters, and quite often it was necessary that we boys sleep out in a tent, or some place in the open. I think that was the best thing that could have happened to me, and I overcame the cough."

William spent forty-three years working for the Dixie Power Company. He was very active in the Church during all those years. "I was [the] first secretary of that group and later president of the elders group.

"We accomplished some things during that time. We sent a man on a mission. For that small group it was quite a struggle. Then I was made ward clerk in the Veyo Ward in 1935, when Bishop Andrew Seitz was made bishop. Since that time, I have been clerk, counselor, and ward clerk. When I was bishop the first time, I had a full twenty-four-hours-a-day job. I could be called out anytime during the day or night, so that was a little harder for me to serve as bishop. I think I got along fairly well. But it has been much easier in my second term because I have been retired most of the time. While I work just about the same and don't get paid for it, I still can stop when I want to and can do the Church work that I need to do and put off other things. So it has been a lot easier for me to handle the bishop's job in the second term than it was in the first term. However, both times I have enjoyed the work. There are a lot of headaches to it. There is a lot of work to it. But there are a lot of things that compensate for all of those situations. I have enjoyed especially my closeness to the young people of the ward. In my interviews with them and the way a young girl comes up and hands me her tithing, I feel so warm inside at the look that she gives me when she hands me the tithing. There are a lot of things, I will tell you, which compensate for all of the headaches and of the extra work that a bishop has to do."[48]

ISAAC ERVIN RIDDLE

Isaac Ervin Riddle was born on 21 June 1894 in Manti, but spent his life in Escalante, Cedar City, and Las Vegas. Much of his life was devoted to Church service. After he married Abby Smith and had three children, he decided he wanted to go on a mission. His wife and children stayed with his father in Escalante for three years, while he served in Oakland and San Francisco. He was the conference president for an area from Carmel to Eureka. His mission president was Joseph W. McMurrin.

"I fulfilled a very honorable mission there. I came home in the spring of 1923. From then on, I have had constant activity in the Church. I have hardly been relieved of one responsibility until I have been given another one. From 1923 to 1960 I was active continually. I remember being selected to be counselor in the Young Men's Mutual Improvement Association, and the stake MIA, immediately after I went back to Cedar City. In a year, President William R. Palmer elevated me to be the superintendent of all the stake MIAs. Finally, in 1939, President Palmer asked me to be bishop of the newly organized Fourth Ward. During that time, we promoted genealogy and things of that sort. We had a committee of twenty-four people in that ward. We used to come down in great swarms to the St. George Temple."

Riddle will long be remembered because he was a successful fundraiser. "There was a six-thousand-dollar debt hanging over the ward building from 1930, when it was built, to almost 1940. The bishop, who was Samuel L. Leigh, called a meeting. I was always a hand at talking and suggested we form a committee, have some big dinners, and raise some money. It wasn't long before we were out of debt and had the chapel paid for. The next thing after we got it out of debt and dedicated, was the institute. They had to have someone to be chairman of the institute and so President William R. Palmer asked me to be the finance chairman. We went on having these five-dollar dinners. We would hold them two nights [a week] with three dinners a night. We fed as many as 1,800 people. We gathered up our half of $300,000 to build that beautiful stake house on Ninth Street in Cedar City as well as the institute."[49]

CIVIC SERVICE

Civic service was essential to community life. Each town needed a mayor and council. There had to be postmasters and water boards, street builders and cemetery sextons. The villages did not have budgets for this work and depended on volunteers. There was a huge need for women to volunteer for things like the Red Cross and historical societies as well as work as midwives. Although these interviewees did not dwell on these matters, they did mention them.

WILLIAM BROOKS

One example is William Brooks, who spent most of his life in civic service. He was born on 23 April 1881 in St. George and spent his life there. He completed high school in St. George and worked in Modena and then went to BYU with his brother, George Brooks. He married Nellie Marie Stephens, who he met at Woodward School as a student. They had six children, two of whom died very young. After Nellie's death he married Juanita Leavitt Pulsipher, who was widowed after she had one son. They then had three boys and one daughter. He narrated his civic service:

"I served eight years on the city [of St. George] council—[two] four-year terms. I was elected to the [Washington] County clerk's office. I was unopposed the first term. The second year I [was] on the Democratic ticket and was elected. I was never defeated after that. I served two two-year terms and one four-year term. I had opposition, but I never was defeated. I had been the county clerk for a number of years, [when the commissioners] thought that one man could run the assessor's office and the sheriff's office. The county commissioners combined the two offices and appointed me sheriff and county assessor.

"It was a hard job; it was a tough job. I was the sheriff for seven years. I was appointed by the commissioners, then I was elected twice by the commissioners and didn't quite finish the last term when I was appointed the postmaster, where I served for twenty years. [The sheriff job] was very interesting. I liked it better than I thought I would. I would get up in the morning [and] go to work. I might be in Idaho or I might be in Arizona the whole night. It was a lot of traveling. I had to have a new car every year. The roads were rough and hard to travel. [I was] allowed ten cents a mile [for expenses]. I could keep my car with the fees that were paid in mileage.

"John Cottam and I were in the bishopric together here. We had a good ol' bishop. He used to caution us all the time, 'Don't be too careless,' and he was right. We would generally be [careful]. Prohibition was very popular at that time. We teamed as the [enforcers] of the law, John and I did. John was less cautious than I was. He would go when he was called. He was the city officer, and I was the county sheriff. They would generally call me if it was the county sheriff's job [or] call him if it was a city job. I would always go with him, and he would always go with me. If there was a car coming, he knew where I would meet him over at the summit, [and] he would always go with me. We would go out and meet them, and we would generally stop them.

"Frankie Wilson was one of the very prominent bootleggers. We got word that he was coming from Mesquite, Nevada. We went out on the road to get Frankie. He was a nice little fellow, and we pushed him out of the road and stopped him. 'I'll be damned! How the hell did you know I was coming?' I said, 'We have friends down this way, and we knew about it.' He wanted to know, 'I know, but how did you find out? You know I come whistling along the road with fifty gallons of white eye on my buckboard. There wasn't anybody in the world [who] knew about it.' I said, 'We got word out while you were whistling on that barrel of whiskey, and we came out and met you.' He said, 'That is not surprising. If you want to, take it. I know what the law is.' We took him into St. George and put him in jail, and he served his term until he could pay it out. He paid it out and went on his way. All his good friends [helped him]. We had lots of [times when] it worked out that way."[50]

THERESA CANNON HUNTSMAN

Here is a woman's tale of community service. It is from Theresa Cannon Huntsman, who was born on 20 October 1885 in St. George. She also lived in Enterprise. After teaching school for five years, she married Lamond

Huntsman on 3 May 1914, and together they had six children. Her father was the president of the St. George Temple. Theresa was a dynamic and active woman: "I was the literature leader for fifteen years [or more in Enterprise]. I was the theology teacher for a good many years. I have lived away [for a while] so that there was a time I was not active. We lived [for] seven years out in the desert and seven years up at the ranch. Part of that time I could not go [to Church]. I did teach some [classes] in Sunday School, but not too much. I was [the] theology teacher [for the adult class], and I was really needed there. I taught Primary some there. I was the chairman of the girls committee when they organized that. I filled two stake missions for the Church in Enterprise.

"When my mother-in-law [Mary Ann 'Terry' Huntsman] was crippled [and] in a wheelchair, I took care of her for thirty-six months. I was the town clerk [in Enterprise] for eighteen years. When grandma died, at age ninety-four, I was town clerk, taking care of her, had most of the children at home and was a stake missionary."[51]

EMMA BRADSHAW CORNELIUS

Emma Bradshaw Cornelius was born in Woodruff, Arizona, to a family of seventeen children. She married her second husband, Henry Cornelius, on 1 May 1914. She had ten children in total. She gave a brief account of Henry's civic work: "He was quite active in civic affairs in [the town of] Virgin. He helped to develop a canal and was president of [the Virgin Canal Company] for several years. In earlier times, he did a lot of [work on] the Dixie Springs project. They were going to put it up here [in] Virgin. He helped on that [project]. He helped survey the Kolob Reservoir [on Cedar Mountain above the Virgin River]. He worked on the Hurricane Canal when he was a boy. He had more interest in the Hurricane Canal than most anybody when they finished it. He sold his interest here and traded for homes up in Virgin because he liked [the area] up that way."[52]

ALVIN HALL

Alvin Hall (mentioned in another chapter) was born on 17 October 1890 in Rockville. Here his comments are included on civic life: "I have been [very] active in the Republican Party. I do a lot of canvassing for the party, [and I] attend the meetings and support the ticket. I have some good friends who are Democrats. I also worked during Peach Days [in Hurricane], when we used to put on Peach Days. I worked on the [Church] welfare farms quite a lot. I told them [something] in priesthood meeting not so long ago. I said, 'I have never refused a job in the Church until it came to thinning peaches.' I just told them that I was too old for that kind of [activity].

"I have done a lot of the work [for the fair]. I was not the leader, [but] it did not bother me at all. I [would] just as soon somebody else would have those leadership positions. It felt good to work on [programs] that I believed in."[53]

GLENN WAITE

Glenn Waite was born on 27 Janury 1906 in Bunkerville, Nevada. He graduated from the eighth grade there and then went to high school in nearby Mesquite but would spend his senior year in Fallon, Nevada, where his brother taught. He went there so he could play on all of the athletic teams. He spent much of his adult life in manual labor, but later on he held public office. He reported, "When I was in the town of Bunkerville, they only had one or two government jobs, or county jobs, civic jobs—justice of the peace and constable. Those two more or less ran the affairs of the town. The crimes that were committed there were taken care of by the constable and the justice of the peace. I ran for the office of justice of the peace and [was elected] and [served] for four years. In the four years I was in there, I married only two people in the town of Bunkerville and had a half a dozen cases to try. I was called three or four different times to act as justice of the peace in Las Vegas. The first time, I was there for Saturday and Sunday. The first Saturday that I was in Las Vegas, I married sixty couples. [During] the two days [I was] there, it was close to a hundred couples that I married [as] justice of the peace in Las Vegas.

"That was about the average [number of marriages] they were [performing] at that time. They [had] in the neighborhood of 10,000 or 12,000 couples married there a year. I was called down several different times to act as justice of the peace. I was on several trials there as a judge. It was good experience to be [in that] position, where you could have the lawyers come in and argue their cases. [Then] you would then have to decide which was right and which was wrong. You had to know a little about the law to be able to do this. It was a good experience that I had in those four years [when] I was justice of the peace."[54]

LILLIAN ORTON COX

Lillian Orton Cox told about the service of her husband, Leroy Henderson Cox. She worked in his law office and could observe it firsthand: "My husband, through the services he had rendered to his political party, was appointed to [be] a member of the Board of Regents of the University of Utah. He held this office for eight years, until [George Dewey] Clyde was elected [governor]. He [served] under Governor [J. Bracken] Lee. Frequently, I went to Salt Lake with him, and there was always some nice [event] to go to. I was all for moving to Salt Lake. I did not care whether we made any money or not. I just wanted to be where there were nice people to meet and nice things to do.

"I participated a good deal [with him]. He was admitted to the Utah State Bar in 1924. He served as county attorney in Washington County from 1924 to 1928. He served as judge of the Fifth Judicial District [for] eight years, beginning in 1928. He was elected [to the bench] at the age of thirty-two. People raised their eyebrows. How could such a young man take such a heavy burden? Something happened in Fillmore that changed their mind. It was at the time when all the banks were going broke. People said, 'He will never do anything about so-and-so [because] he is in the same political party.' That did not turn out to be true, because Roy was a man of principle. It did not make any difference to him. If that had been his own brother, he would have given the same decision. The man was taken out of his position in the bank. The banks were going broke. It goes to show that you cannot judge a man by his age.

"He was the city attorney for twenty-eight years and was on the utility commission for sixteen years. Church-wise, he was not home too much. He was superintendent of Sunday School. He was [an] officer in Mutual [and] participated as much as he could.

"[They] had decided to build the Kolob Reservoir. He was [involved in] a great deal of paperwork that had to be done on all these affairs. When it was away from here, the court clerk [took care of the paperwork], but there was a good deal of paperwork when he had [cases] come up here.

"When we came back from Chicago and we decided to settle in St. George, he became interested in the water situation as it was at the time. The gophers would eat holes [in the ditches], and the water would waste. It was his idea that they cement the ditches so that they would not be losing that water. It did not happen all at once. He was a board member for over twenty-five years for the St. George Valley Irrigation company and the St. George and Washington Canal Company. He was secretary and attorney for the Dixie Project and Development Association Incorporated.

"He was president of the Virgin River Water Users Association from the date of its organization. He was secretary and treasurer for Kolob Reservoir and Storage Association from the date of its organization. He also wrote up all the necessary papers for the Ash Creek Project. It has never amounted to much until this year. If you went over where the Ash Creek waters are, [it] is full of water this year."[55]

CLARENCE JACOB ALBRECHT

Clarence Jacob Albrecht was born on 7 April 1904 in Fremont, Wayne County. As a boy, he herded sheep. He farmed for many years, and raised a family with his wife, Elizabeth Delilah Albrecht. They raised six children (one died as a child). He served in several Church positions, including bishop. His civic life was singular: "I was elected to the Utah State Legislature for the 1949 session. I was green as grass! This was kind of wished on to me because I didn't know anything about politics. The fellows came up to my place and said, 'We are going to run you.' I said, 'I am not a Democrat.' They said, 'You can. We are going to run you anyway.' I didn't take any part, and the first thing I knew, here came a paper stating that I was on the Democratic ticket for state representative from Wayne County. I knew I would be defeated because the person who had been the representative was our stake president, and he was a good man. But I didn't do anything. I went to two or three meetings. I never did go out and talk or stump or campaign. I don't know what happened, but I was elected.

"The fifty-first session came along, and I ran again. I didn't have any opposition. When I was elected in 1951, we had thirty Democrats and thirty Republicans. We sat up there for four days and nights, and we couldn't organize. Every time we would vote, it would be a tie. Governor J. Bracken Lee was hollering his head off at us. On the morning of the fifth day, I stepped to the mike. This was definitely an answer to [a] prayer. I didn't realize until it was half over what I had done. I had prayed that something would happen and we would get going, because I thought it was a waste of time and money. In my proposition, I proposed that the Republicans should have their choice of people by electing Clifton Kerr from Tremonton as speaker of the house, and that the Democrats should have their choice of four major committees. I had lots of mean things said about me and a lot of good things said about me."

Clarence did not run in 1953 or 1955. "I thought I had had enough. About the first of September of 1956, I was down in my meadow irrigating. Here came about ten men down to the water on Sunday morning. They said, 'We are going to run you on the Independent ticket.' He was elected and ran again in 1959. A few years later, he and his wife retired to St. George, where they ran a motel. That is where he was interviewed.[56]

CONCLUSIONS

These three categories of service—military, church, and community—give a broader view of these people, their interaction with others beyond their family, and their work. The issues surrounding military service show that both young men and married men served; some married men even had children at home. The war was well under way before the United States entered. The men went through basic training and some received specialized training. The lateness of the United States' entry meant that they arrived in Europe near the end of the war. They experienced life in England, France, and Germany, but some did not ever leave the United States. In both the homeland and in Europe, many of the troops faced the worldwide flu epidemic. One report mentioned fifteen deaths from flu in one unit. Another told of a soldier who avoided going to the hospital because he felt he was more likely to die there. Very similar things were occurring in the homeland.

Another observation was that some of these troops experienced the beginning of motorization. They were trained to support the artillery.

With equipment drawn by horses, the soldiers backed up the cannon and long-range guns. Soon, motorized tractors arrived and they quickly adapted to a much faster support work. Despite such improvements, they still had to delouse their sleeping quarters regularly. There were some who had children who fought during World War II.

The reports these people gave about their Church service gives a picture of how the whole community was involved. Though some people did not attend, they were part of the community, a community whose values were closely attached to gospel principals. It is clear that there was a difference between male and female roles. The men were called to the priesthood, almost all of them. This meant that they presided at Church functions. The bishop had both spiritual and temporal responsibilities. The LDS bishop is the equivalent of a pastor, but the Church has no paid clergy. The calling was very demanding. Nonetheless, some men remained in that office for several years; one even served for fifteen. It must have occupied twenty or more hours a week. Because it was an unpaid position, the bishop and all other men serving continued their normal occupations to support their families. Male members also carried out ward teaching, which meant they visited a few families each month and reported their visits to their quorum leaders. The boys became Aaronic Priesthood holders at the age of twelve and went with the older men on ward teaching visits. They also carried out other assigned responsibilities. In many cases, that included physical labor. The aim of the bishops was to assign every member over the age of twelve a calling in the ward.

Women comprised the membership of the Relief Society. The duties of this organization included visiting all the women each month. The Relief Society president was the key figure in helping the bishop with welfare needs of families in difficult circumstances. The Primary was a teaching and activity program for children up to age twelve. It was entirely led by women and held midweek. Ladies led the young women in the Mutual Improvement Association, also held midweek, and often directed the choir. Women were the main workers in genealogy research and were active in temple work. Men participated in the temple also. These interviews show that women served in Church callings during their whole adult lives and were participants in the programs as youth also. They reported that they enjoyed their service as a sisterhood.

Serving as full-time LDS missionaries was the most demanding calling in the Church. Like all other callings, this was volunteer service even though it was full-time. The norm for this calling was that young men would be called to serve, though occasionally, a young woman was called. In the earlier decades, most of the missionaries were married men, a tradition that continued after 1900. Several of these interviews described family fathers serving for two years at a distant place, while their families had to support themselves. Funding a mission was a challenge; families carried the main responsibility, but sometimes friends also contributed. Some of the young men were assigned to labor without purse or scrip.[57] It meant that they depended on members in their area, investigators, or friends to feed them. Those missionaries have many tales to tell. Others tell that they received about thirty dollars per month from their families for their support.

It is interesting to note where they served. Most were called to labor in the United States. One served in the Southern states, one in Texas and Louisiana, three in the eastern states, one in North Dakota, one in the Ozarks, one in Alabama, and one in the central states. Two served in Switzerland and one in the new efforts in Japan and Korea. It is clear that the LDS Church missionary efforts were concentrated mainly in North America and Europe. The service in the developing nations came later.

Missionaries reported fascinating experiences, some spiritual, some adventurous. These experiences included considerable opposition. Some missionaries were attacked. A few were even jailed. They often had to find their way alone in a strange land. Some reported the kindness of people who were not Church members in helping them.

Those who reported community service included both volunteer work and paid service. The latter included being the town postmaster, though in the villages the pay was minimal and usually for women. There was a report from Will Brooks, who served full-time as a sheriff. Most of the positions were held by volunteers; a major position was managing the irrigation system. Reservoirs, canals, and ditches had to be built and inspected, and the water-turn system had to be regulated. This work was for men and some gave their life to it. The building of the Hurricane and La Verkin Canals were decade-long efforts, involving scores of men. There had to be a justice of the peace and a town council. Three reported serving in the state legislature. The county fair and the Hurricane Peace Days also needed dozens of volunteers. Some served as a cemetery sexton. This effort to maintain thriving communities was not unique to the Mojave Desert residents: It is a vital feature of American life. The involvement of these people in this way is just one more example of how they were implanting that American system in this location, despite its arid challenges.

This completes the personal statements of a portion of those interviewed. Hopefully the reader has employed historical skills, reading these statements critically. Now we turn to a statistical analysis of the 425 people interviewed.

NOTES

1. Nels Anderson, *Nels Anderson's World War I Diary*, ed. Allan Kent Powell (Salt Lake City: University of Utah Press, 2013).

2. Anderson, *Nels Anderson's World War I Diary*, 35.

3. Anderson, *Nels Anderson's World War I Diary*, 36.

4. Anderson, *Nels Anderson's World War I Diary*, 37.

5. Anderson, *Nels Anderson's World War I Diary*, 41.

6. Anderson, *Nels Anderson's World War I Diary*, 41.

7. Anderson, *Nels Anderson's World War I Diary*, 59.

8. Anderson, *Nels Anderson's World War I Diary*, 66.

9. Anderson, *Nels Anderson's World War I Diary*, 69–70.

10. Anderson, *Nels Anderson's World War I Diary*, 148.

11. Douglas D. Alder and Karl F. Brooks, *A History of Washington County: From Isolation to Destination* (Salt Lake City: Utah State Historical Society, 1996).

12. Elwood Mead and Ray Palmer Teele, ed., *Report of Irrigation Investigations in Utah* (Washington, DC: Government Printing Office, 1903).

13. Frank Adams, "Agriculture Under Irrigation in the Basin of Virgin River," in *Report of Irrigation Investigations in Utah*, ed. Elwood Mead and Ray Palmer Teele (Washington, DC: Government Printing Office, 1903), 212.

14. Douglas D. Alder and Karl F. Brooks, *A History of Washington County*, 187.

15. Douglas D. Alder and Karl F. Brooks, *A History of Washington County*, 180.

16. David Orin Woodbury, VOR File 68-006.

17. Frederick Cheney Van Buren, VOR File 69-098.

18. Benjamin was a cook and helped feed the soldiers he associated with.

19. Benjamin Bringhurst, VOR File 70-054.

20. Homer Young Englesteadt, VOR File 69-185.

21. On 18 July 1917, the national army camp at American Lake, Washington, was named Camp Lewis in honor of Captain Meriwether Lewis, commander of the Lewis and Clark Expedition.

22. Grant Zenis Keyes, VOR File 69-175.

23. Earl Tolton Harris, VOR File 68-103.

24. Charles "Charlie" Richard Sullivan, VOR File, 69-097.

25. Harmon Gubler Jr., VOR File 69-042.

26. Glenn Wilcox Steed, VOR File 69-010.

27. Della Elizabeth McCune Steed, VOR File 69-009.

28. Milo Golden Campbell, VOR File 68-109.

29. Frank Barber, VOR File 69-161.

30. Lafayette Hall, VOR File 69-177.

31. Joseph Fielding Hardy, VOR File 69–080.

32. Alvin accepted a call to serve for six months.

33. Alvin Hall, VOR File 69-136.

34. Joseph Alma Terry, VOR File 69-102.

35. Janet Bracken Keyes, VOR File 69-174.

36. Gilbert became more active in the Church when they moved to St. George.

37. A band of the Paiutes.

38. Gilbert Delos Hyatt, VOR File 70-050.

39. This was still while they lived in their home ward.

40. Mata Gubler Ence, VOR File 70-029.

41. Melvina Belle Hammond Bringhurst, VOR File 70-078.

42. Laura Stucki Gray, VOR File 69-173.

43. Matthew Gray, VOR File 69-169.

44. Nina Venice Spendlove Stratton, VOR File 70-044.

45. Lydia Amelia Barlocker Hunt, VOR File 69-118.

46. Amelia Cooper Woodard, VOR File 69-153.

47. William Malen Cox, VOR File 68-050.

48. William Vaughn Jones, VOR File 69–163.

49. Isaac Ervin Riddle, VOR File 68-090.

50. William Brooks, VOR File 68-101.

51. Theresa Cannon Huntsman, VOR File 69-115.

52. Emma Bradshaw Cornelius, VOR File 70-016.

53. Alvin Hall, VOR File 69-136.

54. Glenn Waite, VOR File 69-106.

55. Lillian Orton Cox, VOR File 69-124.

56. Clarence Jacob Albrecht, VOR File 68-042.

57. Luke 22:35.

Appendix

STATISTICS OF THE VOICES OF REMEMBRANCE INTERVIEWS

OBSERVATIONS ABOUT INTERVIEWEES

First, 425 people were interviewed between 1968 and 1970 by Fielding H. Harris. At that time, they were living in Washington County, Utah, or nearby. Of these interviews, 17 were either not completed or were inaudible, leaving 408 completed ones. The chart allows readers to find the names, birth dates, locations, number of siblings, years they attended school, number of children, number of marriages, health difficulties (if any), involvement level in the LDS Church, work skills, and other items.

Second, these people were born between 1870 and 1933. Out of the 408 people interviewed, 11 were born between 1870 and 1879, 83 between 1880 and 1889, 157 between 1890 and 1899, 110 between 1900 and 1909, 36 between 1910 and 1919, and 11 between 1920 and 1933. Therefore, these stories come from people who were born mostly between 1880 and 1910. Some who were interviewed were elderly, even in their late nineties. They and even their younger contemporaries might have had some memory limitations which impacted the interview. All of the interviews were dependent on memory. Memory is usually enlightening but can

Births by Years

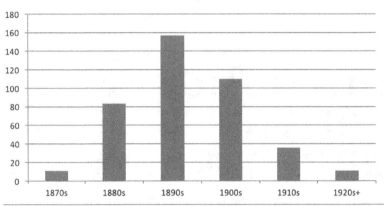

color the comments, even to the point of eulogy or blame. Readers of these interviews have to act as critical readers.

Third, all of these people were survivors. They perpetuated the village system and the values promoted by their parents and grandparents. They made it through the flu epidemic of 1918–19. They survived in the desert. They knew how to produce food, build modest homes and villages, irrigate, herd, barter, work timber, and wander to find seasonal and domestic jobs when they were not involved in agriculture. Manual labor was the way of life for both men and women. They mastered the use of herbal medicine and the creation of fabric. However, many of their children and even parents did not survive.

Fourth, they were often born in families of many children, mainly 5 to 13 siblings. The following group listed only siblings, thus excluding themselves from the total. All total, 382 of them listed 2,808 siblings, 24 did not list any siblings at all, 8 listed 1, 23 listed 2, 19 listed 3, 22 listed 4, 30 listed 5, 22 listed 6, 30 listed 7, 36 listed 8, 32 listed 9, 42 listed 10, 31 listed 11, 28 listed 12, 16 listed 13, 3 listed 14, 1 listed 15, 4 listed 16, 0 listed 17, 2 listed 18, and 28 listed 0.[1]

Some of those interviewed also listed siblings who died: 21 reported that 1 of their siblings died, 22 reported that 2 died, 9 reported that 3 died, 5 reported that 4 died, 5 reported that 5 died, and 1 reported that 6 died.

Chart on siblings

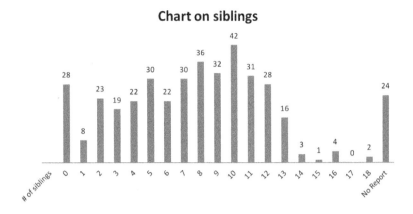

Fifth, they lived in villages. Most of the villages were established before 1900, and a few—Veyo, Central, Ivins, Hurricane, La Verkin, and Enterprise—were established by 1910. Several villages had been abandoned, such as Hebron, Bloomington, Price, Atkinville, Heberville, and Duncan's Retreat. Those people interviewed mainly reported that they loved their childhood. They always had enough to eat, largely because families had a large garden and produced ample food. They loved being with their numerous siblings and the many friends in neighboring homes that also had many children. By living in a village, their lives were different from many people in other western states who lived on homesteads, a long distance from neighbors. Adults from the villages often reported on the vitality of community life, celebrations, water companies, church life, and neighborhood cooperation.

Sixth, the majority of these people were the offspring of the original Mormon settlers in southern Utah, southern Nevada, and northern Arizona—the area named the Mojave Desert and the Colorado Plateau, an arid climate mostly at about 2,500 feet elevation. The original settlers, the interviewees' parents or grandparents, began arriving in 1852, and then the big immigration started in 1861–62. Harmony was the first village, followed by Washington and Toquerville, then Santa Clara, Pine Valley, Gunlock, Hebron, and Hamblin on the west side. Virgin, Grafton, Rockville, Springdale, and Shunesburg were established on the upper Virgin River approaching Zion Canyon. Some temporary villages also existed there, like Duncan's Retreat. In Long Valley, north of Springdale and Mount Carmel on the Virgin River, the towns of Orderville and Glendale were founded. St. George was established in December 1861 and January 1862. Bloomington, Price, Atkinville, and Heberville existed for a while south of St. George but were later abandoned. Leeds, Harrisburg, and Pintura were established north of St. George on the route to Harmony. Pinto was west of Pintura, high in the Pine Valley Mountains. Bunkerville, Mesquite, and Las Vegas were early Mormon settlements in Nevada, south of the Utah boundary. Pioche, Nevada, was a mining town on the western border of Utah where some Mormons went, but Caliente, Panaca, Logandale, Glendale, Modena, and Beaver Dam were founded by Mormon settlers in Nevada and Arizona, near the western border of Utah. Fredonia and Mount Trumbull were in northern Arizona. Several of the people interviewed lived in the counties north of the Mojave Desert in Iron and Garfield Counties, some even farther north. A few were from Panguitch, north of Cedar City, as well as Cedar City and Beaver. About 20 of the interviewees were born in other states in the US and Canada but later moved to southern Utah. At least a dozen interviewees were born in Europe before immigrating to southern Utah from Norway, England, Germany, and Switzerland. About 25 came to southern Utah from villages in Mexico that Mormons had settled some twenty years before the Mexican Revolution of 1910–12.

Seventh, almost all of the interviewees attended school, mainly in the villages where one teacher taught all grades, usually spending fifteen minutes per day with each grade while the others did their assignments. Woodward School in St. George opened in 1901 and offered eight grades, and soon after, ten. Dixie Academy opened in 1911 and offered four years of high school until 1916, and then it added the first year of college; and in 1917, the academy added the second year. A high school was started in Hurricane in 1917. Until that time, those desiring to attend high school had to go to Cedar City or Beaver. A select few went to Brigham Young University in Provo, the University of Utah in Salt Lake City, or Utah State Agricultural College in Logan. Only about ten attended any of those colleges. The others attended schools in their hometowns. The chart shows how far a student progressed in the grade system: 1 through first grade; 1 through second

Years of School Completed

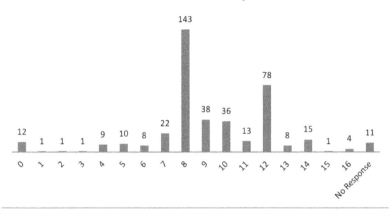

grade; 1 through third grade; 9 through fourth grade; 10 through fifth grade; 8 through sixth grade; 22 through seventh grade; and 143 through eighth grade. Most students who completed school through the eighth grade did so in the villages. By leaving their villages, 38 students progressed through ninth grade, 36 through tenth grade, 13 through eleventh grade, and 78 graduated from high school in the twelfth grade. Many of these graduates were born in the twentieth century. Beyond this, some reported attending school after high school graduation: 8 progressed through grade 13 (freshman in college) and 15 through fourteenth grade (sophomore), which could be completed at Dixie College after 1917. And after freshman and sophomore years, 1 progressed through fifteenth grade (junior) and 4 through sixteenth grade (senior), undoubtedly at a university. Out of the remaining interviewees, 11 gave no answer, and 12 said they did not attend school at all. All total, the number reported was 411.

Eighth, all but one of the people on this list were married, and many of them were married by age 16. Most had children, but had somewhat fewer than their parents had: 21 people listed 1 child, 28 listed 2, 31 listed 3, 55 listed 4, 55 listed 5, 52 listed 6, 34 listed 7, 33 listed 8, 18 listed 9, 25 listed 10, 14 listed 11, 6 listed 12, 7 listed 13, 5 listed 14, 1 listed 16, 5 gave no report, and 15 listed 0. That is the report of 408 people. The total number of births was 2,300. In the column that listed the number of children, some parents, but not all, also noted the number who died,

Number of Children

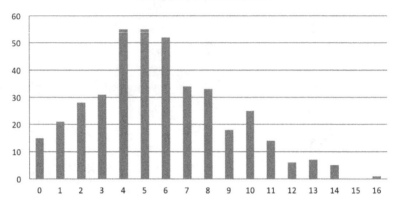

by putting a slash after the number of children born. The total number of children who died was 191. The death of husbands or wives before the age of 40 was not unusual. One woman reported being a widow for 35 years. Most remarried within two or three years, likely because they had many young children to raise and a farm and garden to maintain. Of those interviewed, 85 listed having more than one spouse, and most of those were the result of the death of a spouse.

Ninth, many of the interviewees faced serious health challenges, either in themselves or in their families. They reported the deaths of 116 children, and 237 of the interviewees said that they either had health challenges personally or saw them in their children or spouse. Medical doctors were seldom available in the rural villages where most of the people lived. There were two in St. George and one in Hurricane, but the people in the villages seldom had access to them. Some of those interviewed reported increased health care in the 1930s to the 1950s. A few were even able to travel north to hospitals by that time.

Tenth, the "Church," "Mission," and "Temple" columns give a picture of religious life in this Mormon region in the period between 1880 and 1970. This was a time before the cultural and religious diversity that is present today. Mormonism was dominant in the region. There were two small Presbyterian congregations with schools, and after 1956, a Roman Catholic Church was established in St. George the Catholic Church has a large congregation now. There was a Catholic congregation for a decade in Silver Reef in the 1880s. Referring again to the table, the 348 people who said "Yes" in the "Church" column were responding as Latter-day Saints. Of those, 248 went through the temple. This means that the latter group included the most committed members. It is unlikely that all of the members attended their village religious service every week. There were varying degrees of commitment. Some who lived on ranches were rarely able to travel to the nearest village for services. There were also varying levels of obedience to such commandments as the Word of Wisdom. Nonetheless, every village had an active ward with a bishop and many others serving in various callings as teachers, musicians, visiting and home teachers, and clerks. The members carried out spiritual and secular assignments, including building churches. There was a stake president with two counselors and a high council of twelve men who supervised most of the villages, traveling there frequently. From this report it is clear that most of the people considered themselves as Latter-day Saints.

During those days, the central Church leaders in Salt Lake City requested a few people to serve full-time proselyting missions, generally for two years. They had to support themselves. Sixty-nine people said that they accepted and completed such a calling. Some of them were married men who left a wife and children at home while they served away from home. The family had a garden and farm to help support them, but the children who were old enough had to work nearly full-time to support the family. Often, uncles and aunts helped. The majority of the missionaries were young men, though a few young women also served. Both groups went before they were married. They served mainly in the United States—New England, the South, California, Oregon, Wyoming, and Kansas. A few served in England and Switzerland, 1 went to Hawaii, and another to Korea. This required a strong commitment and generally had a major positive impact on their lives. Being married in the temple and attending the temple thereafter was another measure of religious commitment. Those who checked that column numbered 264. Some of them went to the temple for their initial marriage. Others went there a few years later to seal their civil marriage. Quite a few of those interviewed became active temple attendees, daily or weekly, in their senior years, often when they moved to St. George to be nearer to the temple.

Eleventh, the column listed "Other" mentions many things, including service. About a dozen served in World War I and 2 in World War II. Scores of the people served in volunteer community activities such as the Red Cross and the Daughters of Utah Pioneers. Some also volunteered as election judges, and several worked at the United States Post Office. Many men served on the canal water companies or cattlemen associations, which often took many hours of their time. Some maintained cemeteries. Others were civil servants, including four men who served terms in the Utah State Legislature. One man was in the Civilian Conservation Corps. A few women were midwives, often without pay. Others prepared bodies for burial. Several men were mayors. Many folks played in community bands. the chart does not detail all of this service, the individual interviews included in the book do.

Remember, the words of these interviews are firsthand accounts. As with many memoirs, they are both insightful and biased. These accounts are so important because little has been written about laborers, maybe because they seldom wrote memoirs or articles. Furthermore, little has been written about this middle period between the pioneering and the industrialized consumer society for which this area has become famous—tourism and retirement living in the southwest desert. Now, the region's higher education is widespread, its medical facilities are among the nation's best, its highways are sophisticated, and it abounds with technology. In 1910, survival was marginal. Nonetheless, the people who then lived in that area furthered the implantation of Western civilization that is thriving. Though this study is limited to the arid region of the Mojave Desert, the stories these people tell are very similar to the other 450 Mormon villages in the intermountain region. Those areas were semiarid and used the same village system. Their focus on community, family, service, and hard physical labor is very similar.

NOTE

1. This means that rather than not listing any siblings at all, this group of people confirmed that they had zero siblings. The other group, "29 did not list any siblings at all," simply means there were no siblings on record, but it is possible that they may have had siblings.

STATISTICS OF THE VOICES OF REMEMBRANCE INTERVIEWS

#	Birth Year, Name	Siblings, from Each Marriage/ Died	School	Children from Each Marriage Born/Died	Spouse	Health Challenges	Church	Mission	Temple	Residence	Other
68-001	1894, Lucy Hinton Ruesch	1	8	6/2 + 8	3		Strong		Yes		
68-002	1894, Oren Ruesch	12	8	8	1	Yes	Yes				Farmer, mail deliverer, miller, infections, operations
68-003	1892, Sarah Agnes Hardy	8	?	8/3	1		Yes		Yes		
68-004	1892, Minnie Sainsbury	?	8	12	3		Yes +			Lava Hot Springs	
68-005	1893, Martin C. Wallace Heaton	?	11	4/1	4		Yes		Yes	St. George	
68-006	1895, David O. Woodbury,	1+8	12	3	1	Yes	Yes	Yes	Yes	Salt Lake City, St. George	1915 Dixie College graduate
68-007	1897, Laura S. Woodbury	?	12	4	1	Yes	Yes	England	Yes	St. George	Father was Ed H. Snow

#	Birth Year, Name	Siblings, from Each Marriage/Died	School	Children from Each Marriage Born/Died	Spouse	Health Challenges	Church	Mission	Temple	Residence	Other
68-008	1896, Mary Jane Truman Holt	5	8	8	3: Morris T. Holt		Yes		Yes	Holt's Ranch, Enterprise	Nurse who attended to flu patients
68-009	1885, Joseph Woodruff Holt		8	11/1	3		Yes		Yes	Holt's Ranch	Childhood in Gunlock
68-010	1896, John, Volney Bailey		12	8	1			Yes	Yes	St. George and Idaho	
68-011	1902, Helma C. W. Bailey	8	8	6+2	1	Yes	Yes		Yes	Norway and Idaho	Came to US with parents
68-012	1888, Albert E. Fitzpatrick		8	2	1: 1912	Yes	Convert	Yes	Yes	Wisconsin and St. George	Lived in Oakland for 10 years
68-013	1888, Martha R. L. Fitzpatrick	9	?	2	1: 1912	Yes	Yes			Portage, Salt Lake City	Lived in many California Cities
68-014	1900, Irvin Bryner		8	5	1	Yes	Yes		Yes	St. George, Enterprise	Worked on AZ Strip & railroad, also electrician

#	Birth Year, Name	Siblings, from Each Marriage/ Died	School	Children from Each Marriage Born/Died	Spouse	Health Challenges	Church	Mission	Temple	Residence	Other
68-015	1901, Lola Belle DeMille Bryner	7	12	5	1	Yes	Yes +		Yes, 1920	Rockville	Had speech defect
68-016	1898, Emilie E. Gerlach			5			Convert		Yes	Born in Germany	Retired to St. George
68-017	1893, Charles G. Sanchez	1	8	1	2	Yes	Yes			Born in Chicago, St. George	Worked on railroad & as electrician
68-018	1889, Layton U. Smith	1	8	1	1		Convert in Florida		Yes, 1948	Born in Georgia	Worked as plumber and farmer
68-019	1900, Mertice E. D. Smith	2	8	1	1	Yes	Yes		Yes, 1948	Born in Georgia	
68-020	1905, Hazel M. Brankam		7	5+1	1	Yes	Yes, 1927		Yes	Born in Wisconsin	
68-021	1902, Cecil V. Brankam		8	6	1		Convert age 10			Kentucky, Arizona	Moved often and had many jobs
68-022	1890, Matilde W. Reusch	1	14	5	1		Yes		1916, St. George	St. George, Salt Lake City, Springdale	Homesteader & taught at Dixie Junior High

#	Birth Year, Name	Siblings, from Each Marriage/ Died	School	Children from Each Marriage Born/Died	Spouse	Health Challenges	Church	Mission	Temple	Residence	Other
68-023	1890, Julia M. W. Wilkinson	1	12	6/2	1: 1913	Yes	Yes			Kanarraville	Husband died young
68-024	1901, Mearl D. Carson		6	6/2	2: 1st wife died 1952		Yes		Yes	Washington	Had 50 jobs
68-025	1903, Viola A. J. F. Carson		8	6/2	3	Yes, Typhoid	Yes		Yes	Logan, St. George	
68-026	1887, Donetta M. I. Bundy	2	7	12/1	1	Yes	Yes		Yes	Mexico, Mount Trumbull	
68-027	1891, Joseph H. Johnson Jr.		8+1	6	2		Yes		Yes	Tropic	Worked in dairy, mill, sugar beet factory
68-028	1899, Myrtle I. M. Johnson	2	8	4/2	2	Yes	Yes	Yes	Yes	Mission as widow	Also lived in Uinta
68-029	1894, Addie Oliva A. Truman	7	11	4	1		Yes			Beaver, St. George, Enterprise	Attended Beaver Academy
68-030	1891, Omer Dick Bundy	5	no	10/1	1	Yes	Yes	Mexico	Yes	St. George, Las Vegas	Lived in Mount Trumbull, Bunkerville

#	Birth Year, Name	Siblings, from Each Marriage/Died	School	Children from Each Marriage Born/Died	Spouse	Health Challenges	Church	Mission	Temple	Residence	Other
68-031	1896, Clara M. Woods Terry	8	8	2 adopted	1	Yes	Yes	Husband	Yes	Enterprise, Beaver Dam	Childhood in Provo
68-032	1894, Rowena W. Bundy	?	5	10/1	1	Yes				Born in Springville	Lived in St. George, Mount Trumbull, Las Vegas
68-033	1896, Dorothy J. M. P. Talbot	2	12	2	2	Yes+	Yes			Midwest, Salt Lake City, Logan, St. George	Homesteader
68-034	1892, Lloyd B. Jennings	10	8	5	1		Yes			St. George, Salt Lake City, California, Tintic, Levan	Worked as farm contractor
68-035	1882, Mariah D. Alldredge	8	8	4	1		Yes+			Old Mexico, Aurora,	41 grandchildren, 82 great-grandchildren
68-036	1887, Gordon W. Mathis	2	12	3	1	Yes	Yes	Yes	Yes	St. George	Owned Mathis Market

#	Birth Year, Name	Siblings, from Each Marriage/ Died	School	Children from Each Marriage Born/Died	Spouse	Health Challenges	Church	Mission	Temple	Residence	Other
68-037	1892, Georganna B. Jennings	9	12	5	1	Yes	Yes			Washington, Overton, Salt Lake City	Attended the University of Utah, taught in Washington
68-038	1873, Robert P. Woodbury	9	12	8	1		Yes	Yes	Yes	Hurricane, St. George, Cedar City	Taught elementary school, farmer, St. George mayor
68-039	1888, Chloe G. V. L. Bundy	8	10	14/1	2	Yes	Yes		Yes	Aurora	Had asthma, nurse, had sixteen children, many hard births, son is Lincoln Bundy
68-040	1887, James Bundy	4	13	14/1	1	Yes	Yes		Yes	Old Mexico, Mount Trumbull	Worked as pipe fitter and mechanic
68-041	1885, Marie H. S. LeBaron			2	2		Yes		Yes	Germany, Evanston	Converted in Evanston

#	Birth Year, Name	Siblings, from Each Marriage/ Died	School	Children from Each Marriage Born/Died	Spouse	Health Challenges	Church	Mission	Temple	Residence	Other
68-042	1904, Clarence J. Albrecht	8	12+	6/1	1	Yes	Yes+		Yes		Legislator, bishop, taught at University of Utah and Hanksville
68-043	1910, Elizabeth Delilah Day	9	12	7	1	Yes	Yes		Yes	Circleville, Antimony	
68-044	1899, Vera Hinton Eagar	2	8	7/2	1	Yes	Yes			Hurricane, Las Vegas, Salt Lake City	Also lived in Hinckley and Virgin
68-045	1898, Thomas Eagar	?	8	7/2	1	Yes	Yes			Hurricane and Mexico	Worked as dry farmer and raised sheep and cattle
68-046	1885, Vernon Worthen	7	10	4/2	1		Yes		Yes	St. George	Bishop, taught 41 years in St. George
68-047	1898, Lorna P. Worthen	11	12	4/2	1		Yes		Yes	Overton, St. George, Logandale	Lived in Lincoln, Nevada, and St. George

#	Birth Year, Name	Siblings, from Each Marriage/ Died	School	Children from Each Marriage Born/Died	Spouse	Health Challenges	Church	Mission	Temple	Residence	Other
68-048	1891, LeRoy Elmer Davis	4	?	?	3				Yes		Ran away from home, worked rail-road, beets, lumber
68-049	1909, Inez G. D. L. Davis	7	8	8	2	Yes			Yes	Old Mexico, Cedar City	Polygamist mother
68-050	1896, William Malin Cox	?	9	4/1	2	Yes			Yes		Legislature, Postmaster, Cattle/farm Association
68-051	1886, Hanna E. H. Roundy	14	8	13/several	1	Yes	Yes+		Yes	Orderville, Panguitch	Lived on Alton farm, raised children
68-052	1886, Charles H. Knell	7	9	4/1	2		Yes		Yes	Pinto, Newcastle	Washington musician
68-053	1894, Agatha W. M. Knell	24 in polygamy	12	6	2		Yes		Yes	St. George, Bicknell, Washington	C. Walker, J. McAllister
68-054	1902, Le Roy J. Bailey	?	University 13	2	2	Yes	Convert 1924				Scientist, chemist in New York, convert, 1924

#	Birth Year, Name	Siblings, from Each Marriage/ Died	School	Children from Each Marriage Born/Died	Spouse	Health Challenges	Church	Mission	Temple	Residence	Other
68-059	1893, Ann G. Wulfenstein	11	8	7	1	Yes	Yes		Yes	Springville, St. George, Nevada	Husband was killed
68-060	1894, Verna M. I. Gifford	10	8	10/1	1	Yes	Yes		Yes	St. George, Cedar, Springdale	Also lived in Hurricane and Virgin
68-061	1904, Reba R. LeFevre	8	8	4 adopted Indians	1: married late	Yes	Yes		Yes	Kanar- raville, St. George	Also lived in New Mexico
68-062	1890, Lena R. N. Johnson	11	8		2		Yes	Yes			9 stepchildren
68-063	1909, George C. Thompson	?	14	4	1			Yes	Yes	St. George	Worked in heating, air- conditioning
68-065	1898, Ralph A. Brown	13	9	6	1		Yes+	Yes	Yes	Mexico	Served in temple
68-066	1917, Hannah C. C. Hiatt	?	11	8/1	1	Yes	Yes		Yes	Caliente, Las Vegas	Colorado Hawthorne Company
68-067	1877, Godfrey Lee Neese		5		2		Convert 1955			St. George, Florida	Policeman

#	Birth Year, Name	Siblings, from Each Marriage/ Died	School	Children from Each Marriage Born/Died	Spouse	Health Challenges	Church	Mission	Temple	Residence	Other
68-068	1907, Eliza J. S. Thompson	5	1	4	1		Yes+	Yes	Yes	Missions for 3 children	
68-069	1913, Edwin M. Hiatt	6	?	8/1	1	Yes	Yes	No	Yes	Beaver	Also lived in St. George & Henderson
68-070	1891, Inez H. Hoyt	5	10	8/2	1	Yes	Yes		Yes	Orderville	Husband was Frederick Hoyt
68-071	1890, Frederick C. Hoyt	14	10	8	1		Yes		Yes	Orderville	Spiritual experience (see pages 22–26)
68-072	1900, Alta R. P. Wilcox	13	8	2/1	2	Yes	Yes		Yes	Mexico	Farmer, cook, second husband was Delbert Wilcox
68-073	1884, Joseph B. Swapp			8/3	1				Yes	Enterprise St. George, Ogden	Worked with cattle, sheep, and machines
68-074	1896, Claude S. Rowley	12/5	7	8	1					Mexico, St. George, Blanding	Also lived in Panguitch and Hurricane
68-075	Not in file										

#	Birth Year, Name	Siblings, from Each Marriage/ Died	School	Children from Each Marriage Born/Died	Spouse	Health Challenges	Church	Mission	Temple	Residence	Other
68-076	1894, Nellie F. Eagar Jensen	4		4	2		Yes		Yes	Ogden, St. George	Also lived in Wyoming, worked in motels and hotels
68-077	1907, Callie D. E. Stewart	7	12	2	1	Yes	Yes			Lovell, Salt Lake City, Tooele, St. George	Also lived in Sandy and farmed
68-079	1893, John M. Larson Jr.	2+4 half-siblings	8	3	1		Some		Yes	Bloomington, Beaver Dam	Also lived in St. George and raised cattle on Arizona Strip
68-080	1896, Louise S. L. P. Crosby	4		4	3		Yes		Yes	Idaho, Moroni	Also lived in Perry and St. George as farmer
68-081	1891, Emma L. L. N. Larsen	11/4		4	1	Yes				Beaver Dam	Lived in St. George & Bloomington
68-082	1892, Ernest W. Cardon			7/1	2	Yes	Yes	Yes	Yes	St. George, Ogden	Lived in Carbon, Utah, and Nevada, missionary in Denver

#	Birth Year, Name	Siblings, from Each Marriage/Died	School	Children from Each Marriage Born/Died	Spouse	Health Challenges	Church	Mission	Temple	Residence	Other
68-083	1894, Esther M. Swapp Cardon	9	8	2+	3	Yes	Yes	Yes	Yes	Kanab, Tropic	Also lived in Overton, Nevada
68-084	1873, Samuel C. Dutson	2	2	7/3	2	Yes				Roberts, Idaho; Circleville	Raised sheep
68-085	1917, Jesse A. Callahan	13/2	8	4	2	Yes	Yes			Loa	Called himself a hillbilly, carried mail
68-087	1921, Ruth E. C. Callahan	9/1	8	4	1	Yes	Yes		Yes	Idaho, California, Montana	Also lived in Oregon and St. George
68-088	1891, Harriett W. B. C. Moss	8	8	8	4	Yes	Yes			St. George, Leeds, Mesquite	Also lived in Beaver Dam and Logandale
68-089	1889, Irene L. P. C. Johnson	13/2	8	10/2	2	Yes	Yes+			Deseret, Hinckley, St. George	
68-090	1894, Isaac Ervin Riddle	2,2/2,0	12	4	2	Yes	Yes+		Yes	Cedar City, Escalante	Lived in Wyoming as a homesteader

#	Birth Year, Name	Siblings, from Each Marriage/Died	School	Children from Each Marriage Born/Died	Spouse	Health Challenges	Church	Mission	Temple	Residence	Other
69-091	1890, Minnie Mae Tromley	12	8	10	3		Little			Vernal, Roosevelt	St. George
69-092	1909, George W. McConkie	3	12+	4	1		Yes	Yes	Yes	Moab, La Sal, Salt Lake City, Elko	Also worked in St. George as surveyor. Engineering degrees from Brigham Young University and Utah State University
68-093	1904, Margaret D. Paul	5	12	6	1	'	Yes		Yes	Sharon, Idaho; Logan, Salt Lake City	
68-064	1904, George Wm. Paul	5	12+	6	1		Yes			Salt Lake City	SLC bishop and railroad electrician for the Utah Oil Company
68-095	1897, Mabel H. Muir	3	12	5	1		Yes+			Panguitch, Hatch	

#	Birth Year, Name	Siblings, from Each Marriage/ Died	School	Children from Each Marriage Born/Died	Spouse	Health Challenges	Church	Mission	Temple	Residence	Other
68-096	1903, Blanch M. McComb		12+	3	1		Yes			St. George	Worked at service station
68-097	1889, Lucy M. Osborn	15	8+	7`	1	Yes	Yes+			Beaver, Minersville	Worked in Kanesville, Murdock Academy
68-098	1901, Robert C. McComb	6/1	SLC 12?	3	1		Yes			Missouri, Pocatello, Salt Lake City	Also in St. George, worked at Standard Oil Company
68-099	1885, Selma E. Humphries	12/4	5	3	2	Yes	Yes		Yes	Bull Valley, St. George	
68-100	1877, Mary Hafen Leavitt	5	8	13	1	Yes	Yes	Yes	Yes	Santa Clara, Bunkerville	Husband was Dudley Leavitt
68-101	1881, William Brooks	11	7+ BYU 9	10/1	2	Yes	Yes		Yes	St. George	Was sheriff and postmaster, second wife was Juanita
68-102	1886, Edward Sirls Terry	8	4	1	1: Florence Woodbury	Yes	Yes		Yes	Mesquite	Was a farmer and told cowboy stories

#	Birth Year, Name	Siblings, from Each Marriage/ Died	School	Children from Each Marriage Born/Died	Spouse	Health Challenges	Church	Mission	Temple	Residence	Other
68-103	1889, Earl T. Harris	7	9	6/1	1	Yes	Yes+	Yes	Yes	Oak City, Delta,	WWI service, had scurvy, served in temple
68-104	1885, Clara R. A. Nisson	6/1	8	6	1	Yes	Yes		Yes	Washington	Ranching
68-105	1882, Walter H. Iverson	6	Yes 8?	3	1		Yes			Littlefield, Arizona; Washington	Farming
68-106	1897, Victor Iverson	10/2	8+	3	1		Yes		Yes	Washington	Teacher 40 years and bishop
68-107	1884, Annie Day L. Iverson	7	6–8	6/1	1		Yes		Yes	Littlefield, Washington	Brother was Andrew K. Larson
68-108	1912, Fern M. Hafen	9	12	11/1	1	Yes	Yes		Yes	Ivins	McArthur Jewelers and postmistress
68-109	1908, Milo G. Campbell	7	12	12/3	1					Escalante, Kingston	St. George
68-110	1894, Niels N. Tobiason	11	Several 5	16/7	2	Yes				Logandale, St. George	Also in Oregon, farmer

#	Birth Year, Name	Siblings, from Each Marriage/Died	School	Children from Each Marriage Born/Died	Spouse	Health Challenges	Church	Mission	Temple	Residence	Other
68-111	1908, Lalla W. Tobiason	6	12	11/several	1	Yes	Yes			Bunker-ville, Logandale	Las Vegas
68-112	1891, Ida E. A. Terry Sullivan	6	8	4/1 + step-children	2					Brigham City, Ephraim	St. George
68-113	1878, Miriam A. W. Riding	12	4	10/2	2	Yes	Yes		Yes	Sanpete, Mexico	Sealed in Mexico
68-115	1910, Alporta A. Campbell	12	10	12	1	Yes	Yes			Milo G. Campbell	Moved from Job to job
68-116	1893, Hazel J. Mackel-prang	5	16	13/2	1	Yes	Yes		Yes		
68-119	1883, Powell J. Stratton	11	8+1	7/1	1	Yes	`Yes		Yes	Cedar City	Farmer, no doctors
68-120	1912, Mabel S. McConkie	9	12	4	1	Yes	Yes		Yes	Rockville, Hurricane	Taught Indian Branch School
68-121	1890, Harriet L. Wade Blake	?	10	9	2		Yes				

#	Birth Year, Name	Siblings, from Each Marriage Born/Died	School	Children from Each Marriage Born/Died	Spouse	Health Challenges	Church	Mission	Temple	Residence	Other
68-124	1888, Lafayette Alrey	11	7	11/3	2	Yes	Some		Yes	Escalante, Las Vegas	Also in St. George, did roadwork and ranching
68-125	1888, Isabelle Dean Fullerton	8	9	2	1	Yes	Yes			Vernal, St. George	Married late
68-126	1902, Alvin Carl Hardy	5+4/2	8	5/1	1	Yes	Yes	Yes	Yes	St. George, Springdale	Bishop whose wife was Della Humphries
68-127	1881, Thomas B. Robinson	11	12	4	2		Yes		Yes	Paragonah, Enterprise	Sheep
68-128	1905, Daniel Winder	13/2	10	9	1: Myrtle Crawford	Yes, heart			Yes	Mount Carmel, Springdale	Winder Ranch, bishop 15 years
68-129	1908, Myrtle C. Winder	8/1	Yes 8?	10	1	Yes	Yes		Yes	Springdale	Husband was Leonard Dan Winward
68-131	1881, LoraAnn G. Christensen	12	8	11/several	1		Yes		Yes	Springdale	Widow 45 years
68-132	1885, Fannie C. Gifford	10	8	13/1	1	Yes	Yes			Oak Creek	Near Springdale

#	Birth Year, Name	Siblings, from Each Marriage/Died	School	Children from Each Marriage Born/Died	Spouse	Health Challenges	Church	Mission	Temple	Residence	Other
68-133	1897, Ruth P. Howard	8	8	1	1					School in England	Methodist
68-134	1893, Arthur Delano Cox	11/6	8	8/1	1	Yes	Yes		Yes	Orderville, Rockville	Also Mexico, wife was Cora Haight
68-135	1894, Cora Haight Cox	5	U of Utah 14	4	1	Yes	Yes		Yes	Cedar City, Salt Lake City, Orderville	Also in Rockville
68-136	1882, James Addison Cluff	10/2	8	9	1		Yes		Yes	Near Pima, Arizona	Worked in sawmills and brick plants
68-137	1889, Jessie Helen J. Gibson	5	12	8/1	1	Yes	Yes	Yes	Yes	Rockville, Hurricane	Husband served mission
69-001	1906, Margaret A. B. Stauffer	5	12	4	1		Yes		Yes	Moroni, Salt Lake City, Leeds	Nurse
69-002	1896, Bertha W. Woodbury	13	8	5	1	Yes	Yes			San Juan, Colorado; Monticello	Husband was Grant Woodbury
69-003	1898, Susan C. Ruesch	11	10	10/1	1	Yes	Yes			Springdale, Orderville	Husband was Howard Ruesch

#	Birth Year, Name	Siblings, from Each Marriage/ Died	School	Children from Each Marriage Born/Died	Spouse	Health Challenges	Church	Mission	Temple	Residence	Other
69-004	1894, Samuel K. Gifford	10	12	8/2	1		Yes		Yes	Springdale, Cable Mountain	Also worked in Salt Lake City as a musician and at Auerbach Retail
69-005	1899, Althea G. Gifford	11/3	7	10/5	1	Yes	Yes		Yes	Springdale Cedar, Salt Lake City	Married her cousin
69-006	1898, Grant Woodbury	?	8	5	1		Yes			Cedar City Springdale La Verkin	Story about posse killing Navajos
69-007	1908, Della H. Hardy	4	8	4	1	Yes	Yes		Yes	Virgin, Hurricane	Also in Springdale as domestic worker
69-008	1904, Lucy C. Schiefer	3	8	6/1	1	Yes	Yes+		Yes	Springdale, Zion Park	
69-009	1895, Della E. M. Steed	5/2	8	2	1	Yes	Yes	Yes	Yes	Nephi, Salt Lake City, Santaquin	Springdale
69-010	1896, Glen Wilcox Steed	12	12	3	1		Yes	Yes	Yes	Rockville, Las Vegas, Salt Lake City	Also in Syracuse as dairy worker

#	Birth Year, Name	Siblings, from Each Marriage/ Died	School	Children from Each Marriage Born/Died	Spouse	Health Challenges	Church	Mission	Temple	Residence	Other
69-011	1922, Sarah I. W. Crawford	10	12	0	1	Yes	Yes	Yes	Yes	Idaho, Monroe	St. George teacher
69-012	1901, Newell K. Crawford	8	8	0	0	Yes	Yes	Yes	Yes	Springdale	Hard of hearing
69-013	1895, Lia-Viola Stucki Tobler	12/2	8	3	1	Yes	Yes	Yes	Yes	Santa Clara, Ivins, Salt Lake City	Missionary as widow
69-014	1891, Victoria S. T. Winsor	12	8 Hebron	10 +5 adopted	1	Yes	Yes			Logandale, Enterprise, St. George, Hebron	Described Icelandic genealogical research
69-015	1880, Wilford W. Cannon	10	16 UofU	2	1	Yes+	Yes		Yes		Father was David H. Cannon, mining engineer
69-016	1892, Pearl C. C. Spendlove	5/2	?	2	3	Yes+	Yes		Yes	St. George, Arizona Strip	School lunch worker and temple worker
69-017	1887, Owen W. Clark	10/2	8	6	1			Yes	Yes		

#	Birth Year, Name	Siblings, from Each Marriage/ Died	School	Children from Each Marriage Born/Died	Spouse	Health Challenges	Church	Mission	Temple	Residence	Other
69-018	1892, Erastus S. Gardner	12/1	10	4/1	2	Yes				Pine Valley	Rancher, described early July 24 childrens fun
69-019	1886, Sarah E. H. Clark	10	10	6	1	Yes	Yes			Panguitch, Cannonville	Taught 34 years
69-020	1911, Agnes F. Greenhaugh	7	12	5	1	Yes	Yes		Yes	Glendale, St. George, Kanab	Widow and rancher
69-021	1896, Hazel O. M. Gardner	7	9	2+ adopted	2		Yes			St. George, Leeds	Mentions Milton Moody & E. S. Gardner
69-022	1881, Zora Smith Jarvis	5	14	8/1	1		Yes				Polygamy
69-023	1891, William Allen Keller	12/5	4	8	1	Yes+	Yes		Yes	Deseret	Began work at age 13, homesteader with cattle, worked on railroad
69-024	1907, Mable Geneva (Robb) Jones	9	9	4	1	Yes	Yes		Yes	Paragonah, St. George	Spent time in state mental hospital

#	Birth Year, Name	Siblings, from Each Marriage/ Died	School	Children from Each Marriage Born/Died	Spouse	Health Challenges	Church	Mission	Temple	Residence	Other
69-025	1897, Lillian L Keller	2/1	8	6	1	Yes	Yes		Yes	Logan, Idaho, Hinckley	Husband had leg amputated
69-027	1915, Evan E. Cooper	7	10	5	1		Yes	Yes	Yes	St. George	Cooper Rest Home
69-028	1889, Evalena Belle Albrecht	9	8	6	1				Yes	Sanpete	Earl Albrecht was a cattle rancher and legislator
69-029	1888, Ida May L. Jackson	11/2	8	5	1	Yes	Yes+		Yes	Kanar-raville, Teasdale	Mentions Indians & Robbers Roost
69-030	1911, Margaret Lillian Starks	?	?	3	1	Yes	Convert in Kentucky		Yes	California, Salt Lake City, St. Louis	Husband worked 25 years as tailor, aunt raised her
69-031	Wilford Root Fife (missing)										
69-032	1902, Lodicia E. T. W. A. Fife	4		2 Adopted	2	Mother died	Yes			Annabelle, Utah; Idaho; Mesquite	Husband died

#	Birth Year, Name	Siblings, from Each Marriage/ Died	School	Children from Each Marriage Born/Died	Spouse	Health Challenges	Church	Mission	Temple	Residence	Other
69-033	1910, Lula D. H. Pifer	12	8	8	1	Father died	Yes			Idaho, Wyoming	Farmers
69-034	1909, Emily L. Livingston	6	7	8	1	Father				Rigby, Idaho	
69-035	1887, Athole J. Milne	8	4	10/1	1	Yes				St. George, Washington	Mines, cotton factory
69-036	1883, Amanda H. Milne	8	4	10/1	1		Yes			Washington, Provo, Ogden, Salt Lake City	Cotton factory
69-037	1885, Joseph Arnold Hannig	6/1	4	11/1	1		Yes		Yes	Washington	Cotton factory, Washington Canal, mine
69-038	1908, Laura H. Ernst Newman	0	8	7/3	1	Yes	Convert		Yes		Farmed, café work
69-039	1883, John Ephraim Tanner	?	8	5	1		Yes	Yes, Swiss	Yes	Washington	Cotton factory
69-040	1899, Samuel Richards	11/5	10	4	2	Yes	Yes	Yes	Yes		Farm, worked job to job

#	Birth Year, Name	Siblings, from Each Marriage/ Died	School	Children from Each Marriage Born/Died	Spouse	Health Challenges	Church	Mission	Temple	Residence	Other
69-041	1906, Dora L. H. R. Larson	10/4	11	6/1	3	Yes	Yes		Yes		School lunch worker
69-042	1880, Harmon Gubler Jr.	12	10+	4	2	Yes+	Yes	Yes	Yes	Ivins, Santa Clara	Lawyer, farmer, town council president
69-043	1892, Mary Espe Geoul	?	?	6	1	Yes	Yes		Yes	Minnesota, North Dakota, Utah	Worked in Hawaii
69-044	1890, Lehi F. Earley	5	8	0	1	Flu				St. George, Round Valley	Also in Rupert, Idaho
69-045	1896, John Henry Zohner	12	10	6	1	Sibs	Yes		Yes	Switzer-land, Kanarraville	Also in St. George and Rexburg, Idaho
69-046	1904, Mons N. Johansen	?	10	5/1	1	Yes	Yes+	Yes	Yes	Mount Pleasant, St. George	Farmed, mentioned Indians and especially Utes, had a Danish parent

#	Birth Year, Name	Siblings, from Each Marriage/ Died	School	Children from Each Marriage Born/Died	Spouse	Health Challenges	Church	Mission	Temple	Residence	Other
69-047	1905, Ardath V. R. Johansen	?	8+4	5/1	1	Yes	Yes	Stake	Yes	Vernal, St. George, Benita, Ikoa	Mentioned Indian reservation
69-048	1905, Ida Adams Duell	10	8	5/1	1					Canada, St. George in old age	Cooked for ranchers
69-049	1900, Edwin L Duell	?	9	5/1	3					Canada Alberta	Farmer, city council
69-050	1880, Karolina E. G. Erickson	10/3	8	0	1		Yes			Sweden	Swedish born housekeeper, raised chickens and painted
69-052	1897 Ethel O. A. N. S. Midgley	10/5	10	9	2	Yes					Swiss father, parents died, was adopted
69-053	1919, Mildred J. G. Taylor	6	10	7	1					Salt Lake City, Moroni, Mesa	Mother died when she was age 10
69-054	1893, Eliza C. C. Crane	9/3	8	4/1	1	Yes	Yes			Gunnison, Salina	Farmed and had typhoid fever

#	Birth Year, Name	Siblings, from Each Marriage/ Died	School	Children from Each Marriage Born/Died	Spouse	Health Challenges	Church	Mission	Temple	Residence	Other
69-055	1892, Walter M. Willis	10/4	8	8?	2	Yes+	Yes	Yes	Yes	Henrieville Delta, Las Vegas	Also in Vernal, farmer, miner, plasterer
69-056	1899, Louis Romell Reber	13	7	4+7	2					Santa Clara, Littlefield	Endured flood in 1910, was sheriff
69-057	1919, Lorna Leavitt Reber	?	9	7	1	Yes+	Yes		Yes	Mesquite, Beaver Dam	Also in Littlefield
69-058	1888, John Jensen	5	9	14/2	1	Yes	Yes		Yes	Mexico, Fredonia	Pig and grain farmer
69-059	1881, George F. Campbell	6	8	5/1	1	Little	Yes		Yes	Cedar City, Hurricane	Also in Virgin and Kolob, did construction work
69-060	1903, Leamo West Peterson	4	12	2	1	Yes	Yes		Yes		Worked many jobs, had tobacco habit, injured hand, spoke with lisp

#	Birth Year, Name	Siblings, from Each Marriage/ Died	School	Children from Each Marriage Born/Died	Spouse	Health Challenges	Church	Mission	Temple	Residence	Other
69-061	1904, Verda B. Peterson	12	8	2	1	Yes	Yes			Hebron, Enterprise	Also in Pioche, did laundry and farm work
69-062	1899, Vincent Elias Leavitt	10	13	7	1		Yes		Yes	Bunkerville	Farm and Highway Department work, was bishop
69-063	1893, Elmer Leavitt	10/1	8	5	2	Eyesight	Yes			Bunkerville	Horseman and freighter
69-064	1902, Evelyn H. L. B. Leavitt	Yes	8	3+2/1	3	Yes	Yes			Bunkerville, Pine Valley	Also in Gunlock and Modena
69-065	1890, Ivie J. Cox Leavitt	3	9	11/2	1		Yes	Yes			Husband Alma D. Leavitt, teacher was Martha Cragun Cox
69-066	1909, Alma A. L. Huffman	10	8	5	1	Yes	Yes				Husband was Donald K. Huffman

#	Birth Year, Name	Siblings, from Each Marriage/ Died	School	Children from Each Marriage Born/Died	Spouse	Health Challenges	Church	Mission	Temple	Residence	Other
69-067	1913, Myrtle J. Reber	13	12	7	1		Yes		Yes	Mesquite	Husband was Ralston V. Reber
69-068	1903, Ralston Virden Reber	13/1	10	7	1		Yes		Yes	Bunkerville, Mesquite	Farmer and peddler
69-069	1902, Veda B. Leavitt Cox	9	4	5	1	Yes	Yes		Yes	Bunkerville	Teacher
69-070	1923, Leah Bundy Jensen	3	10	10	1	Yes				Mount Trumbull, Mesquite	Dairy work, shared story about accidents
69-071	1894, Agnes M. L. Leavitt	2/1	8	9/1	1	Yes	Yes		Yes	Bunkerville	Community service, mentioned polygamy
69-072	1909, Lorin Abbott Leavitt	10	12	7	2		Yes	Yes, Chicago	Yes	Bunkerville	
69-073	1916, Ethel Leavitt	?	8	6	1	Yes	Yes		Yes	Bunkerville	Community service, parents died

#	Birth Year, Name	Siblings, from Each Marriage/Died	School	Children from Each Marriage Born/Died	Spouse	Health Challenges	Church	Mission	Temple	Residence	Other
69-074	1933, Eleanor F. L. Nielson	10	10	4	1					Arizona Strip, Bunkerville	Kanosh, Mesquite, Nevada
69-075	1927, Lewis Darne Nielson	11	10	5	1	Yes	Yes		Yes	Leamington, Bunkerville	Railroad and dairy work
69-076	1909, Gertha B. L. Novell	13/3	10 ½	10	2		Yes				Husband was Norris Novell, supported family, café work
69-077	1925, Iona B. Barnum Reber	13/3	12	3?/1	1	Yes	Yes		Yes	Mesquite	Husband was Clarence Reber
69-078	1900, Rhoda H. Leavitt	8	12	3/1	1	Yes				Caliente, Bunkerville	
69-079	1909, Ardice Bunker Hardy	7	12	3	1	Yes	Yes	Yes	Yes	Veyo, Bunkerville	Husband was Joseph F. Hardy, teacher was Ardice
69-080	1908, Joseph Fielding Hardy	3	12	3	1	Yes	Yes	Yes	Yes	Bunkerville	Eastern states missionary

#	Birth Year, Name	Siblings, from Each Marriage/Died	School	Children from Each Marriage Born/Died	Spouse	Health Challenges	Church	Mission	Temple	Residence	Other
69-081	1927, Rosalie W. Bunker	2	13	4	1	Yes				Great Britain	Attended British school and Utah State University
69-082	1894, Mattie L. G. Hawkins	11	7	13	1		Yes		Yes	Alabama	Wrote poetry
69-083	1907, Bertha Miles Pymm	10	8	5/1	1		Yes		Yes	Diamond Valley Ranch	Mentioned nervous breakdown
69-084	1895, Walter Pymm	10	8	5/1	1	Yes	Yes		Yes	St. George	Ranching, son killed
69-086	1907, Shanna G. H. Wadsworth	8/2	12	2	2		Yes			Los Angeles, Chicago	Taught school in Idaho
69-087	1870, Neil Snow Forsyth	9	9	8	2	Yes	Yes	Yes	Yes		First wife was Chloe Rose Hatch, married in 1911, British Mission

#	Birth Year, Name	Siblings, from Each Marriage/ Died	School	Children from Each Marriage Born/Died	Spouse	Health Challenges	Church	Mission	Temple	Residence	Other
69-088	1892, Ruth S. R. Forsyth	?	Mexico 5?	6	2	Yes eye	Yes+			Mexico	Fruit and store work, mentioned polygamy
69-089	1902, Jetta M. L. Huntsman	12	12	1	1	Yes	Yes		Yes	Bunker-ville, Provo, Las Vegas	Husband was Ralph Huntsman
69-091	1898, Ellen J. A. Kleinman	3	13	4	1	Yes	Yes	Husband	Yes	New Mexico	Father had three wives, parents died
69-092	1898, David C. Kleinman	9	14	4	1		Yes+	Yes+ Tennes-see	Yes	Mesa, retired in St. George	Built temples and chapels
69-093	1906, Hilda G. Thacker	4/2	9	14/3	1						
69-094	1902, Claude M. Thacker	10	?	14/3	1	Yes	Yes				Mom died when he was 9½, raised by relatives
69-095	1910, Juanita S McQuaid	?	8	2/1	1	Yes	Yes			St. George	Husband disabled, JC Penney worker

#	Birth Year, Name	Siblings, from Each Marriage/ Died	School	Children from Each Marriage Born/Died	Spouse	Health Challenges	Church	Mission	Temple	Residence	Other
69-096	1918, Helen Hammond Jones	3	12	4	1		Yes		Yes	New Harmony	Raised sheep
69-097	1895, Charles R. Sullivan	6	?	7/1	1		Yes	Yes	Yes	Arizona Strip, St. George	Didn't like school, story: swear or not
69-098	1883, Frederick C. Van Buren	6	11	5	1	Yes	Yes			Los Angeles, Manti	WW1 vet, teacher, sheep rancher
69-099	1890, Effie C. H. Bates	10	5	13/2	1	Yes	Yes		Yes		Convert in Florida, son was Joe Bates
69-100	1891, Mabel L. Leavitt Rushton	10/2	8	10+7	1		Yes	Yes	Yes	Bunkerville	Dudley Leavitt had 55 children, singer & farmer
69-101	1896, Christine Elaine G. Shafer	5	9	0	1	Yes					Christian

#	Birth Year, Name	Siblings, from Each Marriage/ Died	School	Children from Each Marriage Born/Died	Spouse	Health Challenges	Church	Mission	Temple	Residence	Other
69-102	1882, Joseph A. Terry	12	12	2	1		Yes		Yes		Terry's Ranch, bishop for fifteen years, mentioned Nels Anderson
69-103	1909, LaVon LeFevre Jones	5	9	4/1	2: Divorced 1st wife	Yes				Uinta, St. George, Bloomington	Sheep peddling
69-104	1911, Clyde A. McQuaid	?	7 Leeds	2/1	1	Yes	Yes			Nevada, St. George, Leeds	Multiple sclerosis
69-105	1911, Eliza C. Jones	8	Bloomington 5?	0	1: married at 40		Yes	Yes	Yes	St. George	Broom factory, librarian, husband was LaVon Jones
69-106	1906, Glen Waite	?	12	5/2	1		Yes		Yes	Las Vegas, Kanab, Lehi	Bunkerville teacher
69-107	1910, Lulu Mae H. H. White	3	8 Veyo	5	3		Yes		Yes	Enterprise, St. George, Veyo	Also in Washington, wrote four books

#	Birth Year, Name	Siblings, from Each Marriage/ Died	School	Children from Each Marriage Born/Died	Spouse	Health Challenges	Church	Mission	Temple	Residence	Other
69-108	1894, Mary Ann W. J. Allen	5	5	5	2	Yes	Yes		Yes		Peddler
69-109	1884, Franklin Richard Bates	4/1	7	11/1			Yes		Yes	Canada	Sister was burned
69-110	1902, Doris Eliz Nay Whitney	3	8	6	3		Yes		Yes	Enterprise, St. George, Veyo	Also in Washington, Virgin floods
69-111	1921, Ruth Olsen Freeman	4/1	10	7	1		Yes	Yes	Yes		
69-112	1888, Lorenza Barnum Day	5	9	1	1	Yes	Yes		Yes		
69-113	1888, John Mathew Holt	14	9	?	1	Yes	Yes		Yes	Hebron	Annie G. Bauer, married in 1913, farmer
69-114	1890, LaMond W. Huntsman	2	12	6	1: Teresa Cannon					Enterprise St. George Shoal Creek	St. George and Murdock Academies

#	Birth Year, Name	Siblings, from Each Marriage/ Died	School	Children from Each Marriage Born/Died	Spouse	Health Challenges	Church	Mission	Temple	Residence	Other
69-115	1885, Teresa C. Huntsman	10	14	6	1		Yes+			Enterprise, St. George	Teacher, father was David H. Cannon
69-116	1890, Neils I. B. Clove	4	10	9	1	Yes	Yes			Enterprise, Hatch, St. George	Postmaster
69-117	1894, Dora M. H. Clove	9	8 Hebron	9/2	1	Yes	Yes			Holt's Ranch, Enterprise	Worked in store
69-118	1893, Lydia A. B. Hunt	3	8	8/2	1	Yes	Yes+		Yes	Enterprise, Toquerville	Also in Harrisburg, Leeds, Washington
69-119	1879, Anson P. Winsor III	1	6	2 adopted	1	Yes	Yes	Yes	Yes	Enterprise, Logan	Homesteader, railroad worker & poultry farmer
69-120	1891, Ernest A. Pickering	10	8	4/1	1	Yes	Yes		Yes		Farmer
69-121	1876, Walter W. Bowler	11	?	12/1	1		Yes		Yes	Hebron, Enterprise, England	Rancher

#	Birth Year, Name	Siblings, from Each Marriage/ Died	School	Children from Each Marriage Born/Died	Spouse	Health Challenges	Church	Mission	Temple	Residence	Other
69-122	1893, Anna G. Bauer Hunt	2	8	1	1	Yes	Yes		Yes	Hebron	Adopted
69-123	1901, Marie Blake Gubler	8/1	12	6	1	Yes	Yes		Yes		Mother died when Marie was age five
69-124	1898, Lillian Orden Cox	8/1	12	4	1		Some			Parowan, Pine Valley	Husband was Judge Cox
69-125	1907, LaFave Jones Leany	7	12	2/1	1	Yes	Yes		Yes		
69-126	1912, Norma B. Empey	6	12	5	1: Howard Empey	Yes+	Yes+		Yes	Toquerville, Hurricane, St. George	Farmer, clerk, Indians, teacher
69-127	1891, Martha M. L. McKnight	10	8	9/1	1	Yes	Yes		Yes		Husband was Wiliam C. McKnight
69-128	1900, LeGrande C. Pendleton	2	10	1	2		Yes				

#	Birth Year, Name	Siblings, from Each Marriage/ Died	School	Children from Each Marriage Born/Died	Spouse	Health Challenges	Church	Mission	Temple	Residence	Other
60-129	1895, Emily M. H. Williams	5	8	9/1	1	Yes	Yes	Yes	Yes		Served a senior mission
69-130	1890, Harvey A Jackson	10	11sd BNS Toquerv	6/1	1	Yes	Yes	Stake	Yes	Toquerville	Polygamy, farms, WWI, parents died
69-131	1893, Irma S. Jackson	4	10	6/1	1: Harvey A. Jackson	Yes	Yes+	Father, she was 3	Yes	Toquerville	Mother died when she was age six
69-132	1890, Elizabeth Leany Cox	10	14	6/1	1	Yes	Yes		Yes	Teacher	Husband was Dr. W. C. Cox
69-133	1906, Laura H. Pendleton	9	9	2	1		Yes		Yes	Hatch	Husband was LeGrand C. Pendleton
69-134	1908, Fred Booth	7	8	5	1		Yes		Yes	St. George, Leeds	Railroad, trucking, mine, and auto work
69-135	1916, Myrza Marie Booth	7	9	5	1		Yes		Yes	St. George,	Hawthorne Company, cook, civic leader, Woodward School

#	Birth Year, Name	Siblings, from Each Marriage/Died	School	Children from Each Marriage Born/Died	Spouse	Health Challenges	Church	Mission	Temple	Residence	Other
69-136	1890, Alvin Hall	9	14	10/2	1		Yes+	Yes	Yes	St. George, Rockville, Hurricane	Utah State University
69-137	1910, Ella Banks Graham	8	12	5	1	Yes	Yes				Flu
69-138	1906, Merrill Russell	4	8 Grafton	1	1					Grafton	Hurricane Canal, rawhide, alcoholic
69-139	1890, Lucinda E. H. Jackson	2	8	5	3	Yes	Yes		Yes	Washington, Enterprise	
69-140	1908, Delbert W. Pfoutz	2	12	3	1					Ohio	Not LDS
69-141	1885, Nathan B. Jones	9	5	7	1		Yes		Yes		Wife was Susanna H. F. Jones, married in 1911
69-142	1891, Susanna H F. Jones	10	8	7	1		Yes		Yes		Marriage in 1911

#	Birth Year, Name	Siblings, from Each Marriage/ Died	School	Children from Each Marriage Born/Died	Spouse	Health Challenges	Church	Mission	Temple	Residence	Other
69-143	1892, Temperence Mason Davis	10	12	4	1		Yes		Yes	Idaho, Las Vegas	Met husband on mission
69-144	1896, Ruth D. P. Davis	16	8	5/1	1		Yes		Yes	Panguitch, Mexico	Mother was sick, Ruth cared for family,
69-145	1903, Maralta D. Talbot	?	8	4/1	1	Typhoid Fever	Yes		Yes	Panguitch	Husband was Ed Talbot
69-146	1887, Nancy M. T. Kokerhans	7	12	4/1	1	Typhoid Fever	Yes				Hit in head by axe
69-147	1898, Eva M. P. Tebbs	16	8	?	1	Typhoid Fever	Yes			Panguitch	Farmer, had cancer
69-148	1907, Amelia Deuel Smith	13	8	5	1	Yes	Yes		Yes	Panguitch	Farmer, husband was Albert D. Smith
69-149	1909, Parley Grant Lee	7	12	2+4	1		Yes	Yes	Yes	Panaca	Mercantile store, civic activity

#	Birth Year, Name	Siblings, from Each Marriage/ Died	School	Children from Each Marriage Born/Died	Spouse	Health Challenges	Church	Mission	Temple	Residence	Other
69-150	1900, Jean W. LeFevre	7	14	7/2	1	Yes	Yes		Yes	Cardston, Salt Lake City, Panguitch	University of Utah, teacher
69-151	1893, Peter LeFevre			7/2	2		Yes		Yes	Panguitch, Garfield	Farm, sheep & road work, civic activity
69-152	1893, Elizabeth B. B. Dickinson	16	8	10	2		Yes			Panguitch, Joseph	Cook, second marriage
69-153	1896, Amelia C. Woodward	4	8	4	1	Yes	Yes			Panguitch, Salt Lake City, Pine Valley	Husband in WWI
69-154	1880, Olive M. N. M. LeFevre	8/2	8	8	2		Yes		Yes	Panguitch	Husband was Daniel J. LeFevre, rancher
69-155	1893, Daniel J. LeFevre	10	12	1	2		Some		Yes	Panguitch, Hurricane	Rockville, ranch and trucking work
69-156	1890, Mildred Prince Deuel	9/2	12	4	1: Wallace Deuel	Yes			Yes	Panguitch	Missions

#	Birth Year, Name	Siblings, from Each Marriage/Died	School	Children from Each Marriage Born/Died	Spouse	Health Challenges	Church	Mission	Temple	Residence	Other
69-157	1902, Arvel T. Webb	?	11	1	1: Vialate Leavitt	Yes	Yes+		Yes	St. George	Mill burned
69-158	1898, Gwendolyn B. Schmutz	3+	12	4	2: Donald Schmutz 2d	Yes	Yes convert		Yes	Swiss	Age seven, father died
69-159	1889, Donald Schmutz	7/1	14	4	2	Yes	Yes+	2	Yes	New Harmony	Teacher, bishop
69-160	1903, Vilate Leavitt Webb	10	12 Gunlock	11	1	Yes ear eyes	Yes		Yes	Gunlock, Mesquite	Also in Veyo & Las Vegas, farm, milk
69-161	1882, Frank Barber	10/1	6	5	2	Yes	Yes	Yes Texas	Yes	Centerville, Hurricane	Served mission without purse or scrip
69-162	1881, Susan I. B. Leavitt	8+2	7	11	1: Lemuel S. Leavitt	Yes	Yes+			Bicknell, Veyo, Gunlock	Postmistress
69-163	1900, William V. Jones	5/1	8	5	1: Isabel L. Jones	Yes	Yes+		Yes	Enterprise, Holt Ranch	Also in St. George and Veyo, bishop twice
69-164	1901, Isabel L. Jones	11	12 To 8 in tent	5	1		Yes+		Yes	Gunlock, Las Vegas	Also in Mesquite

#	Birth Year, Name	Siblings, from Each Marriage/ Died	School	Children from Each Marriage Born/Died	Spouse	Health Challenges	Church	Mission	Temple	Residence	Other
69-165	1910, Florence M. Leavitt	8	14	9/1	1	Yes	Yes+	Stake	Yes	Veyo, St. George	Siblings were Eldon and Tony McArthur, Annie Jennings
69-166	1882, Emma J. C. McArthur	7	9	6/1	1	Yes	Yes+	Stake	Yes	St. George	Shivwits, taught school
69-167	1907, Delilah Seitz	11	10	5/1	1: Andrew N. Seitz died					Gunlock, St. George, Mesquite	Raised family alone
69-168	1905, Lemuel G. Leavitt	11	9	9	1		Yes		Yes	Gunlock, Veyo, Mesquite	Also in Ox Valley, St. George, Las Vegas
69-169	1890, Matthew Gray	11/1	8	1	1	Yes	Yes		Yes	Pine Valley, Central	Farm and ranch work, civic activity
69-170	1912, Mildred B. Bowler	12	12	5	1		Yes		Yes	St. George, Mesquite, Veyo	Flu, mother died 1918
69-171	1908, Maggie V. H Rasmussen	2	11 Vernal	1	1					Veyo, Bull Valley	Father died when she was 7

#	Birth Year, Name	Siblings, from Each Marriage/ Died	School	Children from Each Marriage Born/Died	Spouse	Health Challenges	Church	Mission	Temple	Residence	Other
69-172	1909, Willis L. Rasmussen	11	10+	1	2	Yes	Yes				US Army, vegetarian, Word of Wisdom devotee
69-173	1903, Laura Stucki Gray	5	8	3/1	1: Matthew Gray		Yes+		Yes	Veyo, Santa Clara	
69-174	1897, Janet B. Keyes	9	8	8	1: Grant Z. Keyes	Yes	Yes			Pine Valley, Central, Veyo	Raised siblings, postmaster
69-175	1895, Grant Zenis Keyes	7/2	8	8	1					Sevier Valley, Pioche, St. George	Also in Ogden, France in WWI, civic Activity
69-176	1889, Mary B. Wood Hall		8	7	1: Lafayette Hall	Yes	Yes		Yes	Grafton, Hurricane	Grafton school
69-177	1888, Lafayette Hall	9/1	12	7/1	1		Yes+	Yes	Yes	Rockville	Dixie College, basketball, farming
69-178	1881, Anna Crawford Isom	13	Yes 8?	12/2	1: George H. Isom	Yes	Yes			Virgin, Springdale	Justice of peace

#	Birth Year, Name	Siblings, from Each Marriage/Died	School	Children from Each Marriage Born/Died	Spouse	Health Challenges	Church	Mission	Temple	Residence	Other
69-179	1889, Johanna H. S. Jaensch	?	7	3	2	Yes	Yes				Hurricane	Husband was imprisoned in WWII
69-180	1894, Ina Bundy Gifford	8	7+	10/1 + 15	1: Cyrus Gifford		Yes	Indiana	Yes	La Verkin, Salt Lake City, Mexico	Also in Mount Trumbull, telephone operator
69-181	1892, John Sevy Thompson	6	8	7/1	1: Ina Alvey Thompson		Yes		Yes	Panguitch	World War I, cowboy
69-182	1906, Ina Alvey Thompson	8	8	7/1	1: John Thompson	Yes	Yes		Yes	Escalante	Farmed, brothers left, and mother died
69-183	1917, Neucile B. Henrie	6	8	4	1: G. Champ Henrie	Yes	Yes		Yes	Richfield, Panguitch	Waterboard recreation, Red Cross
69-184	1912, George C. Henrie	6	12	5	1	Yes	Yes	California	Yes	Panguitch, Richfield, Salt Lake City	Road, welding, and livestock work
69-185	1900, Homer Y. Engelstead	8	12		1: Josephine Engelstead		Yes		Yes	Denmark, Panguitch	Also in Orderville, WWI

#	Birth Year, Name	Siblings, from Each Marriage/ Died	School	Children from Each Marriage Born/Died	Spouse	Health Challenges	Church	Mission	Temple	Residence	Other
69-186	1887, Charles Merrill Hall	10	8	6	1	Yes				Rockville, Hurricane	Hurricane Canal, cattle
69-187	1893, Nancy L. E. Roundy	10	8	5	1: Jesse C Roundy	Yes	Yes				Mentioned polygamy
69-188	1889, Clarence M. Engelstadt	8	8	5	1		Yes	Yes England	Yes		Sheep, WWI
68-189	1896, LaVerna T. Englestead	3	13	5	1	Yes	Yes	Yes	Yes		Age 7 when mother died, teacher
69-190	1887, James Lorenzo Prince	4	8	8	1		Yes	Yes, after marriage	Yes	Arizona Strip	
69-191	1923, Patrice Eleanor Knobe	2	9	2	1	Yes	Catholic				Father died
69-192	1902, Josiah A. Haslem	?	8	2	1	Yes					Mining caused emphysema
69-193	1896, Zesta S. Dallen	1	13	3	1		Yes		Yes	Loa	Son in WWII, father farmed

#	Birth Year, Name	Siblings, from Each Marriage/ Died	School	Children from Each Marriage Born/Died	Spouse	Health Challenges	Church	Mission	Temple	Residence	Other
69-194	1894, Mabel C. L. Williams	9/2	8	4	1		Yes		Yes	Kanar-raville, Canada	Tough life
69-195	1909, Ethel B. Haslam	6	10	2+1	1	Yes	Yes+		Yes		Kannaraville
69-196	1899, Mary Lucy Talbot	11	9	5/1	1	Yes				Paragonah	Farmed, had whooping cough
69-197	1902, Mary Ann Adams Starr	8	8	2	1	Yes	Yes			Cedar City	Mining and freighting
69-198	1900, Maude H. Robinson	8/4	10	6	1	Diphtheria	Yes		Yes	Reed, Caliente	Cedar City
69-199	1889, Orson Haight	9/1	12	4	2	Yes	Yes		Yes	Toquerville	Farming, brand inspecting, civic activity
69-200	1895, Mary A. D. P. Haight	1	8	4	2		Yes		Yes	Canada, Cedar City	Election judge
69-201	1897, Leland H. Bringhurst	8/1	8+1	10/4	2				Yes		

#	Birth Year, Name	Siblings, from Each Marriage/Died	School	Children from Each Marriage Born/Died	Spouse	Health Challenges	Church	Mission	Temple	Residence	Other
69-202	1911, Alena W. Berry		4	11/4	1: Glade A. Berry died	Flu	Yes				Civic activity
69-203	1901, Harriet A. F. Woodbury	6	10	7	1: Hartley A. Woodbury	Husband died	Yes			Kanarraville, Cedar City, Arizona	Husband was in WW1
69-204	1901, Archie R. Stokes	12	7	9	1	Yes, eye	No			Moab	Cattle
69-205	1910, Donevea H. Prisbrey	2	9	4/1	2		Convert			Kanab	
69-206	1905, Reid Prisbrey	10 + 1	6	3	1		Yes			New Harmony, Washington	Sheep
69-207	1893, Cyris "Cy" Gifford WWI	13	12	10						Delta, Mount Trumbull	Also in St. George, Las Vegas, La Verkin
69-208	1896, Hyrum W Loutensock	2	8 Payson Fordham	3	Myrtle M. Loutensock	Flu	Yes		Yes	Salt Lake City, Payson	WWI, Hawaii, Payson Coop, cows, carpet

#	Birth Year, Name	Siblings, from Each Marriage/ Died	School	Children from Each Marriage Born/Died	Spouse	Health Challenges	Church	Mission	Temple	Residence	Other
69-209	1885, MaryAnn R. R. Mackley	11	8	10	2/1	Yes				New Mexico, St. George	Ranch, cook, 75 grandchildren
69-210	1916, Sarah Heston Porter	8	6	6	1: 54 years old	Yes	Yes			Orderville, Cedar City	
69-211	1890, Sarah Ann B. H. Pulsipher	18	8	9	2		Yes		Yes	Hebron	Father on mission
69-212	1892, Samuel Frei Davis	5 + 2 half	15	5?	1		Yes	1912, Chicago	Yes	Las Vegas, Idaho, St. George	8 years as teacher, worked at post office
70-001	1885, Isaac Loren Covington	6/2	10	6	1: Anna Eager		Yes		Yes	Hurricane, Orderville, Las Vegas	Farmer, art, BYU
70-002	1893, Hort- ense E. S. B. Hinton	12	6	4	2	Yes`	Yes+	2 w/ husband	Yes+	Virgin, Hurricane	Farm, peaches
70-003	1911, Iola Lamb Tait Leany	7/2	11	3	2	Yes	Yes		Yes	Mount Carmel, Orderville	Laundry, DUP, band
70-004	1903, Vida P. Curry Jensen	3	12	6	2	Yes	Yes		Yes	Heber City, Charleston	Mom was Norwegian

#	Birth Year, Name	Siblings, from Each Marriage/ Died	School	Children from Each Marriage Born/Died	Spouse	Health Challenges	Church	Mission	Temple	Residence	Other
70-005	1870, Alice A. P. McCune	10	8	7/2	George McCune	Yes	Yes		Yes	American Fork, St. George	
70-006	1896, Myrtle Loutonstock	3/1	8	3	Hyrum Loutens	Yes	Yes Convert	Stake Mission	Yes	Payson, Salt Lake City, Magna	Also in California
70-007	1896, Anna E. Covington	4	8	6	Isaac L.		Yes		Yes	Mexico	Kept house from 8th grade on, polygamy
70-008	1896, Beulah M. Hoyt Parris	4	?	3	George H. Parris	Yes				Idaho	School guard, café, ice
70-009	1887, George Leo Cluff		8	9/2	Clara Sheffer	Yes				Provo, Mexico	Price, coal mining
70-010	1894, Clara Sheffer Cluff	6/3	8	9/2	George L. Cluff	Yes				Juárez Mexico	Panaca
70-011	1889, William Nutter Hinton	11	?	6/1	Mary	Yes	Yes		Yes	Colonia Morales	Son killed in World War II
70-012	1893, Mary W. Hinton	3	4	6/1	Wm. N. Hinton		Yes		Yes		

347

#	Birth Year, Name	Siblings, from Each Marriage/ Died	School	Children from Each Marriage Born/Died	Spouse	Health Challenges	Church	Mission	Temple	Residence	Other
70-013	1890, Erma Crawford Bell	5/2	7		1, cousin	Yes				Springdale	Rest home, married there
70-014	1889, Sylvia A. M. H. Krause	12	12	2	2	Yes	Yes		Yes	Salt Lake City, Mesa, St. George	
70-015	1892, Edward A. Davis	8	11	8	Lorena V. Stephens	Pneumonia	Yes		Yes	Circleville, Parowan	Also in Vernal, St. George
70-016	1889, Emma G. Cornelius	16/3	7	10/1	2: Henry	Yes	Yes		Yes	Virgin, Mexico	Three children by first marriage
70-017	1883, Vivian G. M. Christensen	5	11	7/1		Typhoid	Yes	Father, Carolina		Emery	Emery Academy, Father was bishop and Danish
70-018	1889, Marius M. Miller	5	14	?	Euzella L. Hill	Yes+	Yes	Montana	Yes	Emery County	Wagon accident at age 22, Ricks College
70-019	1899, Evan Squire Lee	12	8 (after harvest)	3	Lillian Lee	Yes	Little		Yes	Virgin	Virgin mayor, farmer, service station

#	Birth Year, Name	Siblings, from Each Marriage/ Died	School	Children from Each Marriage Born/Died	Spouse	Health Challenges	Church	Mission	Temple	Residence	Other
70-020	1903, Martha V. H. Knight	5	7	4/1	1	Yes	Yes+		Yes	Mesquite	Mentioned smallpox, fun activities
70-021	1898, Jesse Victor Knight	7	7	4/1	1	Yes	Yes+		Yes	Mesquite, Knightville	
70-022	1905, Eunice Leavitt Leavitt	12	8	5	Vincen Leavitt		Yes		Yes	Bunkerville	
70-023	1913, Bertha M. H. Dimick	2+3	8	4	1: Vernon M. Dimick	Yes	Yes		Yes	Gunlock, Las Vegas, Veyo, Manti	Also in Bunkerville, Pocatello
70-024	1887, David C. Okelberry	9	5+	7	Florence Crane	Yes	Yes+	Yes	Yes	Idaho, St. George	Tuberculosis, mission
70-025	1885, Lucy J. Barnum Isom	13	12	10	3: Calvin Barnum +2		Yes		Yes	Virgin	Hurricane Canal, James Jepson
70-026	1894, Artemesia Jeppson Reeve	?	9	5/1	1	Yes	Yes			Virgin	Raised by Strattons, Son was Leo Reeve

349

#	Birth Year, Name	Siblings, from Each Marriage/Died	School	Children from Each Marriage Born/Died	Spouse	Health Challenges	Church	Mission	Temple	Residence	Other
70-027	1901, Lora Leavitt Reber	3	8	7	Arthur S. Leavitt +1	Yes	Yes		Yes	Bunkerville, Mesquite	Widowhood, worked
70-028	1896, Cora M. Leavitt	5/2	9	11	Joseph Leavitt	Yes	Yes+		Yes	Mesquite, Gunlock	Farmer, school, cook
70-029	1897, Meta Gubler Ence	10	9	7/1	Ernest R. Ence	Yes	Yes+		Yes	Santa Clara, Pine Valley	Also in Ivins, Shivwits, Daughters of Utah Pioneers
70-030	1906, Margaret M Drochy	4	16	1	Otis Dauchy					Vermont, Mesquite	Teacher
70-031	1889, William S. Black Sr.	7	8	8/1	2	Typhoid	Yes		Yes	Mexico, St. George, Hinckley	Dairy farmer
70-032	1899, Marva May S. Black	2 half sibs	14	0	3	Typhoid	Yes		Yes	Provo, St. George	
70-033	1899, Claude Giles	7	9	3	Bessie Crane	Yes	Some		Yes	Miguel, Nevada	Used tobacco, worked at power plant
70-034	1909, Bessie J. Crane Giles	11/1	12	3	Claude Gay Giles		Yes+		Yes	Miguel, Nevada	Father died when she was 11

#	Birth Year, Name	Siblings, from Each Marriage/ Died	School	Children from Each Marriage Born/Died	Spouse	Health Challenges	Church	Mission	Temple	Residence	Other
70-035	1890, Bodil M. J. Pulsipher	4 Family Polygamy	7	6	1: John L. Pulsipher		Yes		Yes	Mexico, Mesquite	Nephi Jenson
70-036	1895, William Pulsipher	12	8	6	Nevada Hardy	Hearing	Yes	`	Yes	Hebron, Mesquite	Also in Gunlock, farmer
70-037	1897, William Moroni Jones	8	8	4	3	Flu	Yes			Gunlock, Las Vegas	Railroad, mine, hauled wood
70-038	1923, Allene H. Carter Jones	9	7	2	2	Yes	Yes		Yes	Mesquite	
70-039	1881, Nancy E. Holt Bowler	9	8	13	George H. Bowler	Finger	Yes		Yes	Gunlock, Holt's Ranch	Also in Mesquite, ranching
70-040	1892, Dorothy E. A. Frehner	12	7	6	Alfred Frehner	Yes	Yes+		Yes	Bunkerville	Farm
70-041	1903, May L. Jorgensen	6	6	9/1	1	Yes	Yes		Yes		

#	Birth Year, Name	Siblings, from Each Marriage/Died	School	Children from Each Marriage Born/Died	Spouse	Health Challenges	Church	Mission	Temple	Residence	Other
70-042	1900, Ephraim J. Jorgenson	4+5	8	9/1	1	Arthritis, heart	Yes		Yes	Mexico, La Verkin	Farm
70-043	1895, Elmer Rodney Gibson	4/3	8	9	Edna Stout	Yes	Yes	Yes	Yes	Hurricane, Virgin	Father died when Elmer was 1½, lumber
70-044	1912, Nina V. S. Stratton	13	12	1	Wm. C. Stratton		Yes		Yes	Hurricane	Fruit, cattle, 5-year courtship
70-045	1907, William C. Stratton	9/1	14	1	Nina Stratton	Weak eyes	Yes	Yes	Yes	Virgin, La Verkin, Hurricane	Raised siblings, grew strawberries
70-046	1904, Minerva J. S. Tidwell	5	8	5	1	Scarlet Fever	Yes		Yes	Ogden	
70-047	1905, Elmer Tidwell	4	11	5	1		Yes, later		Yes	Wyoming, Vernal	Also in Ogden
70-048	1903, Riley Flynn	?	6	3	Vera Flynn +1		Yes			Vernal, Uintah, Hawaii	Father killed when Riley was 14

#	Birth Year, Name	Siblings, from Each Marriage/ Died	School	Children from Each Marriage Born/Died	Spouse	Health Challenges	Church	Mission	Temple	Residence	Other
70-049	1905, Vera H. Flynn	11	12	0	1	Yes	Yes	Yes	Yes	Salt Lake City, Wyoming, Nevada, Washington, DC	Seminary teacher
70-050	1889, Gilbert D. Hyatt	12	12+	5	Mary L. Holt Hyatt		Yes		Yes	Parowan, St. George, Cedar City	Dentist, teacher
70-051	1892, Leah B. Christensen	11	10	11	1	Measles	RS quote		Manti	Delta	Flu epidemic
70-052	1902, Mary A. De Friez Williams	3	8	4	Kuman D. Williams	Silicosi father	Yes+'		Yes	St. George, Kanarraville	WWI, WWII, homesteader
70-053	1893, Allen Joseph Stout	6	8	3	Mina Stout +Kate Isom	Mother killed	Yes+ Bishop		Yes	La Verkin, Hurricane	Farmer, fruit peddler
70-054	1891, Benjamin Bringhurst	?	8	7	Bernice Gates		Yes		Yes	Toquerville	Looking for jobs
70-055	1907, Lucile C. Fish	7	12	8	Joseph Fish	Yest	Yes+	Yes	Yes	St. George, Pioche	Also in Toquerville

#	Birth Year, Name	Siblings, from Each Marriage/Died	School	Children from Each Marriage Born/Died	Spouse	Health Challenges	Church	Mission	Temple	Residence	Other
70-056	1903, Jessie Lewis Fish	10	13	8	Lucile Fish	Yes	Yes	Yes	Yes	Pioche, Toquerville	Lumber, mines, peddling
70-057	1919, Gerald M. Stout	2+2	14	6	Evelyn LeBaron	Pneumonia	Yes	Yes	Yes	Hurricane, Las Vegas	Alcoholism
70-058	1898, Rulon Langston	8	10	3	2	Typhoid	Yes		Yes	Grafton, Hurricane	Lumber, Cable Mountain, sheep
70-059	1912, Caroline E. C. Langston	11/5	9	5 adopted?	1		Yes		Yes	Cane Beds, Arizona, Mexico	Also in Hurricane and Rockville
70-060	1877, Moroni McArthur	5	Yes 8?	10	1		Mission pres.	Scotland	Yes	St. George	
70-061	1887, Albert Larsen Jones	7	8	4	1	Leg amputated	Yes		Yes	Overton	Farmer, store worker
70-062	1878, Elizabeth A. Johnson	8	3	0	0	Yes	Yes			Rotterdam, Holland	92 years of age at interview
70-063	1888, Era Lehi Conger Jones	6	7	4	1	Small pox	Yes		Yes	Alabama Overton	Store

#	Birth Year, Name	Siblings, from Each Marriage/ Died	School	Children from Each Marriage Born/Died	Spouse	Health Challenges	Church	Mission	Temple	Residence	Other
70-064	1896, Carrie S H Anderson	9	12	5	Fay Anderson	Dipth eria	Yes	Yes	Yes	Overton, Nevada	
70-065	1894, Fay E. Anderson	11	10	5	Carrie Anderson	Typhoid	Yes	Yes	Yes	Overton	Farming and building work
70-066	1888, Emma S. B. Ballard	11/2	Yes 5	6	1	Yes	Yes		Yes		Husband died when Emma was 6
70-067	1903, Freda E. K. Spilsbury	3	10	1	2	Yes				Swit- zerland, Toquerville	Widow for 28 years
70-068	1907, George L. Brinkerhoff	9	8	1	Emily	Yes	Yes	Mesa, Mocca- sin, AZ	Yes	Kanab, Glendale	Mining, Civilian Conservation Corps
70-069	1899, Emily R. F. Brinkerhoff	8	13	1	George	Yes	Yes		Yes		Mother died at Emily's birth, teacher for 32 years
70-070	1921, Lillian Jones Isom	6	12	7	1	Yes	Yes		Yes	Enterprise	
70-071	1905, Ianthus Spendlove	12	12	6	Blanch Sullivan		Yes		St. George	Virgin, Hurricane	Hurricane Canal

#	Birth Year, Name	Siblings, from Each Marriage/Died	School	Children from Each Marriage Born/Died	Spouse	Health Challenges	Church	Mission	Temple	Residence	Other
70-075	1910, Minnie Hulet Dalley	6	9	2	1	Yes	Yes				Healing of son
70-076	1893, Otto Pidding Dalley	8	11 BAC	1	Cora H. Dalley		Yes	Yes	Yes		Farmer, sheep raiser
70-078	1887, Melvina V. H. Bringhurst	6	8	7/1	Harriet Bringhurst		Yes, Relief Society president			Toquerville	Farmer, odd Jobs
70-079	1902, Leland Taylor	10	8	4	Esta Smith	Yes	Some, smoking			New Harmony	Farmer, barber
70-080	1908, Adelia M. Wilson Stratton	7+7 halfs	12	4	3 husbands: Petit, Wetzl, Stratton	Yes	Yes		Yes	Hurricane, St. George, Tropic, Mexico	
70-081	1908, Leslie Lee Stratton	9	10	10	1	Blind	Yes		Yes	Hurricane	Accidents, story deleted
70-082	1909, Franklin Hunter Grimshaw	9	8	8	Lillian Adams, 1934	Yes	Yes			Enoch	Farmer, sewing machine operator, plumber

ABOUT THE COMPILER

Douglas D. Alder was born in Salt Lake City. He graduated from the University of Utah with a bachelor's degree in history and German and a master's degree in history and political science in 1959. He completed a PhD in modern European history at the University of Oregon, Eugene, in 1966, including a Fulbright Scholarship to the University of Vienna, Austria. He taught European history at Utah State University from 1963 to 1986, where he was director of the honors program. He completed an internship in higher education administration with the US Council of Education in 1973–74 at Indiana University, Bloomington. He became president of Dixie College in St. George, Utah, in 1986, and served until 1993, at which time he returned to teaching at the college.

Dr. Alder completed a mission in Austria for two and one-half years and has been a bishop twice in Logan, Utah, and on five high councils in various places he has lived. He was in the St. George Temple presidency from 1998 to 2001 and is a sealer there now. He currently teaches in the Road Scholar and Institute for Continued Learning (ICL) programs at Dixie State University.

He has served on the Utah Arts Council, Utah Humanities Council, Utah Historical Society, Mormon History Association, and local history organizations. He was the chair of the Washington County Library Board and is active in community affairs, including the St. George Book Festival and the Celebrity Concert Series. He has published academic articles on Austrian history, Utah history, social studies education, and Mormon history. He coauthored *A History of Washington County* for the Utah Statehood Centennial in 1996 and added an update in 2008. He is a founder of the "Historic St. George Live!" tours, which began in 1996 as a service in the community. He wrote *A Century of Dixie State College of Utah* to commemorate its centennial in 2011 and was one of three authors of *All That Was Promised: The History of the St. George Temple*. He compiled the Juanita Brooks Lecture Series entitled *Honoring Juanita Brooks*. He is married to Elaine Reiser, and they have four married children, twelve grandchildren, and three great-granddaughters.

INDEX